Mountain Biking Colorado's Front Range

A Guide to the Area's Greatest Off-Road Bicycle Rides

Second edition

Stephen Hlawaty

FALCON GUIDES ®

GUILFORD, CONNECTICUT
HELENA, MONTANA
AN IMPRINT OF GLOBE PEQUOT PRESS

To buy books in quantity for corporate use
or incentives, call **(800) 962-0973**
or e-mail **premiums@GlobePequot.com.**

FALCONGUIDES®

FalconGuides is an imprint of Globe Pequot Press.
Falcon, FalconGuides, and Outfit Your Mind are registered trademarks of Morris Book Publishing, LLC.

Maps by Trailhead Graphics Inc.
All photos by Stephen Hlawaty unless otherwise noted.

Library of Congress Cataloging-in-Publication Data
Hlawaty, Stephen.
   Mountain biking Colorado's Front Range: from Fort Collins to Colorado Springs/by Stephen Hlawaty.—2nd ed.
      p. cm.—(A Falcon guide)

   1. All terrain cycling—Front Range (Colo. and Wyo.)—Guidebooks. 2. Front Range (Colo. and Wyo.)—Guidebooks. I. Title. II. Series.
ISBN 978-0-7627-8672-5

Printed in the United States of America

Contents

The Rides

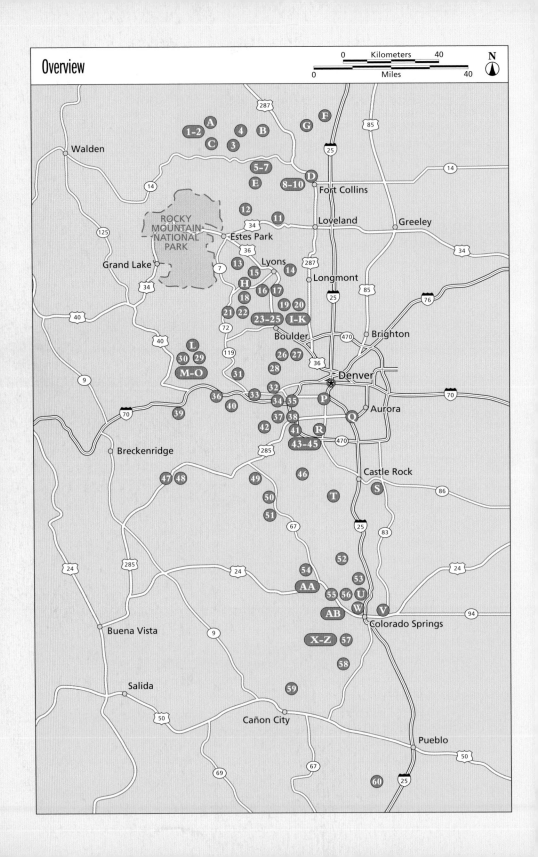

Kilometers

0   40

Miles

0   40

N

Walden

1-2 A
C   3   4 B

G F

85

25

14

5-7
E
8-10 D   Fort Collins

ROCKY
MOUNTAIN
NATIONAL
PARK

12
11   Loveland
34

Greeley

Estes Park
36

Grand Lake

13   Lyons
15   14
H
16 17
18
21 22
23-25 I-K
19 20

7

125

40

40

9

L
30 29
M-O
31

Longmont

85

Boulder

287

Brighton

470

76

26 27
28

36

Denver

P

70

Aurora

Q

Breckenridge

36   33
40   32
34 35
37 38
42   41   R
43-45   470

285

39

70

47 48   49
50
51   67

46

Castle Rock

S

86

T

25   83

94

52

24

54
AA
55 56
AB
X-Z 57

285

53
U
W   V

24

9

Buena Vista

58

Colorado Springs

Salida

59

50

Cañon City

69

67

Pueblo

60   25

50

PREFACE

I do not despair for the future of the human race
when I see an adult on a bicycle.

—H. G. Wells

I first laid tracks in Colorado in 1991. Armed with a packed duffel bag, a pair of skis, and Muddy Fox's steel-framed "Seeker Mega" mountain bike, I staked my claim in Colorado's Front Range. While Muddy Fox may have been the company to first bring mountain biking to Britain in 1981, it held little presence in Colorado's market share. It seems fitting then that I, fresh from the paved streets of New York City, as much a newbie to Colorado as one to mountain biking, should start my mountain biking career as a foreigner both in bike and body.

My introduction into mountain biking was most certainly a baptism by fire. On an early spring day in 1993, after portaging our bikes over some boulders in Walker Ranch, my friends and I decided to sit along the banks of the Boulder Creek and enjoy the fierce moving water of the spring runoff. When it came time to continue our ride, I reached for a nearby rock for leverage but pulled it directly onto my leg. The weight of the rock forced me to fall into the creek. Had it not been for the speedy reactions of my friends, I could have taken quite a tumble in that turbulent water. What I remember most of that day isn't the icy cold water of the creek nor the pain in my leg, but rather the passing of the trees' canopy overhead while being carried out on my back on a stretcher by Rocky Mountain Rescue. This perspective offered me insight into riding the hills surrounding the Front Range. To mountain bike safely requires more than just being safe while on your bike. It demands being safe all the time, always being aware and mindful of your surroundings.

While not attempting to cover all of the rides within the Front Range, I tried to gather a sampling of the variety of rides and terrain in the region, rediscovering old favorites and exploring new possibilities. And so, I present *Mountain Biking Colorado's Front Range* as a kind of trailhead from which to explore new heights, with the understanding that reaching the summit is one thing, but sharing the view—sublime.

ACKNOWLEDGMENTS

Grand Master Morihei Ueshiba, the founder of Aikido, once wrote that "the form and beauty that is the world of heaven and earth has become one family." One meaning that we might glean from O Sensei's words is that we all share a kinship with our natural surroundings and each other. And with that, I gratefully acknowledge the participants in the first and future editions of this work.

To my parents Hans and Maria Hlawaty, Papa and Mama, thank you for all the love and encouragement that you provide. Your selflessness knows no boundaries and has no equal. Papa, thanks for joining the boys and me at Betasso Preserve. I hope you enjoyed seeing your son and grandsons do their thing on two wheels instead of two planks. Thanks also for assisting with some of the logistics of this work.

Many thanks go to my younger sister Ingrid and older brother Roland for their continued support. You two have always set the standard by which I judge the quality of my work.

I've had the pleasure to meet a variety of new and interesting people who have all graciously given of their time and talent in preparation for this book. Ever mindful that a good time shared makes friends of us all, thanks to all those I met along the trail.

It was great to meet with the entrepreneurial geniuses of Don and Vi O'Connor, Randy Wittmer, and Dan French of Any & All Bikes, Denver's only one-stop mobile bike shop. Thanks again for the Singletrack Club. And thank you, Demetrius, for the photos of the big bike and the new fleet.

The mountain biking community at large owes much to the diligent efforts of the International Mountain Bicycling Association (IMBA). Thank you, Tim Blumenthal, former executive director of IMBA, for sharing your thoughts on mountain biking, IMBA, and the environment. It was as much a privilege as it was an education spending time with you. Much appreciation also goes to Judd De Vall, then international coordinator for IMBA, for drawing my attention to the "bicycle challenge area" of Eaton Park.

Thank you, Dirk Vinlove, executive director of the Boulder Off-road Alliance (BOA), which has evolved to become the Boulder Mountainbike Alliance, for clueing me into some of the prospective trail systems for Boulder County. The efforts of you and your staff are greatly appreciated. Likewise, a nod goes to Michael Barrow, Boulder Mountainbike Alliance's advocacy director, for suggesting where I can go for rides in Boulder.

Thank you, Pascal Reid of Boulder County Parks and Open Space, for providing me with the helpful Heil Valley Ranch information.

Much appreciation goes to Austin Clark, president of Southern Colorado Cycling Club, formerly the Southern Colorado Trail Builders, for your information on the 12-foot wall of water that destroyed the 1-year-in-the-making and 1-month-old bridge that crossed Rock Creek in Lake Pueblo State Park. "Pretty amazing" is one way to describe it. Good luck on the floatable and retractable bridge project, plans for future trails, and the restructuring of your organization.

And now, the Come-Back-Kid Award goes to Jeff Williams. We all winced when you put down your mountain bike for your golf clubs. It's good to see you back on the bike again and better than ever. Thanks more recently for joining me on Coulson Gulch, Picture Rock, Centennial Cone Park, Falcon Trail, and Lake Pueblo State Park, where our 21.7-mile ride was complemented by pig rolling, hurricane slinging, flash-flooded Rock Creek rerouting, trailside rattlesnake charming, and impromptu bridge building.

And to Joanna Williams, the strongest mountain biking novitiate I've seen in a long time, thanks for playing along.

Thanks also goes to Creighton Grof-Tisza, backcountry buddy and colleague, for the miles of smiles on all things vertical . . . whataya gonna do—you're %^#&@!

Speaking of which, a respectful bow goes to my old Stumpjumper and Enduro Pro for keeping me rolling. Steel and aluminum unite.

To my long-standing friend, spiritual copilot, and soul avenger John Gray, thanks for the music, 'gammon, and good times. July 2013 brought a scare to our hearts with your trifecta flatlining. Bobcat Ridge has nothing on your bionic self. Railroad.

A huge beaming smile and pats on the back go to my two boys, Ethan and Benjamin. Ethan, you crushed the climb at Doudy Draw. And Benjamin, you owned Betasso Preserve's Benjamin Loop.

Naturally, nothing I do would be complete without the presence of my astonishing wife, Amanda. From the pucker-pinching, back-to-back rides of the Switzerland Trail and Apex Park to dodging lightning bolts atop Rollins Pass to keeping one eye on the trail and another on the kids at Doudy Draw—sorry I didn't do the same at Betasso Preserve—you've shone your smile every step of the way. Were it not for your strength, confidence, and good humor over the years of feast, famine, fire, and flood, this project may have become tired and worn. Thank you for sharing with me that smooth singletrack trail to happiness.

And finally, thank you, fellow riders, for allowing *Mountain Biking Colorado's Front Range* to be your guide. I hope you enjoy what you see.

INTERNATIONAL MOUNTAIN BICYCLING ASSOCIATION

The International Mountain Bicycling Association (IMBA) grew from five California advocacy clubs that had banded together to appease widespread mountain bike trail closures under consideration by the California State Parks. Hearing of crowded trails and trail-user tensions worldwide, the newly formed group decided to adopt a global perspective. And on what certainly must have been a sunny California day in 1988, the International Mountain Bicycling Association was born.

Combining mountain bike advocacy with environmental and social considerations, IMBA includes a network of 35,000 individual members in all fifty states, in most Canadian provinces, and in thirty other countries. With more than 750 chapters, clubs, and patrols, and 200 corporate partners, IMBA continues to add new local, national, and international affiliates. Some of IMBA's projects include the Subaru/IMBA Trail Care Crew, the National Mountain Bike Patrol, IMBA Trailbuilding Schools, Federal Agency Mountain Bike Partnerships, IMBA Epic Rides, Government Affairs, Instructor Certification Program (ICP), Mapping Initiative, and Public Lands Initiative. "In some ways," former IMBA executive director Tim Blumenthal admits, "we've grown into our name."

In the beginning, IMBA was a completely volunteer-run organization. Faced with ever-increasing population growth and development, it became clear that both IMBA and mountain biking needed professional leadership.

As the editor-in-chief for *Mountain Bike* magazine, Tim Blumenthal occupied a seat on IMBA's board of directors in 1989. He offered to become executive director if IMBA would relocate its headquarters to Colorado, the home to major offices of the USDA Forest Service, the Bureau of Land Management (BLM), and the National Park Service. Perhaps more important, according to Tim, "So much of the energy and the enthusiasm for the sport of mountain biking was based in the Rocky Mountains." Thus, IMBA moved to Boulder, Colorado, in the summer of 1994.

By "blending national and international leadership with grassroots support," IMBA strikes a balance between its local and international constituency. IMBA works with the BLM and the Forest Service to promote and manage mountain biking on public lands. The Wilderness Society regularly consults IMBA during the shaping of new wilderness area proposals. Along with the National Park Service, IMBA works to get people out of their cars and onto their bikes to improve the quality of air and visitor experience in national recreation areas. IMBA also speaks at the National Bike Summit, a gathering for all bicycling advocacy groups in the country, to discuss federal leadership projects.

Moreover, IMBA offers strategic advice to local groups with sensitive mountain bike issues, gives cash grants to its member clubs, and donates thousands of trail-work tools for construction and maintenance of trails worldwide. IMBA regularly conducts trail-building schools and provides information on how to build sustainable, heavy-use trails, how to obtain 501c3 nonprofit status for local groups, how to address liability concerns, how to work with other trail-user groups, and how to educate new mountain bikers. In short, says Blumenthal, "IMBA is a marvelous blend of cycling, environmental conservation, [and] education."

It's no wonder that the Forest Service and the BLM have partnered with IMBA. At one point the BLM ran a campaign to include mountain biking in its draft Off-Highway Vehicle (OHV) Strategy released December 4, 2000.

BLM proposed that mountain bikes be considered OHVs and subject to the same kind of regulations and restrictions. Managing 264 million acres of US public land, the BLM was poised to dramatically affect mountain biking as we know it. Blumenthal visited with the BLM in Washington, D.C., in January 2001 to convince the agency to remove mountain biking from the plan. Coupled with roughly 14,000 letters in support of mountain biking, IMBA persuaded the BLM to remove mountain bikers from OHV designation.

On a more local level, good things are happening for Front Range mountain biking. New trail designs are providing increasing sustainability for the environment, as well as for the future of mountain biking in general.

As of this writing, IMBA's Board of Directors includes Elayna Caldwell, Mike Cachat, Chris Conroy, Howard Fischer, Jim Grover, Kent McNeill, lden Philbrick, Luther Probst, David Treinis, Robert Winston, and David Zimberoff. The Boulder office staff includes President and U.S. Executive Director Mike Van Abel, Director Kerri Salazar, Controller Tim Peck, Finance Administrator Tiffanie Beal, Communications Director Mark Eller, Development Department Director Rich Cook, Interim Policy Director Jeremy Fancher, Trails Solutions/Field Programs Director Chris Bernhardt, and a host of regional/associate directors.

International Mountain Bicycling Association (IMBA)
4888Pear East Circle, Suite 200E
Boulder, CO 80301
Phone: (303) 545-9011 or (888) 442-4622
Website: www.imba.com

INTRODUCTION

In the mountains there is a strange market where you can barter the vortex of life for boundless bliss . . .

—Milarepa, 11th-century Tibetan yogi

The length of the Rocky Mountain foothills running south from Fort Collins to Colorado Springs, where amber waves of grain meet the purple mountains' majesty, is generally referred to as the Front Range. It is Colorado's most populated region (home to nearly 80 percent of the state's population). The Front Range's terrain is predominantly semiarid and rocky. Offering cacti, steep grades, and loose rocks, the Front Range delivers some of the most technical riding in the state. Although the views are not as dramatic as the ones found in our inner Rocky Mountains, the trails here are just as good, albeit somewhat more crowded.

Colorado's Front Range is made up of four key communities: Fort Collins, Boulder, Denver, and Colorado Springs. The stellar trails in and around these towns have made us one of the premier mountain bike regions in the country. The 2 million acres that comprise the Arapaho, Roosevelt, and Pike National Forests boost the appeal even more. And while the Front Range's landscape tends to naturally draw attention, the people who call the Front Range home are equally deserving of natural wonder status. The resiliency of these people during the unprecedented fires and floods of 2012 and 2013 is inspiring. We all owe countless individuals our thanks for their efforts in mending the trails and lives damaged by fire and flood.

The Four Regions

Fort Collins carries with it a certain northern Colorado vibe that is best described as "laid-back authenticity." Not as populated or as diverse as its Front Range counterparts, Fort Collins, nevertheless, includes more than 30 miles of multiuse recreational trails, more than 3,000 acres of open space, and more than 280 miles of designated bikeways, including paved trails, bike lanes, and bike routes. While the Poudre Canyon, Horsetooth Reservoir, and Lory State Park offer the best-known mountain biking trails, there are some gems that require slightly more of an effort getting to but are worth every bit of time it takes getting to them. Some of these trails include those around the Red Feather Lakes area, as well as those around Masonville. With such cycling traditions as the Tour de Fat, its hosting a stage in the 2013 USA Pro Challenge, services like the Bicycle Ambassador Program, and being home to Tour de France racer Teejay van Garderen and Olympic bronze medalist Georgia Gould, Fort Collins is an upwardly mobile and forward-thinking bicycle community. In fact, in 2013 the League of American Bicyclists designated Fort Collins as a Platinum Bicycle Friendly Community.

Roughly 60 miles southwest of Fort Collins lies Boulder, perhaps the reigning king of recreational mountain towns. With the steep sandstone walls of the Flatirons as a backdrop, Boulder provides a dramatic setting for some of mountain biking's best trails. To accommodate the number of bicycle commuters in Boulder (which, incidentally, is seven times greater than the national average), the city and county boast more than 160,000 acres of open space (much of which is closed to the public) and 150 miles of trails.

The presence of the International Mountain Bicycling Association's (IMBA) headquarters testifies to Boulder's preeminence as a serious mountain biking town. Likewise, the mission of the Boulder Mountainbike Alliance to improve the trail experiences for riders by organizing social rides and events, advocating for sustainable mountain biking, and building trails has been a tremendous asset. Such commitment manifests itself—among other places—on the trails of Hall Ranch, near the small town of Lyons, which provides some of the sweetest and nearest available singletrack riding, while the recent additions to Heil Valley Ranch assure riders that Boulder County is committed to the future of mountain biking, as well as the sustainability of its trails.

Minutes southeast of Boulder lies Denver, Colorado's state capital. Denver provides all the art, shopping, and dining that any other major city does, but where it differs leaves many other city dwellers wishing they lived in Colorado. Rated number fourteen by *Bicycling* magazine in its 2012 "America's Top 50 Bike-Friendly Cities" feature for cities whose populations were greater than 95,000, Denver certainly does its part in contributing to Colorado's healthy lifestyle. Denver's Jefferson County has a particularly enlightened and excellent trail management system, ever keeping in tune with issues surrounding mountain biking. The new Centennial Cone Park is one of the Denver area's finest mountain bike destinations. The sinuous Cherry Creek Singletrack through downtown Denver passes within minutes of such cityscapes as Neiman Marcus, Saks, and Tiffany's. The lush Hayden/Green Mountain Park trail is another ride destination just minutes from downtown Denver. No wonder, then, that Denver boasts being the thinnest city in the nation, whose residents make up the smallest percentage of overweight adults in the United States.

Just over an hour's drive south of Denver is Colorado Springs, the state's second-largest city, at the base of Pikes Peak. The Springs also does its part in keeping up with Colorado's active lifestyle. It is home to USA Cycling, the national governing body of bicycling, which includes the National Off-Road Biking Association (NORBA) and the US Olympic Training Center. Some of the better rides in the area include the Falcon Trail, Captain Jack's Trail, and trails found in Cheyenne Mountain State Park.

A short 40-minute drive south from Colorado Springs lies Pueblo. This onetime steel mill town is making a bid for itself as a Front Range mountain biking destination in its own right. With the trails that abound in Lake Pueblo State Park, as well as the work being done by the Southern Colorado Cycling Club, Pueblo seems to be redefining itself as an up-and-coming recreational hotbed.

Unlike most major metropolitan areas, Fort Collins, Denver, Boulder, Colorado Springs, and Pueblo are all within an easy 30 minutes' drive of incredible riding. Because trails along the Front Range typically receive a higher volume of use, their routes tend to be considerably easier to follow. That's not to say, however, that Front Range riding is all user-friendly. Few of the trails can be accessed without driving unless you enjoy riding pavement with heavy traffic. Front Range trails oftentimes travel through rattlesnake and mountain lion habitats, something to consider if you are ever riding alone.

Moreover, the Front Range's semiarid terrain is an ideal growing environment for the weed commonly referred to as "goathead" or "puncturevine" (*Tribulus terrestris*). The fruits that these weeds produce are also known as goatheads. After these goatheads fall from their host weeds, they harden and dry (with the seed of the weed inside). Becoming a three-pointed, thorn-like enemy on the trail, goatheads have an uncanny ability of finding their way into your tires. Their pervasion throughout the Front Range demands that riders carry spare tubes, pump, and a stocked patch kit.

Because the Front Range abuts the Continental Divide, riding here includes the rigors of routinely negotiating up and down steep, sandy, and rocky slopes. Added to this is the dustier, hotter, and more exposed terrain of the Front Range at large. However, while riding in Colorado's interior Rockies may require more sustained lung and leg power, Front Range riding requires that you have enough stored energy for short bursts and tight switchbacks. Rhythms are broken very easily and quite frequently. To us is left the fortunate task of surpassing these challenges.

Mountain Biking Guidelines

If every mountain biker always yielded the right-of-way, stayed on the trail, avoided wet or muddy trails, never cut switchbacks, always rode in control, showed respect for other trail users, and carried out every last scrap of what was carried in (candy wrappers and bike-part debris included)—in short, if we all did the right things—we wouldn't need a list of rules governing our behavior.

The fact is, most mountain bikers are conscientious and are trying to do the right thing; however, thousands of miles of dirt trails have been closed due to the irresponsible habits of a few riders.

Here are some basic guidelines adapted from the IMBA Rules of the Trail. These guidelines can help prevent damage to land, water, plants, and wildlife; maintain trail access; and avoid conflicts with other backcountry visitors and trail users.

1. **Only ride on trails that are open.** Don't trespass on private land, and be sure to obtain any necessary permits. If you're not sure if a trail is closed or if you need a permit, don't hesitate to ask. Likewise, always stay on the trail.

2. **Keep your bicycle under control.** Watch the condition of the trail at all times, and follow the appropriate speed regulations and recommendations.

3. Yield to others on the trail. Make your approach well known in advance, either with a friendly greeting or a bell. When approaching a corner, junction, or blind spot, expect to encounter other trail users. When passing others, show your respect by slowing to a walking pace. Otherwise, always yield to hikers and equestrians. If you're on the descent, yield to all uphill traffic. Uphill traffic has the right-of-way.

4. Don't startle animals. Animals may be easily scared by sudden approaches or loud noises. For your safety—and the safety of others in the area as well as the animals themselves—give all wildlife a wide berth. When encountering horses, defer to the horseback riders' directions. As a general rule, dismount from your bikes and wait on the side of the trail for the equestrians to pass. If mountain biking in a group, it's a good idea that all members of the riding party dismount and wait on the same side of the trail.

5. Zero impact. Be aware of the impact you're making on the trail beneath you. You should not ride under conditions in which you will leave evidence of your passing, such as on certain soils after rain. If a ride features optional side hikes into wilderness areas, be a zero-impact hiker, too. Whether you're on bike or on foot, stick to existing trails, leave gates as you found them, and carry out everything you brought in.

6. Be prepared. Know the equipment you are using, the area where you'll be riding, and your cycling abilities and limitations. Avoid unnecessary breakdowns by keeping your equipment in good shape. When you head out, bring spare parts and supplies for weather changes. Riders should know how to use and pack spare tubes, patch kit, tire pump, multi-tool, tire levels, shock pump, extra derailleur hanger with mounting bolts, extra link of chain with a master link, chain lube, zip ties, lip balm, sunscreen, phone, first aid kit, rain jacket, and snacks. Be sure to wear appropriate safety gear, including a helmet, and learn how to be self-sufficient.

Map Legend

Transportation

70	Freeway/Interstate Highway
34	U.S. Highway
83	State Highway
300	Forest Road
	Paved Road
	Gravel Road
	Unimproved Road
	Railroad

Trails

	Selected Route
	Trail
	Doubletrack Trail
→	Direction of Route
	Turnaround

Water Features

	Body of Water
	River or Creek
	Intermittent Stream
	Spring
	Waterfall

Symbols

	Boat Launch
	Bridge
▪	Building/Point of Interest
▲	Campground
⊛	Capital
∩	Cave
•–•	Gate
P	Parking
	Picnic Area
•—•	Powerline
	Ranger Station
	Scenic View/Overlook
	Tower
○	Towns and Cities
20	Trailhead
	Tunnel
?	Visitor Center

Land Management

	National Park/National Forest
	State/Local Park/Open Space

● Easy	■ Moderate	◆ Difficult	◆◆ Very Difficult

Fort Collins Region

Situated in northern Colorado at the foot of the Rocky Mountains, Fort Collins lies in the Cache la Poudre (pronounced "cash la puder") River Valley. The Cache la Poudre River begins in Rocky Mountain National Park and flows through the Poudre Canyon to meet the South Platte River east of Greeley. From its headwaters to the confluence with the South Platte, the Poudre drops roughly 7,000 feet. Sitting at an elevation of 4,984 feet and boasting more than 300 days of annual sunshine, Fort Collins offers mountain bikers a great access point to the foothills and the higher mountains to the west.

In 1862 Camp Collins was established and served as a fortification for travelers and settlers along the Colorado branch of the Overland Trail. On August 20, 1864, Lieutenant Colonel William O. Collins of the Eleventh Ohio Volunteer Cavalry established a new and permanent post to replace Camp Collins. This post became what is now known as Fort Collins and served to protect a strategic trading post. By 1867 the area around Fort Collins was deemed safe from Native tribes, and the fort was abandoned.

By the 1870s and 1880s construction of irrigation canals was complete and led to the development of the area's long-standing agricultural industry. The newly irrigated and the semiarid lands around Fort Collins proved to be a perfect blend for growing wheat, oats, and barley; no wonder that Fort Collins is noted for having the most microbreweries per capita in Colorado, producing 70 percent of the state's craft beers. Fort Collins owes much of its initial growth explosion to these early agricultural years. In fact, many of the elegant and showcase houses (many of which are listed on the National Register of Historic Places) in Fort Collins today were built during the growth years of the 1880s.

Today, Fort Collins has grown into a thriving community of more than 100,000 and boasts an expanding technology sector as well as a healthy tourism industry. With Horsetooth Mountain Park, Lory State Park, and Roosevelt National Park all lying within minutes west of Fort Collins, the town offers an impressive display of outdoor opportunities. The foothills west of Fort Collins are laced with trail networks. Comprising 5,545 acres of foothills, wetlands, prairies, riparian areas, and urban sites, the city of Fort Collins maintains thirty-nine natural areas. Thanks to the open-space sales tax, more than 12,000 acres of land have been preserved in Larimer County alone. But Fort Collins's commitment to riding isn't only found in the foothills. Transfort, the Fort Collins municipal bus service, equips all its buses with bike racks that can carry two bikes. Available on a first-come, first-served basis, there is no extra charge for using the bike racks. It's no wonder that the League of American Bicyclists awarded Fort Collins the Platinum designation for being a bicycle-friendly community.

Local Bike Shops

The Phoenix Cyclery, Fort Collins; (970) 493-4517; www.phoenixcyclery.com/

Peloton Cycles, Fort Collins; (970) 449-5595; http://peloton-cycles.com/

ProVelo Bicycles, Fort Collins; (970) 204-9935; www.provelobikes.com/

Full Cycle, Fort Collins; (970) 484-1800; www.fullcyclebikes.com/

Lee's Cyclery, Fort Collins; (970) 482-6006 and (800) 748-BIKE or (970) 226-6006; http://leescyclery.com/

Brave New Wheel, Fort Collins; (970) 416-0417; www.bravenewwheel.com/

Road 34 Bike Shop, Deli, & Tavern, Fort Collins; (970) 491-9934; www.road34.com/

Niner Bikes, Fort Collins; (970) 682-2241; www.ninerbikes.com/

1 Killpecker Trail

The Killpecker Trail is a rip-roaring ride that sees little mountain bike traffic as it travels from the North Fork Poudre Campground to FR 517 (Elkhorn Baldy Road). The route described here follows Deadman Road, FR 300 (Killpecker Road), and FR 517, which accesses a variety of other motorized trails, such as Bald Mountain and Green Ridge Trails, before reaching Middle Bald Mountain, the second-highest of the three bald peaks in the area, at 11,002 feet. Two thirds of this route involves climbing steadily along these three roads for a total of roughly 10 miles. While the road riding seems long in comparison to the time on the singletrack—and it is—there's good reason for that. The singletrack burns a direct and steep line from the top, at the base of Middle Bald Mountain, to the bottom, south of the North Fork Poudre Campground. Between top and bottom, riders are offered rock- and root-filled singletrack along sometimes narrow terrain.

Start: The Killpecker trailhead
Distance: 14.5-mile loop
Elevation gain: 1,480 feet
Riding time: Advanced riders, 2 hours; intermediate riders, 3 hours
Fitness effort: Physically moderate to challenging due to extended periods of climbing at high elevations
Difficulty: Moderate with some more technically challenging sections of steep grades and large rocks
Terrain: Dirt road and singletrack that reaches elevations in excess of 10,000 feet. While most of the trail runs its course through thick forest, the top of the trail climbs through a very exposed and open meadow, so be aware of any inclement weather that might be rolling in as you near 10,000 feet.
Seasons: June-Oct
Maps: *DeLorme: Colorado Atlas & Gazetteer*, page 19; *USGS:* South Bald Mountain, CO; *Trails Illustrated:* #111, Red Feather Lakes, Glendevey, CO
Nearest town: Red Feather Lakes
Other trail users: Hikers, motorcyclists, horseback riders, and campers
Dog friendly: Yes, but beware of traffic.
Trail contact: Arapaho and Roosevelt National Forests, Canyon Lakes Ranger District, Fort Collins; (970) 498-2770

Getting there: From Fort Collins drive north on US 287. After passing Ted's Place and the intersection with CO 14, continue driving north on US 287 for 11 miles before turning left onto Red Feather Lakes Road (Larimer CR 74E) by the Forks Restaurant. Drive west on Red Feather Lakes Road for 24.6 miles before the road turns to dirt and becomes Deadman Road. Drive on Deadman Road for another 7 miles before bearing left (south) into the Killpecker Trail pullout on the left, across from the North Fork Poudre Campground. Trailhead GPS: N40 48.815' / W105 42.567'

The Ride

Riders begin by climbing up Deadman Road, heading in a northeasterly direction toward the lookout tower. The original wooden tower was built by the Civilian Conservation Corps in 1937 to spot forest fires. The tower was one of eight fire

A successful crossing of the Killpecker Creek.

lookouts in the Front Range, extending from southern Wyoming south to Denver. The wooden tower was replaced by the existing metal structure in 1961. In service for more than 35 years, the Deadman Lookout Tower was the last of the eight Front Range towers to retire, as spotter planes took on the responsibility of locating fires.

In 1991 the National Historic Lookout Register recognized the Deadman Lookout Tower as one of historic and cultural significance. Today, Roosevelt National Forest volunteers oversee the tower. Visitors can still climb to its top to enjoy 360-degree unobstructed views that extend north into Wyoming and south to the Mummy Range and the Rawah Wilderness Area.

With the thought of fire in mind, the climb up Deadman Road makes for a good warm-up to the rest of the day. Within 2 miles of beginning your ride, you pass through what was once the Killpecker Fire, which careless campers started on June 12, 1978, and burned 1,200 acres.

After intersecting with FR 300, you're offered stellar views of West Lake and the Red Feather Lakes area. This section of trail follows the same route as the North Lone

Pine Trail. After roughly 5 miles of riding, FR 300 will come to its first intersection with the Killpecker Trail. From this first intersection the climbing becomes more physically challenging as you make your way into the route's higher elevations. After 6.5 miles the trail levels off a bit and will intersect with the Killpecker Trail two more times. Many area riders will access the Killpecker Trail at its third intersection with FR 300 because from here you begin to lose elevation before having to climb again.

At 10 miles you connect with the Killpecker Trail at a brown trail-marker sign identifying it as a multiple-use trail. Once connecting onto this singletrack, the trail is both technically and physically challenging as it makes its way over rocky and steep terrain to the base of Middle Bald Mountain. You'll eventually come out of the forest into a clearing. The trail climbs alongside the western edge of the clearing, passing a large cairn on your left.

The climb to the top of Middle Bald Mountain (11,002 feet) is well worth the effort, as it offers 360-degree views of Red Feather Lakes to the east, Wyoming to the north, the Rawah Wilderness and Medicine Bow Range to the west, and the Mummy Range to the south. The Mummy Range lies in the northeast corner of Rocky Mountain National Park. Early prospectors to the area decided the range resembled a mummy lying on its back with its hands folded across its chest. The Mummy Range comprises seven prominent peaks: Mount Dunraven (12,571 feet); Mount Chiquita (13,069 feet); Mount Chapin, the mummy's head (12,454 feet); Mummy Mountain (13,425 feet); Mount Fairchild (13,502 feet); Ypsilon Mountain (13,514 feet); and Hague's Peak (13,562 feet). After climbing through the clearing, you'll reenter the forest and negotiate over rocky terrain before intersecting with FR 300.

The descent along the singletrack from its first intersection with FR 300 is fast and moderately technical, providing a variety of more rutted and rockier sections along the way. The middle section of singletrack offers a fast run through a mixed conifer forest and delivers some tighter terrain. Tight rocks, big drop-offs, and steep terrain greet you as you begin the final section of singletrack. Beyond this section the trail descends to meet Killpecker Creek. The rest of the route is fast and furious as the trail weaves alongside, as well as crosses, the creek from time to time. After roughly 13.5 miles you arrive at a rock garden, where you will have to hike-your-bike. Crossing the creek at again 13.9 miles brings you to one last technical section, replete with rocks and steep grades, before returning you to your vehicle.

Miles and Directions

0.0 Start from the Killpecker trailhead and begin climbing in a northeasterly direction on the dirt Deadman Road.

1.7 Pass through the area burned by the Killpecker Fire.

2.1 Deadman Road intersects with FR 300 (Killpecker Road) on your right. Bear right onto FR 300.

3.5 Pass through a gate and continue riding on FR 300.

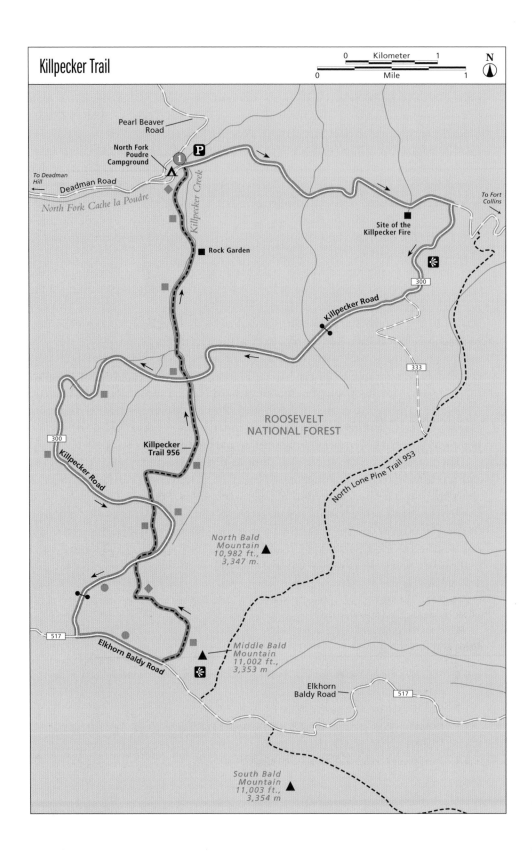

4.9 FR 300 crosses Killpecker Creek and intersects with the singletrack of the Killpecker Trail. Continue riding on FR 300.

7.5 FR 300 once again intersects with the singletrack of the Killpecker Trail. Continue riding on FR 300.

7.6 Pass through a gate and continue on FR 300.

8.6 FR 300 intersects with the singletrack of the Killpecker Trail for the third time. Continue riding on FR 300.

9.3 FR 300 intersects with FR 517 (Elkhorn Baldy Road). Bear left onto FR 517.

10.0 FR 517 passes a foot-travel-only trail on your left. Just past that on your left will be your connection with the Killpecker Trail, marked by a brown, multiple-use trail sign. Bear left onto the Killpecker Trail.

10.3 Arrive at a clearing as you near Middle Bald Mountain, and continue climbing along the clearing's western side. Middle Bald Mountain will be on your right.

11.0 The Killpecker Trail intersects with FR 300. Cross FR 300 and continue descending on the singletrack Killpecker Trail.

11.7 Intersect with FR 300. Cross the road and continue descending on the trail on the other side of the road.

12.7 Intersect with FR 300 again. Bear left on FR 300 for roughly 30 feet, and connect with the singletrack again on the other side of FR 300.

13.0 Cross Killpecker Creek.

13.9 Cross Killpecker Creek again.

14.5 Arrive at your vehicle.

Ride Information

Trail Information

Diamond Peaks Mountain Bike Patrol, a service of Overland Mountain Bike Club; (970) 430-5336; www.overlandmtb.org/

Local Events and Attractions

Creedmore Lakes, north of Red Feather Lakes Road, off CR 180, via CR 73C

Deadman Lookout Fire Tower, west of Killpecker Trail on Deadman Road

Red Feather Lakes, off Red Feather Lakes Road (CR 74E)

Restaurants

Western Ridge Restaurant & Resort, Livermore; (970) 482-4401

The Forks Mercantile, Livermore; (970) 221-2080

Pot Belly Restaurant and Lounge, Red Feather Lakes; (970) 881-2984

2 North Lone Pine Trail

The North Lone Pine Trail is predominantly used by hikers and horseback riders. But owing to the trail's relatively smooth singletrack, which runs underneath a thick canopy of green for its entire length, North Lone Pine offers us "velocipedestrians" one sweet ride. While the entire North Lone Pine Trail continues along the east side of Middle Bald Mountain, at 11,002 feet the second-highest of the three bald peaks in the area, this trail description concerns itself only with the lower half of the trail. The upper half requires too many hike-a-bikes to be enjoyable. While mostly hidden by dense lodgepole pine and aspen forests, the trail does open up near its end to offer easterly views of Red Feather Lakes village. Recreational campers, four-wheelers, and hunters regularly use all the Forest Service roads listed in this description, so be careful as you ride.

Start: The North Lone Pine trailhead
Distance: 4.8-mile loop
Elevation gain: 500 feet
Riding time: Advanced riders, 30-45 minutes; intermediate riders, 1-1.5 hours
Fitness effort: Physically easy to moderate due to the lack of any significant climbing
Difficulty: Technically easy to moderate due to a few rockier and steeper sections
Terrain: Dirt road and singletrack. The single-track runs over mostly smooth terrain under a dense evergreen canopy and alongside North Lone Pine Creek. While most of the trail is smooth and wide singletrack, there are some exposed root sections with which you will have to contend.
Seasons: June-Oct
Maps: *DeLorme: Colorado Atlas & Gazetteer,* page 19; *USGS:* South Bald Mountain, CO; *Trails Illustrated:* #111, Red Feather Lakes, Glendevey, CO
Nearest town: Red Feather Lakes
Other trail users: Hikers, horseback riders, campers, and hunters (in season)
Dog friendly: Yes
Trail contact: Arapaho and Roosevelt National Forests, Canyon Lakes Ranger District, Fort Collins; (970) 498-2770

Getting there: From Fort Collins drive north on US 287. After passing Ted's Place and the intersection with CO 14, continue driving north on US 287 for roughly 11 miles before turning left onto Red Feather Lakes Road (Larimer CR 74E) by the Forks Restaurant. Drive west on Red Feather Lakes Road for 24.6 miles before the road turns to dirt and becomes Deadman Road. Drive on Deadman Road for another 4.5 miles before bearing left into the North Lone Pine overlook and trailhead parking lot area. Trailhead GPS: N40 48.502' / W105 40.232'

The Ride

From your vehicle bear left onto Deadman Road (a dirt road) and climb in a southerly direction to FR 300 (Killpecker Road). FR 300 follows the same route as the Killpecker Trail, a longer, more technical area trail. Once on FR 300, you'll be offered beautiful easterly views of the Red Feather Lakes area.

The area around Red Feather Lakes was first settled as a mining camp in 1871. Although no minerals were ever found, local residents turned their attention to the area's natural beauty. Originally called Westlake, the Red Feather Lakes would then be developed as a mountain resort. Local developers constructed a series of dams and ditches to form the area's many lakes in hopes of attracting Front Range city folk in need of high country diversions. As expected, the city folk came, with not as many leaving. Indeed, the town's first school district was formed in 1895, with a post office following only a year later at the nearby Percy ranch. With an education system and a post office firmly established, the little mountain community was evolving into a full-fledged town. The town's first cabin, built by Nettie Poore along the banks of the smooth Ramona Lake, still stands today. By the early 1900s Westlake was renamed Red Feather Lakes after "Princess" Tsianini Redfeather, a singer who was part Cherokee and part Creek.

Kevin Lam with John Gray close behind wrapping up a smooth run on the North Lone Pine Trail's singletrack.

Once on FR 333, you climb gradually in and out of mixed conifer forests. The trail passes through some old clear-cut fire lines. FR 300 will eventually meet with FR 333A. You'll ride on FR 333A for a very short while before intersecting with the North Lone Pine Trail (953). You'll notice that the trail extends from either side of FR 333A. The section of trail on the right continues to climb to Middle Bald Mountain, while the section of trail on the left descends along North Lone Pine Creek.

The North Lone Pine Trail was once a stock driveway, which was reconstructed as a hiking trail in 1979. After bearing left onto the North Lone Pine Trail, you'll enjoy a fast cruise over smooth singletrack.

About 3.5 miles into your ride, the trail runs down a moderately steep and technical hill to meet North Lone Pine Creek. This section makes for a great watering hole for you, your friends, or some other such faithful companion. You'll cross the creek a couple of times before arriving at a dilapidated shack made of mesh wire. The shack

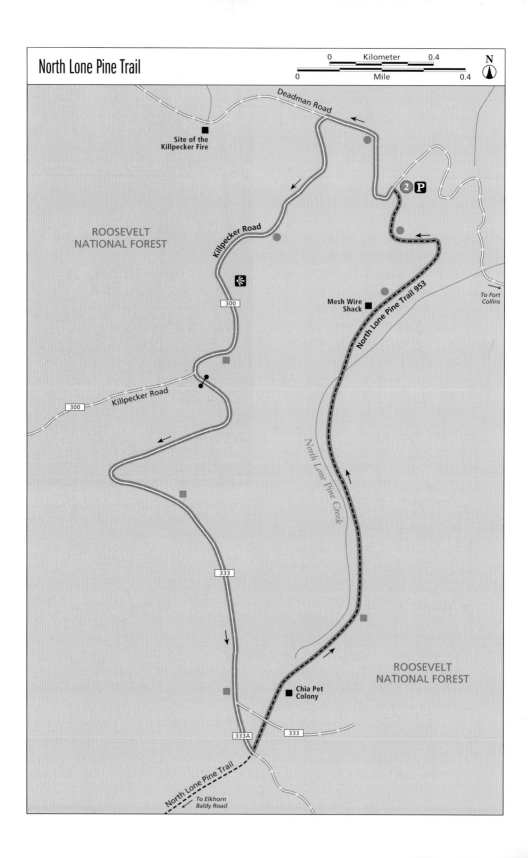

North Lone Pine Trail

Kilometer 0 — 0.4
Mile 0 — 0.4

N

Site of the
Killpecker Fire

ROOSEVELT
NATIONAL FOREST

Deadman Road

2 P

Killpecker Road

300

To Fort
Collins

Mesh Wire
Shack

North Lone Pine Trail 953

Killpecker Road

300

North Lone Pine Creek

333

ROOSEVELT
NATIONAL FOREST

Chia Pet
Colony

333A   333

North Lone Pine Trail

To Elkhorn
Baldy Road

is probably a remnant of when this trail was used as a stock drive for resident ranchers. Nowadays it's more familiar to see stock drives along Red Feather Lakes Road than on nearby area trails. After 4 miles into your ride, the forest will open up briefly to offer glimpses of the Red Feather Lakes area. From here it's a short and fast trip to your vehicle and the end of your ride.

Miles and Directions

0.0 Start by riding out of the parking lot and bearing left onto Deadman Road.

0.5 Deadman Road intersects with FR 300 (Killpecker Road). Bear left onto FR 300, riding in a southerly direction.

1.3 FR 300 intersects with FR 333. Bear left onto FR 333, pass through the iron gate, and continue riding in a southeasterly direction.

2.8 FR 333 bears left and intersects with FR 333A. Continue riding straight on FR 333A and intersect the singletrack trail of the North Lone Pine Trail (953). Bear left onto the cairn-marked singletrack of the North Lone Pine Trail.

2.9 Cross FR 333 and continue riding on the North Lone Pine Trail.

3.6 Arrive at North Lone Pine Creek and continue descending on the trail.

3.9 Pass a dilapidated shack of mesh wire on your left and continue descending on the trail.

4.8 Arrive at your vehicle.

Ride Information

Trail Information

Diamond Peaks Mountain Bike Patrol, a service of Overland Mountain Bike Club; (970) 430-5336; www.overlandmtb.org/

Local Events and Attractions

Creedmore Lakes, north of Red Feather Lakes Road, off CR 180, via CR 73C

Deadman Lookout Fire Tower, west of Killpecker Trail on Deadman Road

Red Feather Lakes, off Red Feather Lakes Road (CR 74E)

Restaurants

Western Ridge Restaurant & Resort, Livermore; (970) 482-4401

The Forks Mercantile, Livermore; (970) 221-2080

Pot Belly Restaurant and Lounge, Red Feather Lakes; (970) 881-2984

3 Elkhorn Creek Trail System

The Elkhorn Creek Trail system is a work in progress, so be mindful of trail indicators such as cairns, dead logs strewn across social trails, or makeshift arrows of branches identifying where to travel and where not to. As of this writing, the trail system includes four completed trails that total over 15 miles. Several other trails within the system will also be opening. Riders can choose from a few options to either shorten or lengthen the ride described here. Indeed, by riding north on Lady Moon Trail to its terminus at CR 74E (Red Feather Lakes Road), riders might choose to link up with the Mount Margaret Trail system. As it is, the ride described here is an out-and-back that combines the Lady Moon Trail and the Granite Ridge Trail. Riders would be well advised to check for updates to this trail system. Throughout the ride mountain bikers are offered intermittent views of the Mummy Range and North and Middle Bald Mountains. Additionally, there are a variety of interesting rock formations with vertical cracks, making it somewhat inviting for bouldering and climbing enthusiasts.

Start: The Elkhorn Creek trailhead off CR 68C (Boy Scout Camp Road)

Distance: 10.8-mile out-and-back, with several side trails that make loops with the main trail

Elevation gain: 734 feet

Riding time: Advanced riders, 1 hour; intermediate riders, 1.5 hours

Fitness effort: Physically easy to moderate due to an initial climb from the trailhead

Difficulty: Technically easy with a couple of more moderately technical sections of single-track and sand

Terrain: Singletrack and doubletrack that deliver rocky and sandy terrain, as well as wider and smoother terrain for a significant portion of the trail's length, passing through open meadows and mixed stands of ponderosa pine and aspen

Seasons: July–Nov

Maps: *USGS:* Red Feather Lakes, CO; *Trails Illustrated:* #111, Red Feather Lakes, Glendevey, CO; *DeLorme: Colorado Atlas & Gazetteer,* page 19, B- and C-6 and -7

Nearest town: Red Feather Lakes

Other trail users: Hikers, equestrians, campers, and climbers

Dog friendly: Yes

Trail contact: Arapaho and Roosevelt National Forests, Canyon Lakes Ranger District, Fort Collins; (970) 498-2770

Getting there: From Fort Collins drive north on US 287. After passing Ted's Place and the intersection of CO 14, continue driving north on US 287 for roughly 11 miles before turning left onto Red Feather Lakes Road (Larimer CR 74E) by the Forks Restaurant. Drive west on Red Feather Lakes Road for roughly 15.7 miles before bearing left onto the dirt CR 68C (Boy Scout Camp Road). Drive on CR 68C for roughly 4.3 miles before turning right into the Elkhorn Creek Trail parking lot. Trailhead GPS: N40 44.782' / W105 32.414'; trailhead terminus/turnaround GPS: N40 46.085' / 105 36.331'

Creighton Grof-Tisza taking it cool and steady along the Granite Ridge Trail 991 underneath the backdrop of Middle Bald Mountain.

The Ride

From the trailhead riders begin riding in a northerly direction on the Lady Moon Trail 985. Originally named Catherine (Katie) Gratton Lawder, Moon arrived in America with Irish immigrant parents in 1865, was orphaned at age 12, and moved to Colorado at 18. Working at Elkhorn Lodge, located near the onetime gold mining town of Manhattan, Katie married miner Frank Gartman, a man several years her senior. Taking a cue from her pilgrim's progress at an early age, Katie divorced Gartman and in 1888 married Oxford graduate and English nobleman Cecil Ernest Moon.

Habitually drinking whiskey and hanging out with ranch hands and miners, Lady Moon would seem to be an unlikely match for Sir Cecil. Accounts of the couple's repeated crossings between Colorado and England are retold in numerous media: in the book *The Lady from Colorado* (1957) by Homer Croy; in the opera (1964) by the same name, composed by Pulitzer Prize winner Robert Ward; and in Fort Collins's Openstage Theater's production of the one-act play *Lady Moon* (2002-2003).

Upon meeting her in-laws for the first time, Moon insisted on bringing her horse Moses and riding gear. Moon also wore cowgirl garb among England's aristocratic

The Great Stupa of Dharmakaya Which Liberates upon Seeing, as seen from the Lady Moon Trail 985.

social elite. When his family and Victorian aesthetics deemed her unacceptable, Lord Cecil divorced and sued Lady Moon for $61,000. Returning to Colorado, Lady Moon insisted on being referred to by her aristocratic title even though she lost it in the divorce. Lady Moon continued to be an interesting character throughout the area, dyeing her hair and dressing in flamboyant attire, until her death in 1926.

As suggested by the life of its namesake, Lady Moon Trail 985 starts out somewhat rocky, crossing Elkhorn Creek and climbing moderately through a mixed conifer forest to an open knoll at roughly 0.5 mile. Riders bear left at the knoll and descend the singletrack that leads over a wider section of embedded granite to a tree-lined meadow. Lady Moon Trail 985 cuts right to climb in a northerly direction over hard-packed, very narrow singletrack through open meadows, aspen, and mixed conifer forests.

Several times in the first mile, the white and golden spire of the Great Stupa of Dharmakaya is visible to the south. The Shambhala Mountain Center's Great Stupa honors Vidyadhara the Venerable Chogyam Trungpa Rinpoche, the great Tibetan guru who taught in the West and realized his own inherent nature, putting him on a par with the Buddha himself. In Buddhist tradition, a stupa functions as a funerary monument, an expression of the living essence of a teacher, and as a sacred center or pilgrimage site. It's believed that anyone who gazes at this stupa sees the body of the Buddha, bringing harmony to the environment and radiating enlightened energy.

With increased harmony and energy, riders continue their moderate climb, passing through meadows awash with purple horsemint, alpine daisies, white alpine yarrow, black-eyed susans, and clucking grouse. Large boulders flank, while columbine complement, the dark and shaded aspen grove through which riders soon pass. Arriving at the Lady Moon Trail 985 (east terminus), riders bear left to intersect the Granite Ridge Trail 991.

Continue west on the generally level Granite Ridge Trail 991, passing through intermittent views to your left of the Mummy Range, which lies on the east boundary of Rocky Mountain National Park. Otherwise the trail is a steady spinner through open meadows and aspen groves, prime habitat for a growing moose population.

You'll eventually arrive at westerly views of the South (11,003 feet), Middle (11,002 feet), and North (10,982 feet) Bald Mountains. North Bald Mountain is the least "bald" of the three, as its rocky summit barely reaches above the tree line. Nevertheless, the summit of North Bald Mountain offers views of Middle and South Bald Mountains, as well as the Mummy Range to the south, the Never Summer Range to the southwest, the Medicine Bow Mountains to the west, the Park Range to the northwest, Wyoming's Snowy Range to the north, and the foothills to the east.

The trail descends to pass several trailheads to its terminus near Manhattan Road. You can really rip the return from here to the intersection with Lady Moon Trail 985 (west terminus), but be aware of the sandier sections. Likewise, the descent on the Lady Moon Trail 985 is fast, but since the singletrack is narrow with tall grass encroaching on both sides, riders will have to invoke their Jedi-riding skills to return safely to their vehicles.

Miles and Directions

0.0 Begin riding north on the Lady Moon Trail 985, climbing over sandy and rocky terrain on wide doubletrack.

0.1 Cross Elkhorn Creek. Stay on the main trail as it passes a campsite on your right. A very narrow singletrack veers off to the left and follows the creek, bearing right and continuing on the wider doubletrack of Lady Moon Trail 985.

0.4 After an initial climb, arrive at an unnamed trail T intersection. A wide doubletrack veers right and descends in an easterly direction. Bear left (west) here, continuing your steady climb on the Lady Moon Trail 985. At the time of this writing, a cairn off to the left marks your route.

0.5 The Lady Moon Trail 985 crests the top of a rocky knoll. Bear left here and descend to the west over sandier and rockier terrain to a meadow. This section of trail shares its route with the Disappointment Falls trail, which continues south through the meadow. (Another wider doubletrack trail leads north and climbs the knoll over steeper and rockier terrain, but this trail has been covered with tree branches in recent months, indicating where the route is not. Should one mistakenly take this route, know that it will eventually connect with the Granite Ridge Trail at another T intersection in a mile. Bearing left at the T intersection will

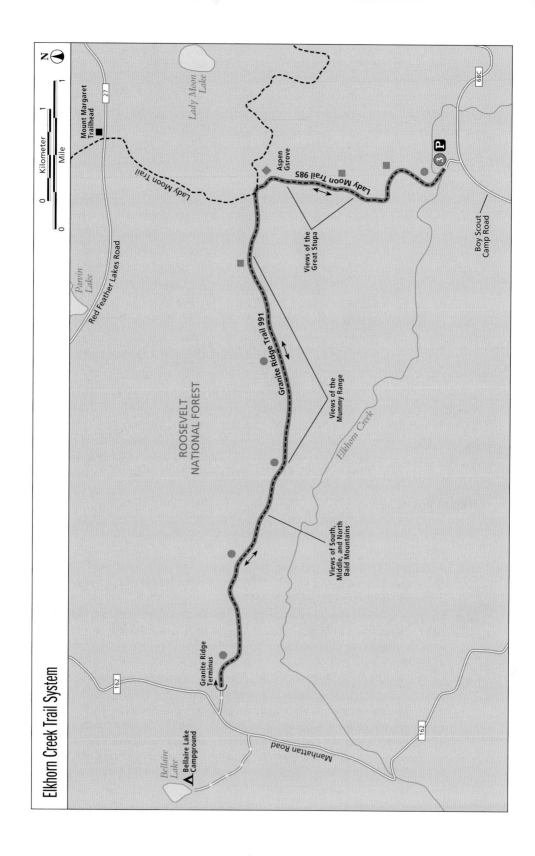

Elkhorn Creek Trail System

deliver you to the properly posted signage for the Lady Moon Trail 985 on the left after another 0.5 mile of riding.)

0.7 The Lady Moon Trail 985 buttonhooks right and climbs moderately in a northerly direction over hard-packed singletrack. Bear right and continue a moderate northerly climb. The meadow will lie behind you to the south. At the time of this writing, an arrow of branches on the left side of the singletrack points the correct way.

0.8 Pass a sign that reads Disappointment Fall 985-2 and Lady Moon 985 on your left.

1.7 Passing through a gate, the Lady Moon Trail 985 (east terminus) intersects with the Granite Ridge Trail 991. Bear left and ride west on the Granite Ridge 991.

1.8 The Granite Ridge 991 intersects with the Lady Moon Trail 985 (west terminus). Continue west on the Granite Ridge 991 trail, passing through the access gate. (**Option:** Bearing right and continuing on the Lady Moon Trail 985 will eventually lead to Red Feather Lakes Road and the Mount Margaret Trail.)

3.4 Pass through another access gate.

3.9 The Granite Ridge Trail 991 intersects with the Molly Moon Trail 991-2 on your left and right. Continue riding west on the Granite Ridge Trail.

4.1 Pass through another access gate.

4.2 The Granite Ridge Trail 991 intersects with the Elkhorn Creek Trail 994 on the left. As of this writing, Elkhorn Creek 994 has yet to be completed. But once completed, it will return to the trailhead from which you started your ride.

4.6 Granite Ridge 991 intersects with the Molly Lake Trail 991-1 on the right. Continue riding on the Granite Ridge 991.

5.4 Arrive at the Granite Ridge Trail 991's western terminus and turnaround. From here, return the way you came.

10.8 Arrive at your vehicle.

Ride Information

Trail Information

Arapaho and Roosevelt National Forests, Canyon Lakes Ranger District; (970) 498-2770 or (970) 295-6700

Local Events and Attractions

Shambhala Mountain Center, Red Feather Lakes; (970) 881-2184

Deadman Lookout Fire Tower, west of the Killpecker Trail on Deadman Road

Red Feather Lakes, off Red Feather Lakes Road (CR 74E)

Creedmore Lakes, north of Red Feather Lakes, off CR 180, via CR 73C

Restaurants

Western Ridge Restaurant & Resort, Livermore; (970) 482-4401

The Forks Mercantile, Livermore; (970) 221-2080

Pot Belly Restaurant and Lounge, Red Feather Lakes; (970) 881-2984

4 Mount Margaret Trail

The Mount Margaret Trail now trades roughly 1.5 miles of doubletrack for as many miles of singletrack. This trail is widely used by equestrians, hikers, and mountain bikers. Its fairly level terrain is well suited for those new to mountain biking. The trail passes by a number of campsites and through a variety of open meadows and quiet stands of aspen and ponderosa pine on its way to the top of Mount Margaret, which overlooks the North Lone Pine Creek drainage. The huge giant rock walls that stand alongside parts of the Mount Margaret Trail offer mountain bikers ample amounts of rock scrambling diversion. Except for the last leg of the trail, which is tight singletrack, the trail follows an old roadbed. Several side trails lead to Dowdy Lake and make loops with the main trail.

Start: The Mount Margaret trailhead
Distance: 7.3-mile out-and-back, with several side trails that make loops with the main trail
Elevation gain: 400 feet
Riding time: Advanced riders, 45 minutes; intermediate riders, 1 hour
Fitness effort: Physically easy due to a lack of any significant elevation gain
Difficulty: Technically easy with a couple of more moderately technical sections of tight singletrack and rockier terrain
Terrain: Singletrack and doubletrack that deliver tighter and rockier terrain toward the end of the trail, as well as wider and smoother terrain for most of the trail's length, as it passes through open meadows and mixed stands of ponderosa pine and aspen
Seasons: Apr-Oct
Maps: *USGS:* Red Feather Lakes, CO; *Trails Illustrated:* #111, Red Feather Lakes, Glendevey, CO; *DeLorme: Colorado Atlas & Gazetteer,* page 19, B- and C-6 and -7
Nearest town: Red Feather Lakes
Other trail users: Hikers, equestrians, and campers
Dog friendly: Yes
Trail contact: Arapaho and Roosevelt National Forests, Canyon Lakes Ranger District, Fort Collins; (970) 498-2770

Getting there: From Fort Collins drive north on US 287. After passing Ted's Place and the intersection of CO 14, continue driving north on US 287 for roughly 11 miles before turning left onto Red Feather Lakes Road (Larimer CR 74E) by the Forks Restaurant. Drive west on Red Feather Lakes Road for roughly 20.5 miles before bearing right into the Mount Margaret Trail parking lot on the north side of the road. Trailhead GPS: N40 46.836' / W105 32.288'; trailhead terminus/turnaround GPS: N40 49.059' / W105 31.676'

The Ride

The trail begins at an easy access along the Red Feather Lakes Road and weaves its way along sinuous singletrack through stands of ponderosa pine and aspen on its way to the South Lone Pine Creek drainage. At 0.7 mile into the ride, the singletrack forks at a sign that points hikers to the right to cross South Lone Pine Creek via a

Author Stephen Hlawaty weaving through a rocky singletrack section, returning from the top of Mount Margaret. AMANDA HLAWATY

footbridge, while stock and mountain bikers bear left and ride through the creek. After crossing the creek, bear left, continuing on the singletrack before connecting to the doubletrack at 1.1 miles.

After passing through the gate at 1.3 miles, the Mount Margaret Trail intersects with Trail 503A on your left. From this intersection continue riding in a northerly direction on the wide doubletrack of the Mount Margaret Trail as it descends moderately over rockier terrain and through a thick patch of aspen. Soon after passing through the aspen, riders can take a break and check out the awesome granite rock formations that stand on either side of the trail. From here riders will pass a variety of campsites and other side trails.

Local Livermore ranchers lease this area for grazing, so it is likely you will pass a few cattle, as well as their droppings, along the way. Adolphus Livernash and Stephen Moore founded the town of Livermore in 1863 when the two of them built a one-room cabin and started prospecting for minerals. With the search not panning out, Livermore soon started growing its ranching roots. Many would-be prospectors turned ranchers came to Livermore from England as remittance men and women.

Ranching took on a life of its own with the opening of a ranching school to train young ranchers in 1880. Ranching is still a part of Livermore; indeed, the town retains a certain ranching community character to this day.

After roughly 2.5 miles the Mount Margaret Trail intersects with two other trails. The East Dowdy Lake Trail lies to your immediate left and cuts back toward the direction from which you came and heads southwest toward Dowdy Lake. Frog Pond, formerly referred to as North Dowdy Lake Trail and Loop A, crosses the Mount Margaret Trail. To the left, Frog Pond heads in a northwesterly direction toward Dowdy Lake, while to the right it heads east before turning north to loop back to the Mount Margaret Trail. At 120 acres, with a shoreline of roughly 3 miles and a maximum depth of 28 feet, Dowdy Lake is the largest of all the lakes in the Red Feather Lakes area. Sitting at an elevation of 8,365 feet, Dowdy Lake makes for a great camping, fishing, and boating spot. The Loop A Trail lies to your immediate right and heads eastward through quiet stands of aspen before reuniting with the Mount Margaret Trail in 1.2 miles. Loop A is a worthwhile diversion from the main trail.

About 3 miles into the ride, riders will pass along the eastern flank of a meadow with a small pond at its center. Once past the intersection with Loop B, riders begin descending on singletrack through a mixed conifer forest. This last leg of the trail offers more rocks and tighter sections, making this section moderately challenging. The singletrack begins to climb as it makes its way to the top of Mount Margaret, which has a hitching post at its base, over tight and moderately technical terrain.

From here riders can see the Maxwell Ranch below in the North Lone Pine Valley. Looking into the North Lone Pine Valley from atop Mount Margaret, riders can see the U-shaped formation of the valley created by the earth's last major glacial period. The Pleistocene or Ice Age began about 2 million years ago, and massive ice sheets covered much of the Northern Hemisphere. In North America, the higher altitudes of the Rocky Mountains were site to the Pleistocene glaciers' first formations, which advanced and retreated multiple times as the climate changed. Today's glacial retreat started some 14,000 years ago and is known as the Holocene epoch.

After taking in the sights, it's time to make a retreat of your own. The initial descent from the top of Mount Margaret is fast and moderately technical with rock, sand, and tighter sections. Be aware of upcoming hikers and equestrians as you return to your vehicle.

Miles and Directions

0.0 Begin riding north on the Mount Margaret Trail on wide and smooth doubletrack for roughly 250 feet before bearing left onto the singletrack.

0.7 The singletrack comes to a fork. Mountain bikers bear left and ride through South Lone Pine Creek; hikers bear right, crossing the creek via a footbridge. After riding through the creek, bear left and continue on the singletrack.

1.1 The singletrack connects with doubletrack. Bear left onto the doubletrack.

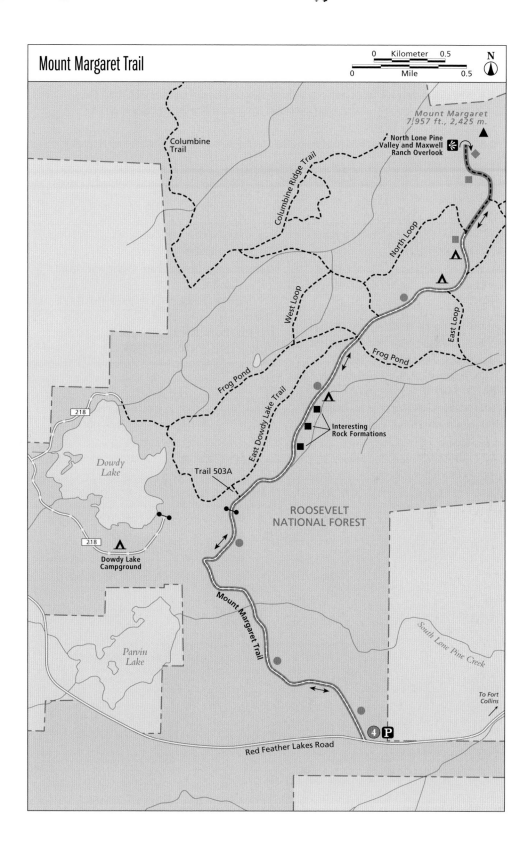

Mount Margaret Trail

Kilometer 0 — 0.5
Mile 0 — 0.5

N

Mount Margaret
7,957 ft., 2,425 m.

North Lone Pine
Valley and Maxwell
Ranch Overlook

Columbine
Trail

Columbine Ridge Trail

North Loop

East Loop

West Loop

Frog Pond

Frog Pond

East Dowdy Lake Trail

Interesting
Rock Formations

218

Dowdy
Lake

Trail 503A

ROOSEVELT
NATIONAL FOREST

218

Dowdy Lake
Campground

Mount Margaret Trail

Parvin
Lake

South Lone Pine Creek

To Fort
Collins

4 P

Red Feather Lakes Road

1.3 Pass through the gate, closing it behind you, and continue riding in a northerly direction on the wide doubletrack. Here the Mount Margaret Trail intersects with Trail 503A on your left.

2.3 The Mount Margaret Trail interesects with the East Dowdy Lake Trail and Frog Pond. From here, continue riding northward on the Mount Margaret Trail, following the sign on your right that reads Mount Margaret-1.5 miles.

2.8 The Mount Margaret Trail intersects with the East Loop on your right. Continue riding on the Mount Margaret Trail.

3.6 Reach the top of Mount Margaret and then return the way you came.

7.3 Arrive at your vehicle.

Ride Information

Trail Information

Arapaho and Roosevelt National Forests, Canyon Lakes Ranger District, Fort Collins; (970) 498-2770

Local Events and Attractions

Deadman Lookout Fire Tower, west of the Killpecker Trail on Deadman Road

Red Feather Lakes, off Red Feather Lakes Road (CR 74E)

Creedmore Lakes, north of Red Feather Lakes, off CR 180, via CR 73C

Restaurants

Western Ridge Restaurant & Resort, Livermore; (970) 482-4401

The Forks Mercantile, Livermore; (970) 221-2080

Pot Belly Restaurant and Lounge, Red Feather Lakes; (970) 881-2984

5 Lower Dadd Gulch Trail

The Lower Dadd Gulch Trail has become more popular among mountain bikers due to trail maintenance. From CO 14 to Salt Cabin Park Road, this trail winds through Dadd Gulch as it follows a stream through thick forests of juniper, ponderosa pine, aspen, and Douglas fir trees. The shade provided by the heavily wooded terrain and a plentitude of creek crossings make this trail a good choice on one of those savagely hot Front Range days. Upon reaching Dadd Gulch Road, riders have the option of either returning to their vehicles the way they came or continuing into Salt Cabin Park to make a loop.

Start: The Lower Dadd Gulch trailhead

Distance: 11.2-mile lariat, with an option to shorten the ride to a 7.0-mile out-and-back

Elevation gain: 1,435 feet

Riding time: Advanced riders, 1 hour; intermediate riders, 1.5 hours

Fitness effort: Physically easy to moderate due to a moderate gain in elevation

Difficulty: Technically easy to moderate due to some rockier and steeper sections

Terrain: Singletrack, doubletrack, and dirt road, which follows a stream in the bottom of a gulch through a heavily wooded mixed conifer forest. The terrain is mostly hard-packed singletrack, with a variety of rockier sections.

Seasons: Apr-Nov

Maps: *DeLorme: Colorado Atlas & Gazetteer,* page 19; *USGS:* Rustic, CO; *Trails Illustrated:* #112, Poudre River, Cameron Pass, CO; Arapaho and Roosevelt National Forests map

Nearest town: Rustic

Other trail users: Hikers and horseback riders

Dog friendly: Yes

Trail contact: Arapaho and Roosevelt National Forests, Canyon Lakes Ranger District, Fort Collins; (970) 498-2770

Getting there: From Fort Collins drive north on US 287. Turn left onto CO 14 at Ted's Place, following signs for the Poudre Canyon, and drive west on CO 14 for 29.5 miles before turning left into the Lower Dadd Gulch trailhead parking lot, just after passing the trailhead to Indian Meadows. A wooden and wired gate marks the beginning of the trail. After passing through the gate, please be sure to close it behind you. Trailhead GPS: N40 41.898' / W105 32.528'

The Ride

The Lower Dadd Gulch Trail winds its way through a mixed conifer forest following the old stock drive up and out of the Poudre Canyon toward the southwest. The first half mile of the trail requires a variety of creek crossings over moderately ascending terrain. You'll follow alongside the creek for the first mile before having to climb steeply uphill away from the creek. After roughly 1.5 miles the trail becomes increasingly tighter as it courses its way through thick, leafy vegetation. By 2 miles you're facing a physically challenging climb, which soon levels off into a grassy meadow with large boulders off to your right. From here the trail climbs more moderately over smooth singletrack; then it will begin to level off through an open area. Once

Salt Cabin Park Road.

beyond the barbed-wire fence, you'll pass through a pine forest clear-cut before intersecting with Dadd Gulch Road.

The climb to Salt Cabin Park Road is moderate, a welcome relief from the singletrack climb through lower Dadd Gulch. As you connect with the Salt Cabin Park
Road, you'll find the descent is fast over large rocks and loose sand. Burned trees
recall the Hourglass Fire of July 1, 1994, which started with a lightning strike in
Pingree Park, southwest of here. Over a dozen buildings were lost on a campus of
Colorado State University. Luckily, no one was injured during the 4-day blaze that
consumed 1,275 acres and cost $10.5 million to fight.

Interestingly, the lodgepole pine has developed its own natural defense against forest fires. Lodgepole pine has both closed (serotinous) and open (nonserotinous) cones.
Closed cones require the intense heat of a forest fire to melt resins and expose the
seeds within, allowing for natural revegetation of the lodgepole pine in the wake of a
forest fire. In periods of no forest fire activity, nonserotinous lodgepole pine regener-
ate the species at a much slower rate. Thus, the dominant tree species in the forests
surrounding Dadd Gulch will survive with or without fire.

In an effort to curb future wildfire hazards, nearby forests have been thinned,
while grass seeding and tree planting have aided in erosion control efforts. Evidence
of reseeding and planting can be seen as you pass through a variety of revegetation
sites around Salt Cabin Park. Bear in mind that there is vehicular traffic on Salt Cabin
Park Road once you pass through the iron gate at 4.4 miles.

After descending to Salt Cabin Park and connecting with the much-improved,
dirt Crown Point Road, you make a smooth, speedy descent, with Bennett Creek to
your right, before reconnecting with Dadd Gulch Road. Riders should watch their
mileage, as there are no real identifying signs for this part of Dadd Gulch Road. Keep
your eyes open for a large dirt pullout at the intersection of Crown Point Road and

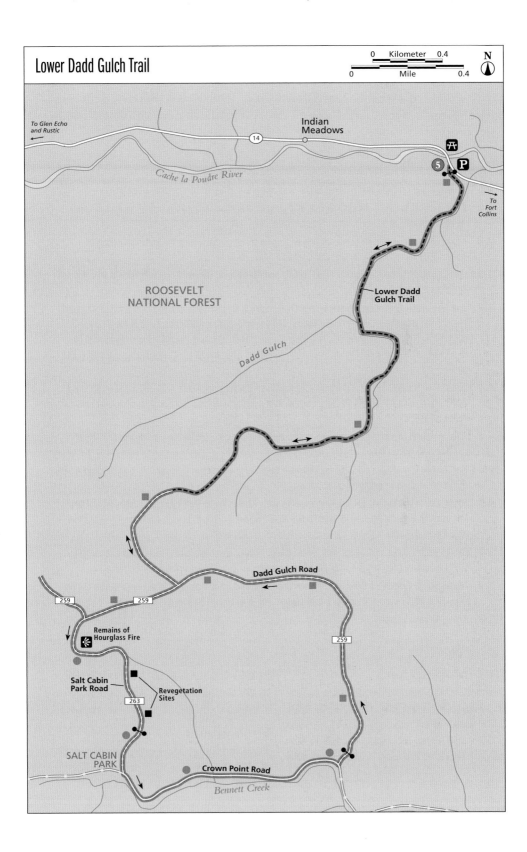

Lower Dadd Gulch Trail

0   Kilometer   0.4

0   Mile   0.4

N

To Glen Echo and Rustic

Indian Meadows

14

Cache la Poudre River

To Fort Collins

ROOSEVELT NATIONAL FOREST

Lower Dadd Gulch Trail

Dadd Gulch

Dadd Gulch Road

259

259

259

Remains of Hourglass Fire

Salt Cabin Park Road

263

Revegetation Sites

SALT CABIN PARK

Crown Point Road

Bennett Creek

Dadd Gulch Road. Be sure to stay on the main Dadd Gulch Road, as there are many crisscrossing roads throughout your climb to the Lower Dadd Gulch Trail. Once you've reconnected with the Lower Dadd Gulch Trail, the descent is fast, with many tight turns and a number of whoop-di-doos off which to catch air (should you be so inclined).

Miles and Directions

0.0 Begin riding on the Lower Dadd Gulch Trail, heading in a southwesterly direction.

1.9 After a short grunt of a climb, arrive at a grassy meadow and continue riding in a south-westerly direction toward Dadd Gulch Road.

2.6 Arrive at another meadow with a row of aspen trees off to your left. Continue riding in a southwesterly direction on the Lower Dadd Gulch Trail.

3.3 Pass through a barbed-wire fence, and continue riding toward Dadd Gulch Road on a wide doubletrack.

3.5 The southern terminus of the Lower Dadd Gulch Trail intersects with Dadd Gulch Road (FR 259). Bear right onto Dadd Gulch Road, and climb moderately in a westerly direction. (**Option:** Where Dadd Gulch Road (FR 259) and the southern terminus of the Lower Dadd Gulch Trail intersect, riders can choose to turn around and retrace the route to their vehicles.)

4.0 Dadd Gulch Road (FR 259) intersects with Salt Cabin Park Road (FR 263). Bear left onto Salt Cabin Park Road (FR 263), heading in a southeasterly direction, and descend toward Salt Cabin Park.

4.4 Pass through the iron gate and continue descending on Salt Cabin Park Road (FR 263) toward Salt Cabin Park.

4.6 Salt Cabin Park Road (FR 263) will come to a fork at a clearing. Bear left, descending on the road in a southeasterly direction.

4.9 Salt Cabin Park Road (FR 263) intersects with Crown Point Road at Salt Cabin Park. Bear left onto the much-improved, dirt Crown Point Road, and descend in an easterly direction with Bennett Creek to your right. Beware of vehicular traffic.

6.0 Crown Point Road intersects with Dadd Gulch Road. Bear left onto Dadd Gulch Road (FR 259), passing through the iron gate, and begin climbing in a northerly direction.

7.7 Dadd Gulch Road (FR 259) completes the loop and intersects with the Lower Dadd Gulch Trail. Bear right onto the Lower Dadd Gulch Trail and return to your vehicle.

11.2 Arrive at your vehicle.

Ride Information

Trail Information

Diamond Peaks Mountain Bike Patrol, a service of Overland Mountain Bike Club; (970) 430-5336; www.overlandmtb.org/

Diamond Peaks Mountain Bike Patrol, Timnath; (970) 482-6006 ext. 22; DPMBP@aol.com

Local Events and Attractions

Mishawaka Amphitheater, Fort Collins; (970) 482-4420

Restaurants

Glen Echo Resort and Restaurant; Rustic, CO; (970) 881-2208

6 Young Gulch

Young Gulch is a great ride for those who like to get wet. During the spring thaw the trail crosses a number of larger creeks. Since this route travels through mixed conifer forests and under thick canopies, the trail remains quite cool, so don't expect to be warm or to dry too quickly. In fact, it's best that you bring a towel and an extra pair of shoes and socks. There are a few rocky and steep technical sections, but for the most part this out-and-back is well suited for the beginner and intermediate rider. The advanced rider will find some of these steeper, rockier sections a challenge and the descent back to his or her vehicle a riot.

(*Note:* As of this writing, Young Gulch remains closed as part of the continuing effort to restore forest trails following the High Park Fire of 2012. Contact local authorities for the latest status of this trail.)

Start: The south side of CO 14, at milepost 109, 3.2 miles west of Poudre Park
Distance: 10.3-mile out-and-back
Elevation gain: 1,179 feet
Riding time: Advanced riders, 1.5 hours; intermediate riders, 2.5 hours
Fitness effort: Physically moderate due to its mellower elevation gain: 5,800-7,040 feet
Difficulty: Technically moderate to challenging due to its rocky but short climbs and descents
Terrain: Singletrack, traveling through a gulch, with many creek crossings under forest cover
Seasons: Apr-Nov

Maps: *DeLorme: Colorado Atlas & Gazetteer*, page 19; *USGS:* Poudre Park, CO; *Trails Illustrated:* #101, Cache La Poudre, Big Thompson, CO; Arapaho and Roosevelt National Forests map
Nearest town: Poudre Park
Other trail users: Campers, hikers, and horseback riders
Dog friendly: Yes
Trail contact: Arapaho and Roosevelt National Forests and Pawnee National Grassland, Forest Supervisor Office, Fort Collins; (970) 498-1100

Getting there: From Fort Collins head north on US 287. Turn left onto CO 14, following signs for the Poudre Canyon. Drive on CO 14 for 13 miles. The dirt road turnoff to Young Gulch is 3.2 miles past the tiny town of Poudre Park and will be on the left, at milepost 109. Drive up the dirt road to the parking area and trailhead. A wooden and wired gate marks the beginning of the trail. After passing through the gate, please be sure to close it behind you. Trailhead GPS: N40 41.317' / W105 20.890'; trailhead terminus/turnaround GPS: N40 38.611' / W105 21.985'

The Ride

The Young Gulch Trail is located in Roosevelt National Forest's Poudre Canyon. In 1918 the Forest Service granted the town of Fort Collins permission to develop Young Gulch as a place where people could picnic, camp, and hike. Three years later Young Gulch was opened. Today, it stands as a reminder of Colorado's early commitment to mountain recreation.

Amanda Hlawaty displaying a stable hold while carrying her bike.

Convict labor built the original road leading to Young Gulch—now CO 14. The Poudre Valley Good Roads Association constructed a masonry fireplace to celebrate the completion of the road to that point. Located just beyond the turnoff for Young Gulch, the fireplace was left for others to use in the future.

Just before the old fireplace, a Forest Service sign marks the Cache la Poudre River as a "Wild and Scenic River System." The Poudre is the only river in Colorado to receive protection under the National Wild and Scenic River Act. Covering an estimated 150 miles, the Poudre River originates from Poudre Lake (an alpine lake located high in the mountains of Rocky Mountain National Park) and extends to the South Platte River just east of the town of Greeley.

The Poudre Canyon is dedicated to a variety of outdoor activities: mountain biking, hiking, camping, rock climbing, four-wheeling, kayaking, and rafting. Local citizens groups, like Friends of the Poudre, have worked to develop boat chutes at diversion structures on the river so kayakers and rafters can run the entire river in the lower canyon without having to portage their crafts. These chutes are estimated to cost between $200,000 and $300,000 each—further evidence of Colorado's commitment to recreation.

Just 3 miles up CO 14 from the Young Gulch trailhead stands the Mishawaka Inn (Mishawaka means "sweet water"), a laid-back, riverside complex including an inn, amphitheater, and restaurant serving locally brewed beer. The name probably comes from the sweet sounds of the nearby Poudre River. The property is a summer venue for the likes of John Gorka, Otis Taylor, Martin Sexton, and the David Grisman Quintet—to name but a few. In February of 1916, Walter S. Thompson, a musician from Fort Collins, purchased the surrounding land with the intent of operating a self-supporting home. Within 3 years Thompson had built himself a very comfortable house, several cabins, a general store, and a dance hall. More than 90 years later, the music continues to play throughout the Poudre Canyon, keeping time with the rocking and rolling of our bikes through Young Gulch.

Rocking and rolling do well to describe this trail. Young Gulch offers a vast array of terrain for any level mountain biker. Its steep-sided, narrow, and rocky terrain offers challenges for even the best riders, while its many creek crossings allow the novice mountain biker many chilling thrills. The creek crossings, along with dense forests, make this trail ideal for those hot summer days. Unfortunately, the heavy forest cover causes the snow at

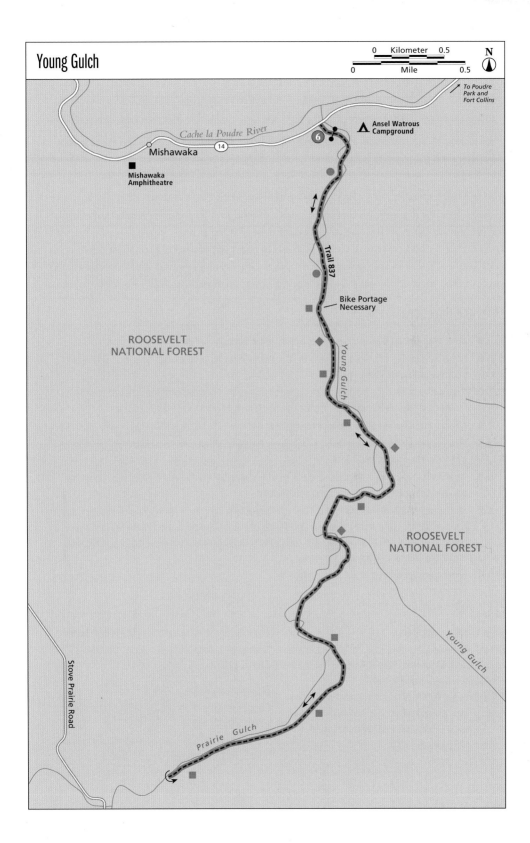

Young Gulch

Young Gulch to melt late, creating a potentially cold and wet environment late into the spring. These spring conditions can be tricky to ride in. Deep creek crossings, wet rocks, and slippery roots can all cause loss of significant braking power.

The last 3 miles of Young Gulch is smoother and wider, making for a fast descent on your way back. Take care on your return, as rocky approaches into creeks come up on you fast. The rocky downhills can be hairy if not approached carefully—but oh! the fun.

Miles and Directions

0.0   Start from the gate at the trailhead. Begin riding through the thickly forested gulch.

0.6   Arrive at a sweet, shaded spot, just to your right—ideal for a quick rest or snack. Blooming cacti abound creekside.

1.3   Reach one of two short but technical climbs. Climb this section with thoughts of your returning descent. Picking the line to your right on your return is probably best.

1.4   A rocky impasse requires a bike portage.

3.5   Pick up the trail by walking upcreek for approximately 50 feet. From here the gulch widens out with fewer rocks and roots.

5.0   The trail merges with a four-wheel-drive road heading up the hillside to your left. Climb for another 0.2 mile to reach the turnaround point.

5.2   As the top of this climb levels out, bear an immediate right for a short grind to the top of a knob of stone. From here there is a good view of the gulch and Stove Prairie Road. Private property begins beyond the gate. Do not cross without permission. After resting, backtrack and enjoy the fast and rocky descent.

10.3   Arrive back at your vehicle.

Ride Information

Trail Information

Diamond Peaks Mountain Bike Patrol, a service of Overland Mountain Bike Club; (970) 430-5336; www.overlandmtb.org/

Diamond Peaks Mountain Bike Patrol, Timnath; (970) 482-6006 ext. 22; DPMBP@aol.com

Forest to Grassland Information Center, Fort Collins; (970) 498-2770

Local Events and Attractions

Mishawaka Amphitheater, Fort Collins; (970) 482-4420

Restaurants

CooperSmith's Pub & Brewing, Fort Collins; (970) 498-0483

Rio Grande (the best margaritas you'll ever drink), Fort Collins; (970) 224-5428

7 Hewlett Gulch

Hewlett Gulch is a favorite among mountain bikers in and around Fort Collins. Its fast singletrack, big drop-offs, creek crossings, killer climbs, and one very rocky descent will satisfy any mountain biker's idea of a good ride. Although technically and physically moderate to challenging, the ride serves first-time mountain bikers well as it can be ridden at any pace. For those who like to grab air, there's a great spot at the 2.3-mile mark where the trail dips into a small gully. With enough speed, you'd swear you were flying. An alternate route to the steep and rock-laden descent that arrives at 5.4 miles has been built; however, this area has received much damage by way of fire and flood.

Start: The trailhead parking lot, just past Poudre Park in the Poudre Canyon

Distance: 8.5-mile lariat, with an additional 4 miles if one opts for the 4-mile out-and-back

Elevation gain: 1,195 feet

Riding time: 2 hours

Fitness effort: Physically moderate to challenging due to an extended climb midway through the ride

Difficulty: Technically challenging due to a very rocky and steep descent on the return

Terrain: Rough doubletrack and singletrack. This trail has many creek crossings and weaves in and out of mixed conifer forests before climbing up through a meadow. Although most of this ride is manageable by the intermediate rider, there are big drop-off sections as well as one of the rockiest singletrack descents in all of the Front Range.

Seasons: Apr-Nov

Maps: *DeLorme: Colorado Atlas & Gazetteer,* page 19; *USGS:* Poudre Park, CO; *Trails Illustrated:* #101, Cache La Poudre, Big Thompson, CO; Arapaho and Roosevelt National Forests map

Nearest town: Poudre Park

Other trail users: Campers, hikers, hunters, and horseback riders

Dog friendly: Yes

Trail contact: Arapaho and Roosevelt National Forests and Pawnee National Grassland, Forest Supervisor Office, Fort Collins; (970) 498-1100

Getting there: From Fort Collins head north on US 287. Turn left onto CO 14, following signs for the Poudre Canyon. Drive on CO 14 for 10 miles. After passing the tiny town of Poudre Park, you'll spot a bridge to the north crossing the Cache la Poudre River. Cross the bridge and continue up the road to the trailhead parking lot. Respect residents of the Poudre Canyon by not parking in front of their driveways or mailboxes. Trailhead GPS: N40 41.370' / W105 18.622'

The Ride

As the Cache la Poudre River crashes through the Poudre Canyon in Roosevelt National Forest, the echoes of a distant pioneering past resound from its granite walls. The very name of the canyon recalls the struggles that the early pioneers had to endure in order to come to terms with this western wilderness.

In November 1836 a party of French-Canadian trappers and traders, led by Antoine Janis of John Jacob Astor's American Fur Company, was en route to a rendezvous on

The author splashes down after managing the rocky drop behind him. AMANDA HLAWATY

the Green River when bad weather hit. The snowstorm made it impossible for the group to safely ford the Poudre Canyon's river, so Janis gave the order to lighten the wagon loads. The men dug a large pit, lined it with pine boughs and animal skins, and filled it with what could be spared from each wagon. After backfilling the pit, the trappers burned a large fire on top to disguise the site from Arapaho and Cheyenne Indians. Included in the buried supplies were several hundred pounds of gunpowder. The French-speaking trappers called this place cache la poudre ("the hiding place of the powder"). Some months later the party returned to the Poudre Canyon and recovered all of their supplies. The name stuck.

Typical of the mountain biking trails of Colorado's Front Range, Hewlett Gulch delivers smooth, fast-riding singletrack; rocky, uncompromising climbs and descents; and a dizzying array of creek crossings. The trail begins as an overgrown doubletrack, which soon turns to singletrack within half a mile. There are four creek crossings within the first mile of the trail. To slow erosion, water bars lie across the trail for the first 2 to 3 miles, making for some steep drop-offs and tough, "taco-bending hill hops" (jumps that can bend your front wheel like a taco). The water bars have effectively made Hewlett Gulch more technical than ever before.

Within the first mile you encounter the remnants of Horace Huleatt's old homestead. Huleatt settled the gulch in 1870 on land he later found out was sacred to Ute

Indians. When Horace realized this, he quickly moved on, leaving his homestead as a parting gift. Today, a stone chimney and a concrete foundation are all we have of old Horace Huleatt, but his name lives on, though slightly corrupted, in Hewlett Gulch. After the homestead the trail leads into a lush, pine-covered sanctuary awash with thousands of wildflowers.

The trail continues through intermittent fields and groves of cedar and pine. The canyon narrows here. Sheer granite walls climb the sides of the canyon in a vain attempt to pierce the sky. The surroundings become more rugged, save the yellow flowering cacti.

After about 2 miles into the ride, the trail comes to a T before a big gully, offering the opportunity for "sick air," or a long jump. Bear left and climb the side of the hill. The hit or jump is on the right side of the trail as you scream up the other side of the gully. From there the trail meanders through alternating stands of lodgepole pine and spruce, offering occasional short, rocky, and steep climbs. After one such climb the trail lets out onto a broad grassy hill completely devoid of trees. A half mile to the north of this hill stands a beautiful house boasting an even better southerly view. Turn around and enjoy an inspiring view of the canyon through which you've just ridden.

The 2-mile climb to the top of this hill is deceiving, as there is a false summit at mile 4.2. This false summit does, however, offer a great opportunity to dismount and take in the views. Although Hewlett Gulch does have its challenging, short, steep climbs, it rewards the persistent rider with incredible, rocky singletrack descents. After arriving at the second gully, the trail once again comes to a T. Here you have the option to bear right for a rugged 4-mile out-and-back or simply bear left and continue on the main trail. This optional trail ends at the national forest boundary and overlooks some private homes in Hewlett Gulch.

The descent from this point is famed for its technical riding, although recent trail maintenance efforts have built an alternate route to this one. The alternate route avoids the steep grades and loose, football-size rocks that once made for one of the sickest singletrack descents on Colorado's Front Range. This notwithstanding, recent fire and flood have considerably affected this trail. Once you arrive at the bottom, bear right and backtrack for the remaining 2.3 miles.

Miles and Directions

0.0 Start from trailhead and bear onto a rough doubletrack, entering Roosevelt National Forest.

0.4 The singletrack begins.

1.1 The trail crosses the creek for the fourth time and leads into a lush pine forest carpeted with wild poppies. A great place for a picnic or resting spot.

2.3 Sick air. The trail T's. Bear right.

3.3 An extremely difficult and rocky descent delivers you to a broad and grassy 2-mile hill climb.

4.2 Don't be fooled. This is a false summit, albeit an ideal resting spot for those in need.

4.3 A short but fast stretch of singletrack highlighted by a couple of rocky sections rewards the patient hill climber.

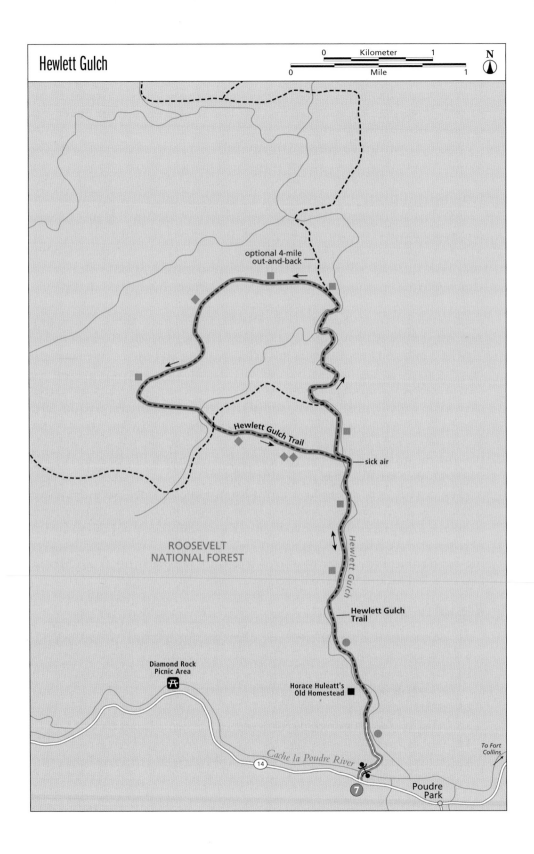

Hewlett Gulch

optional 4-mile
out-and-back

Hewlett Gulch Trail

sick air

ROOSEVELT
NATIONAL FOREST

Hewlett Gulch
Trail

Hewlett Gulch

Diamond Rock
Picnic Area

Horace Huleatt's
Old Homestead

Cache la Poudre River

To Fort
Collins

14

7

Poudre
Park

0   Kilometer   1
0   Mile   1

N

John Gray takes flight over the Hewlett Gulch Trail.

5.3 The trail leads into a deep gully. You'll need your speed getting out of it, as the trail continues up a steep but short ascent. At the top of this short climb, you'll once again come to a T in the trail. Bear left here on the main trail toward your eventual descent. (**Option:** Bear right for a 4-mile out-and-back option.)

5.4 Beginning of the onetime rugged, sick descent. An alternate route now skirts the hillside to the bottom.

6.2 You arrive at the bottom, where you caught the sick air. Bear right and backtrack the first part of Hewlett Gulch Trail.

8.5 Arrive at your vehicle.

Ride Information

Trail Information

Diamond Peaks Mountain Bike Patrol, a service of Overland Mountain Bike Club; (970) 430-5336, www.overlandmtb.org/

Diamond Peaks Mountain Bike Patrol, Timnath; (970) 482-6006 ext. 22; DPMBP@aol.com

Forest to Grassland Information Center, Fort Collins; (970) 498-2770

Local Events and Attractions

Mishawaka Amphitheater, Fort Collins; (970) 482-4420

Restaurants

CooperSmith's Pub & Brewing, Fort Collins; (970) 498-0483

Rio Grande (the best margaritas you'll ever drink), Fort Collins; (970) 224-5428

8 Mill Creek Trail

Lory State Park/Horsetooth Mountain Park is prime real estate for some of the area's best mountain biking. The Mill Creek Trail is arguably one of the most technically and physically challenging rides in all of Fort Collins, but it has recently undergone some trail renovations to deliver a more flowy ride. Added to this is the Kimmons Trail, which connects the Timber Trail to the West Valley Trail. Likewise, a variety of repair work was completed to ten bridges and various trails affected by the Galena Fire of 2013. With gorgeous views of Colorado's great plains and Horsetooth Reservoir to the east, riders climb into the semiarid woodlands of Colorado's Front Range, the first step into the Rocky Mountains. This route offers rolling terrain alongside Horsetooth Reservoir, a burly climb to Horsetooth Mountain, and a sweet descent down the Mill Creek Trail. An experience reaching biblical proportions, the Mill Creek Trail is David to the Goliath-like trails of the giant Rocky Mountains.

Start: Entrance to Lory State Park, at the guard station, just beyond the stop sign

Distance: 13.3-mile lariat

Elevation gain: 1,500 feet

Riding time: Advanced riders, 1.5-2 hours; intermediate riders, 2.5-3 hours

Fitness effort: Physically moderate to challenging—3 miles of rolling singletrack runs south along Horsetooth Reservoir, while 3 miles of steep and arduous hill climbing takes you to the top of Horsetooth Mountain and the trailhead of Mill Creek

Difficulty: Technically moderate to challenging due to its rocky and steep singletrack descents—a trademark of Front Range mountain biking

Terrain: Rocky and rolling terrain on both singletrack and dirt road surfaces

Fees and permits: $3 individual park pass must be purchased (price subject to change)

Seasons: Apr-Nov

Maps: *DeLorme: Colorado Atlas & Gazetteer*, page 20; *USGS:* Horsetooth Reservoir, CO; Colorado State Parks maps: Lory State Park; Larimer County Parks Department map: Horsetooth Mountain Park

Nearest town: Fort Collins

Other trail users: Hikers, campers, horseback riders, and those enjoying various forms of water recreation

Dog friendly: Yes, but beware the horseback riders.

Trail contact: Larimer County Parks and Open Lands Department, Loveland; (970) 679-4570

Getting there: From downtown Fort Collins at the junction of College Avenue and Mountain Road, drive north on College Avenue out of Fort Collins for 6.3 miles, heading toward La Porte and Lory State Park. After driving through La Porte, veer left onto Larimer CR 52E. Drive on 52E for approximately 1 mile before making a left onto CR 23 by the red flagstone Bellvue Senior Center. At 8.7 miles turn right onto CR 25G and follow signs to Lory State Park. Drive another 1.6 miles to the entrance of Charles A. Lory State Park. Leave your vehicle outside of the park, as you will begin your ride by the guard station. Trailhead GPS: N40 35.420' / W 105 11.050'

Amanda Hlawaty runs through the lower valley of Lory State Park amid the backdrop of Arthur's Rock.

The Ride

The over 5,000 acres that make up Lory State Park and Horsetooth Mountain Park boast a venous system of trails. This network, running along the transitional ecology of the Rocky Mountain foothills, weaves its way through a variety of terrain and vegetation: unique rock outcroppings, sandstone hogbacks, grassy open meadows, cacti-laden hillsides, and ponderosa pine forests. To the northwest Arthur's Rock (6,780 feet) marks the high point in Lory State Park and overlooks the city of Fort Collins. Its jutting granite foundation stands as a testament to the strength of will and the indomitable character of the people of Fort Collins.

On July 29, 1997, Fort Collins's local newspaper, the *Coloradoan*, ran the headline "Torrential Rain Floods City." In a 5-hour span, Fort Collins received 8.41 inches of rain. The ensuing flood washed trains off their tracks. Ninety-two mobile homes were destroyed; 145 houses and 116 apartments were damaged; and five lives were lost. The city suffered millions of dollars in damages. It was Fort Collins's worst natural disaster to date.

The deluge dropped in excess of 10 inches of rain on nearby Lory State Park, wreaking havoc on the park's trails. By September of 1997 a massive reconstruction effort of the park's trails was under way, involving the efforts of the Diamond Peaks Mountain Bike Patrol, trail design professionals from the International Mountain Bicycling Association, and local residents and riders.

Prior to becoming a state park in 1967, this area was primarily ranch land. The trails most likely started as game trails. Over the years, and after much use, they've evolved into mountain bike trails. Unfortunately, the trails had never received proper erosion-proofing or design. And so, when the flood of '97 hit, Lory State Park's trail system sustained substantial damage. Since the flood, a concerted effort has been devoted to redesigning and preserving these natural trails.

At this point, all of the damage has been rectified. The lower stretches of trail—those hardest hit by the flood—which lie just west of Horsetooth Reservoir in Lory State Park's valley, offer ideal riding conditions for beginners practicing their techniques. Advanced riders wanting to increase their heart rates will enjoy them as well. The first 4.7 miles of West Valley Trail meanders through rolling, open meadows and past a number of Horsetooth Reservoir's coves and bays. There's Santanka Cove, named for the red sedimentary formations in the area, and Soldier Cove, located at the base of Soldier Canyon—so-called because a skeleton and three US Army buttons were found there. Eltuck Bay was named after Elton Collins, who with the help of Tuck (J. Morris) Howell helped build the reservoir as part of the Colorado–Big Thompson Irrigation Project in the late 1940s. Before the waters of the reservoir swept in to cover them, Quarry Cove was a sandstone quarry and Orchard Cove a cherry orchard. Dixon Cove gets its name from a local landowner of the mid-1900s.

Once you arrive at the service road (aka Sawmill Trail), you begin your 2.4-mile climb to the top of Horsetooth Mountain—the Front Range's answer to those lung-busting climbs of the Colorado high-country interior. While climbing, you pass beneath Horsetooth Rock, which resembles a horse molar, hence its name. According to an Arapaho Indian legend, this formation is the heart of the Great Red Warrior who was killed by the Great Black Warrior in a long and bitter struggle in the heavens. The blood shed in the battle is said to have stained the rock red.

With the grind to the top accomplished, it's time for a sick ride down the singletrack of the Mill Creek Trail. The trail begins through a dense ponderosa pine forest. Heading south, as you hug the east face of Horsetooth Mountain, you'll have to negotiate your line through some steep and rocky sections, all within the first mile of starting the Mill Creek Trail. Remember, the straightest line is always your strongest line. At mile 9.6 you cross Mill Creek—so-called because the Latham Mill once operated on it—behind Horsetooth Reservoir. The mill provided lumber for bridges in the early history of Larimer County. Nothing of the mill remains.

As you cross the creek and begin your climb out, notice the small wading pond to your left. If you don't cool off here, the next leg of the trail may toss you. Just 0.2 mile ahead is the tight switchback section of the trail. Although the approaches to

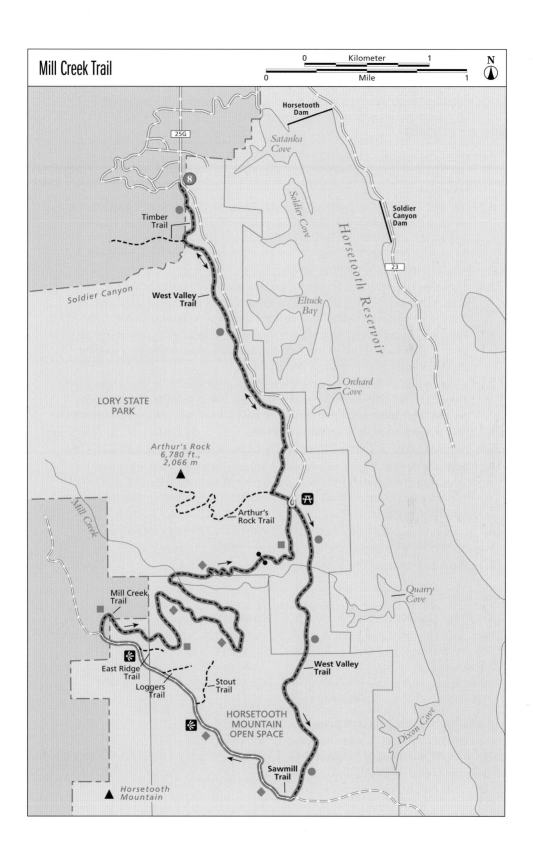

Mill Creek Trail

Kilometer
0   1

Mile
0   1

N

Horsetooth
Dam

*Satanka
Cove*

25G

8

Timber
Trail

*Soldier
Cove*

Soldier
Canyon
Dam

23

West Valley
Trail

Soldier Canyon

Horsetooth Reservoir

*Eltuck
Bay*

LORY STATE
PARK

*Orchard
Cove*

*Arthur's Rock
6,780 ft.,
2,066 m*

Mill Creek

Arthur's
Rock Trail

*Quarry
Cove*

Mill Creek
Trail

West Valley
Trail

East Ridge
Trail

Loggers
Trail

Stout
Trail

Dixon Cove

HORSETOOTH
MOUNTAIN
OPEN SPACE

Sawmill
Trail

*Horsetooth
Mountain*

each switchback can be ridden quickly, check your speed, as the switchbacks come up quickly. The remaining descent through Lory State Park to return to your vehicle comes complete with short, rocky sections and smooth-running singletrack.

Miles and Directions

0.0 Start on the singletrack by the visitor center and entrance to the park, just beyond the stop sign. Daily park passes must be purchased before entering the park. Follow the singletrack to the group picnic area.

0.3 Ride right into the Timber Trail group area and pick up the singletrack of the Timber Trail to the left of the sign. Within 0.2 mile from where Timber Trail started, the singletrack will Y. Bear left at the Y onto West Valley Trail (Timber Trail continues to the right, where bikes are not allowed). Note that West Valley Trail will cross a number of other trails leading into the hills. Do not veer right on any offshoots.

2.3 Reach the group picnic area. From here there are a number of routes that branch left to coves at Horsetooth Reservoir. Following the rolling terrain of West Valley Trail, continue through the meadow, paralleling the sandstone hogbacks of Horsetooth Reservoir to your left.

4.7 Reach the junction of West Valley Trail and Sawmill Trail. Look for a frog pond to your right. Head right, climbing up Sawmill Trail. Note that Sawmill Trail is a rough service road and marks your entrance into Horsetooth Mountain Park.

7.1 Having climbed for 2.4 miles, passing the tempting singletracks of the Stout, Loggers, and East Ridge Trails, you'll see the trailhead to Mill Creek Trail on your right. Note that there are a number of offshoots to your left, leading down the west side of Horsetooth Mountain. Reserve taking any of these trails for another day.

9.1 Reach the junction of Loggers Trail and Mill Creek Trail. Veer left, continuing on Mill Creek Trail.

10.2 Arrive at a red gate, marking your reentrance into Lory State Park. Close the gate behind you, and enjoy the views of Fort Collins and Horsetooth Reservoir to the east. Ride for 0.1 mile to the sign for Arthur's Rock, Horsetooth Mountain, and the parking area. Ride straight ahead past the sign.

10.8 Arrive at the sign that marks the trailheads for Bridal and Arthur's Rock Trails. From here return by either the road or the singletrack to your vehicle.

13.3 Reach the entrance of Lory State Park and the ranger station.

Ride Information

Trail Information

Diamond Peaks Mountain Bike Patrol, a service of Overland Mountain Bike Club; (970) 430-5336; www.overlandmtb.org/

Diamond Peaks Mountain Bike Patrol, Timnath; (970) 482-6006 ext. 22; DPMBP@aol.com

Local Events and Attractions

Horsetooth Mountain Park, 4 miles from Fort Collins; contact Larimer County Parks and Open Lands Department at (970) 679-4570

Lory State Park, Bellevue; (970) 493-1623

Restaurants

CooperSmith's Pub & Brewing, Fort Collins; (970) 498-0483

Rio Grande (the best margaritas you'll ever drink), Fort Collins; (970) 224-5428

9 Bobcat Ridge Trail

Bobcat Ridge is one of the biggest rides in the Fort Collins area. Riders are offered commanding views of red rock cliffs, the west face of Horsetooth Rock, and the foothills and eastern plains. It provides riders of any ability with a variety of route options. The route described here captures much of what the area offers and is a burly ride by any standard. Joining the Valley Loop, Power Line, and Ginny Trails, this route incorporates most of the trails in the Bobcat Ridge area with the exception of the Eden Valley Spur Trail and the D.R. Trail (closed to mountain bikes). Riding the loop in a counterclockwise direction delivers a strenuous slog up the Power Line Trail, which offers much to this route's physically challenging rating, before intersecting with the technically challenging Ginny Trail. Along the way riders are rewarded with miles of meadows dotted with yucca plants and extraordinary views of the remains of a 2000 wildfire. Due to the exposed nature of the area, it is best to ride during the earlier hours of the morning or the later hours of the day. For anyone wanting a tough, technical, full-day ride, Bobcat Ridge is it.

Start: The Valley Loop trailhead
Distance: 10.0-mile loop, with several side trails that make shorter loops, lariats, and out-and-back trails
Elevation gain: 1,405 feet
Riding time: Advanced riders, 2 hours; intermediate riders, 3 hours
Fitness effort: Physically challenging due to considerable elevation gain
Difficulty: Technically challenging with a few bike-portaging sections of steep, sandy, and rocky terrain
Terrain: Singletrack and doubletrack that deliver exposed steep, sandy, and rocky terrain

Seasons: Apr-Oct
Maps: *USGS:* Masonville, CO, and Drake, CO; *DeLorme: Colorado Atlas & Gazetteer,* page 30, A-1
Nearest town: Masonville
Other trail users: Hikers, equestrians, and picnickers
Dog friendly: No; dogs are not permitted at Bobcat Ridge.
Trail contact: City of Fort Collins Natural Areas Program Office; (970) 416-2815; www.fcgov .com/naturalareas/

Getting there: From Fort Collins drive west on Harmony Road until it turns into CR 38E at the intersection of Harmony Road and Taft Hill Road. From this intersection drive on CR 38E, heading around Horsetooth Reservoir and passing the Blue Sky Trail and Horsetooth Mountain Park on your right, for roughly 9.5 miles before turning left (south) onto CR 27 by the Masonville Mercantile. Drive on CR 27 for roughly 0.6 mile before bearing right (west) onto the dirt CR 32C. Drive on CR32C for roughly 0.5 mile before arriving at the Bobcat Ridge Natural Area. Trailhead GPS: N40 28.757' / W105 13.595'

John Gray making his descent along the Ginny Trail.

The Ride

Originally the Bobcat Ridge area was the cool-weather stomping grounds of the Ute Indians who descended from the mountains in search of the large game that would congregate near the area's red, rocky ridges. These rocky areas were also the site of conflict between the Ute and their enemies the Arapaho, as it was once part of traditional migratory routes.

Traversing a 2,600-acre area, Bobcat Ridge is one of the most technically and physically demanding rides in the Fort Collins region. The route described here begins on the wide and smooth doubletrack of the Valley Loop Trail. Biking in a northerly direction, riders are rewarded with a smooth ride through open meadows, but such mountain biking civility does not last for long. After passing the intersection with the Power Line Trail and carrying on for roughly 1.2 miles, the wider double-track of the Valley Loop Trail turns into a more dedicated dirt singletrack trail. From this point riders begin their ascent, with the first moderate climb arriving at roughly 1.8 miles. Shortly thereafter the Valley Loop Trail intersects with the D.R. Trail, which is closed to mountain biking. And, perhaps, this is as it should be.

The D.R. Trail is named after David Rice (D.R.) Pulliam, who, along with his wife, Virginia, owned the Bobcat Ridge property. As the Valley Loop Trail continues to ascend from this intersection, riders come to a beautiful overlook where there is a stone sitting bench, an ideal location to honor the memories of past family members, be they kin or canine: rock on, Pooh and Moab. Shortly after this overlook riders are given a considerable wakeup call as they intersect and begin climbing the Power Line Trail.

The intersection of the Valley Loop Trail and the Power Line Trails offers riders a few options: the route described here directs riders to climb the Power Line Trail. However, riders wishing to shorten their ride and ease their efforts can continue riding in a southerly direction on the Valley Loop Trail, which skirts the lower, tree-lined valley slope. Otherwise, bear right onto the Power Line Trail and begin the long slog to the top and Mahoney Park. The climb is considerable, and the trail's namesake is well deserved: a rider will need to have power and pick the right line. The trail itself follows an old and rutted utility road that is steep, rocky, and sandy.

Three miles into the ride, riders are offered views of the remains of the 2000 Bobcat Gulch Fire and 2009 Bobcat Ridge Fire. The fires burned over 70 percent of the mixed coniferous stands that covered most of this area, consuming more than 10,000 acres: an eerie but spectacular sight. The former fire started in June when flames from an abandoned campfire ignited dry grasses. The more recent fire started on the morning of June 12, burning north and east from Bobcat Gulch and northwest to Masonville.

From the Power Line Trail and after nearly 4 miles of riding, riders intersect with the Ginny Trail, which leads to Mahoney Park. The Ginny Trail is a welcome gift for riders, as it was for D.R. Pulliam when his wife, Virginia (Ginny), surprised him with a birthday present of the building of a narrow dirt road to Mahoney Park—one of the couple's favorite spots. The Ginny Trail is Bobcat Ridge's sweetest section, and its singletrack runs through open meadows and some stands of ponderosa pine. The exposed white granite along the trail stands in stark relief against the boulders and burnt trees that pepper the area.

Some of the visible rocks illustrate a process known as spalling. This occurred when the Bobcat Gulch Fire heated the rock's outer surface, causing part of the rock's surface to flake off and fracture. Erosion ultimately rounds the edges of the rocks to create the smooth and rounded boulders that you pass along the trail.

After riding for roughly 5.5 miles, riders are delivered to an expansive view as the trail continues over tight, rocky singletrack. Once arriving at the Ginny Trail's most technical descent section, you'll encounter some more extreme sections, so take care when descending. After connecting with the Valley Loop Trail, it's a fast and smooth singletrack descent back to your vehicle.

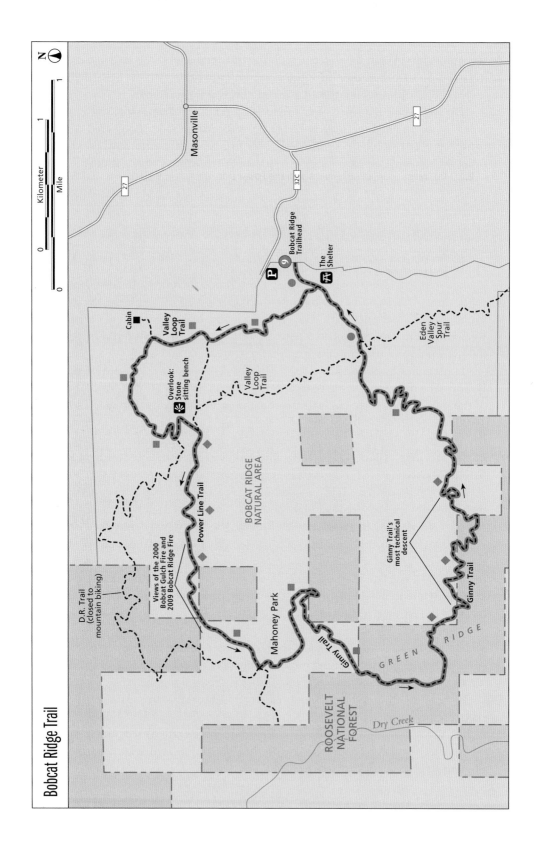

Bobcat Ridge Trail

Miles and Directions

0.0 Begin riding on the Valley Loop Trail.

0.1 Bear right, continuing on the Valley Loop Trail.

0.9 The Valley Loop Trail intersects with the Power Line Trail for the first time on the left. Continue riding on the Valley Loop Trail, heading north.

2.0 The Valley Loop Trail intersects with the D.R. Trail (no bikes allowed on the D.R. Trail).

2.3 The Valley Loop Trail intersects with the Power Line Trail for the second time on the right. Bear right and climb on the Power Line Trail. (**Note:** The Power Line Trail can only be ridden in a counterclockwise direction. Riders are prohibited from descending on the Power Line Trail.)

3.3 The Power Line Trail levels out slightly.

3.8 The Power Line Trail intersects with the D.R. and Ginny Trails. Bear left onto the Ginny Trail and begin riding in a southerly direction.

6.3 Reach the beginning of the Ginny Trail's most technical descent section, where a sign reads uphill users have right of way. Descend with care.

9.4 The Ginny Trail intersects with the Valley Loop Trail. Bear right onto the Valley Loop Trail.

10.0 Arrive at your vehicle.

Ride Information

Trail Information

City of Fort Collins Natural Areas Program Office; (970) 416-2815; www.fcgov.com/naturalareas/

Bobcat Ridge Ranger Office; (970) 461-2700

Local Events and Attractions

Masonville Mercantile, 9120 CR 27, Masonville; (970) 667-4058

Horsetooth Reservoir; www.horsetooth reservoir.com/Horsetooth_Reservoir/Home .html and www.larimer.org/naturalresources/ horsetoothconditions.cfm

Blue Sky Trail; http://larimer.org/parks/ bluesky_brochure.pdf

Horsetooth Mountain Park; www.co.larimer .co.us/parks/htmp.cfm

Restaurants

Masonville Mercantile, 9120 CR 27, Masonville; (970) 667-4058; open daily from dawn to dusk

10 Blue Sky Trail

The Blue Sky Trail, which shares its route with Horsetooth Mountain Open Space and Devil's Backbone Open Space, is a gem of a mountain bike ride, particularly on a sunny day. The route described here includes the Indian Summer Trail, which provides riders with additional singletrack climbing and descending. Due to the exposed nature of the area, the Blue Sky Trail can get hot in the middle of the day, so start early. Otherwise, its sinuous singletrack rolls over hard-packed, rocky, and sandy terrain. While there are a few sections of more technical terrain, Blue Sky is generally moderate in nature and provides mountain bikers with a fast and fun ride.

Start: The Blue Sky trailhead off CR 38E

Distance: 15.0-mile out-and-back, with several side trails that make loops with the main trail

Elevation gain: 1,645 feet

Riding time: Advanced riders, 1.5 hours; intermediate riders, 2 hours

Fitness effort: Physically moderate due to a lack of significant elevation gain

Difficulty: Technically moderate with a few technically challenging sections of steep and rocky singletrack

Terrain: Singletrack and doubletrack that deliver exposed rocky and sandy terrain

Fees and permits: A daily entrance permit (fee charged) is required of all vehicles and provides access to the Blue Sky Trail as well as the other trails in Horsetooth Mountain Open Space. Annual entrance permits are also available.

Seasons: Apr-Nov

Maps: *USGS:* Horsetooth Reservoir, CO, and Masonville, CO; *DeLorme: Colorado Atlas & Gazetteer,* page 30, A-1

Nearest town: Fort Collins

Other trail users: Hikers, runners, and equestrians

Dog friendly: Yes

Trail Contact: Natural Resources Department, Loveland; (970) 679-4570; http://larimer .org/parks/

Getting there: From Fort Collins drive west on Harmony Road until it turns into CR 38E at the intersection of Harmony Road and Taft Hill Road. Continue driving west on CR 38E, around Horsetooth Reservoir, for 5.5 miles before turning right into the Blue Sky parking lot. Trailhead GPS: N40 31.104' / W105 10.070'; trailhead terminus/turnaround GPS: N40 26.822' / W105 09.283'

The Ride

The Blue Sky Trail gets high marks for its flow factor in both directions. Running north-south, it serves as a corridor trail that runs through a valley between Horsetooth Reservoir and the Devil's Backbone. The Blue Sky Trail itself is only 5.5 miles long, but since it connects with Horsetooth Mountain Park, Coyote Ridge Natural Area and Rimrock Open Space, and the Devil's Backbone Open Space, riders can turn this 15-mile route into an extended epic ride.

Riders begin their day on the pristine singletrack of the Blue Sky Trail. The singletrack is twisty as it weaves its way around tight rock outcroppings over relatively smooth terrain. Otherwise, the trail is lined with juniper, sage, and yucca plants. It isn't

Creighton Grof-Tisza expertly negotiating "The Stairs" for the Blue Sky Trail.

until 1.2 miles into your ride that you have to negotiate a steep, technical climb—a hike–a–bike for all but the toughest riders.

By 3.5 miles you reach a slow and steady climb to the intersection with the Rimrock Trail, which is a more technical loop and connects to the Coyote Ridge Natural Area and the 472-acre Rimrock Open Space to the east, beyond the top of the ridge. No dogs are allowed in the Coyote Ridge Natural Area, which includes 2.3 miles of natural surface trails at an elevation gain of roughly 600 feet. Though the climb is a bit of a grunt, the views of the towering red rock cliffs and hogback valleys are worth the sweat. From this intersection riders can also make out part of the Devil's Backbone off to the southwest. Its stegosaurus–like ridgeline is the hardened remains of an ancient anticline of sedimentary rocks that were thrust skyward as the Rocky Mountains were formed over 200 million years ago when this area was covered by a vast inland sea of the Jurassic period.

The Blue Sky trail descends westward from this vantage point to the valley floor, avoiding a raptor nesting area in the cliffs. The descent is fast and furious over tight and rocky singletrack. Riders should take care as they near the bottom as the terrain becomes sandier and tighter in sections.

At the west side of this valley, riders connect with the Indian Summer Trail, which climbs moderately westward. After a fast descent over a mix of smooth and rocky terrain, riders arrive at a technical section at roughly 5.3 miles, which is doable for more advanced riders. Shortly thereafter, riders reach the high point of the Indian Summer Trail, offering views of the Indian Peaks to the southwest and Boyd Lake to the east. The Indian Peaks were summer hunting grounds for the Arapaho Indians for thousands of years.

From here the Indian Summer Trail curves south to descend once again to the valley floor and reconnect with the Blue Sky Trail roughly 6.2 miles into your ride. Riders will then pass a tempting shady cottonwood tree and bench, but don't stop pedaling. Nearing 7 miles into your ride, Longs Peak (14,255 feet) and Mount Meeker

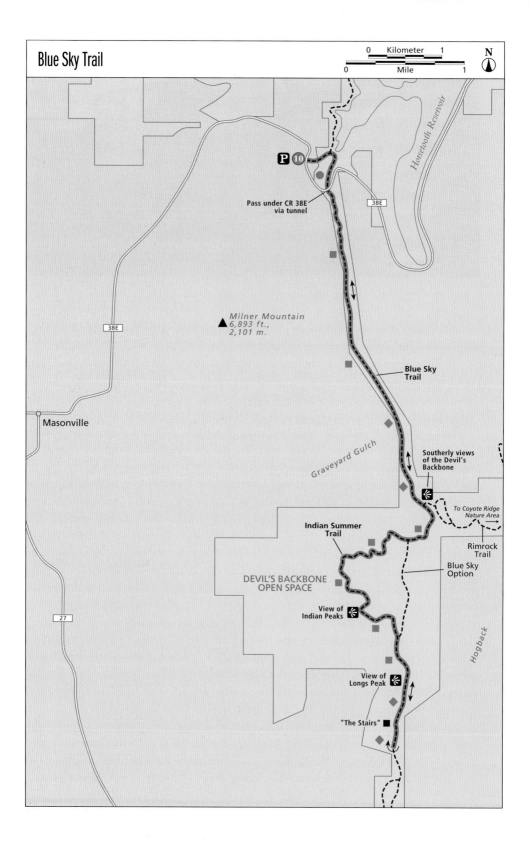

Blue Sky Trail

0   Kilometer   1

0   Mile   1

N

Horsetooth Reservoir

P 10

Pass under CR 38E
via tunnel

38E

38E

▲ Milner Mountain
6,893 ft.,
2,101 m.

Blue Sky
Trail

Graveyard Gulch

Masonville

Southerly views
of the Devil's
Backbone

To Coyote Ridge
Nature Area

Indian Summer
Trail

Rimrock
Trail

Blue Sky
Option

DEVIL'S BACKBONE
OPEN SPACE

View of
Indian Peaks

27

Hogback

View of
Longs Peak

"The Stairs" ■

(13,916 feet) come into view. These are the two most prominent peaks in northern Colorado. Taking in these views, you're off again to meet with "the Stairs." The Stairs serve up technically challenging terrain for advanced riders, but they are well worth the scramble to the top and the Blue Sky's turnaround point 7.5 miles into your ride.

From here you have the option to return the way you came or continue on to the Laughing Horse Loop. If you go for it, be sure to bear right and ride counterclockwise, or the loop will deliver highly technical and big hike-a-bike sections. Otherwise, take care descending the Stairs; they are technical and rocky. Similarly, the descent and return to your vehicle combines fast terrain with tight turns that are often being used by others coming in the opposite direction. Be mindful, but enjoy the ride nonetheless.

Miles and Directions

0.0 Begin riding south along the Blue Sky Trail.

0.5 Pass under CR 38E via a tunnel.

3.6 The Blue Sky Trail intersects with the Rimrock Trail, a more technically challenging loop for riders who want to test their mountain biking mettle. Rimrock Trail also connects riders with the Coyote Ridge Natural Area. From here continue on the Blue Sky Trail and descend to its intersection with the Indian Summer Trail.

4.1 The Blue Sky Trail intersects with the Indian Summer Trail. Bear right onto the singletrack of the Indian Summer Trail and begin climbing. (**Option:** Riders can continue riding on the wide dirt road of the Blue Sky trail to avoid the climb.)

5.4 The Indian Summer Trail reaches its high point. Take some time to enjoy the views before continuing your ride on the Indian Summer Trail and descending to its intersection with the Blue Sky Trail.

6.2 The Indian Summer Trail intersects and reconnects with the Blue Sky Trail. Bear right onto the Blue Sky Trail and continue riding in a southerly direction. (For riders who are tired or who might have mechanical issues, bearing left onto the Blue Sky Trail will return them to the Indian Summer trailhead via a flat service road.)

7.5 Reach the top of the Stairs of the Blue Sky Trail. This is the turnaround point. (**Option:** Continue riding south toward the Laughing Horse Loop, a 1.5-mile romp in the Devil's Backbone Open Space. See Ride 11.)

15.0 Arrive back at your vehicle.

Ride Information

Trail Information

Natural Resources Department, Loveland; (970) 679-4570; http://larimer.org/parks/

Local Events and Attractions

Horsetooth Reservoir, contact Larimer County Parks and Open Lands Department, Loveland; (970) 679-4570

Horsetooth Mountain Park, contact Larimer County Parks and Open Lands Department, Loveland; (970) 679-4570

Lory State Park, Bellevue; (970) 493-1623

Restaurants

Rio Grande (the best margaritas you'll ever drink), Fort Collins; (970) 224-5428

Equinox Brewing Company (best beer in town), Fort Collins; (970) 484-1368

11 Devil's Backbone

Aside from offering views of an interesting geological formation, as well as swirling raptors overhead, the aptly named Devil's Backbone delivers mountain bikers a technically challenging trail in exposed and rocky terrain. Due to the trail's exposure, be sure to drink enough water, wear plenty of sunscreen, and try to complete the ride before or after the hottest hours of the day. This trail runs along the lower eastern flank of the Backbone and includes two possible loops: the southern Hunter Loop and the northern Laughing Horse Loop. This description covers both loops. The northernmost tip of the Laughing Horse Loop connects with the Blue Sky Trail.

Start: The Devil's Backbone trailhead
Distance: 6.5-mile double lariat
Elevation gain: 400 feet
Riding time: Advanced riders, 1 hour; intermediate riders, 1.5-2 hours
Fitness effort: Physically moderate due to its exposed terrain and steep climbing sections
Difficulty: Technically moderate to challenging due to some steeper ascents and descents over large rocks, big drop-offs, and loose sand
Terrain: Dirt road and singletrack, which runs over intermittent hard-packed and rockier terrain. The trail is very exposed with little to no shade, so temperatures can get quite hot in the summer months.

Seasons: Seasonal wildlife closures in effect Mar 1 to June 15
Maps: DeLorme: Colorado Atlas & Gazetteer, page 30; USGS: Masonville, CO; Devil's Backbone Open Space trail map; Larimer County Parks and Open Lands map
Nearest town: Loveland
Other trail users: Hikers and horseback riders
Dog friendly: No—there is little to no water or shade available on the route. Rattlesnakes have also been spotted in this area.
Trail contact: Larimer County Parks and Open Lands Department, Loveland; (970) 679-4570

Getting there: From Fort Collins drive south on I-25 for roughly 12 miles and exit at 257B and US 34 in Loveland. Bear right and drive west on US 34 for 8.5 miles before bearing right onto Wild Lane (Larimer CR 22B), marked by the large, cement Loveland water tank on your right. Drive on Wild Lane for 0.2 mile, crossing a creek, and bear right into Peep-O-Day Lane and the Devil's Backbone parking lot. Trailhead GPS: N40 24.702' / W105 9.155'

The Ride

In 1998 Larimer County acquired the Devil's Backbone Open Space through a sales tax passed by voters to help protect important area natural resources. The beginning of the Devil's Backbone Trail rolls over smooth and wide singletrack as it parallels a fence and crosses a couple of footbridges, one of which spans the Louden Ditch. A native of Louden, Iowa, Aaron Benson settled in the Big Thompson Valley in 1878. Benson built the ditch to carry water from the Big Thompson River to irrigate 12,000-plus acres of area farmland. While constructing the ditch, workers unearthed

Author Stephen Hlawaty enjoys the fast descent, with the Devil's Backbone in the background.
AMANDA HLAWATY

a soft, white material that absorbed much of the water passing through it. The material turned out to be high-quality gypsum ($CaSO_4$), the same material used in the manufacture of plaster of paris, drywall, and fertilizers.

As you ride from the ditch, you can still notice the abandoned gypsum mines to the east. These mines also bore several mammal fossils, including a prehistoric elephant with 5-foot-long tusks and a jawbone with seven teeth. While these remains were of mammals of the Cenozoic era, much of the Devil's Backbone rock is from the Morrison Formation, which dates back more than 150 million years. By touching the gray rock of the Backbone, you may well be touching the same stones once trod upon by dinosaurs. But due to the extremely fragile and unstable nature of the Devil's Backbone, do not climb on the rocks.

Once past the first, short climb, the trail bears north and runs alongside the eastern flank, over relatively smooth singletrack, through a low-lying valley of Morrison and Entrada rock outcroppings, as well as mountain mahogany shrublands and needle grasslands. After 0.5 mile of riding, the "multiuse" trail intersects with the foot-only portion of the Devil's Backbone Trail. Taking the left fork, this hiking trail climbs steeply and travels north along the base of the Backbone before descending and returning to the multiuse portion of the trail.

Shortly after intersecting with the northern terminus of the Devil's Backbone's Foot-Only Trail, you begin a medium-length climb over rocky and steep terrain.

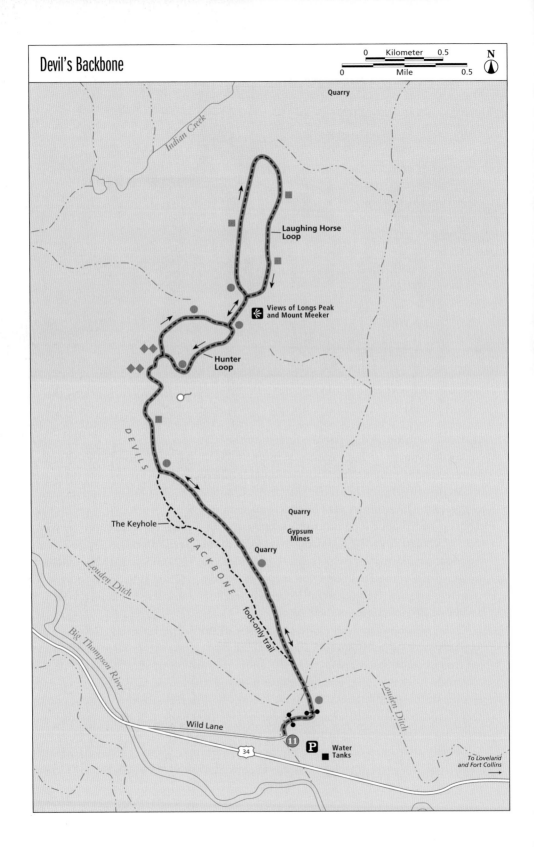

Devil's Backbone

0   Kilometer   0.5

0   Mile   0.5

N

Quarry

Indian Creek

Laughing Horse
Loop

Views of Longs Peak
and Mount Meeker

Hunter
Loop

DEVILS

The Keyhole

BACKBONE

Quarry

Gypsum
Mines

Quarry

foot-only trail

Louden Ditch

Big Thompson River

Louden Ditch

Wild Lane

11

P

Water
Tanks

34

To Loveland
and Fort Collins

The climb is physically challenging over technically moderate terrain of sand and loose rock. Just before reaching the 2-mile mark of your ride, you come to the trail's most technical section, which combines a steep climb with loose rock.

Continuing from the intersection of the Hunter Loop, you ride over moderately rolling terrain, heading in a northerly direction. From here the trail becomes increasingly rocky. Upon connecting with the Laughing Horse Loop, you'll begin climbing in a westerly direction over embedded rock and narrow singletrack. This is an enjoyable section of the trail for a number of reasons. Not only does it present technically moderate terrain, but it also runs along the rim of a small plateau, offering westerly views of the Devil's Backbone rock formation. The erosive forces of wind and water have produced openings in the formation, such as the Keyhole.

From these views and roughly 3 miles into your ride, you descend over

The author working his way through some of the more ridiculously technical sections of the Devil's Backbone. AMANDA HLAWATY

rocky terrain that delivers a variety of bigger drop-offs. The trail eventually veers to the south, offering some technically challenging terrain over tight, embedded rock, and returns to where you began the Laughing Horse Loop. After finishing this loop, you're offered views of Longs Peak and Mount Meeker to the west as you race toward the trail's southern loop.

The Hunter Loop is short but sweet. Upon intersecting with the main trail again, take care in descending. The terrain offers loose rock and sand over steeper slopes before letting out to the more moderate terrain. With the Backbone to your right, it's a fast cruise back to your vehicle.

Miles and Directions

0.0 From the parking lot begin riding up the dirt road underneath the cottonwood trees in a northerly direction. Shortly thereafter, bear right onto the Devil's Backbone singletrack, following signs to the Devil's Backbone Trail.

0.1 Pass through a wooden gate, and continue north on the singletrack.

0.3 Pass through an iron gate, and begin a short climb in a northwesterly direction over moderately steep terrain.

0.5 Arrive at the intersection of the foot-only portion on your left and the multiuse portion of the Devil's Backbone Trail on your right. Bear right, continuing on the multiuse portion of the trail.

1.3 The Devil's Backbone multiuse trail intersects with the northern terminus of its foot-only trail on the left. Continue right on the multiuse singletrack.

2.0 Arrive at the Hunter Loop. (This will be the second loop you complete.) Bear left here, continuing in a northerly direction.

2.3 Arrive at the second intersection of the Hunter Loop on your right. Bear left here.

2.6 Arrive at the Laughing Horse Loop, the beginning of the trail's northernmost loop. Bear left here and begin riding the loop in a clockwise direction.

3.1 Pass a sandstone bench off to your right.

3.8 Arrive at the intersection and end of the Laughing Horse Loop. Bear left here and return from where you came to the Hunter Loop.

4.1 Arrive at the intersection with the Hunter Loop. Bear left and begin climbing in a southerly direction.

4.5 Arrive at the intersection and end of the Hunter Loop. Bear left here and return the way you came.

6.5 Arrive at your vehicle.

Ride Information

Trail Information

Larimer County Parks and Open Lands Department, Loveland; (970) 679-4570

Local Events and Attractions

Estes Park and Rocky Mountain National Park, west through the Big Thompson Canyon Rocky Mountain National Forest; recorded message, (970) 586-1333; general information, (970) 586-1206. For additional information or correspondence, write to Rocky Mountain National Park, Superintendent, Estes Park, CO 80517. A fee is charged for backcountry permits in the summer months; reservations are recommended. For reservations or bivouac permits, call (970) 586-1242.

Restaurants

Backbone Gourmet Grub & Brewhouse, 1480 Cascade Ave., Loveland; (970) 622-8008

12 Crosier Mountain Trail

The Crosier Mountain Trail offers riders primal mountain biking appeal that may not be best suited for those who enjoy a smooth-rolling ride. Although riders can link routes to lessen the distance and technical aspects of the ride, the route described here includes all aspects of what the Crosier Mountain Trail has to offer: nearly 6 miles of road biking; roughly 200 feet of dirt road biking; technical switchback ascents and descents along rocky, root-filled, and tight singletrack terrain; as well as soft and smooth singletrack through pristine meadows, aspen groves, and mixed conifer forests and past juniper, bitterbrush, yucca, and prickly pear. Added to this is a short, 1-mile out-and-back hike to the top of Crosier Mountain, which offers an awesome panoramic view. On the other side of this spectrum lie a fair number of hike-a-bike sections that will test your stamina and strength. In the end, this 14-mile loop offers it all for anyone willing and able to tear off as much as he or she can chew.

(**Note:** As of this writing, Crosier is closed as a result of the flooding of 2013. Contact local authorities for latest status of this trail.)

Start: The Garden Gate 931 trailhead off CR 43

Distance: 14.0-mile loop, with options to shorten

Elevation gain: 2,802 feet (this includes the hike to the top of Crosier Mountain)

Riding time: Advanced riders, 2 hours; intermediate riders, 2.5 hours

Fitness effort: Physically challenging due to considerable elevation gain

Difficulty: Technically challenging with a few sustained bike-portaging sections of steep, sandy, and rocky terrain

Terrain: Paved road; singletrack and double-track that deliver steep, sandy, and rocky terrain with little running water nearby

Seasons: Apr-Nov

Maps: *USGS:* Glen Haven, CO; *DeLorme: Colorado Atlas & Gazetteer,* page 29, A-7; *Trails Illustrated:* #101, Cache La Poudre, Big Thompson, CO

Nearest town: Glen Haven

Other trail users: Hikers, equestrians, and picnickers

Dog friendly: Yes, but little to no water

Trail contact: Canyon Lakes Ranger District, Fort Collins; (970) 295-6700; www.fs.usda .gov/goto/arp/clrdrecreation

Getting there: From Loveland drive west on US 34. Roughly 7.5 miles past the Dam Store, turn right onto CR 43 (Devil's Gulch Road). Drive north on CR 43 for roughly 2.1 miles before turning left into the pullout parking spaces of the Garden Gate trailhead #931. Parking is limited with room for only seven vehicles. Trailhead GPS: N40 26.541' / W105 22.699'

The Ride

There are three access points to the Crosier Mountain Trail along CR 43: the Garden Gate, Rainbow Pit, and Glen Haven trailheads. This route connects the easternmost Garden Gate trailhead to the westernmost Glen Haven trailhead, before looping to the start along the Crosier Mountain Trail, to incorporate the most mileage. For a shorter ride you can choose to do one of the shorter loops from any of the three trailheads.

As described, the Crosier Mountain Trail is a beast of a ride, so riders should know what they're in for: steep climbs, switchbacks, and body-pounding bike portages over rocky terrain and big drop-offs. Aside from this, the route includes a nearly 6-mile run on CR 43 that parallels the sweet-sounding waters of the North Fork of the Big Thompson River, butter-smooth singletrack through forests and meadows, and a 1-mile out-and-back hike to the summit of Crosier Mountain and panoramic views.

The initial run on CR 43 offers a good warm-up to what lies ahead. The sounds of the North Fork of the Big Thompson River blend with the sounds of the wind rushing past your ears to create a Zen-like flow to your ride. Appreciate it now, as this route will eventually take you to the opposite extreme.

Upon reaching the town of Glen Haven, your road ride ends as you connect with the Crosier Mountain Trail just beyond the red horse stable on the south side of the road. Glen Haven was named and founded in 1903 by Reverend W.H. Shureman, who wanted to make the area a summer retreat for Presbyterians. Shureman was a prolific leader of the religious faithful who traveled thousands of miles by horse, buggy, stagecoach, railroad, and automobile to organize 215 Sunday schools and 25 churches in northern and eastern Colorado, make 14,500 pastoral visits, and participate in 13,600 church programs between the years 1898 and 1933.

After connecting with the Crosier Mountain Trail, riders begin their southerly climb over several switchbacks and through forests dominated by ponderosa pine, Douglas fir, and juniper trees. Having ridden nearly 6.5 miles, you'll reach the top of a ridge and the intersection with the H-G Ranch Trail on your right and Knapps Knob Trail on your left.

The H-G Ranch Trail is a loop that eventually reconnects with the Crosier Mountain Trail at the southern tip of Piper Meadows. The ruins of a cabin belonging to Robert and Amanda Anderson, who homesteaded here in 1906, are on the H-G Ranch Trail. Four years later the Andersons mysteriously fled their homestead for New Mexico, leaving their furniture and baking still on the kitchen table. Supposedly their abrupt departure was due to the overwhelming grief at the sudden death of their infant daughter, whom they wrapped in a blanket before leaving. Knapps Knob Trail owes its namesake to Ira Knapp, who in 1896 set up a sawmill along the North Fork of the Big Thompson River across from the horse stable in Glen Haven. A year later the Knapps laid claim to the land that is Glen Haven, which at that time was known as Knappville.

From here riders continue their ascent through Piper Meadows, which offers sweeping views of the Mummy Range. Harry Piper operated a dairy here from 1913 to 1930. Near the lower end of the meadow was located the milk house, now a hole in the ground with a rock foundation. The larger hole nearer the trail was the barn, where Piper lived after his home burned down in the early 1930s. Continue climbing

View from the top of Crosier Mountain with Longs Peak in the background.

to the meadow's southern tip before cutting sharply to your left to climb a series of switchbacks. Climbing in a more northerly direction, you'll intersect with the Crosier Rainbow Trail 981 to your left. The ride from here to the intersection with the Crosier Mountain Summit Trail delivers another tough climb.

After reaching the Crosier Mountain Summit Trail, park your bike and hike the 0.5 mile to the 9,250-foot summit. Views at the top include the Twin Sisters Peaks and Longs Peak to the south, Estes Park and Rocky Mountain National Park to the southwest and west, Signal Mountain to the northwest, and the Front Range to the east. A plastic jug with the words crosier mountain log written on it and an "all-weather memo book" invite you to record and register your name, thoughts, and sightings.

From the Crosier Mountain Summit Trail, it's a fast and tight singletrack descent through True Gulch before hitting a couple of arduous and sustained hike-a-bike sections, so get in touch with your primal roots. Once you pass the cave to your left at roughly 13.1 miles, the descent to your vehicle is fast and furious.

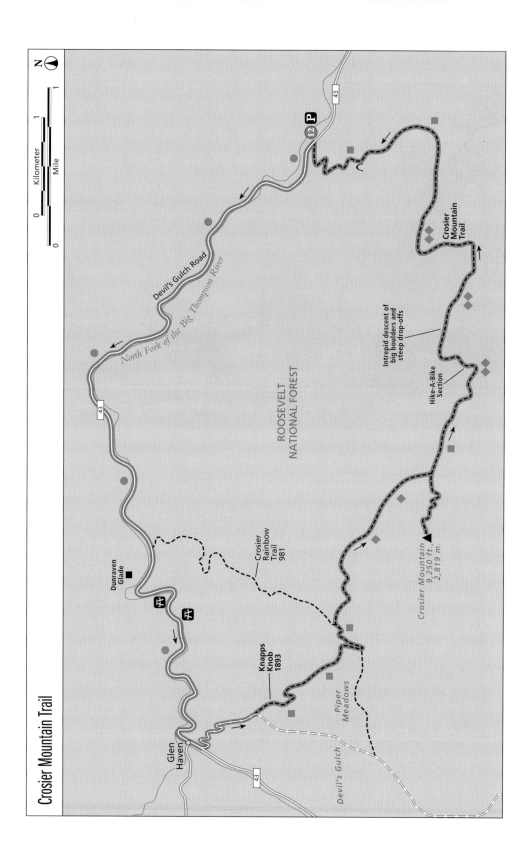

Crosier Mountain Trail

N

Kilometer
0   1

Mile
0   1

ROOSEVELT
NATIONAL FOREST

Devil's Gulch Road

North Fork of the Big Thompson River

43

Dunraven
Glade

Glen
Haven

43

Devil's Gulch

Crosier
Rainbow
Trail
981

Knapps
Knob
1893

Piper
Meadows

Crosier Mountain
9,250 ft.
2,819 m.

Hike-A-Bike
Section

Intrepid descent of
big boulders and
steep drop-offs

Crosier
Mountain
Trail

12 P

43

Miles and Directions

0.0 Begin riding north on CR 43 toward the town of Glen Haven.

3.7 CR 43 intersects with the Crosier Rainbow Trail 981 (aka Gravel Pit Trail) on your left. Continue riding on the road toward Glen Haven.

5.6 Reach Glen Haven. Ride through the town for another 0.1 mile just past the red horse stable.

5.7 CR 43 intersects with the Crosier Mountain Trail. Bear left onto the dirt road, following the sign to the Crosier Mountain Trail.

5.8 Bear right onto the Crosier Mountain Trail singletrack.

6.4 The Crosier Mountain Trail intersects with the lower H-G Ranch Trail on your right and Knapps Knob Trail 1893 on your left. Continue riding on the Crosier Mountain Trail.

7.5 Reach the top of Piper Meadows and the intersection of the Crosier Mountain Trail and the upper H-G Ranch Trail. Bear left, continuing on the Crosier Mountain Trail.

8.0 The Crosier Mountain Trail intersects with the upper Crosier Rainbow Trail 981 (aka Gravel Pit Trail) on your left. Continue riding on the Crosier Mountain Trail. (**Option:** Riders wishing to shorten their ride can descend the Crosier Rainbow Trail 981 to CR 43, making a lariat loop.)

9.2 The Crosier Mountain Trail intersects with the Crosier Mountain Summit Trail. Biking to the summit is ill advised. Rather, stow your bike and hike the 0.5 mile to the top of Crosier Mountain and an elevation of 9,250 feet. Once returning to your bike, continue riding on the Crosier Mountain Trail for a fast singletrack descent.

11.0 Reach the beginning of a burly hike-a-bike climb.

11.4 Begin an intrepid descent of big boulders, steep drop-offs, tight terrain, and precipitous angles.

12.0 Descend along a smooth singletrack through a meadow before arriving at another very technical descent at 12.7 miles.

13.1 Pass a cave to your left. From this point it's a fast descent to your vehicle.

14.0 Arrive at your vehicle.

Ride Information

Trail Information

Canyon Lakes Ranger District, Fort Collins; (970) 295-6700; www.fs.usda.gov/goto/arp/clrdrecreation

Larimer County Parks and Open Lands Department; (970) 679-4570; www.larimer.org/parks/openlands

Local Events and Attractions

Inn of Glen Haven, Glen Haven; (970) 586-3897

Rocky Mountain National Park, Estes Park; (970) 586-1206

Restaurants

Inn of Glen Haven, Glen Haven; (970) 586-3897

Glen Haven General Store, Glen Haven; (970) 586-2560 (closed in winter)

Honorable Mentions

Fort Collins Region

Seven more rides in the Fort Collins area deserve mention, even though they didn't make the "A" list. They may be a bit out of the way or more heavily traveled, but they still deserve your consideration when choosing a destination.

A Beaver Meadows

Beaver Meadows is a little-known resort ranch situated roughly 4.5 miles northwest of the town of Red Feather Lakes. Surrounded by the Roosevelt National Forest, Beaver Meadows offers outdoor enthusiasts plenty of recreation. Although it is privately owned, the proprietors of Beaver Meadows allow mountain bikers to ride their trails without having to stay at the ranch. Maps of the area are located at the ranch's small bike shop.

Some of Roosevelt National Forest's best and relatively unknown trails can be accessed from Beaver Meadows Resort Ranch. Riders can make the day trip from Fort Collins to enjoy some of northern Colorado's greatest and least traveled mountain biking trails.

To get to Beaver Meadows Resort Ranch from Fort Collins, drive north on US 287. After passing Ted's Place and the intersection with CO 14, continue driving north on US 287 for roughly 11 miles before turning left onto Red Feather Lakes Road (Larimer CR 74E) by the Forks Restaurant. Drive west on Red Feather Lakes Road for 24.5 miles before making a right onto CR 73C by the Pot Belly Restaurant. Drive on CR 73C for roughly 4.5 miles before bearing left into the Beaver Meadows Resort Ranch entryway. There will be a log sign with red and white lettering. Follow the entryway to the main parking lot, and check in at the Beaver Shop or the restaurant.

B Lone Pine Trail

Located 8 miles west of US 287 along Red Feather Lakes Road, the Lone Pine Trail is a popular equestrian trail. While mountain bikers do use the trail, they are certainly in the minority. Managed by the Colorado Division of Wildlife, the Lone Pine Trail is only open to mountain bikers, horseback riders, and hikers from May 1 to September 1. Throughout the rest of the year, the area serves as a winter migratory route for resident elk. However, the area is open to hunters during regular hunting seasons. With this short riding season, it's easy to see why mountain bikers tend to overlook the riding here, but it is a mistake.

The trail offers some stellar singletrack, both ascending and descending, before meeting with the wider doubletrack of an old ranch road that runs along the North

Lone Pine Creek. The doubletrack leads in a northwesterly direction through a series of small valleys and open meadows and crosses the creek a number of times before ending at the Colorado Division of Wildlife boundary. From there riders return the way they came.

To get to the Lone Pine Trail from Fort Collins, drive north on US 287. After passing Ted's Place and the intersection with CO 14, continue driving north on US 287 for roughly 11 miles before turning left onto Red Feather Lakes Road (Larimer CR 74E) by the Forks Restaurant. Drive west on Red Feather Lakes Road for roughly 8 miles, and bear right into the Lone Pine Trail parking lot.

C Kelly Flats Trail

This four-wheel-drive road/trail can be ridden in any number of ways—as a loop, a point-to-point, or an out-and-back. In any way, the trail offers a tough climb of sometimes very technical and always challenging terrain.

The Kelly Flats Trail climbs out of the Poudre Canyon and descends to the Boy Scout Camp Road near the town of Rustic and the Goodell Corner. Riders can access the trail from either the Poudre Canyon or the Boy Scout Camp Road. Either option delivers a physically challenging climb to the top, where riders are rewarded with stunning views of Rocky Mountain National Park's Mummy Range.

The initial climb north out of the Poudre Canyon is extremely strenuous. The trail will veer left near its high point and pass Lonetree Mountain to the north. Heading west, riders will eventually pass through Wintersteen Park before descending to the Boy Scout Camp Road, near the Goodell Corner.

This intersection pays tribute to the area's earliest pioneers. Ermine Robinson and Clark Goodell homesteaded the area in 1886. A year later Fort Collins businessmen named the area Manhattan, as they settled upon mining for gold. The gold mining never proved profitable, so Manhattan was abandoned in 1915.

To reach Kelly Flats from Fort Collins, drive north on US 287. Turn left at Ted's Place onto CO 14, following signs for the Poudre Canyon, and drive west on CO 14 for roughly 27 miles before turning right into the Kelly Flats trailhead parking lot.

D Foothills Trail

The Fort Collins Foothills Trail is a popular and easily accessible trail for mountain bikers and hikers. Upon reaching CR 23 atop Horsetooth Reservoir, there are a variety of other riding options. The Foothills Trail, then, offers willing riders a portal through which to explore other area trails.

Beginning on Fort Collins's western flank, the Foothills Trail extends from the flats of Fort Collins into the foothills to the west. The trail combines wide singletrack with rocky terrain and climbs moderately to Horsetooth Reservoir and its northern dam. From here riders can cross CR 23 and intersect the singletrack to the right of the Skyline Picnic Area. From here it's a steep and rugged descent to Soldier Canyon

Dam. Much of the trail that follows the waterline is eroded, so take caution if proceeding. From here the trail leads south to CR 42C and Dixon Reservoir. Dixon Reservoir also offers a number of networked trails and is worth exploring.

To reach the Fort Collins Foothills Trail, drive west from Fort Collins to the Overland Trail. Drive or ride north on Overland Trail. After passing Lee Lake on the right, Overland Trail curves sharply to the west for 0.1 mile before heading north again. Where Overland Trail again bears north (right), continue driving or riding west (straight) and intersect with Michaud Lane (West CR 50). Drive or ride west on Michaud Lane to its end and the trailhead of the Foothills Trail.

E Old Flowers Road

(**Note:** As of this writing, Old Flowers Road remains closed as part of the continuing effort to restore forest trails following the High Park Fire of 2012. Contact local authorities for the latest status of this trail.)

Old Flowers Road is a long-standing, popular ride that offers incredible views of the Rawah Wilderness Area. While many mountain bikers may have an aversion to riding roads, paved or otherwise, this old wagon road is worth checking out because it delivers one of the best descents in the area and includes 360-degree Rocky Mountain views. This can be ridden as either an out-and-back or as a point-to-point.

Old Flowers Road takes its name from Jacob Flowers, the founding father of the nearby town of Bellvue. The town's first general store, also built by Flowers from local red sandstone, still stands today. It was originally a wagon road that serviced the onetime silver-mining towns of Lulu and Teller Cities, west of Cameron Pass at the headwaters of the Colorado River. One story recalls Flowers's habit of nailing tin cans packed with wildflowers to the trees along the road as a way to set his road apart from all the others.

You can reach Old Flowers Road by driving north on US 287, following signs to Laporte. US 287 will bear right and travel in a more northerly direction. When US 287 bears right, continue driving straight on CR 54G through Laporte. By Vern's Restaurant bear left (west) onto CR 52E and drive through Rist Canyon to Stove Prairie Road 27. Park your vehicle by the old schoolhouse and start riding.

F Soapstone Prairie Natural Area

The Soapstone Prairie Natural Area, which adjoins Red Mountain Open Space, includes over 30 miles of trails that are open to mountain bikes. These trails roll through and past sweeping vistas, high-plateau grasslands, and interesting cultural resources, such as the National Historic Landmark Lindenmeier archaeological site. In the 1930s the Smithsonian and the Colorado Museum of Natural History unearthed evidence of human habitation in the area more than 12,000 years ago. The prehistoric Paleo-Indian Folsom people are noted for their Clovis points, fluted projectiles used to spear bison.

The area is remote and exposed, which may keep some riders away. But if you do decide to check this place out, bring water, as there is none to be had here. Dogs are not allowed at Soapstone Prairie Natural Area. You might also find little use for your cell phone, as reception is spotty at best. Otherwise, some of the trails are restricted to mountain biking, so pick up a trail map at the gate. The Soapstone Prairie Natural Area is closed December through February.

To get to Soapstone Prairie Natural Area, drive from Fort Collins on CO 1/Terry Lake Road to Larimer CR15 north (toward the town of Waverly). From CR 15 turn north onto Rawhide Flats Road and continue to the area's entrance.

G Red Mountain Open Space

Red Mountain Open Space offers riders an additional 15 miles of multiuse trails that can be combined with those of Soapstone Prairie Natural Area. It's a beautiful region of deep crimson- and orange-colored rock, as well as sandy washes and open meadowlands. As such, biking here after a rain shower gives the sandy washes a clay-like consistency and may prove less an experience in mountain biking and one closer to throwing pots on a pottery wheel.

Since this is remote and exposed, bring water, as there is none here. Dogs are not allowed. Likewise, cell phones are of little use out here. Red Mountain Open Space is closed from December through March.

To get to Red Mountain Open Space, drive from Fort Collins on CO 1/Terry Lake Road to Larimer CR 15 north (toward the town of Waverly). Drive north on CR 15 to Larimer CR 78. Bear left (west) onto CR 78 to CR 17. Bear right (north) onto CR 17 to CR 80. Bear left (west) onto CR 80 to CR 19. Bear right (north) onto CR 19—you will pass a gravel pit on the left—to CR 21. Bear left onto CR 21 and drive to the trailhead parking area.

Boulder Region

There's good reason why Boulder earned the title of "America's Number One Sports Town" from *Outside* magazine. The town's over-the-top enthusiasm for healthy living and recreation, along with its prime location, sets it apart from other outdoor towns.

Boulder rests in a broad valley with towering sandstone Flatiron formations leaning against the eastern flanks of the central Rocky Mountains and the Continental Divide. A radical liberal bastion, Boulder is sometimes said to be "25 square miles surrounded by reality."

The Southern Arapaho Indians first occupied the Boulder Valley because of its favorable climate and abundance of elk, bison, and deer. The prospect of gold would later lure nonnative settlers to set up camp near the entrance of Boulder Canyon on October 17, 1858. Known originally as Deadwood Diggings and developed as a supply center for area mining camps, Boulder grew larger and became an officially incorporated city on November 4, 1871. Today, Boulder's central industries include education, research and technology, and tourism.

To its credit, Boulder had the foresight to grow responsibly. While definitely embracing the call from wealth and opportunity, Boulder has developed programs to safeguard its natural riches. After purchasing thousands of acres of open space in 1967, Boulder implemented the Boulder Valley Comprehensive Plan 3 years later, which serves to manage proper land use and development in the Boulder Valley. In 1972 Boulder passed a height restriction ordinance for any newly built structures. These actions, along with several others, have to a large part been the impetus behind the town's continued commitment to its outdoor lifestyle, not the least of which is its commitment to cycling.

Raising the bicycle to anthropomorphic status, all of Boulder's city bus and shuttle services accept bikes in their racks or cargo compartments, accommodating more than 100,000 bicycles—more than one per person—that reside in the town. Moreover, the city offers its cyclists more than 300 miles of bike paths, lanes, and routes, and that's just within the city limits. Likewise, the over 45,000 acres and 146 miles of trails in Boulder's Open Space and Mountain Parks provide excellent biking opportunities.

The fact that bicycles are not allowed in the Boulder Mountain Parks system, however, does irritate the local taxpaying cyclists. The League of American Bicyclists has acknowledged Boulder as a Platinum Bicycle Friendly Community.

Flood of 2013

From September 9 through 16 of 2013, Colorado experienced one of its most catastrophic natural disasters in recorded history. With over 17 inches of rainfall—9 of which fell in a single day, more than half of the state's annual recorded amount—historic rains flooded six major rivers, seventeen counties, and over a dozen cities and towns. Areas affected by the storm received over 600 percent of the average precipitation for September. Such flooding arose as a result of several key factors that rarely occur over the region at the same time: a deep moisture source, a slow-moving low pressure system, instability, and saturated soils. All told, the flood waters spread across 2,830 square miles (larger than the state of Delaware) and caused eight fatalities, required 11,500 evacuations, and damaged or destroyed 20,000 homes and 30 bridges. For more on this "perfect" storm, visit the Colorado Flood 2013 information page at http://coflood2013.colostate.edu/.

Local Bike Shops

Redstone Cyclery, Lyons; (303) 823-5810; http://redstonecyclery.com/
University Bicycles, Boulder; (303) 444-4196; http://ubikes.com/
Boulder Cycle Sport, Boulder; (303) 444-2453; www.bouldercyclesport.com/
CyclHops, Longmont; (303) 776-2453

13 Coulson Gulch Trail

The Coulson Gulch Trail 916 is an out-and-back ride that offers sweet singletrack through meadows, aspen groves, and mixed conifer forests. Along the North Saint Vrain Creek, riders encounter some rockier and sandier descents and ascents. Even though this ride ends with a climb back to your vehicle, you shouldn't let that deter you from riding this trail. It's a gem.

Start: The Coulson Gulch 916 trailhead off Johnny Park Road 118

Distance: 8.3-mile out-and-back

Elevation gain: 859 feet

Riding time: Advanced riders, 1 hour; intermediate riders, 1.5 hours

Fitness effort: Physically moderate due to little significant gain in elevation

Difficulty: Technically easy to moderate with a few steep sections of rock and sand

Terrain: Singletrack and doubletrack that deliver sometimes steep, sandy, and rocky terrain, as well as smooth, pine needle–laden surfaces through shaded forests

Seasons: Apr-Oct

Maps: *USGS:* Raymond, CO; *DeLorme: Colorado Atlas & Gazetteer,* page 29, C-7

Nearest town: Lyons

Other trail users: Hikers, equestrians, picnickers, and campers

Dog friendly: Yes. The trail provides access to water via the North Saint Vrain Creek.

Trail contact: Boulder Ranger District, Boulder; (303) 541-2500

Getting there: From Lyons drive west on US 36 for 10.4 miles. Bear left onto CR 47 and drive for 3 miles. As the pavement turns to dirt, you will arrive at a fork. Bear left at the fork onto the deteriorating Johnny Park Road 118, following a red National Forest sign. Due to the flooding of 2013, Johnny Park Road and CR 47 were considerably damaged. The right fork will take you to Big Elk Meadow subdivision. Driving for 0.5 mile on Johnny Park Road 118 delivers you to a small area on your left for parking your two-wheel drive vehicle before the gate and cattle guard. A short walk up the road that turns to the south leads to the trailhead. Should you have a four-wheel drive, higher-clearance vehicle, you can continue through the gate for 0.1 mile to the trailhead parking lot. Trailhead GPS: N40 14.995' / W105 24.640'; trailhead terminus/turnaround GPS: N40 12.767' / W105 26.055'

The Ride

The fact that this ride is an out-and-back and one that ends with a climb doesn't detract from its pedal appeal. Highlighted by smooth singletrack that sometimes delivers rockier, technical sections, all the while following the North Saint Vrain Creek, the Coulson Gulch Trail is sure to satisfy even the most discriminating mountain bikers.

Riders begin by descending south through a meadow from the Coulson Gulch trailhead. North Sheep (8,278 feet) and Cook (7,540 feet) Mountains stand in stark relief against this meadowlands descent. The initial descent is fast and smooth. Nearing a mile into your ride, the terrain gets considerably steeper and rockier before

Jeff Williams descending along the rockier singletrack of the Coulson Gulch Trail with the North Saint Vrain Creek below.

passing a dilapidated cabin to your right. The cabin is roofless, but it still contains the rusty remnants of a bedspring and stove.

To the east of Higgins Park lies the Button Rock Reservoir (aka Ralph Price Reservoir). Ralph Price was a mayor of Longmont. In 1950, as Longmont's population started to near 8,000 with the majority of its economy resting in agriculture, Price was instrumental in organizing the construction of the Button Rock Dam and Reservoir, which was completed in 1965. The reservoir's atmosphere is pristine, but cyclists are prohibited. The City of Longmont Water Department operates the 2,600-acre watershed of Button Rock Preserve, which is its primary water supply. Anglers need to apply for a special permit—which are in limited supply—to fish the reservoir. Anglers can only fish using artificial flies and lures for brown and rainbow trout, as well as splake, a brook and lake trout hybrid. Tiger muskies also swim these waters, but any muskie less than 36 inches must be returned to the water right away. Fishing season at the reservoir runs from May 1 through October 31.

From here riders bear right to connect with the wide doubletrack of the Button Rock Road Trail. After a mile-long descent, riders cross the North Saint Vrain Creek for the first time and connect with wider singletrack of the Button Rock Trail. The North Saint Vrain Creek, known locally as the Saint Vrain River, is inspiring as it tumbles through the narrow canyon walls. It originates near 12,162-foot Saint Vrain

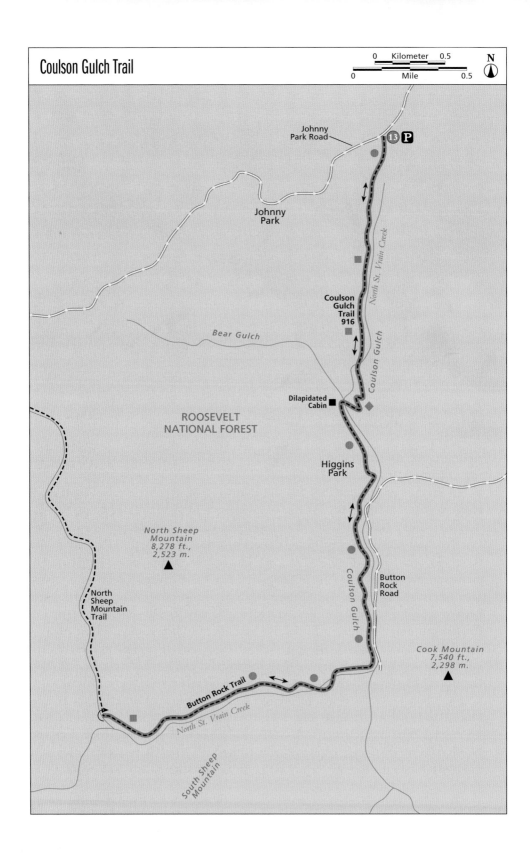

Coulson Gulch Trail

Johnny Park Road

Johnny Park

Bear Gulch

ROOSEVELT NATIONAL FOREST

Coulson Gulch Trail 916

North St. Vrain Creek

Coulson Gulch

Dilapidated Cabin

Higgins Park

North Sheep Mountain 8,278 ft., 2,523 m.

North Sheep Mountain Trail

Coulson Gulch

Button Rock Road

Cook Mountain 7,540 ft., 2,298 m.

Button Rock Trail

North St. Vrain Creek

South Sheep Mountain

0   Kilometer   0.5

0   Mile   0.5

N

Mountain, which sits between the Indian Peaks Wilderness Area and Rocky Mountain National Park.

The singletrack paralleling North Saint Vrain Creek is punctuated by some rockier and sandier sections of moderate technical degree. After crossing the creek for the second time after roughly 3 miles, the trail becomes a more dedicated singletrack. Riders will climb gently, eventually veering away from the creek to the trail's terminus, noticeable by a camping site below and adjacent to the creek. The nondescript North Sheep Mountain Trail veers right and begins to climb in a northerly direction, leading to Johnny Park Road, which is primarily used for off-road driving. The North Sheep Mountain Trail is not ideal for cycling. It's best to turn around here and return to your vehicle.

But while you may have lost some elevation in getting to the turnaround, the ride back doesn't feel like too much of a climb. In fact, there are a fair amount of sinuous, speedy descents with some loose rock and sandier sections. That said, the climb from the cabin in the woods is tough and will most likely require you to hike-a-bike. Otherwise, the last push to the top and your vehicle is easily ridden.

Miles and Directions

0.0 Begin riding on Coulson Gulch Trail 916 in a southerly direction, descending on smooth-running sinuous singletrack.

1.2 The terrain becomes steeper and delivers a fair amount of sandy and loose rock sections.

1.4 Pass a dilapidated cabin on your right, and continue through Higgins Park.

1.8 Reach the intersection of the Coulson Gulch Trail 916 and Button Rock Road, which leads to the Button Rock Preserve on your left. Bear right and continue on the Button Rock Road, which runs south along the North Saint Vrain Creek.

2.8 Cross the North Saint Vrain Creek via a wooden bridge. Once across the creek, Button Rock Road becomes Button Rock Trail.

3.2 Cross the North Saint Vrain Creek a second time via a wooden bridge.

4.1 Reach the intersection of the Button Rock Trail with the North Sheep Mountain Trail. Turn around at this point and return the way you came.

8.3 Arrive back at the trailhead and your vehicle.

Ride Information

Trail Information

Boulder Ranger District, Boulder; (303) 541-2500

Arapaho and Roosevelt National Forests and Pawnee National Grassland, Fort Collins; (970) 295-6600

Local Events and Attractions

Lyons Redstone Museum, Lyons; (303) 823-5271

Summer Public Programs; (303) 441-3950
Planet Bluegrass; (303) 823-0848
Good Old Days, June; (303) 823-5215
Rocky Mountain National Park; (303) 586-2371

Restaurants

Oskar Blues, Lyons's oldest brewery; (303) 823-6685

14 Rabbit Mountain

Rabbit Mountain offers riders a short and accessible network of trails that deliver rocky singletrack, short but steep climbs, and incredible views of the Front Range and Longs Peak. While suited more for beginner to intermediate riders, Rabbit Mountain can easily be enjoyed by more advanced riders who appreciate a variety of terrain within a small amount of space. Restrooms are located in the parking lot. Because this area is exposed to the elements, make sure to bring enough water for you as well as for your dogs.

Start: The Rabbit Mountain trailhead
Distance: 5.8-mile lariat with out-and-back spur
Elevation gain: 650 feet
Riding time: Advanced riders, 30 minutes; intermediate riders, 45-60 minutes
Fitness effort: Physically easy to moderate due to some shorter but steeper climbs, particularly when ascending on the Little Thompson Overlook Trail
Difficulty: Technically easy to moderate due to some rockier and sandier singletrack, particularly on the Eagle Wind and Little Thompson Overlook Trails
Terrain: Dirt road and singletrack that weave through stands of evergreen and over embedded granite, other loose rock, and sand

Seasons: Mar-Oct, although seasonal closures span from Feb 1 through July 31 in the critical wildlife habitat found alongside the Eagle Wind Trail. The route described here, however, never enters the critical wildlife habitat.
Maps: *DeLorme: Colorado Atlas & Gazetteer*, pages 29-30; *USGS:* Carter Lake Reservoir, CO, and Hygiene, CO; ZIA Maps: Boulder County Mountain Bike Map
Nearest town: Lyons
Other trail users: Hikers and horseback riders
Dog friendly: Yes
Trail contact: Boulder County Parks and Open Space, Boulder; (303) 441-6200

Getting there: From Boulder drive on US 36 west (North Foothills Highway) for roughly 13.3 miles, heading north toward the town of Lyons. At a stoplight US 36 comes to a T and intersects with CO 66. Bear right onto CO 66 and drive east for roughly 1 mile before bearing left onto Fifty-third Street, just after passing a brown Rabbit Mountain Open Space sign. Drive north on Fifty-third Street for 2.8 miles before bearing right into the trailhead. Parking spaces are provided at the trailhead. Trailhead GPS: N40 14.798' / W105 13.420'

The Ride

Residents of Boulder County have been visiting Rabbit Mountain Open Space since 1983, but records indicate that humans have inhabited the Rabbit Mountain area for the last 5,000 years. Arapaho Indians favored this locale as an ideal wintering ground, while miners who didn't strike it rich opted to farm in the area.

The first couple of miles along the Little Thompson Overlook Trail and the Eagle Wind Trail climb gradually over rocky and sandy singletrack. As you head up, there

are beautiful views of the Continental Divide and the Flatirons before you plunge into a dense ponderosa pine forest. Here the trail levels and becomes rockier with embedded granite and sandstone. This healthy forest remains so due, in part, to controlled burns, which took place nearby in 1996 and 1997. You might still be able to glimpse the remains of the burns, which help to thin crowded forests and leave a natural mix of trees and plants, thereby maintaining a healthy ecosystem.

Once through the first gate, it's a short ride to the top of Rabbit Mountain, where you're offered majestic views of Longs Peak and Mount Meeker. The name "Rabbit Mountain" may provide riders with a false sense of security, as the mountain was once called Rattlesnake Mountain for good reason. This is rattlesnake country. Some stories report that area developers found "Rattlesnake" to be too much of a PR problem when luring settlers. So they changed the name to

The unique and fun embedded granite of the Eagle Wind Trail.

"Rabbit" because some say the mountain resembles a crouching rabbit with lowered ears when seen from the east.

Once the Eagle Wind Trail levels atop Rabbit Mountain, riders ride alongside a critical wildlife habitat area before making their northerly descent. This critical wildlife habitat marks the park's transitional zone ecosystem, where prairie and foothill montane ecosystems meet. This seasonally closed (February 1 to July 31) area protects wildlife's hunting, eating, sleeping, and breeding grounds. A sign reading ONLY BY OUR COLLECTIVE STEWARDSHIP CAN WE PRESERVE THE INTEGRITY OF THIS PARK stands before the protected area and speaks the truth.

From the Eagle Wind Trail, riders descend to the Indian Mesa Trail. Riders who wish to extend their trip can opt to ride on the Indian Mesa Trail, which leads to the eastern portion of the Open Space. Crossing the Indian Mesa Trail, however, riders connect with the Little Thompson Overlook Trail.

The Little Thompson Overlook Trail was named after David Thompson (1770-1857), an English fur trapper with the Northwest Fur Company. This trail's initial climb is steep and rocky over broken shale and slabs of sandstone, but it offers

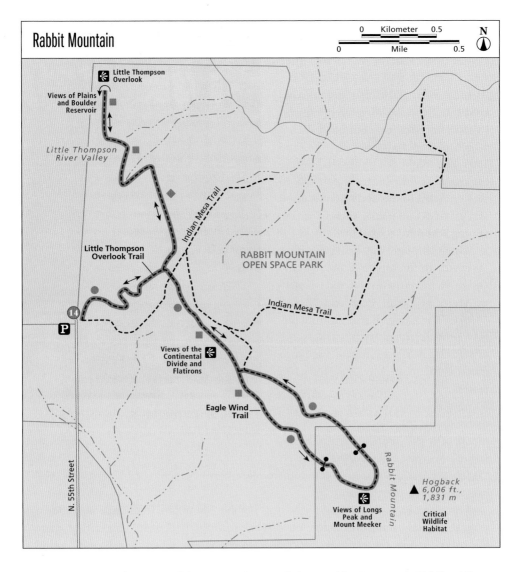

Little Thompson
Overlook

Views of Plains
and Boulder
Reservoir

Little Thompson
River Valley

Indian Mesa Trail

Little Thompson
Overlook Trail

RABBIT MOUNTAIN
OPEN SPACE PARK

Indian Mesa Trail

14

P

Views of the
Continental
Divide and
Flatirons

Eagle Wind
Trail

N. 55th Street

Rabbit Mountain

Views of Longs
Peak and
Mount Meeker

Hogback
6,006 ft.,
1,831 m

Critical
Wildlife
Habitat

0   Kilometer   0.5

0   Mile   0.5

N

panoramic easterly views of the Great Plains and the Boulder Reservoir. While riding, you may notice caves carved by erosion in the mountainside. These caves provide shelter for mountain lions. Nearing 4 miles, the more technical terrain levels off as the trail descends moderately past a barrier that reads STOP: THIS IS NOT A DESIGNATED TRAIL. Stay on the main trail and follow the other sign that points in the direction of the Little Thompson Overlook.

After arriving at the Little Thompson Overlook, take in the beautiful views of the Little Thompson River Valley and the surrounding geological terrain. Sadly, the Little Thompson River often runs dry. This is unfortunate when you consider that the small town of Pinewood Springs, lying directly west of Rabbit Mountain on I-36, depends upon the Little Thompson River for roughly 80 percent of its water. In the past, the town has had to ship in water to fill the shortage left by the drying Little Thompson. However, during the flooding in September 2013, the Little Thompson River turned torrential, covering and destroying US 36 in spots and marooning the 1,200 residents of Pinewood Springs.

From the overlook, descend on the Little Thompson Overlook Trail along technically challenging terrain to your vehicle.

Miles and Directions

0.0   From the Rabbit Mountain trailhead, begin climbing on the upper singletrack of the Little Thompson Overlook Trail, heading in a northeasterly direction.

0.5   The Little Thompson Overlook Trail intersects with the Indian Mesa Trail (the gravel dirt road) and the Eagle Wind Trail. Bear right onto the Eagle Wind Trail, crossing the Indian Mesa Trail, and head southeast.

1.0   The Eagle Wind Trail forks. Bear right at the fork, riding in a counterclockwise direction. (**Option:** You can opt to bear left here and ride the loop in a clockwise direction, thereby descending through a thick ponderosa pine forest.)

1.8   Pass through a gate as the trail starts veering east.

2.3   Pass through another gate and continue descending to the Indian Mesa Trail.

3.5   The Eagle Wind Trail intersects with the Indian Mesa Trail. Cross the Indian Mesa Trail, continuing up the singletrack you had previously ridden down, and connect with the Little Thompson Overlook Trail. Bearing right onto the Little Thompson Overlook Trail, you begin to climb in a northeasterly direction, turning shortly toward the northwest.

4.3   Arrive at the Little Thompson Overlook. Turn around and descend on the Little Thompson Overlook Trail toward your vehicle.

5.3   Reach the intersection of the Little Thompson Overlook, Eagle Wind, and Indian Mesa Trails. Continue descending along the Little Thompson Overlook Trail.

5.8   Arrive at your vehicle.

Ride Information

Trail Information

Boulder County Parks and Open Space, Boulder; (303) 441-3950; www.bouldercounty.org/os/parks/pages/rabbitmtn.aspx

Local Events and Attractions

Lyons Redstone Museum, Lyons; (303) 823-5271

Summer Public Programs; (303) 441-3950

Planet Bluegrass; (303) 823-0848

Good Old Days, June; (303) 823-5215

Restaurants

Oskar Blues, Lyons's oldest brewery; (303) 823-6685

15 Hall Ranch

Opened in 1997, Hall Ranch is one of Boulder County's best rides. As part of the North Foothills Open Space, Hall Ranch has become a favorite among Boulder-area mountain bikers, and deservedly so. Its smooth and wide singletrack leads mountain bikers through varying terrain of open meadow and higher mixed conifer forests. Dramatic hogbacks, exposed sandstone granite domes, and distant cliffs are all to be seen by the curious rider. At one point riders are offered an incredible view of Longs Peak (14,255 feet) and Mount Meeker. A great ride for the intermediate and advanced rider, Hall Ranch offers a short, moderately easy to technical trail system close to Boulder.

Start: The Hall Ranch trailhead along CO 7

Distance: 10.2-mile lariat

Elevation gain: 1,182 feet

Riding time: Advanced riders, 1 hour; intermediate riders, 1.5-2 hours

Fitness effort: Physically easy to moderate due to moderate climbing

Difficulty: Technically easy to moderate due to wide and smooth singletrack. There is a short, rocky, and steeper section that requires more advanced bike-handling skills.

Terrain: Mostly wide and hard-packed singletrack. There are some rockier sections, as well as some sandy patches, as the trail winds through grasslands, shrublands, woodlands, forests, cliffs, and canyons.

Seasons: Mar-Oct; open sunrise to sunset

Maps: DeLorme: Colorado Atlas & Gazetteer, pages 29-30; USGS: Lyons, CO; Boulder County Parks and Open Space Hall Ranch trail map; ZIA Maps: Boulder County Mountain Bike Map

Nearest town: Lyons

Other trail users: Hikers and horseback riders

Dog friendly: No. Dogs are not permitted at the North Foothills Open Space, including Hall Ranch, for wildlife habitat protection purposes.

Trail contact: Boulder County Parks and Open Space, Boulder; (303) 441-6200

Getting there: From Boulder drive on US 36 west (North Foothills Highway) for roughly 13.3 miles, heading north toward the town of Lyons. At a stoplight US 36 comes to a T at its intersection with CO 66. Bear left at the stoplight, continuing west on US 36 for 1.6 miles through the town of Lyons before bearing left onto CO 7 (South Saint Vrain Drive). Drive south on CO 7 for roughly 1.2 miles before bearing right into the Hall Ranch parking lot. Trailhead GPS: N40 12.730' / W105 17.365'

The Ride

With more than 3,200 acres to its credit, Hall Ranch is part of a large block of undeveloped land that includes the North Saint Vrain Canyon, the USDA Forest Service's Coffintop Gulch area, and the City of Longmont's Button Rock Reservoir. Combined, these three large parcels of public land are nearly equal in size to Rocky Mountain National Park.

The author enjoying Hall Ranch's technical side. Amanda Hlawaty

Because the ranch lies at the junction where the Great Plains meet the Rocky Mountains, rock formations dating back roughly 1.7 billion years can be seen near the western side of Hall Ranch. After upward surges of magma powered through the earth's crust during the Precambrian era, the magma gradually cooled into igneous rock roughly 15 miles below the earth's surface. Over time, continental shifting and erosion brought this cooled magma to the surface, exposing large granite shelves.

But what may best characterize the area are the tilted sandstone rock formations that jut skyward near the entrance to Hall Ranch. As the seas that covered Boulder County 260 million years ago receded, they left behind windblown sand dunes that later hardened into quartz sandstone, which is known as the Lyons Formation and is heavily used in construction. Indeed, the sandstone quarry located to the east of Hall Ranch is made up of fifty-two small quarry pits and was started by Edward Lyon. Many of the stones that make up the buildings of the University of Colorado's Boulder campus were taken from these quarries.

As you begin riding, you'll see Hat Rock and Indian Lookout Mountain to the north—they offer the best examples of these prehistoric rock formations. Named

Hall Ranch

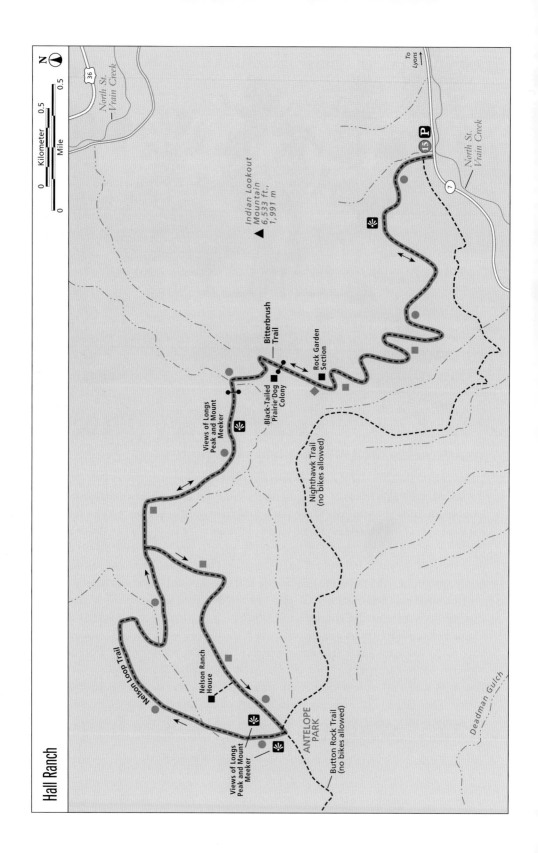

after the area's abundant antelope bitterbrush bushes, the Bitterbrush Trail passes over wide and smooth singletrack. As the trail weaves through meadows and mixed conifer forests, the area's great natural variety becomes quite clear.

Although Edward Lyon patented the land in 1885, there were more than twenty different families that lived and operated businesses in the area. This area had been home to sugar beet farmers who settled here after World War I, as well as those who quarried sandstone and logged ponderosa pine and Douglas fir trees. Hallyn and June Hall, from whom the ranch takes its present name, also operated a ranch here in the mid-1940s, grazing livestock throughout the property for more than 50 years.

Meadows and forests soon fade away as you near your second mile and a challenging rock garden section. This is the toughest section of the entire ride. After climbing out of this section, you pass through a gate before arriving at one of Boulder County's highest (6,200 feet in elevation) black-tailed prairie dog (*Cynomys ludovicianus*) colonies. Specifically built to minimize impact to this area, the Bitterbrush Trail circumvents this one-of-a-kind colony.

After passing the prairie dog colony, you'll descend quickly through the meadow before the trail turns upward again on its way to the Nelson Loop Trail. Ponderosa pines are the most abundant trees in the area. Once you intersect with the Nelson Loop Trail, continue to climb in a clockwise direction (it's equally fun going counterclockwise) through fairly heavily wooded terrain. The trail switches back through mixed conifer forests over rock-embedded singletrack before delivering you to Antelope Park, a beautiful meadow offering incredible views of Longs Peak and Mount Meeker.

Originally homesteaded in 1890 by Richard Clark, the land known as Antelope Park was purchased from Clark in 1922 by the Nelson family, who operated a successful ranch here. A short trail leads to the Nelson Ranch House. The ranch once consisted of a standing house, root cellar, and cement silo.

As you pass through Antelope Park, you begin your speedy descent along the Nelson Loop Trail, heading in a northeasterly direction. The descent passes through mixed conifer forests over relatively smooth singletrack before intersecting with the Bitterbrush Trail. Once you reconnect to the Bitterbrush Trail, it's a fast and wild ride over moderately rocky terrain to your vehicle.

Miles and Directions

0.0 Begin riding in a westerly direction on the wide singletrack of the Bitterbrush Trail.

0.2 The Bitterbrush Trail intersects with the Nighthawk Trail to the left—no bikes are allowed on the Nighthawk Trail. Bear right here, continuing on the Bitterbrush Trail.

2.2 Pass through a gate and continue riding north toward the Nelson Loop.

2.3 Pass a large prairie dog colony on your left.

2.6 Pass through another gate, and ride through a speedy smooth descent through a meadow.

3.6 Enjoy the views of Longs Peak and Mount Meeker.

4.0 The Bitterbrush Trail intersects with the Nelson Loop Trail. Bear left onto the Nelson Loop Trail, traveling the loop in a clockwise direction.

4.2 Cross a small wooden bridge.

4.8 Arrive at the Nelson Ranch House in Antelope Park. Caution: The foundation of the ranch house is unstable, so keep out.

5.0 The Nelson Loop Trail intersects with the Nighthawk Trail to the left. Bear right to continue riding on the Nelson Loop Trail, with views of Longs Peak and Mount Meeker directly in front of you.

6.3 The Nelson Loop Trail intersects with the Bitterbrush Trail. Veer left onto the Bitterbrush Trail, and retrace your path back to the start.

10.2 Return to your vehicle.

Ride Information

Trail Information

Division of Wildlife Headquarters, Denver; (303) 297-1192

Local Events and Attractions

Lyons Redstone Museum, Lyons; (303) 823-5271

 Summer Public Programs; (303) 441-3950

 Planet Bluegrass; (303) 823-0848

 Good Old Days, June; (303) 823-5215

 Rocky Mountain National Park; (303) 586-2371

Restaurants

Oskar Blues, Lyons's oldest brewery; (303) 823-6685

16 Picture Rock

Opened in 2008, the Picture Rock Trail at Heil Valley Ranch is a great example of trail sustainability and, hopefully, the future of mountain biking trail systems. Offering 5.4 miles of high-quality flow factor, the Picture Rock Trail serves up a moderate climb of a consistent angle over variable singletrack terrain that includes smooth-rolling sections, tight and rocky turns, playful technical sections, and very negotiable switchbacks. It stands as a connector trail to Heil Valley Ranch's southern trails and the Hall Ranch trail system to the north near Lyons. In short, the Picture Rock trail is the linchpin for one of the area's epic ride combinations, which this guide has partitioned out into three separate rides: Hall Ranch, Heil Valley Ranch, and the Picture Rock Trail. The route described here includes the Picture Rock Trail and the Wild Turkey Trail, which shares part of its route with the Ponderosa Loop Trail. Completed in 2007, the Wild Turkey Trail offers riders steeper and rockier sections to the south, as well as smother, flatter, and faster singletrack to the north, making this combination of trails one great lariat-loop ride.

Start: The Picture Rock trailhead off Red Gulch Road
Distance: 14.9-mile lariat
Elevation gain: 1,180 feet
Riding time: Advanced riders, 1.5 hours; intermediate riders, 2 hours
Fitness effort: Physically moderate with its steady climb
Difficulty: Technically moderate with a few more advanced rockier sections
Terrain: Singletrack and doubletrack, delivering at times exposed as well as forested trail that rolls over rocky, root-filled, and smooth terrain
Seasons: Apr-Oct

Maps: *USGS:* Lyons, CO; Boulder County Parks and Open Space Heil Valley Ranch trail map; *DeLorme: Colorado Atlas & Gazetteer,* page 30, C-1
Nearest town: Lyons
Other trail users: Hikers, equestrians, and picnickers
Dog friendly: No. Dogs are not permitted in Heil Valley Ranch.
Trail contact: Boulder County Parks and Open Space, Longmont; (303) 678-6200; www.bouldercounty.org/dept/openspace/pages/default.aspx

Getting there: From Lyons drive west on US 36 for roughly 0.8 mile. Turn left onto CO 7 (west) and drive 0.5 mile before turning left onto Old South St. Vrain Road. Drive on Old South St. Vrain Road for 0.3 mile and turn left onto Red Gulch Road. Follow Red Gulch Road for another 0.1 mile to the Picture Rock trailhead. Trailhead GPS: N40 12.682' / W105 16.353'

The Ride

The initial portion of this ride rolls over wide and smooth singletrack as it passes through a meadow. However, by 0.5 mile, the singletrack narrows to deliver rolling terrain with intermittent rockier sections. Among the beauties of this trail are the

Jeff Williams hammering it out on the Wild Turkey Trail.

mileage markers and the signs indicating when the trail narrows and provides limited visibility around corners. In addition, the trail has been constructed with embedded sandstone in parts, making for a unique riding feature, as well as carefully designed and constructed switchbacks that allow riders of any ability to get around.

Initial planning for the trails and management of Heil Valley Ranch began in 1995 and included collecting data on area soils, vegetation, and wildlife. The Picture Rock Trail was designed and built by members of the International Mountain Bicycling Association, the Boulder Mountainbike Alliance, Boulder County Parks and Open Space, and hundreds of volunteer trail builders. The goal: provide riders of all physical and technical abilities with a trail that would be environmentally sustainable and enjoyable.

Picture Rock Trail is named after a type of sandstone that is found locally and has been part of Lyons's quarrying history. Surrounded by red sandstone mountains on three sides, Lyons's rock formations hail from the Permian period and are roughly 260 million years old. This sandstone is considered to be the hardest in the world. Its strength, along with the beauty of its reddish, salmon-like color, helped to establish the town's first quarrying business in 1882 by E.S. Lyon. Picture rock is a specific kind of faulted sandstone sedimentary rock. When this area was awash with a vast inland sea, layers of sand and mud were deposited over millions of years. As a result of this accumulation, the pressure fused the sand grains of the bottom layers together, forming sandstone in a process known as lithification. Riders pass an example of picture rock made into a table roughly 1 mile into the ride.

Past the table the singletrack becomes a wider doubletrack that rolls over an old roadbed used by the Whitestone and Vickery Quarry Complex, which operated from the 1890s to the 1960s. Many of the buildings on the University of Colorado's Boulder campus are built from sandstone mined here. Passing a white silo on the left, riders roll over embedded rock as the trail passes the remains of the Whitestone ranch: a sandstone cabin foundation, a rusted vehicle, an old kitchen stove, and a well just east of the ranch house. Just beyond the ranch the trail delivers some sweet rockier sections that are intermediately technical before turning into a more dedicated singletrack.

Nearing 4 miles into your ride, the trail provides more advanced technical riding over rockier terrain, a bit of a pedal basher for sure. The intersection of the Picture Rock Trail with the Wild Turkey Trail provides a sitting bench and a place to refuel before continuing with the moderate climb over narrower, rockier, and sandy singletrack on the Wild Turkey Trail to its first intersection with the Ponderosa Loop and the overlook.

Once past the overlook the trail delivers some of the sweetest singletrack the Front Range has to offer. The baby-bottom smoothness of this section of singletrack stands in stark contrast to the rockier terrain covered before the overlook and has a tendency to lull riders into a kind of Zen-like flow. However, the rockier terrain that follows soon disrupts your meditative riding and demands attention. The descent on the Picture Rock Trail is awesome because you are not constantly on your brakes. There is a fair amount of pedaling and rolling with intermittent rockier sections. Keep your speed in check, particularly on sections with limited visibility, as other trail users may be on the ascent.

Miles and Directions

0.0 Starting at the Picture Rock trailhead, begin riding in a southerly direction.

1.0 Pass the picture rock table on your left.

3.0 Pass the white silo to your left.

5.4 The Picture Rock Trail intersects with the Wild Turkey Trail. Bear left onto the Wild Turkey Trail, riding this loop in a clockwise direction.

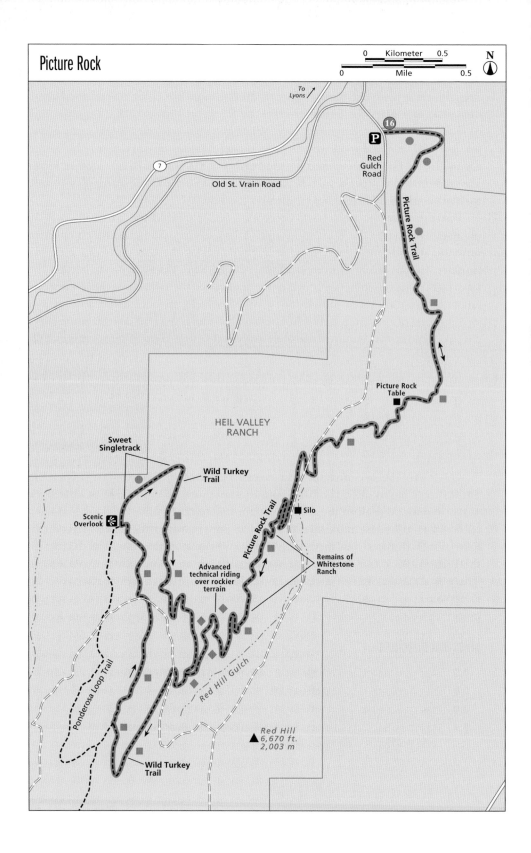

Picture Rock

0 Kilometer 0.5

0 Mile 0.5

N

To Lyons

16

P

Red Gulch Road

Old St. Vrain Road

7

Picture Rock Trail

Picture Rock Table

HEIL VALLEY RANCH

Sweet Singletrack

Wild Turkey Trail

Scenic Overlook

Picture Rock Trail

Silo

Remains of Whitestone Ranch

Advanced technical riding over rockier terrain

Ponderosa Loop Trail

Red Hill Gulch

Red Hill
▲ 6,670 ft.
2,003 m

Wild Turkey Trail

Jeff Williams coming onto an example of picture rock bought by the Boulder Mountainbike Alliance on the Picture Rock Trail.

6.6 The Wild Turkey Trail intersects with the Ponderosa Loop Trail. It is here that the Wild Turkey Trail's northern section shares the same route as the Ponderosa Loop Trail's southern section. Bear right here, continuing on the Wild Turkey Trail's northern section.

7.6 Arrive at the overlook and the second intersection of the Wild Turkey Trail and the Ponderosa Loop Trail. Bear right, continuing on the Wild Turkey Trail.

9.5 Return to the intersection of the Wild Turkey Trail and the Picture Rock Trail. Bear left onto the Picture Rock Trail, and return the way you came.

14.9 Arrive back at the Picture Rock trailhead and your vehicle.

Ride Information

Trail Information

Boulder County Parks and Open Spaces, Longmont, CO; (303) 678-6200; www.bouldercounty .org/dept/openspace/pages/default.aspx

International Mountain Bicycling Association (IMBA), Boulder; (303) 545-9011

Boulder Mountainbike Alliance, Boulder; http://bouldermountainbike.org/

Boulder Bicycle Commuters, Boulder; (303) 499-7466

Local Events and Attractions

Lyons Redstone Museum, Lyons; (303) 823-5271

Planet Bluegrass; (303) 823-0848

Good Old Days, June; (303) 823-5215

Restaurants

Oskar Blues, Lyons's oldest brewery; (303) 823-6685

17 Heil Valley Ranch

The Heil Valley Ranch Open Space Park includes all the furnishings of a carefully constructed trail system. Accessible from Geer Canyon Drive, this route combines the park's western edge of the Lichen Loop Trail, Wapiti Trail, and Ponderosa Loop Trail. Its wide and rocky singletrack climbs moderately through ponderosa pine forests to incredible views of Longs Peak and Mount Meeker, as well as to an overlook of Hall Ranch, to which it connects. Riders will also appreciate the views of the ruddy sandstone hogbacks near Lyons. Heil Valley Ranch provides a fair amount of tame and technical terrain. In short, Heil Valley Ranch is a mountain biker's playground, offering ample opportunities for riding of any level. It is also very popular with hikers due to the close proximity to Boulder.

Start: The Heil Valley Ranch Open Space trailhead

Distance: 8.1-mile lariat

Elevation gain: 847 feet

Riding time: Advanced riders, 45 minutes; intermediate riders, 1 hour

Fitness effort: Physically easy to moderate due to the lack of any significant steep climbing

Difficulty: Technically easy to moderate due to the trail's wide singletrack and thoughtful design

Terrain: Singletrack and dirt road, delivering a mostly smooth-riding and wide surface that courses in and out of ponderosa pine forests and meadows. There are some very rocky sections.

Seasons: Mar-Oct; open sunrise to sunset

Maps: *DeLorme: Colorado Atlas & Gazetteer,* page 30; *USGS:* Lyons, CO; Boulder County Parks and Open Space Heil Valley Ranch trail map

Nearest town: Boulder

Other trail users: Hikers and horseback riders

Dog friendly: No. Dogs are not permitted at the North Foothills Open Space, including Heil Valley Ranch, for wildlife habitat protection purposes.

Trail contact: Boulder County Parks and Open Space, Boulder; (303) 441-6200

Getting there: From Boulder drive north on US 36 to Left Hand Canyon Drive. Make a left onto Left Hand Canyon Drive, and drive west for 0.7 mile. Turn right onto the dirt Geer Canyon Drive, and drive 1.25 miles before bearing right into Heil Valley Ranch Open Space. Park in the designated area at the trailhead. Trailhead GPS: N40 08.958' / W105 18.009'

The Ride

Nestled among the hogbacks of Geer Canyon, the area surrounding Heil Valley Ranch was settled by Solomon Geer in 1888. Bought by the Heil family in 1949, the land grew into a successful ranching business. Purchased by the county in 1996, the Heil Valley Ranch Open Space comprises over 5,000 acres of land and presents a network of trails. In 2001 the Lichen Loop, Wapiti, and Ponderosa Loop Trails opened. Now we have the Wild Turkey Trail, completed in 2007, and the Picture Rock Trail, completed in 2008.

As part of the North Foothills Open Space, Heil Valley Ranch is among a large parcel of undeveloped land that includes the North Saint Vrain Canyon, the Roosevelt

National Forest, and the Trevarton Conservation Easement.

Riders begin on the dirt road of the Lichen Loop Trail's west edge (the only portion of this trail where bikes are allowed). The ease of the Lichen Loop Trail along with the picnic shelter make this area of the ranch ideally suited for mellow family outings.

After connecting with the wide and mostly smooth singletrack of the Wapiti Trail, riders climb moderately in a northwesterly direction. Part of aligning the Wapiti Trail within the greater Heil Valley Ranch involved tracking the migratory animal from which the trail takes its name. Wapiti, a Shawnee Indian word meaning "white rump," is better known as North American elk (*Cervus canadensis*).

Jeff Williams returning from the open views of Longs Peak and Mount Meeker.

The Wapiti Trail also passes through a winter range for elk migrating down from the Indian Peaks Wilderness. This vertical migration represents the only one of its kind for the species. That's good news when one considers that elk were once nearly extinct. Prized for sport, clothing, food, and medicinal value—their canine teeth were once used as charms—elk were nearly eradicated throughout North America, disappearing from 90 percent of their range by 1900. In fact, to this day, elk are no longer present in the eastern United States. Even Boulder County witnessed the elimination of all of its elk population by the turn of the twentieth century. Fortunately, elk were reintroduced into the area from 1913 to 1917.

Nearing a mile into your ride, the trail levels off a bit but continues to climb through a ponderosa pine forest. To its credit, the Wapiti Trail's few switchbacks are well constructed and secured by tight-fitting granite, though it is narrow and rocky in spots. You will see large areas of forest that have been cleared for fire mitigation, an ongoing project that will take years to clean up. Two miles into the ride, riders pass the foundation of an old building on the right, left over from the area's rich ranching and quarrying history.

The Wapiti Trail intersects the Ponderosa Loop Trail, an 8-mile multiuse, stacked loop trail system. With a few exceptions that offer riders views of high peaks, the Ponderosa Loop is contained under a thick cover of forest. Once riders reach the scenic overlook, with a nice bench, they are rewarded with sweeping views of the red sandstone walls of the North Saint Vrain Canyon and Hall Ranch.

From the overlook riders climb gradually through a thick ponderosa pine forest before engaging in a speedy descent nearing 5 miles into the ride. The descent courses through a hillside whose trees are more widely spread apart, offering ample

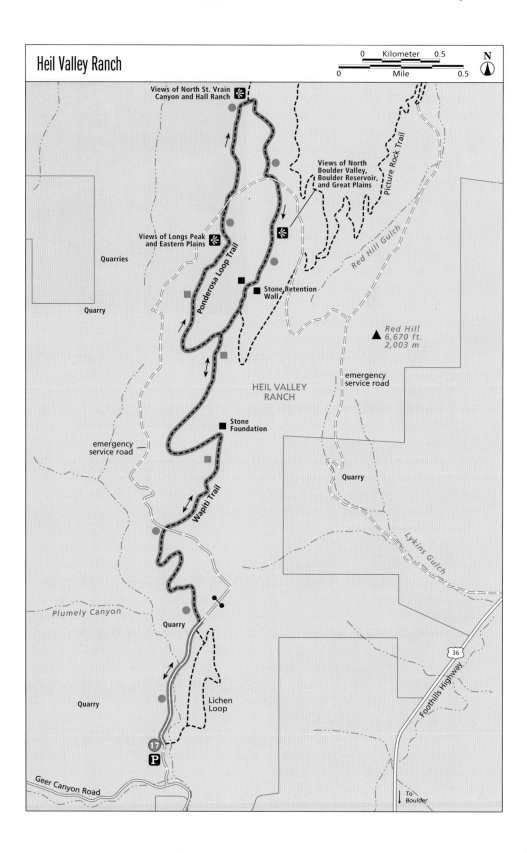

Views of North St. Vrain
Canyon and Hall Ranch

Picture Rock Trail

Views of North
Boulder Valley,
Boulder Reservoir,
and Great Plains

Views of Longs Peak
and Eastern Plains

Ponderosa Loop Trail

Quarries

Quarry

Red Hill Gulch

Stone Retention
Wall

Red Hill
6,670 ft.
2,003 m

emergency
service road

HEIL VALLEY
RANCH

Stone
Foundation

emergency
service road

Quarry

Wapiti Trail

Lykins Gulch

Plumely Canyon

Quarry

Quarry

Lichen
Loop

36

Foothills Highway

17

P

Geer Canyon Road

To
Boulder

views of the North Boulder Valley, Boulder Reservoir, and Great Plains. This overlook also provides continued access to the Wild Turkey Trail (see ride 16: Picture Rock).

After reconnecting with the Wapiti Trail, riders are delivered a fast descent over smooth singletrack. But while the smooth and wide singletrack invites a speedy descent, the trail's closely flanking evergreens, along with its sinuous path and abundant hikers, require attention from riders with a need for speed.

Miles and Directions

0.0 Begin riding north on the dirt road of the multiuse portion of the Lichen Loop Trail. (Bikes are not permitted on the Lichen Loop's singletrack trail, which veers off to the right of the road.)

0.5 The multiuse portion of the Lichen Loop Trail intersects with the Wapiti Trail on the left. Before the iron gate bear left onto the singletrack Wapiti Trail, and then cross a bridge and climb gradually in a northwesterly direction.

1.3 Cross an emergency service road and continue riding straight ahead on a narrower, rocky section of the Wapiti Trail.

2.6 The Wapiti Trail intersects with the Ponderosa Loop Trail. Bear left onto the Ponderosa Loop Trail, riding the loop in a clockwise direction. (Counterclockwise is fun, too.)

3.5 Reach a clearing in the Ponderosa Loop Trail with views of Longs Peak and the eastern plains.

3.8 Cross an emergency service road, and continue riding straight ahead on the Ponderosa Loop Trail. This section was recently buffed out smooth.

4.1 Reach the scenic overlook off to your left.

4.5 Cross the emergency service road, and continue riding straight ahead on the Ponderosa Loop Trail.

5.2 Pass through a stone retention wall before a moderate climb to the Ponderosa Loop Trail's intersection with the Wapiti Trail.

5.4 Reach the intersection of the Ponderosa Loop Trail and the Wapiti Trail. Veer left onto the Wapiti Trail, and retrace your path toward the trailhead.

8.1 Arrive at your vehicle.

Ride Information

Trail Information
Boulder County Parks and Open Space; (303) 678-6200

Division of Wildlife Headquarters; (303) 297-1192

Lyons Chamber of Commerce; (303) 823-5215

Boulder Chamber of Commerce; (303) 442-1044

Division of Wildlife Headquarters, Denver; (303) 297-1192

Local Events and Attractions
Lyons Redstone Museum, Lyons; (303) 823-5271

Planet Bluegrass; (303) 823-0848

Good Old Days, June; (303) 823-5215

Restaurants
Oskar Blues, Lyons's oldest brewery; (303) 823-6685

18 Ceran Saint Vrain Trail

The Ceran Saint Vrain Trail has been popular since the late 1980s. The Boulder Mountainbike Alliance calls this "one of the funnest stretches of creekside singletrack in the county." It leads through a mixed conifer forest along the South Saint Vrain Creek to a road that climbs brutally to Miller Rock. The creek offers amenities for anglers, as well as for those who like to camp out to the sounds of rushing waters nearby. Once arriving at Miller Rock Road, the trail's high point, riders can take in the incredible views of the Indian Peaks Wilderness Area and Pleasant Valley. Take care when riding this area, as there is a vast network of trails that can disorient an unfamiliar rider.

(**Note:** Due to the flooding that occurred in 2013, this trail is closed as of this writing.)

Start: The Ceran Saint Vrain trailhead

Distance: 6.4-mile lariat

Elevation gain: 1,000 feet

Riding time: Advanced riders, 45-60 minutes; intermediate riders, 1.5-2 hours

Fitness effort: Physically moderate to challenging due to the steeper sections and higher elevations of the trail

Difficulty: Technically moderate, with some more challenging sections due to some steeper, rocky climbs and descents. There are sections of this trail where the route passes over precipitously sloping terrain.

Terrain: Doubletrack and singletrack along sometimes rocky, sandy, and rooted trail. The trail follows the South Saint Vrain River through mixed conifer forests.

Seasons: May-Oct

Maps: *DeLorme: Colorado Atlas & Gazetteer,* page 29; *USGS:* Raymond, CO; ZIA Maps: Boulder County Mountain Bike Map; *Trails Illustrated:* #102, Indian Peaks, Gold Hill, CO

Nearest town: Jamestown

Other trail users: Hikers, anglers (fishing in the South Saint Vrain Creek is catch-and-release only), and ATVs

Dog friendly: Yes

Trail contact: Roosevelt and Arapaho National Forests, Boulder Ranger District, Boulder; (303) 444-6600

Getting there: From Boulder drive north on US 36 and make a left on Left Hand Canyon Drive (CR 81). Left Hand Canyon Drive and the Overland Road (CR 94) share the same route for roughly 5 miles before Left Hand Canyon Drive forks sharply to the left on its way to the town of Ward. At this fork bear right, continuing on Overland Road (CR 94), and follow it for roughly 3 more miles to the town of Jamestown. Drive for another 4.7 miles past Jamestown on the paved Overland Road (CR 94) and past the point where the road turns into dirt to the Saint Vrain Trail sign on the right (north) side of CR 94. Park at the trailhead. Trailhead GPS: N40 07.471' / W105 26.517'

The Ride

Along this ride you'll pass under a thick canopy of aspen, pine, and fir and through underbrush of currant, wild rose bushes, aster, wild geranium, and yarrow. Add to this the sound of the crashing South Saint Vrain River, an 8 out of 10 for coolness on Boulder Mountainbike Alliance's scale, and you have one winner of a trail—Colorado-style.

The Saint Vrain Trail takes its name from a fur trader with an illustrious career on the frontier. Born in Missouri, Ceran Saint Vrain arrived in Colorado in 1824. Between 1830 and 1840, Saint Vrain, along with his partner Charles Bent, began setting up a number of forts on the Colorado plains. Among those established was Fort Saint Vrain, near present-day Platteville, which operated as a major trading post until 1845. Another fort built out of adobe along the Santa Fe Trail in eastern Colorado was a premier trading center for travelers to the frontier.

Saint Vrain gained prominence in business, the military, and political circles. Indeed, his partnership with Bent became one of the greatest enterprises in frontier history, with annual earnings of more than $40,000. In a letter to his family describing one of his expeditions to the Boulder area, Saint Vrain wrote, "I equipt sum men to goe trapping, thinking that it will be the most

Amanda Hlawaty riding along the pristine singletrack through the woods.

profitable for me . . . the men I have equipt is all the best of hunters, if they make a good hunt, I will doe verey good business."

The Saint Vrain Trail begins heading through a dark evergreen forest alongside the creek. As you follow the creek in a northerly direction, the trail oftentimes slopes precipitously. Within the first half mile of the trail, you're thrown some moderately technical terrain, including rocks and steeper hits or jumps and drop-offs. After descending to the creek level, the narrow trail continues as a mellow cruise through the forest with the creek to your right. But don't let this mellow meander fool you into believing that this trail is all made up of soft places to fall. Technical hits appear without warning, so you really need to be aware of where the trail leads.

One such technical bit arrives at roughly 2 miles. Riders need to grind up a challenging sandy and rocky section. Upon reaching the trail's high point atop Miller Rock Road, the trail levels out as riders are offered views of the Indian Peaks Wilderness and Peaceful Valley.

Lured by available land in 1907, John and Mildred Roberts arrived at what was then known as Wildcat Gulch. Reportedly, upon seeing their new home for the first time Mildred exclaimed, "Oh, what a peaceful valley." And that was that.

Amanda Hlawaty rolls over some of the trail's smoother terrain alongside the Ceran Saint Vrain.

Legend has it that Miller Rock was named after a horse thief who took refuge there trying to hide from a posse. As you descend from Miller Rock Road, you ride over an assortment of embedded granite sections. Nearing 4 miles into your ride, you'll come to what is known as the 5-Point Intersection. Should you continue straight on the leftmost trail, you will eventually run into private property in the town of Raymond. Rather, take the trail that is immediately to the right of it. This route falls over rocky and root-filled sections.

Upon reconnecting with the trail intersection that you encountered at 2.2 miles, take care in your final descent to your vehicle and enjoy avoiding the sheer drop-offs that come within inches of the trail.

Miles and Directions

0.0 Cross a footbridge of the South Saint Vrain Creek, and begin riding in a northeasterly direction.

0.9 Descend to the creek, where you are offered the chance to soak your bum in a small waterfall runoff.

2.0 The singletrack opens up to a grunt of a climb over sandy and rocky doubletrack as it heads in a northerly direction.

2.2 The trail forks, with one trail leading to your left (northwest) and the other continuing straight ahead (north). Bear left here and climb steeply out of the drainage. You will eventually return to this point after descending from Miller Rock Road.

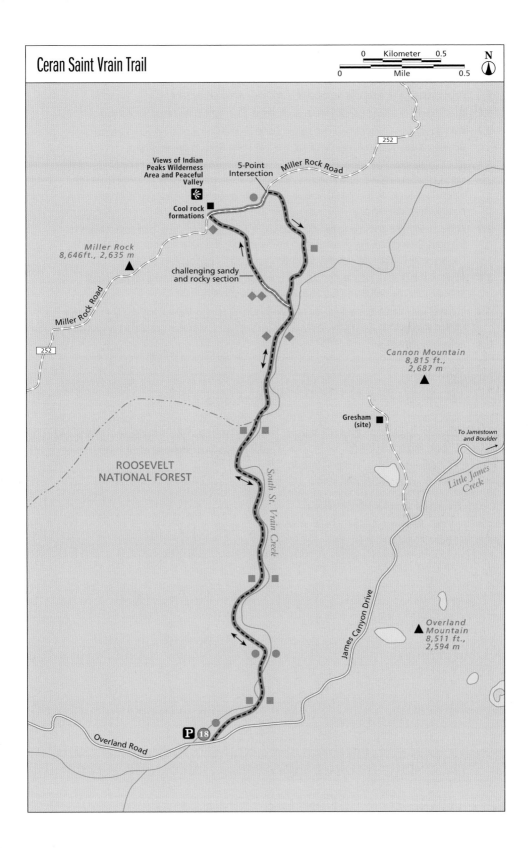

Ceran Saint Vrain Trail

0   Kilometer   0.5

0   Mile   0.5

N

252

Views of Indian
Peaks Wilderness
Area and Peaceful
Valley

5-Point
Intersection

Miller Rock Road

Cool rock
formations

Miller Rock
8,646ft., 2,635 m

Miller Rock Road

challenging sandy
and rocky section

252

Cannon Mountain
8,815 ft.,
2,687 m

Gresham
(site)

To Jamestown
and Boulder

ROOSEVELT
NATIONAL FOREST

South St. Vrain Creek

Little James
Creek

James Canyon Drive

Overland
Mountain
8,511 ft.,
2,594 m

P 18

Overland Road

2.5 The trail arrives at another intersection. Veer left here, heading west and continuing your climb over a challenging sandy and rocky section, toward Miller Rock Road.

2.7 Pass through a dilapidated fence over wide and sandy singletrack.

3.0 The singletrack intersects with Miller Rock Road. Bear right onto Miller Rock Road.

3.2 Pass a rock formation on your left as you continue riding in a northeasterly direction. Climbing these rocks will offer views of the real Miller Rock to the southwest.

3.6 Arrive at another trail intersection. A singletrack trail veers off to the right and heads south, which, if taken, will eventually return to the point where you originally connected with the Miller Rock Road. At this point, however, ride straight ahead, continuing your descent in a northeasterly direction.

3.7 Arrive at an intersection with two dirt roads. One road leads to the left; the other leads to the right. Bear right here, continuing on the main trail, and pass a cairn with a stick in it. The trail now leads in an easterly direction.

3.8 Arrive at the 5-Point Intersection. Do not continue straight (east) on the leftmost trail. Instead, take the trail that is immediately to the south of it.

4.2 Arrive at the intersection where you previously turned toward Miller Rock at 2.2 miles. Now retrace your path to the trailhead.

6.4 Arrive at your vehicle.

Ride Information

Trail Information

Arapaho and Roosevelt National Forests and Pawnee National Grassland, Boulder Ranger District, Boulder; (303) 541-2500

Boulder Convention and Visitors Bureau, 2440 Pearl St., Boulder; (800) 444-0447

Local Events and Attractions

Buchanan Pass Trail and Middle Saint Vrain Creek. See Honorable Mention H

Restaurants

Jamestown Mercantile Company Cafe (The Merc), 108 Main St., Jamestown; (303) 442-5847; www.jamestownmercantile.com/home

19 Boulder Valley Ranch

Still a working cattle ranch, the Boulder Valley Ranch offers a trail system that weaves atop mesas and through rich agricultural fields. Along the route you'll find views of the Flatirons to the west, the Boulder Valley to the north and south, and the Great Plains to the east. Throughout the route a variety of migratory waterfowl can be seen in the many nearby ponds, that is, if not chased by the many dogs out strolling with their families. This is a great beginner's ride, as it meanders casually, save for one trickier singletrack section, through the northern lowlands of the Boulder Valley.

Start: The Eagle Trail at the Foothills trailhead off US 36

Distance: 7.6-mile lariat

Elevation gain: 123 feet

Riding time: Advanced riders, 30-45 minutes; intermediate riders, 1-1.5 hours

Fitness effort: Physically easy due to the lack of any significant elevation gains. A technical section does challenge one's aerobic levels, but it is a short-lived challenge.

Difficulty: Technically easy due to the route's smooth surfaces. There is, however, one rockier singletrack section that descends precipitously down a slope.

Terrain: Farm-access dirt roads, doubletrack, and singletrack that roll over relatively smooth terrain atop plateau-like mesas on the way to the Boulder Reservoir

Seasons: Open year-round from 5 a.m. to midnight

Maps: *DeLorme: Colorado Atlas & Gazetteer,* page 30; *USGS:* Boulder, CO, and Niwot, CO; ZIA Maps: Boulder County Mountain Bike Map

Nearest town: Boulder

Other trail users: Hikers and horseback riders

Dog friendly: Yes

Trail contact: City of Boulder Open Space and Mountain Parks Department, Boulder; (303) 441-3440

Getting there: From Boulder drive north on 28th Street (which turns into US 36, aka Foothills Parkway) for roughly 2 miles to Jay Road. Continue on US 36 for another 1.5 miles past Jay Road before bearing right onto the dirt farm-access road that leads to the Foothills trailhead. Park in the lot provided at the trailhead. Trailhead GPS: N40 04.227' / W105 16.933'

The Ride

John and Maggie Williams were first to own the Boulder Valley Ranch. Since 1874, however, farmers and ranchers, as well as oil companies, owned shares in the ranch. It wasn't until 1973 that the Boulder Open Space finally purchased the land for itself.

The route begins on the Eagle Trail as it climbs to the top of a mesa via a farm-access road. From atop the mesa riders look out onto the wondrous expanse of north Boulder Valley. This area was once prime agricultural land, but before that the native tribes of the Arapaho and Cheyenne Indians roamed these prairies. Granted the rights to hunt and fish in the Boulder Valley in 1851 by the Fort Laramie Treaty Council, these native tribes found the area to be ripe with possibility. So much so that

Climbing toward the top of the mesa on the Eagle Trail, with the Flatirons and a canine watering hole in the background.

the Southern Arapaho Indian Tribe Chief Niwot (Arapaho for "Left Hand") once predicted that anyone who came to live in this area would never be happy living anywhere else. The so-called Niwot's Curse is said to have been partly to blame for the Boulder Valley's expansive growth in recent years.

Returning from your own personal vision quest that being atop Boulder Valley mesa affords, the Eagle Trail eventually turns into a wide doubletrack as it continues heading in an easterly direction toward the Boulder Reservoir. Nearing 2 miles into your ride, you descend from the mesa via a moderately rocky singletrack. Climbing this singletrack will prove a formidable challenge on your return trip. Upon reaching the bottom, the trail continues as a wide doubletrack; however, there is a singletrack carved alongside the doubletrack. Bear right at the bottom of this section as you continue on the Eagle Trail heading northeast.

Once you pass the pond at 2.5 miles, the trail climbs moderately before reaching the Boulder Reservoir. On the return trip from the reservoir, you're offered beautiful views of the entire Front Range, along with the tips of the Indian Peaks. The Sage Trail meanders quietly past farms and fields on its way to its intersection with the

Boulder Valley Ranch

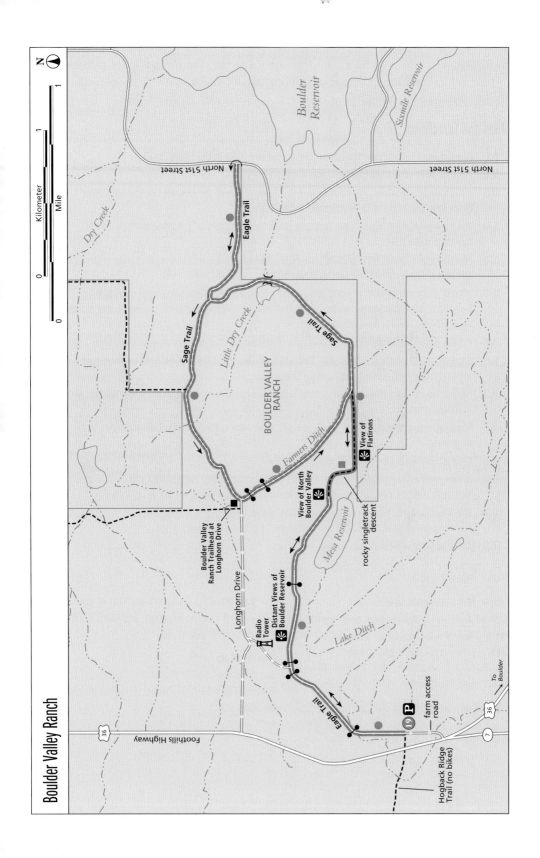

N

Kilometer

Mile

0   1

Dry Creek

North 51st Street

North 51st Street

Boulder Reservoir

Sixmile Reservoir

Eagle Trail

Sage Trail

Sage Trail

Little Dry Creek

BOULDER VALLEY RANCH

Farmers Ditch

View of Flatirons

View of North Boulder Valley

rocky singletrack descent

Mesa Reservoir

Boulder Valley Ranch Trailhead at Longhorn Drive

Longhorn Drive

Radio Tower

Distant Views of Boulder Reservoir

Lake Ditch

Eagle Trail

Eagle Trail

Foothills Highway

36

farm access road

19 P

To Boulder

36

7

Hogback Ridge Trail (no bikes)

Eagle Trail. Once you arrive at this intersection, what remains is a quiet ride back to your vehicle and the challenge of, having feasted your eyes on the Boulder Valley Ranch, trying to live happily elsewhere.

Miles and Directions

0.0   Start riding in a northeasterly direction on the dirt road of the Eagle Trail.

0.5   Pass through a gate as the trail climbs moderately in an easterly direction.

0.8   Pass through another gate where you are offered views of the distant Boulder Reservoir. From here the trail starts descending moderately.

1.0   The trail forks. Bear right at the fork and pass through another gate; the left fork heads toward a radio tower.

1.3   The trail turns into a wide doubletrack by a shaded canopy area. Veer left, passing through another gate, and continue on the Eagle Trail.

1.8   After a moderately rocky singletrack descent, the Eagle Trail intersects with the Sage Trail. Bear right here, continuing on the Eagle Trail. You will be looping back around to this point via the Sage Trail on your return.

2.5   Pass a pond via a footbridge. Here is one of the better places to bring your dog.

2.8   Eagle Trail intersects with the Sage Trail again on the left. Continue straight on the Eagle Trail, heading east toward the Boulder Reservoir.

3.3   Reach the Boulder Reservoir, and then turn around and backtrack to the Eagle and Sage Trails intersection.

3.8   The Eagle Trail intersects with the Sage Trail. Bear right onto the Sage Trail, heading northwest.

4.6   Pass a working cattle farm off to your left.

5.0   Reach the Boulder Valley Ranch trailhead at Longhorn Drive. Ride across the road in a southerly direction. Pass through two gates and continue riding on the Sage Trail.

5.7   The Sage Trail intersects with the Eagle Trail at the bottom of the singletrack. Veer right and climb up the singletrack to the top of the mesa; then retrace your path.

7.6   Arrive at your vehicle.

Ride Information

Trail Information

City of Boulder Open Space and Mountain Parks Department, Boulder; (303) 441-3440; https://bouldercolorado.gov/osmp

Boulder Convention and Visitors Bureau, 2440 Pearl St., Boulder; (800) 444-0447

Local Events and Attractions

Chautauqua, 900 Baseline Rd., Boulder; (303) 442-3282

Valmont Bike Park, intersection of Valmont and Airport Roads, Boulder; (303) 413-7226; www.valmontbikepark.org

Restaurants

The Kitchen, 1039 Pearl St., Boulder; (303) 544-5973; http://thekitchen.com/the-kitchen-boulder

20 East Boulder Trail/White Rocks

The East Boulder Trail of the Teller Farm and White Rocks area provides an easy ride through the pastoral heartland of the Boulder Valley. Hay fields and croplands evidence the rich agricultural heritage here. Streamside areas lush with vegetation and ponds teeming with wildlife make way for the towering sandstone cliffs of the White Rocks Nature Preserve. A great ride for the family, this trail avoids any hill climbs or narrow routes and is a mild day's spin in the saddle. The route offers views of the Boulder Flatirons, Indian Peaks, and Longs Peak.

Start: The East Boulder Trail–South trailhead
Distance: 9.7-mile out-and-back
Elevation gain: 250 feet
Riding time: Advanced riders, 45 minutes; intermediate riders, 1-2 hours
Fitness effort: Physically easy due to the level surface area of the entire route
Difficulty: Technically easy due to the improved gravel surface area and width of the trail
Terrain: Improved gravel farm road, double-track, and wide singletrack

Seasons: Open year-round from 5 a.m. to midnight
Maps: DeLorme: Colorado Atlas & Gazetteer, page 30; USGS: Niwot, CO; ZIA Maps: Boulder County Mountain Bike Map
Nearest town: Boulder
Other trail users: Hikers, bird-watchers, and anglers
Dog friendly: No. Dogs are prohibited.
Trail contact: City of Boulder Open Space and Mountain Parks Department, Boulder; (303) 441-3388

Getting there: From Boulder drive east on Arapahoe Road for roughly 6 miles past 75th Street. After driving another 0.5 mile, turn left (north) onto the dirt road of the Teller Farm trailhead entrance. Drive for roughly 1 mile on this dirt road to the East Boulder Trail–South trailhead. Trailhead GPS: N40 01.310' / W105 09.511'; trailhead terminus/turnaround GPS: N40 03.724' / W105 07.913'

The Ride

The East Boulder Trail and the White Rocks area offer hope in the face of ever-burgeoning development. As an example of responsible land use, this area was once site to numerous gravel pits used in the construction of Boulder-area roads and housing. Nowadays much of the destruction left by the gravel pits has been reclaimed and remains as preserved wildlife and wetland habitats. The great horned owls that nest in the cottonwood trees at the East Boulder Trail–South trailhead serve as a fitting welcome to this area. These raptors have nested here for years and always draw a curious eye.

As the trail meanders alongside numerous irrigation canals and by vast spreads of cropland, you'll pass through a number of gates. After crossing Valmont Drive, you enter into the White Rocks Nature Preserve.

Irrigation ditches run alongside the trail and lend testimony to the area's agricultural history.

The gravel road gives way to wide singletrack through parts of the White Rocks area as the route passes through a variety of riparian habitats. After 3 miles you reach one of several ponds named after Walden "Wally" Toevs, a Boulder County commissioner in the early 1970s who supported land reclamation.

Just after crossing the Boulder Creek, you're offered distant views of the White Rocks to the northwest. Arapaho Indians considered this location a prime hunting ground for pronghorn sheep and used the cliffs of the White Rocks as a bison jump. The rocks are the geological remains of a 135-million-year-old river delta.

The singletrack that passes through the White Cliffs Nature Preserve eventually turns into wide doubletrack as it makes its way to the White Cliffs trailhead at 95th Street. Oftentimes overlooked by riders wanting to venture into the mountains, this trail offers a look into the agricultural lifestyle of the eastern plains. With nearly 100 million acres of this country's farmland lost since the 1900s, it's important that we respect and understand this vital resource. Luckily, areas such as those surrounding the East Boulder Trail are often leased for agricultural purposes. In fact, 35 percent of Boulder's Open Space—35,000 acres—is leased for agricultural uses, thereby preserving our country's heritage.

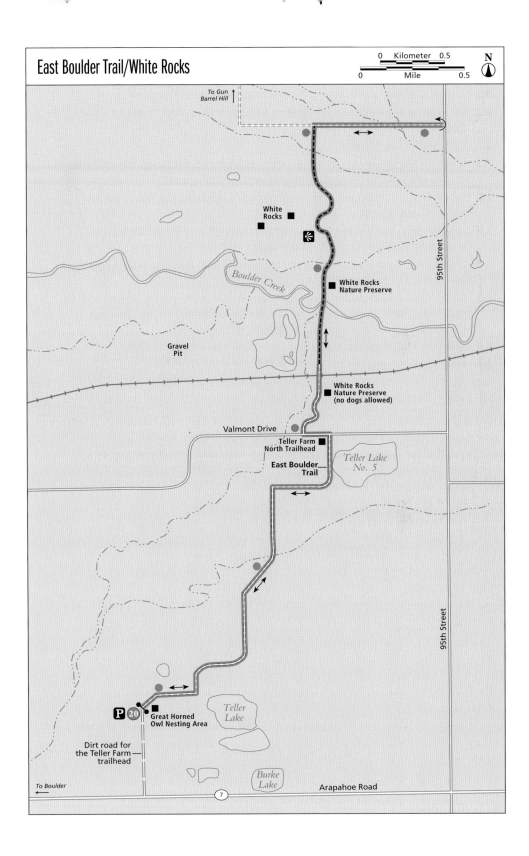

East Boulder Trail/White Rocks

0   Kilometer   0.5

0   Mile   0.5

N

To Gun
Barrel Hill

White
Rocks

Boulder Creek

White Rocks
Nature Preserve

95th Street

Gravel
Pit

White Rocks
Nature Preserve
(no dogs allowed)

Valmont Drive

Teller Farm
North Trailhead

East Boulder
Trail

Teller Lake
No. 5

95th Street

Teller
Lake

P **20**

Great Horned
Owl Nesting Area

Dirt road for
the Teller Farm
trailhead

To Boulder

Burke
Lake

Arapahoe Road

Miles and Directions

0.0 After going through a gate, begin riding east on the wide, gravel doubletrack.

0.2 The route continues in a northerly direction. Riding with a fence now to your left, cross a footbridge.

1.7 Cross over an irrigation ditch.

2.2 Reach the East Boulder Trail Teller Farm–North trailhead. Bear left through the parking lot. The trail picks up again in the northwest corner of the parking area.

2.3 Bear right and cross Valmont Drive (watch for traffic), continuing your ride on the other side and heading north.

2.5 Enter the White Rocks Nature Preserve (no dogs allowed). Here the trail follows wide singletrack before turning into gravel road again.

3.2 Cross Boulder Creek via a bridge. Shortly hereafter the route gives way to singletrack again as it passes a White Rocks information sign.

4.3 Exit the White Rocks Preserve. Cross a private driveway and arrive at the intersection of the East Boulder/White Rocks Trail and the East Boulder/Gunbarrel Farm Trail. Bear right at this intersection, continuing on the East Boulder/White Rocks Trail.

4.9 Reach the White Rocks trailhead at 95th Street, and return the way you came.

9.7 Arrive at your vehicle.

Ride Information

Trail Information

City of Boulder Open Space and Mountain Parks Department, Boulder; (303) 441-3408

Boulder Convention and Visitors Bureau, 2440 Pearl St., Boulder; (800) 444-0447

Valmont Bike Park, intersection of Valmont and Airport Roads, Boulder; (303) 413-7226; www.valmontbikepark.org

Rocky Mountain Raptor Program; (970) 491-0398

Local Events and Attractions

Fishing

Chautauqua, 900 Baseline Rd., Boulder; (303) 442-3282

Restaurants

The Kitchen, 1039 Pearl St., Boulder; (303) 544-5973; http://thekitchen.com/the-kitchen-boulder/

21 Sourdough Trail

The Sourdough Trail skirts the fringes of the beautiful Indian Peaks Wilderness Area. The scenic drive to the trailhead is reason enough to head for this trail. While traveling up the Boulder Canyon, multisport adventurers can stop to enjoy great climbing and hiking opportunities before continuing on Colorado's famed Peak-to-Peak Highway. Once on the trail, the fun really starts. The Sourdough Trail is almost entirely covered by a thick forest canopy, providing cool, shaded relief the whole ride. Although the climb to Brainard Lake is challenging (but enjoyable), the return is why you ride it. A fast and smooth descent through a thick emerald forest will have you screaming with joy.

Start: The Sourdough trailhead off CR 116, the road to the University of Colorado Research Station

Distance: 12.2-mile out-and-back, with an option for a 13.2-mile loop

Elevation gain: 1,350 feet

Riding time: Advanced riders, 2-2.5 hours; intermediate riders, 3-3.5 hours for the out-and-back

Fitness effort: Physically moderate to challenging due to the extended climbing to Brainard Lake Road

Difficulty: Technically moderate due to a relatively smooth trail with little in the way of rocks. There are, however, a few switchbacks that make the riding moderately technical.

Terrain: Singletrack, plus some paved and dirt road if optional loop is taken

Seasons: May-Oct

Maps: *DeLorme: Colorado Atlas & Gazetteer,* page 29; *USGS:* Ward, CO; *Trails Illustrated:* #100, Boulder, Golden, CO; ZIA Maps: Boulder County Mountain Bike Map

Nearest town: Ward

Other trail users: Hikers, campers, snowshoers, and skiers

Dog friendly: Yes

Trail contact: Roosevelt and Arapaho National Forests, Boulder Ranger District, Boulder; (303) 541-2500

Getting there: From Boulder drive west on Canyon Boulevard to the town of Nederland. Canyon Boulevard will become a single-lane highway (CO 119), winding its way through the steep-walled Boulder Canyon. Before reaching Nederland, you'll drive alongside Barker Reservoir and enjoy stunning views of Eldora Ski Resort. From Nederland take CO 72 east (aka the Peak-to-Peak Highway) toward Ward for 7.5 miles until seeing the sign for the University of Colorado Research Station on the right side of the road. Turn left immediately after the sign onto CR 116, and drive another 0.5 mile. The trailhead will be on the right. Trailhead GPS: N40 01.678' / W105 31.494'; trailhead terminus/turnaround GPS: N40 04.799' / W105 32.054'

The Ride

The Sourdough Trail is one of Boulder County's most popular singletrack routes. It's located just half a mile west of the majestic Peak-to-Peak Highway, between the historic tungsten- and gold-mining towns of Nederland and Ward. The trail brings together

The tiny gold-mining town of Ward.

rolling climbs with a number of narrowly negotiable switchbacks through densely mixed forests of lodgepole pine, Douglas fir, and aspen. The forest opens occasionally to reveal outstanding views of the foothills of the Front Range below and the Great Plains to the east. When many of the other trails in the foothills area turn sandy as the summer nears its end, the Sourdough Trail, owing to its superb tree coverage and high altitude, remains ideal with smooth-running, hard-packed singletrack.

The Sourdough Trail begins at 9,220 feet and rises to a lung-notable 10,280 feet. The trail provides some of the highest alpine mountain biking you'll find near Boulder and Denver. With elevations such as these, it's hard to believe that Sourdough's sinewy path skirts only the base of the Indian Peaks—a collection of jagged mountain summits, ragged arêtes, windswept tundra uplands, and cirque glaciers. The range stretches southward for 27 miles and constitutes the crest of the Continental Divide in this part of Colorado.

For years Ellsworth Bethel (1863-1925), a Denver high school botany teacher, enjoyed a view of the peaks from his classroom. Moved by them, Bethel and his students went about naming each of them after various Native American tribes from Colorado's history. Though Bethel didn't succeed with all of his suggestions, he did secure approval from the US Board on Geographic Names for seven tribe names on seven Front Range peaks—which constitute the Indian Peaks.

The snowfields and glaciers of the Indian Peaks are some of the most studied alpine environments in the world. Just west of the Sourdough trailhead lies the University of Colorado's Institute of Arctic and Alpine Research. Above treeline, modest and cramped huts—some of them secured to the mountainside with cables—contain the tools of this world-renowned field station. Rustic buildings resembling early trapper

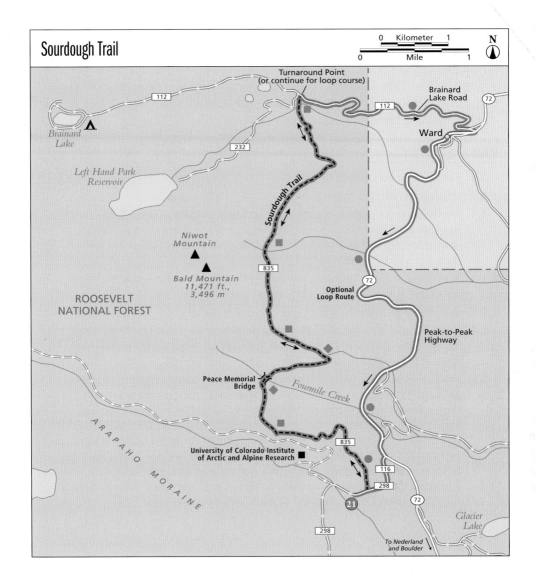

Sourdough Trail

0   Kilometer   1

0   Mile   1

N

Turnaround Point
(or continue for loop course)

112

Brainard
Lake Road

72

112

Brainard
Lake

Ward

232

Left Hand Park
Reservoir

Sourdough Trail

Niwot
Mountain

835

Bald Mountain
11,471 ft.,
3,496 m

Optional
Loop Route

72

ROOSEVELT
NATIONAL FOREST

Peak-to-Peak
Highway

Peace Memorial
Bridge

Fourmile Creek

University of Colorado Institute
of Arctic and Alpine Research

835

A R A P A H O   M O R A I N E

116

298

21

72

Glacier
Lake

298

To Nederland
and Boulder

homesteads are tucked among trees just below timberline, camouflaging modern laboratories that house state-of-the-art meteorological equipment. Studies and classes are conducted on topics such as acid precipitation, climatic patterns, and alpine flora.

Just a few miles from the Sourdough Trail, amid the cutting-edge technology of the Institute of Arctic and Alpine Research, are the small, onetime mining communities of Nederland and Ward. Only 12 miles from Boulder, Nederland was originally named Brownsville after its founder. Because of its proximity to Boulder, Brownsville was also called Middle Boulder. When a homesick Dutch company bought the tungsten mill, the town was renamed Nederland—an archaic spelling for Netherlands. From 1900 to 1918, Nederland produced $23 million worth of tungsten, making

Boulder County the largest tungsten producer in the United States. The town of Ward also boasts a prosperous mining heritage. During Ward's heyday (1860 to 1900), the mining district's population peaked at 5,000 and it was the largest mining camp in northern Colorado. With five hotels, eight lodges, and seven saloons—not to mention the $5 million in gold reserves—Ward achieved a certain Vegas status among Colorado mining towns of the late 1800s and early 1900s.

Miles and Directions

0.0 Start at the Sourdough trailhead.

0.3 Crossing the footbridge begins a short climb through a thick pine forest.

1.4 After negotiating a challenging climb with a number of switchbacks, you reach a spot where the forest opens and the trail continues under a stretch of power lines, offering views of the Peak-to-Peak Highway to the east—a good resting spot before attempting a short, technical section of trail.

1.9 You'll arrive at a sign for Sourdough Trail and Red Rock trailhead. Follow the Sourdough Trail.

2.7 Cross the Peace Memorial Bridge.

5.7 The Sourdough Trail arrives at a trail intersection. Bearing left will take you to the Little Raven Ski Trail and Brainard Lake. Continuing straight will deliver you to Brainard Lake Road via Sourdough Trail.

6.1 Arrive at Brainard Lake Road. At this point you can either bear right onto Brainard Lake Road and do the loop or simply backtrack to your vehicle, going the way you came. I suggest backtracking and enjoying the Sourdough's fast singletrack descent. Although maps make it appear that you can continue north from the Brainard Lake Road, this is highly inadvisable—it soon becomes nightmarish. (**Option: To do the 13.2-mile loop,** turn east onto Brainard Lake Road and follow it to the Peak-to-Peak Highway, where you'll ride south along the paved highway for 6.5 miles until you once again arrive at CR 116. Turn right onto CR 116, and ride for another 0.5 mile to your parked vehicle. This option is a bit faster if the weather is frightful, and it is paved nearly the entire way.)

Ride Information

Local Information
Boulder Ranger District, 2140 Yarmouth Ave., Boulder; (303) 541-2500

Local Events and Attractions
Eldora Mountain Resort, Nederland; (303) 440-8700 or (888) 2-ELDORA
Nederland Old Timer Miner Days, July; (303) 258-3580
Peak-to-Peak Highway, CO 7, 62, and 119, connecting Estes Park and the Black Hawk/Central City gambling district

Lodging
Sundance Lodge & Stables, Nederland; (303) 258-3797 or (800) 817-3797

Restaurants
Millsite Inn, Ward; (303) 459-3308
Black Forest Restaurant, Nederland; (303) 258-8089
Cool Beans Espresso, Nederland; (303) 258-3435
Sundance Lodge & Cafe, Nederland; (303) 258-0804

22 Switzerland Trail

The Switzerland Trail follows an old railroad grade that once served to connect the mining camps in Boulder County. As such, it can be a popular route for four-wheel-drive vehicles. The former rail route offers moderate grades and is a good introduction for beginner riders. The trail descends—a bittersweet treat, as you return this way—initially into the small town of Sunset in Fourmile Canyon before climbing to terrific views of the Continental Divide and the Indian Peaks atop the Mount Alto Picnic Area. From there the trail continues across Gold Hill Road and to an eventual scree field before connecting with Sawmill Road. Along the route you'll find traces of bygone mining activity: old railroad tracks, abandoned mines, and rusted buckets. One of the attractions of this trail is that it passes through a number of cutouts in the hillside through which the terrain gets considerably rockier. These cutouts are a testament to the determination and hardiness of those involved in the area's earlier railroading history.

Start: Trailhead at the base of Sugarloaf Mountain

Distance: 23.1-mile lariat

Elevation gain: 1,800 feet

Riding time: Advanced riders, 2 hours; intermediate riders, 3-3.5 hours

Fitness effort: Physically moderate to challenging due to the extended climbs in exposed areas

Difficulty: Technically easy due to the trail's width

Terrain: Four-by-four road, doubletrack, and singletrack that run over rocky and sandy terrain. With a 4 percent grade in spots, the trail travels through forests of aspen, ponderosa pine, lodgepole pine, and Douglas fir. At one point riders must portage their bikes up a steep talus slope.

Seasons: May-Oct

Maps: *DeLorme: Colorado Atlas & Gazetteer,* page 29; *USGS:* Gold Hill, CO, and Ward, CO; Arapaho and Roosevelt National Forests map; *Trails Illustrated:* #100, Boulder, Golden, CO; ZIA Maps: Boulder County Mountain Bike Map

Nearest town: Gold Hill

Other trail users: Motorbikes, four-by-four vehicles, and hikers

Dog friendly: No, due to the length and motorized vehicular traffic of the trail

Trail contact: Roosevelt and Arapaho National Forests, Boulder Ranger District, Boulder; (303) 541-2500

Getting there: From Boulder at the corner of 28th Street and Canyon Boulevard, drive west on Canyon Boulevard (which will turn into CO 119) for 6.4 miles before turning right onto Sugarloaf Road. At 11.2 miles turn right again onto the dirt Sugarloaf Mountain Road, and drive on this dirt road for another 0.8 mile before reaching its end and the trailhead to Switzerland Trail. Trailhead GPS: N40 01.501' / W105 25.493'

The Ride

The Switzerland Trail begins with a speedy descent to the small town of Sunset. The route follows the old mining rail line of the Greeley, Salt Lake, and Pacific narrow

Author Stephen Hlawaty passes through one of several cutouts through the mountain side on the old Narrow Gauge Railroad bed. AMANDA HLAWATY

gauge railroad, nicknamed Switzerland Trail. The line's inaugural running occurred on April 6, 1883, when it left Boulder for Penn Gulch (later named Sunset) in Four-mile Canyon. This narrow gauge railroad helped in developing the towns of Sunset, Ward, Gold Hill, Salina, and Wallstreet by running gold and silver ore during the mining boom of the late 1800s.

Having reached Sunset after a rocky and speedy descent, you begin climbing along a section of the Switzerland Trail that railroad engineers used to call "Giant's Ladder." Your climb up Giant's Ladder can be a grunt on your way to Mount Alto but one that is rewarded with wonderful easterly views of the Great Plains.

Upon reaching the Mount Alto Picnic Area, the trail begins to level off where a lodge once stood. When the railway gave in to dwindling stocks of gold and silver, and having suffered from the flood of 1894, the Greeley, Salt Lake, and Pacific narrow gauge railroad was reborn as a tourist line. With advertisements reading things like "One need not go to Switzerland for sublime mountain scenery," a new flood began to pour along the Switzerland Trail.

More than 10,000 visitors began to ride the rails in a single summer. These tourist-toting trains would carry beer packed in snow for outings like moonlight walks, wildflower hikes, and aspen viewing. Mount Alto became one of the featured stops on these outings, where tourists would engage in baseball games, while the Mont Alto Lodge served as a fitting venue for concerts, lectures, and dances. A flash flood in 1919 through Fourmile Canyon would end the rail line forever. Today, all that is left of the lodge and rail destination is an old stone chimney.

From the Mount Alto Picnic Area, you continue on the Switzerland Trail as it descends to its intersection with Gold Hill Road. Bearing right onto Gold Hill Road will deliver you to the small town by the same name. Gold Hill was one of the first permanent mining camps in Colorado. The discovery of gold in 1859 led to an influx of more than 1,500 miners less than a year later. Built in 1872, the year that tellurium was also discovered in Gold Hill, the Miner's Hotel still stands today with many of its original furnishings. Unfortunately, a fire reduced much of the town to ashes in 1894.

Once across Gold Hill Road, the trail whips along level doubletrack through beautiful aspen glens. Along this stretch of the trail you can expect to find sunflowers, wild geraniums, yarrow, milkweed, Indian paintbrush, and currant bushes. Such life stands in historical contrast to the 2010 Fourmile Canyon Fire that started on September 6. The fire burned 6,181 acres of the area's steep, rugged terrain and became the third-largest fire in Colorado history, destroying 168 homes and costing over $14.1 million. By mile 11 you have to negotiate over some moderately technical and rocky terrain before reaching the talus field. Take care in portaging your bike atop the talus field, as its steep grade delivers loose rock and sand. As you bear left onto Sawmill Road, it's a bit of a grunt to the road's high point at 12.3 miles.

After reconnecting to the Switzerland Trail from Gold Hill Road, it's a fast and rocky descent to the town of Sunset. Be warned, however, that from Sunset you'll still have to climb nearly 4 miles out of Fourmile Canyon to your vehicle at the base of Sugarloaf Mountain.

Miles and Directions

0.0 Start from the northwest corner of the parking lot and begin a descent over sandy and rocky terrain.

0.5 Pass views of Sugarloaf Mountain and the Indian Peaks off to your right. Stay on the main route at all times.

3.6 Arrive at the intersection of the Switzerland Trail and the Pennsylvania Gulch Trail. Bear right, passing a sign for the small town of Sunset. Cross Fourmile Creek and ride through Sunset on CR 118 (Fourmile Canyon Drive).

3.8 CR 118 intersects with FR 109 (Switzerland Trail). Bear left onto FR 109, climbing in an easterly direction up Giant's Ladder.

7.3 Reach the Mount Alto Picnic Area, where you'll find restrooms and picnic tables. Continue in a westerly direction as you begin to descend moderately.

Switzerland Trail

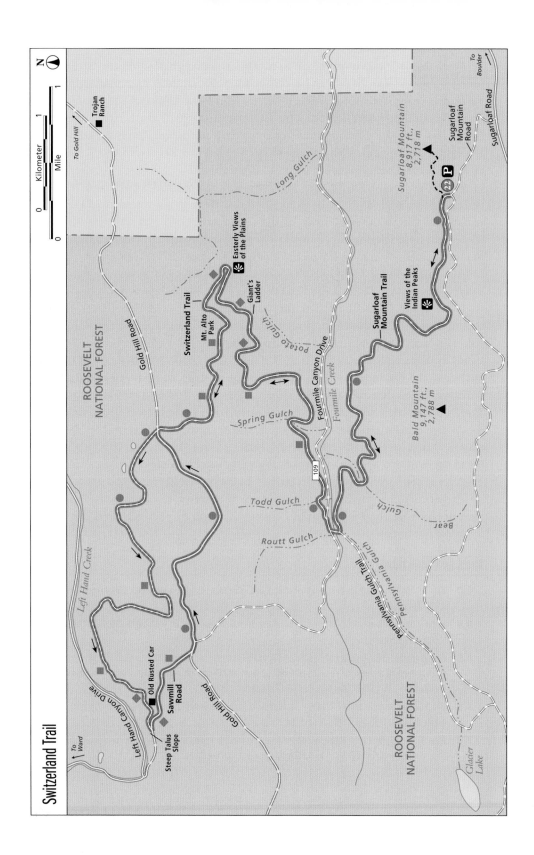

8.5 The Switzerland Trail intersects with Gold Hill Road. Cross Gold Hill Road and continue straight on the Switzerland Trail, heading in northwest.

10.6 Reach a sign that reads DEAD END. Pass beyond the sign and continue your riding on a wide doubletrack through a mixed conifer forest.

11.6 Pass an old, rusted, abandoned car to your left.

11.9 Reach a steep talus slope with Lefthand Canyon Drive off to your right. Portage your bike up the talus slope on your left to Sawmill Road. Bear left onto Sawmill Road.

12.6 Sawmill Road intersects with Gold Hill Road. Bear left onto Gold Hill Road.

14.4 Gold Hill Road intersects with the Switzerland Trail. Bear right onto the Switzerland Trail, and return the way you came.

23.1 Arrive at the parking lot.

Ride Information

Trail Information

Roosevelt and Arapaho National Forests, Boulder Ranger District, Boulder; (303) 541-2500

Local Events and Attractions

Gold Hill General Store, 531 Main St., Boulder; (303) 443-7724; www.goldhillstore.com

Gold Lake Mountain Resort & Spa, near Ward; (303) 459-3544

Peak-to-Peak Highway, CO 7, 62, and 119, connecting Estes Park and the Black Hawk/ Central City gambling district

Restaurants

The Gold Hill Inn & Bluebird Lodge, 401 Main St., Gold Hill, Boulder; (303) 443-6461 or (303) 443-6475; www.goldhillinn.com/

23 Betasso Preserve

In 2011 Betasso Preserve added the Benjamin Loop Trail to its lineup, nearly doubling in size the mountain biking accessibility in the area. Riders can choose to ride this route once for a short and sweet romp through some of Boulder County's sweetest singletrack or ride these loops repeatedly for an extended tour. Combined, the Canyon and Benjamin Loop Trails offer much to riders of any ability. Indeed, my 10-year-old and 7-year-old sons, Ethan and Benjamin, rode this route with tons of giggles while sharing the trail with adult hammerheads out to crush this ride. The wide and smooth singletrack of the Canyon Loop Trail is ideal for beginners wanting to test their singletrack mettle, while the Loop Link and Benjamin Loop Trails deliver somewhat more technical terrain with little margin for error, as the trail can be rocky and sandy in spots and is bench cut on steep slopes. Being so close to Boulder, Betasso Preserve offers an immediate getaway from the hectic pace of Boulder during rush hour. The preserve has been the subject of much public scrutiny and environmental impact studies in the last few years, reminding us to respect our parks, open spaces, and forests.

Start: The Canyon Loop trailhead
Distance: 7.3-mile loop
Elevation gain: 248 feet
Riding time: Advanced riders, 45 minutes; intermediate riders, 1 hour
Fitness effort: Physically easy to moderate due to the lack of significant elevation gain. There are a few shorter hill climbs.
Difficulty: Technically easy due to the wide and smooth singletrack
Terrain: Singletrack and doubletrack that roll over open meadows and hard-packed forest terrain

Seasons: Apr-Nov
Maps: Boulder County Parks and Open Space Betasso Preserve map; *USGS:* Boulder, CO; *DeLorme: Colorado Atlas & Gazetteer,* page 29, D-7; ZIA Maps: Boulder County Mountain Bike Map
Nearest town: Boulder
Other trail users: Hikers, picnickers, and equestrians
Dog friendly: Yes
Trail contact: Boulder County Parks and Open Space, Longmont; (303) 678-6200; www.BoulderCountyOpenSpace.org

Getting there: From Boulder drive west on Boulder Canyon Road (CO 119) for 5 miles to Sugarloaf Road. Bear right onto Sugarloaf Road, and drive for roughly 1 mile to Betasso Road. Bear right onto Betasso Road, by the Betasso Preserve sign, and drive for another 0.5 mile before bearing left into Betasso Preserve. Trailhead GPS: N40 00.952' / W105 20.667'

The Ride

The area surrounding Betasso Preserve was once the town of Orodell, which served as a stage stop for coaches traveling from Boulder to Nederland. Situated at the junction of Boulder and Fourmile Canyons, the town serviced those working in the

Benjamin and Ethan Hlawaty on the charge high atop the Benjamin Loop.

nearby sawmills and mines of Colorado's northeast mineral belt. Tragically, Orodell was lost to fire in 1883, while the sawmill and gold mill were destroyed by flood.

Betasso Preserve is truly a Boulder County gem. It is set atop an underlay of 1.7-billion-year-old Boulder Creek granodiorite (granite to you and me), one of the oldest types of rock in Boulder County. The Bummer's Rock Trail leads to an excellent example of this granite, which contains pink feldspar, mica, and quartz. But Betasso Preserve offers more than just ancient jewels. Its beautiful landscapes, which include 7.3 miles of ideal singletrack, speak to the prevailing land preservation attitudes of public opinion.

Our story begins just west of the Canyon Loop trailhead, when, in 1912, the Blanchard family homesteaded 160 acres. The Blanchards sold their small cattle ranch, equipped with log buildings, to Stephen Betasso in 1915. Stephen was a hard rock miner living in Fourmile Canyon, whose original cabin still exists on the preserve. With earnings saved from his gold and tungsten mining, Stephen built more permanent structures and maintained a prosperous cattle business on the ranch, preparing the land for inheritance by his sons Dick and Ernie. But what Stephen left his sons was more than just a ranch; he left them a legacy steeped in land stewardship.

So ingrained was their mutual respect for the land that Ernie, hoping to preserve the land he had enjoyed for more than 60 years, sold 718 acres to Boulder County in 1976. It's reported that Ernie never once considered moving to town, arguing that "you can't leave the mountains because when you live up there one leg gets shorter than the other," and lived in the mountains until his death in 1983. Since 1976 Boulder County has added on to its original purchase—most recently the Benjamin property in 2007—and now preserves nearly 1,200 acres. Even some of the ranch's original buildings are still standing.

Near the Canyon Loop trailhead, there is a log cabin that was built between 1902 and 1912. Nick Fanti built the brick house for Stephen Betasso in 1918, and Ernie Betasso left his mark in the clapboard house, which he built in 1948.

From the trailhead riders begin by descending on the wide doubletrack of the Canyon Loop Trail. Within the first mile riders pass a picnic table, grill, and sitting benches that offer views of Boulder and its university. After a mile into your ride, the trail becomes narrower and rockier, fast and flowy singletrack as it weaves through a ponderosa forest to its first short climb at 1.5 miles.

After connecting with the Loop Link Trail, riders enjoy a fast and smooth single-track descent to cross a footbridge at roughly 2.6 miles. A short and steady climb delivers riders to the Benjamin Loop. After passing the Fourmile Link Trail on your right, start a steady but easy climb over supple singletrack and through a mixed coni-fer forest. This section of the trail also delivers a fair amount of well-designed switch-backs. Once through with the climb, it's a speedy descent to the intersection with the Loop Link Trail and its intersection with the Canyon Loop Trail. Bearing right onto the Canyon Loop Trail's western hemisphere, riders climb moderately over single- and doubletrack to a sage-filled meadow before the final descent to the parking lot.

Miles and Directions

0.0 Bear right onto the Canyon Loop Trail, riding in an easterly (counterclockwise) direction.

2.1 The Canyon Loop Trail intersects with the Loop Link Trail, which leads to the Benjamin Loop. Bear right onto the Loop Link Trail, riding in a northwesterly direction toward the Benjamin Loop Trail.

2.9 The Loop Link Trail intersects with the Benjamin Loop Trail. Bear right onto the Benjamin Loop Trail, and ride in a northwesterly (counterclockwise) direction.

3.4 The Benjamin Loop Trail intersects with the Fourmile Link Trail on your right. Continue riding on the Benjamin Loop Trail.

4.9 Pass one of several sitting benches on this route.

5.3 The Benjamin Loop reconnects with the Loop Link Trail. Bear right onto the Loop Link Trail, and return the way you came to the Canyon Loop Trail.

6.1 The Loop Link Trail returns to its intersection with the Canyon Loop Trail. Bear right onto the Canyon Loop Trail to complete the loop and return to your vehicle.

7.3 Arrive back at your vehicle.

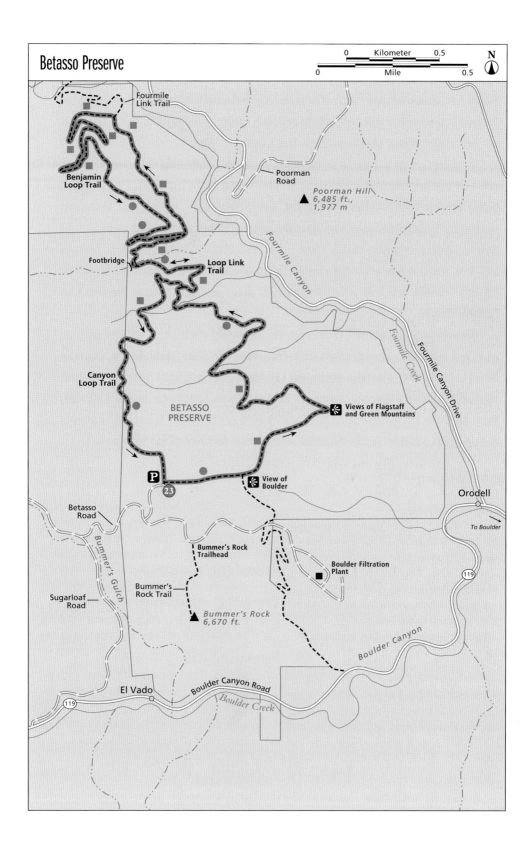

Betasso Preserve

0 Kilometer 0.5
0 Mile 0.5

N

Fourmile
Link Trail

Poorman
Road

Poorman Hill
6,485 ft.,
1,977 m

Benjamin
Loop Trail

Fourmile Canyon

Footbridge

Loop Link
Trail

Fourmile Creek

Fourmile Canyon Drive

Canyon
Loop Trail

BETASSO
PRESERVE

Views of Flagstaff
and Green Mountains

Orodell

To Boulder

View of
Boulder

P
23

Betasso
Road

Bummer's Gulch

Bummer's Rock
Trailhead

Boulder Filtration
Plant

Sugarloaf
Road

Bummer's
Rock Trail

119

Bummer's Rock
6,670 ft.

Boulder Canyon

El Vado

Boulder Canyon Road

Boulder Creek

119

SUPER BETASSO ROUTE

Riders can access Betasso Preserve from downtown Boulder via Fourmile Canyon and the Betasso connector Fourmile Link Trail, once known simply as the Pipeline Trail. However, at the time of this writing, the Fourmile Link Trail was closed. When it is open, riders can begin the Super Betasso route from the corner of Broadway and Canyon Road in Boulder. The Fourmile Link Trail lies roughly 4 miles up the Boulder Canyon on the right side of the road, just before a tunnel. Over the years this trail has been preserved as a historic trail. In the past the Boulder County Parks and Open Space Department, along with the Youth Corps and the Boulder Mountainbike Alliance, has taken on the responsibility of maintaining the Fourmile Link Trail, which is now under the auspices of Boulder County Parks and Open Space. The 0.8-mile Fourmile Link Trail provides riders with direct access to Betasso Preserve from Fourmile Canyon.

Unfortunately, as a result of the new and improved Fourmile Link Trail, we may see additional mountain bike restrictions for Betasso Preserve in the future. As it is, mountain biking is not permitted on Wednesdays and Saturdays, and riders must follow the alternating directions for traveling the Canyon and Benjamin Loops. Check with the Boulder County Parks and Open Space Department at (303) 678-6200 or the Boulder Mountainbike Alliance at bouldermountainbike.org for the latest information regarding this and other trails.

Ride Information

Trail Information

Boulder County Parks and Open Space Department, Longmont; (303) 678-6200; www.Boulder CountyOpenSpace.org

International Mountain Bicycling Association (IMBA), Boulder; (303) 545-9011

Boulder Mountainbike Alliance, Boulder; http://bouldermountainbike.org/

Boulder Bicycle Commuters, Boulder; (303) 499-7466

Local Events and Attractions

The preserve provides a large group area for picnics (50 people maximum) that can be reserved. There are also restrooms and grills at the preserve. Open Apr to Nov from sunrise to sunset. Closed Sat and Wed to mountain bikes. (**Note:** Mountain bikers must travel in the posted direction—clockwise or counterclockwise. Directions change each month. Check directional arrows at trail access points for details. At the time of this writing, mountain bikers were directed to ride these loops in a counterclockwise direction, and the description of this route follows suit.)

Restaurants

The Kitchen, 1039 Pearl St., Boulder; (303) 544-5973; http://thekitchen.com/the-kitchen-boulder/

24 Meyers Homestead Trail

The Meyers Homestead Trail is a great beginner's ride. It offers riders a wide doubletrack trail that doesn't deliver too many rocks, roots, or loose sand sections. The trail gets a bit tougher as it climbs to its terminus. As one arrives at the turnaround point, views of the Indian Peaks, Continental Divide, Boulder Canyon, and Sugarloaf Mountain (at the base of which begins ride 22: Switzerland Trail) can be seen to the north. The end of the trail also borders private property, so do not venture off it. Offering restrooms and picnic tables, the Meyer's Gulch Homestead Trail is a great destination for a family of riders.

(**Note:** As of this writing, Meyers Homestead Gulch is closed as a result of the flooding in 2013. Contact local authorities for the latest status of this trail.)

Start: The Meyers Homestead trailhead by the group picnic area
Distance: 5.3-mile out-and-back
Elevation gain: 750 feet
Riding time: Advanced riders, 30 minutes; intermediate riders, 45-60 minutes
Fitness effort: Physically easy due to the relative lack of elevation gain as well as the trail's short distance. The hill toward the turnaround point offers riders a moderate test of aerobic levels.
Difficulty: Technically easy due to the wider doubletrack that the trail runs over. There is a moderate hill climb over rockier terrain that arrives near the trail's turnaround point.

Terrain: Doubletrack over sand and rock. The trail travels through open meadows and mixed forests to its terminus.
Seasons: May-Oct
Maps: *DeLorme: Colorado Atlas & Gazetteer,* page 39; *USGS:* Eldorado Springs, CO; Boulder County Parks and Open Space Walker Ranch map; ZIA Maps: Boulder County Mountain Bike Map
Nearest town: Boulder
Other trail users: Hikers and picnickers
Dog friendly: Yes
Trail contact: Boulder County Parks and Open Space, Longmont; (303) 678-6200; www.BoulderCountyOpenSpace.org

Getting there: From Boulder drive west on Baseline Road up and over Flagstaff Mountain. Baseline Road turns into Flagstaff Mountain Road after passing Chautauqua Park on your left. This road is crisscrossed heavily by hiking trails, so keep an eye out for pedestrians and cyclists. After roughly 4 miles you'll pass the sign for the Flagstaff Mountain Amphitheater and Green Mountain Lodge. Continue on Flagstaff Mountain Road for roughly another 3.5 miles before bearing right into the Meyers Homestead Picnic Area and trailhead. Trailhead GPS: N39 20.796' / W105 33.871'; trailhead terminus/turnaround GPS: N39 57.961' / W105 33.871'

The Ride

The ambling Meyers Homestead Trail that wanders past hay barn ruins is part of Walker Ranch. As such, Meyers Homestead is included among the 3,778 acres of cultural landscape, the largest parcel in Colorado to receive this designation.

Riding past the dilapidated remains of the historic sawmill built by James Walker.

Not much is known of Andrew R. Meyers, who settled the gulch north of Walker Ranch in 1890. Although Meyers later sold his land to James Walker, this trail still bears his name. Meyers obtained his land during America's campaign to populate its western interior. This expansion west took shape in the Homestead Act of 1862, which called for the opening of public lands to agricultural settlement.

Used primarily for logging and livestock pasture by the Walker family, the Meyers Homestead area became part of the largest cattle ranch in this region of Colorado. To his credit, James Walker built his highly successful ranch by using portable sawmills and bringing in hardy Scottish cattle that could survive in the Rocky Mountain foothills.

The trail begins by descending on a wide doubletrack as it heads in a northwesterly direction to the historic sawmill. After passing the sawmill, riders cruise through a couple of other meadows as the trail begins to climb more moderately. During the autumn months these meadows are crowded with chokecherry and raspberry bushes. In preparation for their dormant season, black bears can feed for nearly 20 hours a day on these berries. In Colorado female bears enter their dens in late October, while

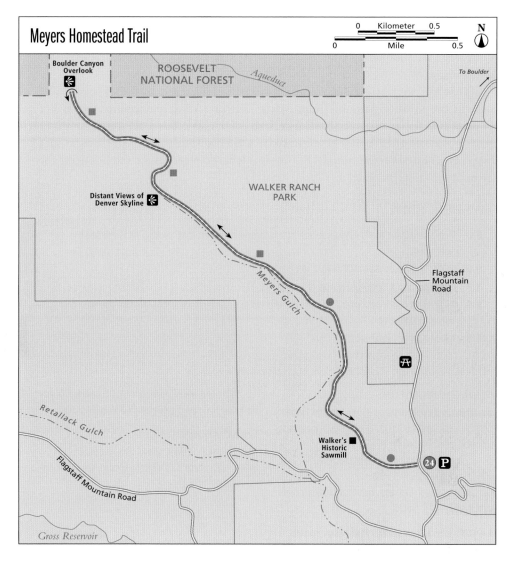

Meyers Homestead Trail

0 Kilometer 0.5
0 Mile 0.5

N

Boulder Canyon
Overlook

ROOSEVELT
NATIONAL FOREST

Aqueduct

To Boulder

Distant Views of
Denver Skyline

WALKER RANCH
PARK

Meyers Gulch

Flagstaff
Mountain
Road

Retallack Gulch

Flagstaff Mountain Road

Walker's
Historic
Sawmill

24 P

Gross Reservoir

male bears retreat to their dens in early November. Encounters with bears are rare, but the possibility still exists. Should you encounter a bear, stay calm and speak softly to make the bear aware of your presence. If on a trail, step off the trail on the downhill slope and back away from the bear slowly.

From the dilapidated sawmill the trail alternates from level to steeper terrain. Nearing 2 miles, riders will begin to climb more steeply as they head in and out of mixed conifer forests. In addition, riders are offered distant glimpses of the Denver skyline through a fissure in the foothills. The final approach to the trail's turnaround point arrives nearly 2.4 miles into the ride. Here you make your final climb through a meadow to the trail's high point and the Boulder Canyon Overlook, offering views of the Continental Divide, Indian Peaks, and Sugarloaf Mountain.

You can't help but notice the charred trees and barren ground of Sugarloaf Mountain. In 1989 a garage fire caused this devastation, destroying forty-four structures along the mountain's hillsides. Now, more than 25 years later, the mountainside still struggles to recover.

From the overlook riders return to their vehicles the way they came. The descent from this turnaround point is fast. Take care when descending, as this is a popular trail for hikers and bikers alike. The route also offers a great many erosion ditches that cross the trail. These can cause a rider to flip if his or her weight isn't properly adjusted on the bicycle. For more advanced riders, these ditches make for great bunny-hop potential.

Miles and Directions

0.0 Begin riding on a wide doubletrack in a westerly direction that shortly turns toward the northwest.

0.5 Pass the historic sawmill to your left.

1.9 Ride through a beautiful stand of aspen.

2.6 Reach the trail's turnaround point and the Boulder Canyon Overlook. Return the way you came to the start.

5.3 Arrive back at your vehicle.

Ride Information

Trail Information

Boulder County Parks and Open Space Department, Longmont; (303) 678-6200; www.Boulder CountyOpenSpace.org

Colorado Division of Wildlife; (303) 291-7227 or (303) 297-1192

USDA Forest Service, Boulder District, Boulder; (303) 444-6600

Local Events and Attractions

Meyers Homestead Trail Group Shelter, accommodates up to seventy-five people; for reservations contact Boulder County Parks and Open Space at (303) 678-6200

Walker Ranch Tours; contact Boulder County Parks and Open Space at (303) 678-6200

Restaurants

The Kitchen, 1039 Pearl St., Boulder; (303) 544-5973; http://thekitchen.com/the-kitchen-boulder/

25 Walker Ranch Loop

The Walker Ranch Loop is a popular ride among Boulder mountain bikers. Its initial singletrack descent to South Boulder Creek is awesome. During the spring thaw South Boulder Creek is an impressive torrent of white water, an exhilarating sound to hear while riding along its banks. This ride weaves in and out of mixed conifer forests and offers a number of rockier singletrack sections. There is one section of the trail that requires you to portage down (or up) a steep hillside, a section that some area riders consider the Walker Ranch Loop's best and worst feature. Mountain lions have been spotted in the area, so pay attention to the mountain lion warning signs. This description is for a counterclockwise ride, but it's equally fun when going clockwise.

(*Note:* Walker Ranch sustained considerable damage as a result of the flooding in 2013 and remains closed as of this writing. Contact local authorities for the latest status of this trail.)

Start: Parking lot of Walker Ranch Open Space at the South Boulder Creek trailhead

Distance: 8.0-mile loop, with other options available in Walker Ranch

Elevation gain: 1,650 feet

Riding time: Advanced riders, 1 hour; intermediate riders, 2 hours

Fitness effort: Physically challenging due to the variety of climbing involved

Difficulty: Technically moderate to challenging due to smooth, fast singletrack coupled with tough rocky sections. (**Note:** There is a section of trail called "Cliff Conditions" that requires you to portage your bicycle down steep steps and over rock faces. Take care.)

Terrain: Singletrack with patches of rocks and sand; improved dirt road

Seasons: May-Oct

Maps: *DeLorme: Colorado Atlas & Gazetteer,* pages 39-40; *USGS:* Eldorado Springs, CO; Boulder County Parks and Open Space Walker Ranch map; ZIA Maps: Boulder County Mountain Bike Map

Nearest town: Boulder

Other trail users: Hikers, anglers, picnickers, horseback riders, and climbers

Dog friendly: Yes, but dogs must be on a leash at all times.

Trail contact: Boulder County Parks and Open Space, Longmont; (303) 678-6200; www.BoulderCountyOpenSpace.org

Getting there: From Boulder drive west on Baseline Road to Flagstaff Mountain Road. Baseline turns into Flagstaff after Chautauqua Auditorium to your left. Stay on Flagstaff Mountain Road for about 8 miles as it winds its way up and over Flagstaff Mountain. The road is crisscrossed heavily by hiking trails, so keep an eye out for pedestrians and cyclists. Following the sign for Walker Ranch, you'll drive past the sign for the Flagstaff Mountain Amphitheater and Green Mountain Lodge after roughly 4 miles. Flagstaff Mountain Road will eventually top out before descending down the other side of Flagstaff Mountain. Pass the Meyers Homestead Picnic Area and trailhead on the right. From there Walker Ranch is roughly 0.5 mile farther on the left. Pull into the dirt road and drive up the short distance to the South Boulder Creek trailhead and parking lot. You can also park and start from the Ethel Harrold Picnic Area and trailhead, where more parking and restrooms are available. Trailhead GPS: N39 57.069' / W105 20.262'

Amanda Hlawaty descending the Cliff Conditions to the South Boulder Creek.

The Ride

Near Flagstaff Mountain and just west of Boulder is an area that evokes a love/hate relationship among many mountain bikers. Walker Ranch's cliff-like descent from the South Boulder Creek Trail to South Boulder Creek has the reputation of being one of the more hazardous portages in Colorado. This section of trail—loved for its uniqueness, hated for its vertigo-inducing incline—has summoned many a masochist. The portage notwithstanding, Walker Ranch offers some exciting singletrack mountain biking and beautiful scenery, set amid a rich local history.

In 1869 James Walker, with only $12 in his pocket and suffering from a life-threatening illness, traveled from Missouri to Boulder on the advice of his physician. Colorado's high, dry climate would prove to be Walker's salvation. His health dramatically improved. Having reclaimed his health, Walker, along with his wife, Phoebe, filed a homestead claim to 160 acres in 1882.

By 1883 Walker Ranch—consisting of a ranch house, barn, blacksmith shop, root cellar, granary, smokehouse, springhouse, chicken and turkey houses, corn storage house, and pig barn—afforded James and Phoebe the self-sufficient lifestyle with which they both would eventually fall in love. With various corrals, fenced pastures, and 160 acres, Walker Ranch was one of the largest cattle ranches in this region and is listed on the National Register of Historic Places.

Today, posted signs of mountain lion territory greet the would-be mountain biker at the South Boulder Creek trailhead. If you decide to park and begin your ride at the Ethel Harrold Picnic Area and trailhead, you will begin by riding up Pika Road to the South Boulder Creek Trail. Otherwise, the route begins on the South

MOUNTAIN LIONS

Residing in areas of piñon pine, juniper, mountain mahogany, ponderosa pine, and oak brush, the mountain lion—cougar, panther, or puma—is one of North America's biggest cats and inhabits much of Colorado, including the Front Range. For this reason it is not uncommon to see mountain lion warning signs at many mountain bike trailheads. Although mountain lion/human encounters are rare because of the big cat's calm, quiet, and elusive nature, such meetings are on the rise as a consequence, in part, of increased mountain biking in lion habitat.

Ranging in size from 7 to 8 feet in length and 90 to 150 pounds in weight, the mountain lion is much larger than other wild cat species in Colorado. According to Division of Wildlife experts, a mountain biker may run a higher-than-normal risk of being attacked. A mountain biker's lowered head posture may spark a lion's curiosity. Also, mountain bikers riding through the forest may be interpreted by the lion as fleeing prey, stimulating its predatory attack response. While bicycling in mountain lion habitat, keep the following information in mind.

- Ride in groups.
- Make noise during times of prime mountain lion activity—dawn and dusk.

If you should encounter a mountain lion:

- Never approach a lion, but keep your bicycle between yourself and the lion.
- Stay calm. Speak calmly but firmly to it.
- Back away from the lion slowly, facing the lion and standing upright; do not turn and run and chance stimulating the lion's predatory instincts.
- Make yourself larger in appearance: raise your arms, open your jacket if wearing one.
- If the lion becomes aggressive, throw stones or branches without crouching down or turning your back.
- If the lion attacks, fight back and avoid falling to the ground.

Boulder Creek Trail, contouring to the south of Langridge Dyke and descending to Tom Davis Gulch and South Boulder Creek at mile 1.0. There are a number of great fly-fishing holes along this patch of the creek. The route to this point is fast on rock-riddled singletrack with varying patches of sand. A number of switchbacks and dips prevent the rider from going too fast. Once it reaches South Boulder Creek, the trail smoothes to soft forest singletrack blanketed with pine needles. Ride upstream to a footbridge that crosses the creek at mile 1.5, whereupon the trail divides. Bear left here and continue your ride. For those requiring a cooling dip, riding straight ahead will deliver you to a wading pond about 50 yards up.

After bearing left, the trail climbs out of the drainage to the Crescent Meadows trailhead at mile 2.7, offering views of the Grande Western Railroad. The climb to

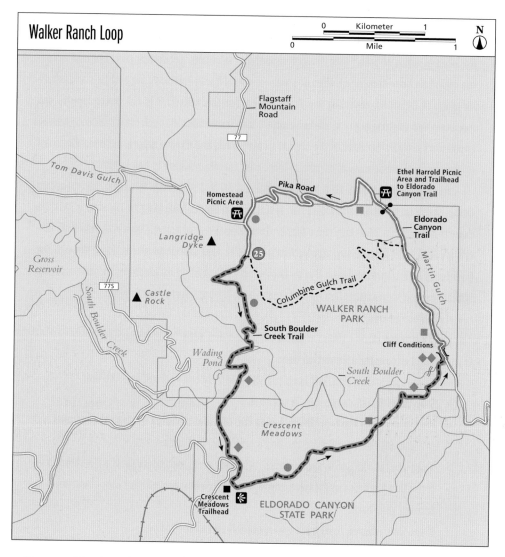

Walker Ranch Loop

0 — Kilometer — 1

0 — Mile — 1

N

Flagstaff
Mountain
Road

77

Tom Davis Gulch

Ethel Harrold Picnic
Area and Trailhead
to Eldorado
Canyon Trail

Pika Road

Homestead
Picnic Area

Eldorado
Canyon
Trail

Langridge
Dyke

Gross
Reservoir

25

775

Castle
Rock

Columbine Gulch Trail

Martin Gulch

WALKER RANCH
PARK

South Boulder
Creek Trail

Cliff Conditions

South Boulder Creek

Wading
Pond

South Boulder
Creek

Crescent
Meadows

Crescent
Meadows
Trailhead

ELDORADO CANYON
STATE PARK

Crescent Meadows is a grunt but one well worth undertaking. It climbs to 7,300 feet and offers a beautiful view of snowcapped peaks to the west. Ride east on the Crescent Meadows Trail as it parallels Eldorado Canyon State Park to the right.

This section of the route begins as a moderate descent through meadows awash with wildflowers and then becomes considerably steeper as it drops to South Boulder Creek. This may be the best section of the entire route. After dropping some big rocky hits, arrive at a sign at mile 4.8 that reads DANGER: CLIFF CONDITIONS. Dismount and carefully climb down the very technical terrain to South Boulder Creek. Once at its shores, scramble over the boulder field directly downstream and head to the bridge that crosses the creek.

After crossing the bridge, the Crescent Meadows Trail connects with the Eldorado Canyon Trail. Mountain bikers are now prohibited from entering Eldorado Canyon

State Park via the Eldorado Canyon Trail from lower Walker Ranch. (Before closures, cyclists could ride up Flagstaff and descend Walker Ranch through Eldorado Canyon and back along the Mesa Trail for an epic loop. Such a loss!) Climbing through Martin Gulch, the Eldorado Canyon Trail intersects with the Columbine Gulch Trail at mile 6.1. Here you have the option of veering left onto the Columbine Gulch Trail and shortcutting over the 1.5-mile trail back to the South Boulder Creek trailhead to your vehicle or continuing straight ahead to Pika Road.

The Columbine Gulch Trail climbs for 400 feet via a number of steep switchbacks. For those seeking the challenge of tough singletrack climbing, this part of the route, which ascends under thick forest cover, delivers all you'll ever want. For spinners who prefer constant pedaling, ride straight past the Columbine Gulch Trail to the Ethel Harrold Picnic Area. Pass the gate, ride out of the parking lot, and intercept Pika Road to the left. Pika Road offers 1.3 miles of gradual cool-down climbing before intersecting with Flagstaff Mountain Road. Turn left onto Flagstaff Mountain Road, and ride to your vehicle.

Miles and Directions

0.0 Start at the South Boulder Creek trailhead. As the trail contours south of Langridge Dyke, descend the switchbacks into Tom Davis Gulch to South Boulder Creek.

1.0 Descend to South Boulder Creek. Follow the creek upstream.

2.7 Reach Crescent Meadows (7,300 feet). From here you can see Gross Dam due west.

5.0 Reach the Cliff Conditions area. Dismount and carefully portage your bike down to South Boulder Creek.

6.1 Meet the junction of Columbine Gulch Trail and Crescent Meadows Trail. (**Option:** The 1.5-mile Columbine Gulch Trail will return you to your vehicle, but the trail is not recommended for bicycles.) Continue straight to the Ethel Harrold Picnic Area and trailhead for the Eldorado Canyon Trail.

6.3 Reach the Ethel Harrold Picnic Area and trailhead for the Eldorado Canyon Trail. Ride straight out of the parking lot and turn left onto Pika Road.

7.6 Reach a stop sign at the intersection of Pika Road and Flagstaff Mountain Road. Bear left onto Flagstaff Mountain Road toward the ride's start.

8.0 Reach the South Boulder Creek trailhead and Walker Ranch parking lot. You're at your vehicle.

Ride Information

Trail Information

Boulder County Parks and Open Space Department, Longmont; (303) 678-6200; www.Boulder CountyOpenSpace.org

Local Events and Attractions

Meyers Homestead Trail Group Shelter, accommodates up to seventy-five people; for reservations contact Boulder County Parks and Open Space at (303) 678-6200

Walker Ranch Tours; contact Boulder County Parks and Open Space at (303) 678-6200

Restaurants

The Kitchen, 1039 Pearl St., Boulder; (303) 544-5973; http://thekitchen.com/the-kitchen-boulder/

26 Marshall Mesa/Community Ditch Trail

The Marshall Mesa and Community Ditch Trail is one of the most popular trails in all of Boulder County. The trail follows an easy route atop Marshall Mesa before crossing CO 93 via a newly constructed underpass for bikes on its way toward Eldorado Springs Canyon. The views of the Flatirons are among Boulder's best. Trail users regularly bring their dogs, as the trail runs alongside a water-filled "community ditch," as well as Marshall Lake. This trail can become quite crowded during the weekends.

Start: The Marshall Mesa trailhead, just east of the intersection of CO 93 and Marshall Road

Distance: 7.7-mile lariat loop

Elevation gain: 25 feet

Riding time: Advanced riders, 30 minutes; intermediate riders, 45-60 minutes

Fitness effort: Physically easy with only a moderate hill climb at the outset from the Marshall Mesa trailhead

Difficulty: Technically easy due to the wide singletrack over smooth terrain. It is ideal for cyclocross bikes.

Terrain: Wide singletrack, doubletrack, and gravel road that roll atop mesas, through sprawling grasslands, and past sandstone cliffs

Fees and permits: Non–Boulder County residents must pay a parking fee of $5, but Boulder Open Space and Mountain Parks is advising Boulder to discontinue the program for a donation collection box.

Seasons: Mar-Nov

Maps: *DeLorme: Colorado Atlas & Gazetteer,* page 40; *USGS:* Louisville, CO, and Eldorado Springs, CO; ZIA Maps: Boulder County Mountain Bike Map

Nearest town: Boulder

Other trail users: Hikers, picnickers, and horseback riders

Dog friendly: Yes

Trail contact: Boulder County Parks and Open Space, Longmont; (303) 678-6200; www.BoulderCountyOpenSpace.org

Getting there: From Boulder drive south on CO 93 for roughly 5 miles before bearing left (east) onto CO 170 (Eldorado Springs Road). Soon thereafter, bear right into the Marshall Mesa Trailhead. Park in the spaces provided. Trailhead GPS: N39 57.157' / W105 13.874'; trailhead terminus/turnaround GPS: N39 56.276' / W105 15.389'

The Ride

Riders begin this route heading in an easterly direction along the Marshall Valley trail. The Marshall Valley trail runs alongside the northern flank of Marshall Mesa, which stands dominant over the site of what once was the mining town of Marshall. In 1859 William A. Kitchens discovered coal in the area and named his mine the Washington Lode, though his customers were more familiar with the term "Kitchens' Bank." The Marshall Mesa area is cut by numerous faults that run northeast-southeast. These faults divide the mesa into several uplifted and down-dropped blocks called horsts and grabens, respectively. Joseph Marshall purchased the mine in 1866

Returning from Eldorado Springs Canyon via the Community Ditch Trail, with the Flatirons in the background.

and soon acquired the rights to all the coal in the area, which led to the development of fifty-one mines on the mesa.

Coal mining flourished in Marshall from 1859 to 1946. The town grew so large that its population outnumbered Boulder's. While by today's standards this area may seem quiet enough, the underground coal fires that have burned since 1869 remain a metaphor for Marshall's more turbulent times. Coal strikes in 1910-14 were so violent that mine owners installed machine guns to protect their property (the location of one is still visible at the Gorham Mine), and state police killed six miners on November 21, 1927, in nearby Erie.

Riders now begin riding along the Community Ditch Trail as it travels to the top of Marshall Mesa. Along the way a variety of informational tablets tell of Marshall's mining history. As you pass Marshall Lake on your left, you'll notice the water-filled ditch to your left. This ditch once channeled water from the South Boulder Creek drainage, near the mouth of Eldorado Springs Canyon, to agricultural lands in the east.

As you connect with the Greenbelt Plateau Trail, the trail will become considerably rockier as it climbs from the community ditch over steep and water-barred terrain. Take caution when descending the gravel road of the Greenbelt Plateau Trail to CO 93. Near its intersection with CO 93, the trail cuts sharply to the left and delivers much loose gravel.

Marshall Mesa/Community Ditch Trail

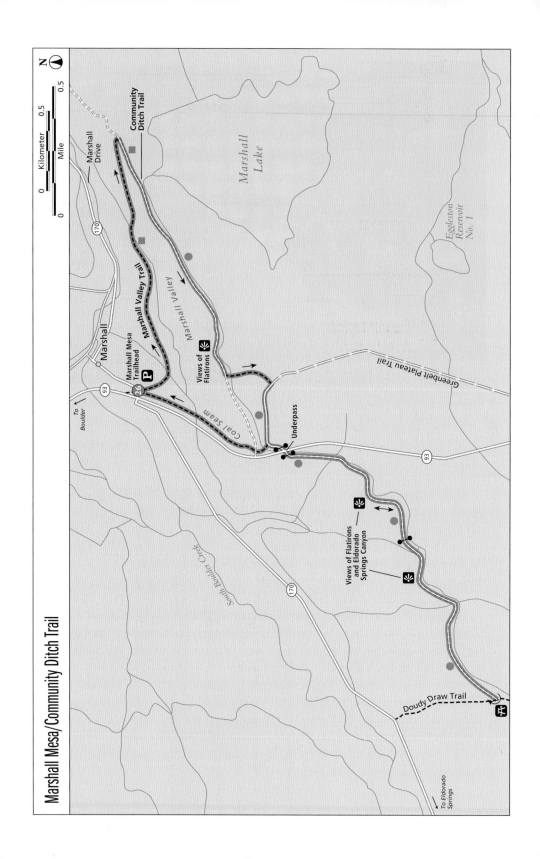

After crossing CO 93, riders rejoin the Community Ditch Trail. The trail delivers a fast descent along a smooth doubletrack. The doubletrack will eventually level off as it weaves through a meadow with spectacular views of the Flatirons directly in front of you.

The intersection of the Community Ditch Trail and the Doudy Draw Trail offers riders and their dogs relief from the hot sun by providing shade from huge cottonwood trees and the cool running water of the South Boulder Creek. From here it's a short ride to the restrooms and the turnaround point.

Miles and Directions

0.0   Begin riding in an easterly direction along the Marshall Valley Trail toward the top of Marshall Mesa and Marshall Lake. (No bikes are allowed in the Marshall Lake area.)

1.1   The Marshall Valley Trail intersects with the The Community Ditch Trail. Continue riding west on the Community Ditch Trail.

1.2   The Community Ditch Trail intersects with the Greenbelt Plateau Trail. Veer left, crossing a bridge, and continue on the Greenbelt Plateau Trail.

1.4   The Greenbelt Plateau Trail comes to a T intersection with a gravel road. Bear right at the T intersection, heading in a westerly direction, and continue on the Community Ditch Trail. (Bearing left here will take you to the Greenbelt Plateau Trail's southern terminus at CO 128.)

1.8   After going through an iron gate, the Greenbelt Plateau Trail ends at its intersection with CO 93. Cross CO 93 via the underpass and continue riding on the Community Ditch Trail.

1.9   Pass through another iron gate.

3.1   Pass through another iron gate, heading toward Eldorado Springs Canyon.

3.5   The Community Ditch Trail intersects with the Doudy Draw Trail. Veer right, continuing on the Community Ditch Trail to the picnic area.

3.7   Reach the western terminus of the Community Ditch Trail. Here you'll find restrooms, as well as picnic tables. From here turn around and retrace your path back to the Coal Seam Trail and the trailhead.

7.7   Arrive back at your vehicle.

Ride Information

Trail Information

Boulder Convention and Visitors Bureau, 2440 Pearl St., Boulder; (800) 444-0447

City of Boulder Open Space and Mountain Parks Department, Boulder; (303) 441-3440; www.osmp.org

International Mountain Bicycling Association (IMBA), Boulder; (303) 545-9011

Boulder Mountainbike Alliance, Boulder; http://bouldermountainbike.org/

Boulder Bicycle Commuters, Boulder; (303) 499-7466

Local Events and Attractions

Cyclists can make a scenic 14.5-mile loop around Marshall Mesa by linking up the various trails. It's mostly doubletrack with fun sections of singletrack and great for cross bikes.

Restaurants

The Kitchen, 1039 Pearl St., Boulder; (303) 544-5973; http://thekitchen.com/the-kitchen-boulder/

27 Doudy Draw Area

Mountain bikers of Boulder County have cause to celebrate the expansion of mountain biking access in recent years in the Doudy Draw area. And many have, as is evidenced by this area's popularity. As such, expect crowded trails on weekends. Nevertheless, the area provides riders from south Boulder near slopeside access to wonderful single-track that any mountain biker, regardless of skill level, would find inviting. In fact, this writer's 10- and 7-year-old sons, Ethan and Benjamin, found their ride in this area to be "bumpy-bumpy" and "awesome." Combining four different trails, this route covers the gamut of what mountain biking can deliver: wide, gravel doubletrack; rockier single- and doubletrack; steep, technical terrain; flat, easy terrain; fast-running, smooth descents; and sweeping views—all within 5 miles of downtown Boulder. The first 4 miles of this route provides user-friendly terrain, although advanced riders also find this section to be a blast. The most technical part of the route arrives between miles 4 and 5, before it levels off atop the Flatirons Plateau and flatter terrain. The descent from the intersection of the Flatirons Vista Trail and the Doudy Draw Trail is a hoot.

Start: The Doudy Draw trailhead off Eldorado Springs Drive

Distance: 10.5-mile double lariat

Elevation gain: 566 feet

Riding time: Advanced riders, 1 hour; intermediate riders, 1.5 hours

Fitness effort: Physically easy to moderate given no significant elevation gain

Difficulty: Technically easy with one or two challenging steeper and rockier sections

Terrain: Singletrack and doubletrack that deliver flat-running singletrack and doubletrack, as well as some rockier and sandier sections

Fees and permits: Non–Boulder County residents must pay a parking fee of $5, but Boulder Open Space and Mountain Parks is advising Boulder to discontinue the program for a donation collection box.

Seasons: Apr-Nov

Maps: *USGS:* Eldorado Springs, CO; *DeLorme: Colorado Atlas & Gazetteer,* page 40, A-1; *Boulder Open Space and Mountain Parks Doudy Draw/Eldorado Mountain Trails* guide

Nearest town: Eldorado Springs

Other trail users: Hikers, equestrians, and picnickers

Dog friendly: Yes, but dogs are required to be on a leash.

Trail contact: Boulder County Parks and Open Space, Longmont; (303) 678-6200; www.BoulderCountyOpenSpace.org

Getting there: From Boulder drive south on CO 93 for roughly 4 miles and turn right onto Eldorado Springs Drive (CO 170). Drive west on Eldorado Springs Drive for 1.6 miles, and turn left into the Doudy Draw trailhead parking lot. Trailhead GPS: N39 56.276' / W105 15.389'

The Ride

The trail begins with an easy climb on wide, gravel-laden doubletrack as it heads in a southerly direction. Once passing the intersection with the Community Ditch Trail

Ethan and Benjamin Hlawaty making their descent along the Spring Brook loop, with the Flatirons in the background.

and immediately crossing the bridge, the climbing continues over a wider dirt trail before the trail becomes narrower over rockier terrain. As this is a very popular trail system, be conscious of other trail users, yielding to hikers and equestrians as well as riders on the ascent.

After riding for roughly 1 mile, you'll turn onto the Spring Brook Trail spur, which leads to the Spring Brook loop, the first in this two-lariat ride. The Spring Brook Trail's diminutive name belies its grander origins. Between 70 and 80 million years ago, the place where you are now riding was once covered by 600 feet of ocean water. The trail made up part of the seabed of a vast inland ocean that covered much of central North America and spanned from the Gulf of Mexico to Canada's Hudson Bay. Sloughing sand and rock from the surrounding shores collected to form a layer of mud more than a mile thick on the seafloor. It is this ancient marine mud, or Pierre Shale, upon which your tires tread. The clay-enriched Pierre Shale is soft and crumbly, making it very susceptible to erosion, so stay on the trail and avoid riding when wet or muddy conditions exist.

By roughly 1.7 miles the trail begins to climb easily through a forest of ponderosa trees, a welcome relief from the exposed landscape of the meadowlands through which you just rode. Once reaching the summit and intersection with the Goshawk Ridge Trail, riders continue along the Spring Brook Trail's northern hemisphere. As the Goshawk Ridge Trail is located in the Eldorado Mountain Habitat Conservation Area, no dogs or bikes are permitted. The trail leading to this area is named after a powerful raptor whose short and broad wings and long tail are well adapted for maneuvering through the trees and forests in which it hunts and nests. And if environmental impact isn't reason enough to respect a goshawk's habitant, the raptor has been known to attack people who come too close to its nest. Once a goshawk has you in its cross-feathers, it's game on, as the goshawk may pursue its prey for up to 60 minutes.

Watching your back for a goshawk attack, descend from the Spring Brook loop summit through a mixed conifer forest before exiting onto a sweeping plateau with expansive views of the Flatirons roughly 3 miles into your ride. Named after the metal irons with which pioneers used to press their clothes, the Flatirons are conglomerate sandstone that is nearly 300 million years old. As the trail curves east, a rockier singletrack descent awaits before the finish of the Spring Brook loop. Be careful on your descent since other trail users may be coming up the trail. Bear left onto the Spring Brook Trail spur to continue your ride in a southerly direction on the Doudy Draw Trail.

The continuation of the Doudy Draw Trail is more technical than any of the terrain previously ridden on this route. After crossing a footbridge at roughly 4.3 miles, riders have to negotiate a challenging climb that delivers steep, sandy, and rocky terrain. This challenge is quickly put to rest once you're connected with the Flatirons Vista Trail at 5.0 miles. This part of the route offers wide and mellow singletrack that delivers some rockier sections over flat terrain as it weaves atop plateau. By 6.2 miles you'll catch easterly views of the National Renewable Energy Laboratory's National Wind Technology Center, the nation's premier wind energy research facility. These 262-foot wind turbines can produce multiple megawatts of electricity.

As this trail loops around to the north, you will eventually arrive at the intersection of the Flatirons Vista and the Prairie Vista Trails. After bearing left onto the Prairie Vista Trail, it's a speedy descent, but watch out for two tight switchbacks. This descent is followed by a short climb on rockier doubletrack after reconnecting with the Flatirons Vista Trail (north). As you travel west over wide doubletrack on generally flat terrain, beautiful views of the Flatirons lie directly in front of you. Upon arriving again at the intersection with the Doudy Draw Trail, you are offered a fast, fun, and speedy 2-mile descent retracing your route back to your vehicle.

Miles and Directions

0.0 From the Doudy Draw trailhead, begin riding south over wide, gravel terrain.

0.4 Once passing the restrooms to your left, reach the intersection of the Doudy Draw Trail and the Community Ditch Trail on your left. Continue riding on the Doudy Draw Trail, crossing the bridge.

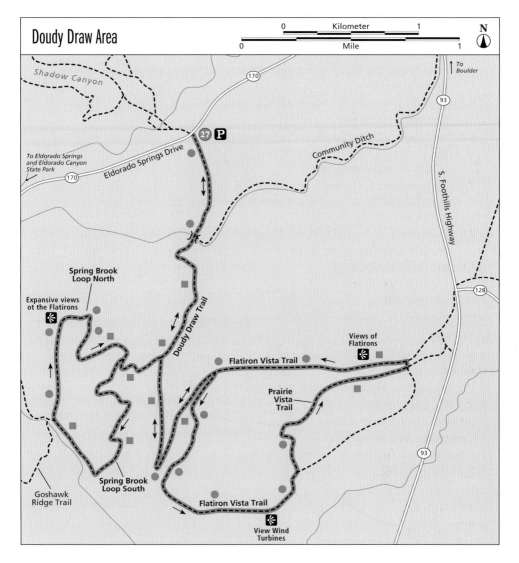

Doudy Draw Area

Shadow Canyon

To Eldorado Springs
and Eldorado Canyon
State Park

Eldorado Springs Drive

Community Ditch

S. Foothills Highway

To
Boulder

Spring Brook
Loop North

Expansive views
of the Flatirons

Doudy Draw Trail

Flatiron Vista Trail

Views of
Flatirons

Prairie
Vista
Trail

Spring Brook
Loop South

Goshawk
Ridge Trail

Flatiron Vista Trail

View Wind
Turbines

1.1 Reach the intersection of the Doudy Draw Trail and the spur trail of the Spring Brook Trail. Bear right onto the Spring Brook Trail spur.

1.4 Arrive at the Spring Brook Trail loop (south and north). Bear left onto loop's southern hemisphere, riding in a clockwise direction.

2.6 Reach the summit of the Spring Brook Trail loop (south and north) and its intersection with the hiking-only Goshawk Ridge Trail. Continue riding on the Spring Brook Trail's northern hemisphere.

3.7 Reconnect with the Spring Brook Trail loop (south and north). Bear left onto the Spring Brook Trail spur, and retrace your route to the Doudy Draw Trail.

4.0 Arrive at the intersection of the Spring Brook Trail spur and the Doudy Draw Trail. Bear right onto the continuation of the Doudy Draw Trail, and begin a short climb in a southerly direction. (**Option:** At this point riders can choose to shorten their ride by bearing left onto the Doudy Draw Trail and return to their vehicles.)

5.0 Pass through the cattle fence and arrive at the Doudy Draw Trail's intersection with the Flatirons Vista Trail. Make an immediate right onto the Flatirons Vista Trail, and ride in a southerly direction.

6.2 Pass through another cattle fence with views of the National Wind Technology Center's wind turbines to the east.

6.4 The Flatirons Vista Trail intersects with the Prairie Vista Trail. Bear left onto the Prairie Vista Trail. (By bearing right onto the Prairie Vista Trail, riders will ultimately reach the same destination as by bearing left.)

7.4 The Prairie Vista Trail intersects with the Flatirons Vista Trail (north). Bear left onto the Flatirons Vista Trail (north), heading in a westerly direction with views of the Flatirons directly in front of you.

8.3 Reach the intersection of the Flatirons Vista Trail and the Doudy Draw Trail. Pass through the fence to continue on the Doudy Draw Trail, retracing your route to your vehicle.

10.5 Arrive back at your vehicle.

Ride Information

Trail Information

City of Boulder Open Space and Mountain Parks Department, Boulder; (303) 441-3440; www.osmp.org

International Mountain Bicycling Association (IMBA), Boulder; (303) 545-9011

Boulder Mountainbike Alliance, Boulder; http://bouldermountainbike.org/

Boulder Bicycle Commuters, Boulder; (303) 499-7466

Local Events and Attractions

Eldorado Canyon State Park; (303) 494-3943

Eldorado Springs Pool; (303) 499-9640

Restaurants

The Kitchen, 1039 Pearl St., Boulder; (303) 544-5973; http://thekitchen.com/the-kitchen-boulder/

28 Eldorado Canyon State Park

Eldorado Canyon State Park offers riders an array of recreational opportunities. The park itself is perhaps best known for its rock climbing. Climbers from around the world enjoy a huge collection of routes along the soaring red sandstone walls, making for an interesting sight along your ride. Standing at 7,240 feet high, Shirttail Peak is the highest within the canyon. The Rattlesnake Gulch Trail follows the narrow and rocky singletrack through Rattlesnake Gulch. Its sand- and rock-filled trail offers an exceptional ride to bikers with moderate to advanced technical ability. The climb through the gulch is also a bit of a grunt as it leads to the historic Crags Hotel ruin and views of the Continental Divide at the trail's westernmost portion.

(*Note:* As of this writing, the Fowler and Rattlesnake Gulch Trails in Eldorado State Park are closed as a result of the flooding in 2013. Contact the park for the latest status on these trails.)

Start: Along the road through Eldorado State Park
Distance: 4.9-mile lariat
Elevation gain: 1,304 feet
Riding time: Advanced riders, 1 hour; intermediate riders, 1.5-2 hours
Fitness effort: Physically challenging due to the narrow climb through Rattlesnake Gulch
Difficulty: Technically challenging with some steeper, rockier sections
Terrain: Singletrack and dirt road that travel through Eldorado Canyon and up the steep Rattlesnake Gulch. The trail doles out much rock and sand as it carries riders out of Eldorado Canyon.

Fees and permits: $3 per cyclist/walk-in; $8 per vehicle (fees subject to change)
Seasons: Mar-Oct
Maps: *DeLorme: Colorado Atlas & Gazetteer,* page 40; Colorado State Parks maps: Eldorado Canyon; *USGS:* Eldorado Springs, CO; ZIA Maps: Boulder County Mountain Bike Map
Nearest town: Eldorado Springs
Other trail users: Hikers, anglers, picnickers, and climbers
Dog friendly: Yes
Trail contact: Eldorado Canyon State Park; (303) 494-3943

Getting there: From Boulder drive south on CO 93 for roughly 5 miles before bearing right (west), after passing a brown Eldorado Canyon Park sign, onto CO 170. Drive west on Eldorado Canyon, through Eldorado Springs, for 2.4 miles before entering the Eldorado Canyon State Park. Parking is available near the entrance to the park. Trailhead GPS: N39 55.766' / W105 17.402'

The Ride

Riders begin by traveling west on the dirt road through the park. The road follows the South Boulder Creek upstream and passes a variety of sandstone walls that tower 800 feet above the canyon. Formations such as the Bastille, Rotwand Wall, Wind Tower, Hawk-Eagle Ridge, Whale's Tail, Redgarden Wall, and Lower Peanuts Wall greet the rider at the outset.

Rattlesnake Gulch Trail in the mouth of Eldorado Canyon, with the eastern plains in the background.

Once riders connect with the Rattlesnake Gulch/Fowler Trails, the route passes over wide and smooth singletrack that travels in an easterly direction. To the left lie the massive sandstone climbing walls of Eldorado Canyon. Glimpses of the eastern plains also come into view through the mouth of the canyon. Watch out for rattlesnakes sunning on trailside boulders.

Where the Rattlesnake Gulch Trail breaks from the Fowler Trail, riders are soon delivered a tight and rocky grunt of a climb through the gulch. After roughly 1 mile riders have to negotiate past a tight and sandy left-handed switchback, after which the trail starts veering in a southerly direction. Below you lie the tracks, if not the train, of the Denver & Rio Grande Railroad. After 1.5 miles the trail switches back to head in a northerly direction. As riders head north, the views of the eastern plains and the thermal pools of Eldorado Springs greet them.

The thermal hot springs found in Eldorado Canyon were once the wintering grounds for resident Ute and Arapaho Indians. When white settlers arrived in 1860, their main interest was logging. As word spread of the hot waters of the springs, the town of Eldorado Springs started receiving visitors, and by 1902 the town had become a spiritualist camp for those in need of healing. Soon thereafter the town would flourish as a tourist resort with the development of the first spring-fed swimming pool in 1904. Dubbed the "Coney Island of the West," the resort attracted as many as 60,000 summer guests, who arrived by train from Denver. Aside from the hot springs, guests would also come for Resort Days, which included the high-wire act of Ivy Baldwin. He walked across a wire suspended 582 feet above the canyon floor eighty-six times before he retired at the age of 82 in 1948.

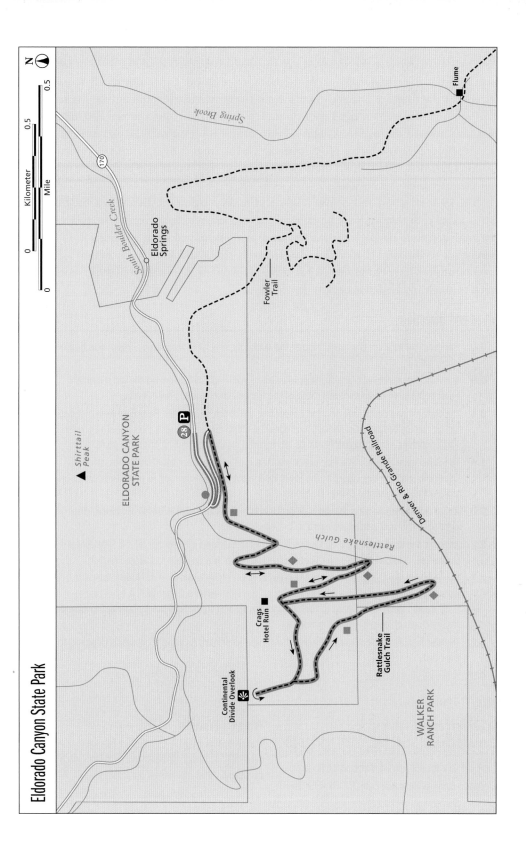

Eldorado Canyon State Park

Once you arrive at the Crags Hotel ruin, which burned down in 1912, a schematic map at the site details where the hotel once stood. Today, not much remains except for the fireplace and the circular foundation where the fountain was located.

From the Crags riders head west through dense mixed conifer forests and hillside meadows toward the overlook. This section of the route provides a welcome relief from the more exposed areas of Rattlesnake Gulch. After arriving at the Continental Divide Overlook, riders climb moderately again on the old railroad bed before making their descent.

The descent is fast and delivers tight and rocky singletrack. Before reaching the worn social path that leads to the railroad and tunnels, which are on private property, the trail descends steeply over narrow and precipitously sloping singletrack. From here it's a technically challenging descent over steep and loose rock before again arriving at the Crags Hotel ruin. What's left is a final descent of tight and sandy singletrack through big boulders back to the trailhead.

Miles and Directions

0.0 Begin riding west on the road through the park, passing the hikers-only Streamside Trail on your right.

0.5 The road intersects with the Rattlesnake Gulch Trail and Fowler Trail on the left. Bear left here, continuing on the shared route of the Rattlesnake Gulch/Fowler Trails.

0.6 The Rattlesnake Gulch Trail and the Fowler Trail split from each other. Bear right here, continuing on the Rattlesnake Gulch Trail, and continue climbing in a westerly direction. The Fowler Trail continues heading east. No bikes are allowed on the Fowler Trail after this point.

1.8 The Rattlesnake Gulch Trail intersects with the Crags Hotel ruin, the Continental Divide Overlook, and the beginning of the loop. Bear right here, continuing in a westerly direction toward the Continental Divide Overlook.

2.0 Arrive at the intersection for the trail that leads to the Continental Divide Overlook. Bear right onto the trail and head north to the overlook.

2.1 Arrive at the Continental Divide Overlook. Return to the loop intersection of the Rattlesnake Gulch Trail, and bear right onto it, continuing your loop in a counterclockwise direction.

2.7 The Rattlesnake Gulch Trail descends sharply and cuts left before a rail fence. Veer left here and continue a northerly descent along the Rattlesnake Gulch Trail. A worn social path travels beyond the gate to the railroad tracks and tunnels of the Denver & Rio Grande Railroad, which are on private property.

3.2 The Rattlesnake Gulch Trail intersects the Crags Hotel ruin. Bear right here and descend to the start.

4.9 Arrive at your vehicle.

Ride Information

Trail Information
Eldorado Canyon State Park; (303) 494-3943

Local Events and Attractions
Eldorado Springs Resort & Pool; (303) 499-9640

Restaurants
The Kitchen, 1039 Pearl St., Boulder; (303) 544-5973; http://thekitchen.com/the-kitchen-boulder/

29 Fourth of July Road

The Fourth of July Road is a widely used access route for campers, hikers, riders, and four-wheel-drive vehicles. Thus, it tends to get crowded during the weekend. Don't let the crowds turn you away, however, from enjoying the cool, refreshing runoff of Hellums Waterfall and the high-mountain scenery of Klondike and Bald Mountains. The trail delivers riders to the Fourth of July Campground and the boundary of the Indian Peaks Wilderness Area, a popular entrance point for backpackers. Located near the quirky old mining town of Eldora, the Fourth of July Road offers riders with a yearn-to-burn attitude a moderate to challenging ascent past the Eldora Ski Area and onto the base of the 11,340-foot Bald Mountain.

Start: The intersection of Hessie and Fourth of July Roads

Distance: 12.0-mile out-and-back

Elevation gain: 1,600 feet

Riding time: Advanced riders, 1 hour; intermediate riders, 1.5-2 hours

Fitness effort: Physically moderate to challenging. Although most of the climbing is gradual, the ride reaches elevations in excess of 10,000 feet.

Difficulty: Technically easy to moderate due to the route following along a dirt, albeit sometimes rutted, road

Terrain: Dirt road that can get considerably rutted as it climbs through mixed aspen and conifer forests

Seasons: July-Oct

Maps: *DeLorme: Colorado Atlas & Gazetteer*, page 39; *USGS:* East Portal, CO, and Nederland, CO; *Trails Illustrated:* #100, Boulder, Golden, CO; ZIA Maps: Boulder County Mountain Bike Map

Nearest town: Nederland

Other trail users: Hikers, backpackers, picnickers, and four-wheel-drive vehicles

Dog friendly: No, due to the vehicular traffic that is on the road

Trail contact: Roosevelt and Arapaho National Forests, Boulder Ranger District, Boulder; (303) 541-2500

Getting there: From Boulder drive west on Canyon Boulevard (CO 119) for 15.1 miles through the town of Nederland. At a roundabout in Nederland, bear left and continue driving south on CO 119 for another 0.6 mile. After passing a brown Eldora Ski Area sign, bear right onto Boulder CR 130. After 1.4 miles CR 130 intersects with 140 Road; 140 Road bears left and continues to the ski area. Bear right here, continuing on CR 130 (which soon turns into Eldorado Avenue) toward the town of Eldora. Drive on Eldorado Avenue for 1.7 miles before entering Eldora. Drive through Eldora for 0.8 mile before Eldorado Avenue turns to dirt road. Stay on the dirt road for 0.7 mile before parking along the side of the road, next to the South Fork of Upper Boulder Creek. Parking is allowed only between signs on the Fourth of July Road. Violators will incur a $50 fine or be towed. Due to the weekend congestion in the area, Boulder County provides bus service to the Hessie Trailhead. For more information contact Boulder County Parks and Open Space at (303) 678-6200. Trailhead GPS: N39 57.094' / W105 35.693'; trailhead terminus/turnaround GPS: N39 59.714' / W105 38.052'

Hellums Waterfall.

The Ride

The Fourth of July Road travels up the steep-walled drainage of the North Fork of Middle Boulder Creek and ends at the boundary to the Indian Peak Wilderness Area at the base of 11,340-foot Bald Mountain. As a result of periodic thundershowers in the area, along with its proximity to the creek, the road can become quite muddy and rutted.

The Fourth of July Road extends from the quirky little mining town of Eldora, past the road that leads to the Hessie Mine, and on to the Buckingham Campground. Although prospectors had been poking around the Eldora area since the 1850s, it wasn't until 1875 that enough gold was discovered to warrant the opening of the Fourth of July Mine. Mining would continue in the area at a modest pace until 1892, when thirteen claims were struck in the same year.

The arising town was first called Happy Valley, after John Kemp founded the Happy Valley Placer Mine in 1897. As the population swelled to 1,500 strong, the residents decided to rename their town Eldorado. This lasted until the discovery that many of their personal letters and payroll checks were being delivered to Eldorado, California. In 1898 the townspeople voted to drop the last syllable of the name, and the town became Eldora.

Upon setting out on the trail, you'll see Eldora Ski Area to your left as you climb in a northerly direction. To the west of the drainage lie the enormous granite walls that stand before the 10,860-foot Chittenden Mountain. Roughly 1.5 miles into the ride, the trail narrows and becomes steeper, falling to meet the creek. From here the trail levels off a bit and enters a dense lodgepole pine and aspen forest.

Beginning just west of Eldora, near where you now ride, a massive forest fire ripped through this drainage in 1899. With much of the surrounding area's timber

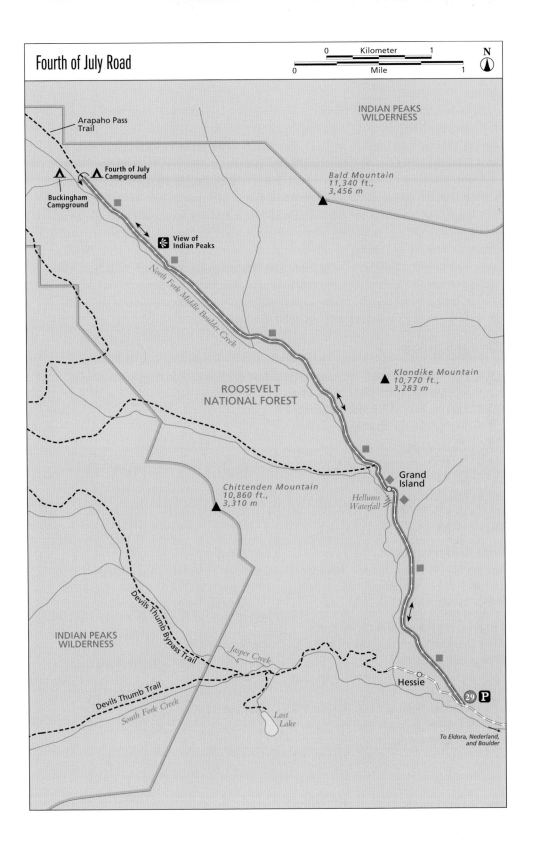

Fourth of July Road

0 Kilometer 1

0 Mile 1

N

Arapaho Pass Trail

Fourth of July Campground

Buckingham Campground

View of Indian Peaks

North Fork Middle Boulder Creek

INDIAN PEAKS WILDERNESS

Bald Mountain
11,340 ft.,
3,456 m

ROOSEVELT NATIONAL FOREST

Klondike Mountain
10,770 ft.,
3,283 m

Grand Island

Hellums Waterfall

Chittenden Mountain
10,860 ft.,
3,310 m

INDIAN PEAKS WILDERNESS

Devils Thumb Bypass Trail

Jasper Creek

Devils Thumb Trail

South Fork Creek

Lost Lake

Hessie

29 P

To Eldora, Nederland, and Boulder

lost to fire, lumber that was vital to mining construction was in short supply. The fire, coupled with the preponderance of low-grade ore, ended Eldora's short-lived bid to become El Dorado.

In recent years there has been renewed interest in mining Eldora, with hopes of reopening the Mogul Tunnel Mine on Spencer Mountain at Eldora, a gold and silver mining operation established in 1897. The fact that the mine's entrance sits only 150 yards from the center of town worries many people.

Upon reaching the trail's terminus, riders are surrounded by the towering peaks of Klondike, Pomeroy, and Bald Mountains. From here the Indian Peaks Wilderness Area begins, where bikes are banned. Picnic areas and restrooms are available at the Buckingham Campground. This takes its name from C.G. Buckingham, whose family donated much of its mining claims around Boulder Falls (you passed it in Boulder Canyon) and offered 30 acres near Eldora to create the campground.

Before turning around and immediately speeding back to your vehicle, take time to relax, have a snack, maybe go on a hike, and then speed down to your vehicle. Take care though, as the road does support vehicular traffic.

Miles and Directions

0.0 From the intersection of the Hessie and Fourth of July Roads, begin riding in a northwesterly direction on the Fourth of July Road.

1.5 Pass the Hellums Waterfall to your left.

3.0 Pass Chittenden Mountain to your left.

5.0 The Indian Peaks come into view.

6.0 Reach the Buckingham Campground and the Indian Peaks Wilderness Area boundary. Turn around to return the way you came.

12.0 Arrive back at your vehicle.

Ride Information

Trail Information

Arapaho and Roosevelt National Forests and Pawnee National Grassland, Boulder Ranger District, Boulder; (303) 541-2500

Local Events and Attractions

Eldora Mountain Resort, Nederland; (303) 440-8700 or (888) 2-ELDORA

Nederland Old Timer Miners' Days, July; (303) 258-0567

Peak-to-Peak Highway, CO 7, 62, and 119, connecting Estes Park and the Black Hawk/ Central City gambling district

Lodging

Goldminer Hotel and Rocky Ledge Cabins, Eldora; (303) 258-7770 or (800) 422-4629

Sundance Lodge and Stables, Nederland; (303) 258-3797 or (800) 817-3797

Restaurants

Black Forest Restaurant, Nederland; (303) 258-8089

Cool Beans at Happy Trails, Nederland; (303) 258-3435

30 Rollins Pass

For years Rollins Pass has been a staple in the lexicon of high-mountain riding near Boulder and Denver. Beginning on the Continental Divide's eastern slope, the ride to the top of Rollins Pass provides a long but relatively moderate hill climb to the summit and the Continental Divide at 11,671 feet. Along the way riders are treated to dynamic views of the Indian Peaks and the Boulder Park Valley before arriving at the top. Following the bed of an old wagon train route, the road passes through mixed conifer forests and around high-altitude lakes before arriving at the caved-in Needle Eye Tunnel and Rollins Pass. Since much of this route travels above timberline, riders should start early in the day to lessen the chances of being caught above timberline during a midafternoon thunderstorm, a common occurrence for this area.

Start: The east portal of the Moffat Tunnel
Distance: 30.2-mile out-and-back
Elevation gain: 2,469 feet
Riding time: Advanced riders, 3 hours; intermediate riders, 3.5-4.5 hours
Fitness effort: Physically moderate to challenging due to the trail's length and high elevations. The trail leading from the Needle Eye Tunnel to Rollins Pass is physically challenging, with steep terrain at high elevations.
Difficulty: Technically easy, although the trail leading from the Needle Eye Tunnel to Rollins Pass is technically challenging, with steep and rocky terrain
Terrain: Two-wheel-drive road, doubletrack, and singletrack that travel through mixed conifer

forests and across hillside meadows to above timberline and the Continental Divide
Seasons: June-Sept
Maps: *DeLorme: Colorado Atlas & Gazetteer,* page 39; *USGS:* Nederland, CO, and East Portal, CO; *Trails Illustrated:* #103, Winter Park, Central City, Rollins Pass, CO; ZIA Maps: Boulder County Mountain Bike Map
Nearest town: Nederland
Other trail users: Hikers, anglers, campers, and two- and four-wheel-drive vehicles
Dog friendly: No, due to the vehicular traffic and the trail's long distance
Trail contact: Arapaho and Roosevelt National Forests and Pawnee National Grassland, Boulder Ranger District, Boulder; (303) 541-2500

Getting there: From Boulder drive west on Canyon Boulevard for 16 miles to Nederland and a roundabout. Bear left at the roundabout and continue driving west on CO 119 for 5 miles to Rollinsville before turning right onto the dirt Rollins Pass Road (RD 16). Continue on Rollins Pass Road for 7.4 miles to the intersection of the road leading to the east portal of the Moffat Tunnel and FR 149 (Moffat Road "Hill Route"). Trailhead GPS: N39 54.322' / W105 37.823'; trailhead terminus/turnaround GPS: N39 56.020' / W105 41.000'

The Ride

Originally a mule trail linking Denver and Winter Park, the route across Rollins Pass served as a major thoroughfare for Native Americans, fur trappers, and miners alike. In 1865 John A. Rollins built a wagon toll road over the original mule trail and laid

Climbing up and over the Needle Eye Tunnel.

the foundation for what was to become the rail line of the Denver, Northwestern, & Pacific Railway, the highest rail line ever built in North America.

Built in 1903 by Denver banker and railroad pioneer David Moffat, the line was actually a compromise, opting for going over Rollins Pass when funding for a tunnel underneath the Continental Divide fell through. The line ran for 23 miles and operated until 1913, when it was bought by William Freeman and renamed the Denver Salt Lake Railroad. Although Moffat, who died in 1911, would never realize his dream of building a tunnel, Freeman considered the idea worth pursuing.

The first few miles of the route climbs gradually and offers expansive views of the Boulder Park Valley. Behind you lies the eastern portal of the Moffat Tunnel, an engineering marvel that required the removal of 750,000 cubic yards of rock by way of 2.5 million pounds of dynamite. The tunnel cost the lives of twenty-nine of the men who routinely worked 90-hour weeks for 4 years. But on February 26, 1928, it secured its first safe passage of a train to Grand County's west portal. Measuring 6.2 miles in length, the Moffat Tunnel is the world's sixth-longest and highest railroad tunnel, passing underneath the Continental Divide at 9,239 feet.

About 8 miles into your ride, the road becomes considerably rockier as it continues to climb in a westerly direction. Here riders are afforded beautiful views of Bryan and Woodland Mountains to the northeast, inviting riders to stop and smell the flowers. Blue lupine, pink mountain globemallow, red fireweed, and yellow meadow goldenrod all blaze along hillsides like islands of fragrant wildfires.

A BYGONE COLORADO TRADITION: DENVER'S SKI TRAIN

For more than sixty years, the Denver Ski Train had been transporting skiers from Denver's Union Station to the Winter Park Ski Resort. But once the snows melt, the town of Winter Park transforms itself from ski resort to Mountain Bike Capital, USA.

It would seem natural, then, for the Ski Train to want to open its doors to mountain bikers. And it had.

In the summer of 2000, the train began transporting mountain bikers and their bikes to Mountain Bike Capital, USA. Fresh off the success of its 2000 summer run, the Ski Train continued its mountain biking services through the summer of 2001.

The Ski Train departed from downtown Denver's Union Station in the morning and returned by late afternoon. A specifically designed car fit all of the bicycles on board, leaving passengers to simply enjoy the ride through the Rockies. As the train paralleled South Boulder Creek, it passed the towns of Pinecliffe and Rollinsville. After going through a barrage of tunnels, the Ski Train would come to the 6.2-mile-long Moffat Tunnel, the highest railroad tunnel in the United States, before coming to a stop fewer than 100 yards from the ski lifts. The trip to Winter Park only took two hours, as much as it would if driven by car.

The Ski—and mountain bike—Train ended its 69-year-old Colorado tradition when it made its last run on March 29, 2009.

The book *The Ski Train* by Steve Patterson and Kenton Forrest provides a comprehensive history of this bygone Colorado tradition.

After the road passes the Jenny Creek Trail, riders continue their gradual ascent northwest, making a 180-degree turn around Yankee Doodle Lake. At 10,711 feet, the lake sits in a basin before Guinn Mountain. A cascading waterfall flows into the lake from the snowfields above.

The long approach to Needle Eye Tunnel suddenly appears around a curve. Once at the tunnel, you must portage your bike up and over it and along a narrow and rocky path through talus fields. During spring thaw boulders from the tunnel's ceiling have been known to pry loose, dropping into the tunnel without warning.

Having safely made it to the top of the tunnel, you are welcomed by two stone foundations that serve as fitting lookouts to views of the Indian Peaks, as well as Yankee Doodle Lake, nearly 1,000 feet below. The tailless, mouse-like creatures that you'll see ducking in and out of surrounding talus fields are called pikas. Now above timberline, riders descend along rocky singletrack to the Boulder Wagon Road.

Below this road lie the Devil's Slide Trestles, also known as Twin Trestles. While an interesting sight to see, the trestles are unsafe and should be avoided. The doubletrack of the Boulder Wagon Road is burdened by steep grades and football–size rocks, making it a physically and technically challenging section of trail.

Upon reaching Rollins Pass, take some time, if you are not hurried by thunder and lightning, to absorb miles of unobstructed views from the Continental Divide. Here lies the site of the small railroad town of Corona. With no food available atop Rollins Pass, riders make their speedy, if not hungry, return. After crossing back over Needle Eye Tunnel, it's a big–ring descent to your vehicle.

Miles and Directions

0.0   Begin riding east on Rollins Pass Road 117 (FR 149).

5.6   Rollins Pass Road intersects with the Jenny Creek Trail (FR 502) on the right. Continue straight, gradually climbing on the Rollins Pass Road. (**Option:** More advanced riders can choose to branch off here and continue on the Jenny Creek Trail as it descends on a narrow, physically and technically challenging four-by-four road to Jenny Creek before making its eventual climb to reconnect with Rollins Pass Road at Yankee Doodle Lake. This route cuts roughly 5 miles off the one-way distance of this ride.)

9.6   Rollins Pass Road reconnects with the Jenny Creek Trail and arrives at Yankee Doodle Lake. You'll be able to spot Needle Eye Tunnel high above the lake on the ridgeline.

10.4   Rollins Pass Road intersects with the Jenny Lake Trail (FR 505) on the right. Continue straight on Rollins Pass Road, climbing in a westerly direction.

11.4   Rollins Pass Road intersects with the foot and horse Trail 809 on the left. Continue climbing on Rollins Pass Road as you approach Needle Eye Tunnel.

13.0   Arrive at Needle Eye Tunnel. Skirt the tunnel to your right, and portage your bicycle over the narrow talus-field trail to the other side.

13.1   Arrive at the top of the Needle Eye Tunnel. Here cairns along a rocky singletrack mark the proper route. Follow the cairns and the singletrack to the intersection with the Boulder Wagon Road.

13.4   The singletrack intersects with the Boulder Wagon Road. Bear left onto the physically and technically challenging Boulder Wagon Road and continue climbing steeply to the north. The road that leads to the Devil's Slide Trestles will be below you on the right, blocked off by logs, and is marked by a devil's trestles sign. (**Option:** Riders can either ride or hike this road to view the trestles before returning and reconnecting with the Boulder Wagon road.)

13.5   The Boulder Wagon Road crumbles into a wider jeep trail as it veers toward the west and Rollins Pass. Continue riding along a moderate grade to the pass, passing a KEEP VEHICLES ON ROAD sign to your left.

14.9   The Boulder Wagon Road intersects with Rollins Pass Road 149 at a T intersection. Bear right here onto Rollins Pass 149 and head to the old town site of Corona and Rollins Pass. FR 149 continues left and descends to Winter Park.

15.1   Arrive at the top of Rollins Pass and the Continental Divide. Turn around here and return the way you came back to your vehicle.

30.2   Arrive back at your vehicle.

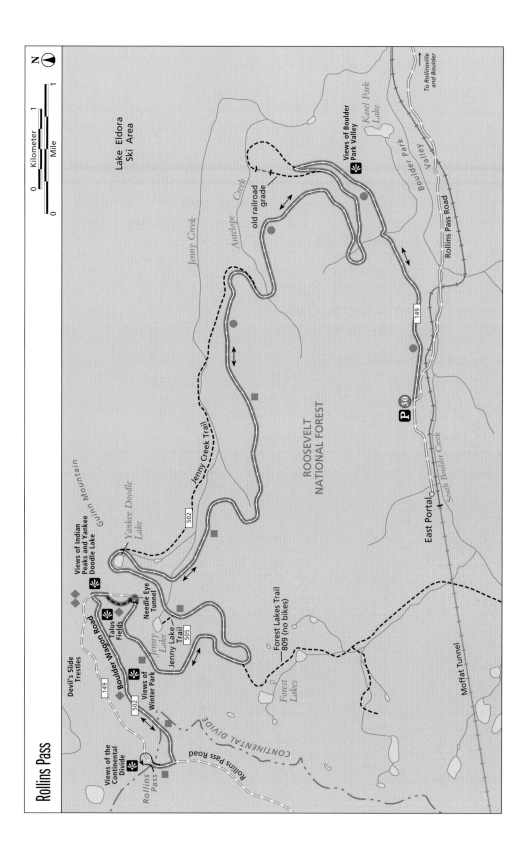

Rollins Pass

N

| 0 | Kilometer | 1 |
| 0 | Mile | 1 |

Lake Eldora Ski Area

Views of Indian Peaks and Yankee Doodle Lake

Gunn Mountain

Yankee Doodle Lake

Jenny Creek

Jenny Creek Trail

Antelope Creek

old railroad grade

Views of Boulder Park Valley

Karel Park Lake

Boulder Park Valley

Rollins Pass Road

To Rollinsville and Boulder

149

ROOSEVELT NATIONAL FOREST

P 30

East Portal

South Boulder Creek

Moffat Tunnel

CONTINENTAL DIVIDE

Rollins Pass Road

Forest Lakes

Forest Lakes Trail 809 (no bikes)

Jenny Lake Trail

Jenny Lake

505

Needle Eye Tunnel

502

Talus Fields

Views of Winter Park

Boulder Wagon Road

149

Devil's Slide Trestles

Views of the Continental Divide

Rollins Pass

502

Jenny Creek Trail

Ride Information

Trail Information

Arapaho and Roosevelt National Forests and Pawnee National Grassland, Boulder Ranger District, Boulder; (303) 541-2500

Local Events and Attractions

Eldora Mountain Resort, Nederland; (303) 440-8700

Nederland Old Timer Miners' Days, July; (303) 258-0567

Self-guided auto tours with a mile-by-mile account of the "Hill Route." Brochures are available at various businesses at Winter Park and Rollinsville.

Lodging

Goldminer Hotel and Rocky Ledge Cabins, Eldora; (303) 258-7770 or (800) 422-4629

Sundance Lodge and Stables, Nederland; (303) 258-3797 or (800) 817-3797

Restaurants

Black Forest Restaurant, Nederland; (303) 258-8089

Cool Beans at Happy Trails, Nederland; (303) 258-3435

Honorable Mentions

Boulder Region

Seven more rides in the Boulder area deserve mention, even though they didn't make the "A" list. They may be a bit out of the way or more heavily traveled, but they still deserve your consideration when choosing a destination.

H Buchanan Pass Trail

Most riders who attempt the Buchanan Pass Trail come away either loving or hating the experience. For rock hounds who enjoy putting their body and bike through battle with boulders, Buchanan Pass lies close to their hearts. For riders who prefer more of a spinner's route, this trail leaves little in the way of smooth sailing.

As part of the 16-mile trail that eventually leads into the Indian Peaks Wilderness Area, the Buchanan Pass Trail begins near the Camp Dick campground and incorporates sections of the South Saint Vrain Trail and the Sourdough Trail. The route parallels the creek over relatively smooth singletrack. This smooth singletrack is short-lived, however, delivering the blows of rocks and roots soon thereafter.

The first eastern 4.5 miles of the Buchanan Pass Trail are open to mountain bikes, after which the trail leads into the Indian Peaks Wilderness Area. Here riders will connect with Coney Flats Road (FR 507) and then with the Beaver Reservoir Cut-off Trail 835. From this cutoff trail, riders will intersect and negotiate the rocky Sourdough Trail before reconnecting with the smoother singletrack trail of the Middle Saint Vrain.

This trail can be quite confusing for riders unfamiliar with the area. Riders would benefit from checking with the Boulder County Mountain Bike Map by ZIA Maps.

For more information contact the Arapaho and Roosevelt National Forests and Pawnee National Grassland, Boulder Ranger District, at (303) 541-2500.

To reach the Buchanan Pass Trail, drive west on Canyon Boulevard (CO 119) to Nederland. In Nederland bear right onto CO 72 and drive north for roughly 15 miles to the turnoff for Camp Dick on the left. Drive for another mile and park at the trailhead on the left.

I Bald Mountain Trail

Next time you think there's no time to go mountain biking, think again. In a word, Bald Mountain is short, 1.1 miles short, but worth riding nevertheless. For beginners who haven't yet conditioned their bodies to Colorado standards, this is a great ride whose singletrack delivers baby-bottom's smoothness in as small a package. For the more advanced riders, Bald Mountain offers mountain bikers the opportunity to run laps, a unique outside reinterpretation of the velodrome.

A Boulder rider goes large and in charge at the Valmont Bike Park.

From Boulder drive west on Mapelton Avenue, which will turn into Sunshine Canyon Drive (CR 52), for 4.6 miles to the Bald Mountain Scenic Area trailhead on the left. Park in the spaces provided by the Bald Mountain Scenic Area trailhead.

For more information contact the Boulder County Parks and Open Space at (303) 678-6200.

J Valmont Bike Park

Make a visit to this world–class bike park a high priority—it's a hoot! The city opened the Valmont Bike Park in June 2011 to wide acclaim. Located at the corner of Valmont and Airport Roads in Boulder, the 42-acre park features 4 miles of wonderful trails. Open 5 a.m. to 11 p.m., weather permitting, the Valmont Bike Park is the region's premier trials–riding area. It provides no–cost riding for all abilities and disciplines. But aside from offering fabricated and natural features; color–coded range of difficulty; and small, medium, large, and extra large jumps, the park also provides lessons and clinics and serves as a rental event center, offering four different event locations. Among its many events, the Valmont Bike Park hosted the 2014 Cyclocross National Championships.

Parking is provided on both Airport Road and Valmont Road. For more information visit www.valmontbikepark.org or call (303) 413-7226.

K Boulder Creek Path

The Creek Path is one of the most recognizable bicycle thoroughfares in all of Boulder. The concrete path parallels the Boulder Creek for roughly 7.5 miles and continues into lower Boulder Canyon, where it eventually becomes a wide, natural-surface trail.

Riders typically access the Boulder Creek Path at the Boulder Public Library on Tenth and Arapaho Streets. From there the path passes the Children's Fishing Pond, an ideal resting spot for littler anglers; the Red Rocks/Settler's Park, where vertical red rock formations jut dramatically skyward; and the Boulder Creek Kayak Course, where boaters brave the rapids during the runoff of late spring and early summer. Later in the season you will often find tubers running the same, if somewhat mellowed, rapids.

For more information on the Boulder Creek Path, contact the Boulder Parks Department at (303) 413-7200.

(**Note:** As of this writing, some portions of the Boulder Creek Path are closed due to the flooding of 2013.)

L Winiger Ridge Dot Trail System

Located in Nederland, the Dot Trail System begins behind the Nederland High School. While there is presently a network of trails in the area, the Forest Service, the Boulder Mountainbike Alliance, and the International Mountain Bicycling Association are in the planning stages of creating a mapped and well-constructed trail system that would extend from Nederland to Boulder, connecting West Magnolia Road to Walker Ranch.

The current network of trails can be ridden; however, due to its circuitous arrangement and spotty trail markings, it's recommended that cyclists ride with someone who knows the area. Riders have been known to get lost here. For more information on the area, visit the Boulder Mountainbike Alliance at bouldermountainbike.org.

M West Magnolia Recreation Area

West Magnolia Recreation Area has been a long-standing favorite for area mountain bikers of Boulder and Nederland. Its closure in the summer of 2012 for fire mitigation prompted a fair amount of redesign and reconstruction. With no real physically or technically challenging terrain, the trail is great for beginners. At several vantage points you're offered beautiful views of the Indian Peaks. The trail offers several routes to Rollinsville and links to the numerous singletrack trails and access roads found in the surrounding Roosevelt National Forest. These trail systems offer mountain bikers, hikers, and horseback riders an easy to difficult route through the densely wooded areas of the Magnolia area.

To reach the West Magnolia Recreation Area, drive south on CO 119 from Nederland toward Rollinsville. After passing the Sundance Cafe Lodge, bear right onto West Magnolia (CR 132W). Park in the pullout provided and begin riding through the densely wooded mixed conifer forest. Roughly a mile farther down CR 132W is another Forest Service road on the left that links with a variety of other roads and singletrack trails.

For more information contact the Preserve Unique Magnolia Association (PUMA) at www.puma-net.org or P.O. Box 536, Nederland, CO 80466.

N Mud Lake Trail System

The Mud Lake Trail System is an easy ride in western Boulder County. Located 2 miles north of Nederland, Mud Lake Open Space is well suited for families and those just getting started in mountain biking. Acquired by Boulder County and the town of Nederland in 1999, this area provides easy accessibility to Colorado's generally less accessible montane life zone, with elevations ranging from 8,300 to 10,000 feet.

The area provides three easy trails that combine to make for roughly 3 miles of riding. Intersecting with the Tungsten Loop, the 0.7-mile out-and-back Caribou Link Trail leads to the Caribou Ranch Open Space, where dogs and mountain biking are not allowed. Caribou Ranch Open Space is closed from April 1 to June 30. The Tungsten Loop is a 0.8-mile effort and skirts around Mud Lake. A short connector trail connects the Tungsten Loop with the 1.1-mile-long Kinnickinnick Loop.

For more information contact Boulder Parks and Open Space at (303) 678-6200.

Denver Region

I f you're looking for proof of Denver's metropolis status, you need only look to the Denver Broncos, the Colorado Rockies, the Denver Nuggets, and the Colorado Avalanche—but even that wouldn't present the whole picture. Consider the $4.3 billion Denver International Airport and the $76 million refurbished Central Library, and you've got one heck of a megalopolis. But what distinguishes Denver from other large US cities isn't its sports teams or the fact that its airport rests on a site larger than Manhattan, but rather that it's only minutes away from some of the sweetest stretches of singletrack in all of Colorado.

Denver is one of the few cities in history that was not founded near a road, railroad, lake, navigable river, or body of water. The discovery of gold in 1858 along the banks of Cherry Creek first brought settlers to the site that would later become Colorado's capital. Prior to the "Pikes Peak or Bust Gold Rush" of the late 1850s and early 1860s, however, the area had already enjoyed a reputation as a meeting place for trappers, traders, and the Native tribes of the Sioux, Cheyenne, Arapaho, Ute, and Crow. But it would be by rail that Denver would secure its dominance as a western city.

Not put off by the Trans-Continental Railroad bypassing its city, Denver residents opted instead to start their own railroad company and connect it with the Union Pacific in Cheyenne, Wyoming. Awarded capital status of the Colorado Territory in 1867, Denver would remain the capital after Colorado was admitted to the union in 1876.

Located nearly 300 miles west of the United States' geographic center and covering more than 154 square miles of land, Denver is the largest city in the region. Nestled between the eastern plains and the central Rocky Mountains, Denver serves as gateway to more than 8.8 million visitors a year, many of whom come to enjoy the area's fine cycling opportunities.

While there are over 20,000 acres of parks in nearby mountains, Denver itself boasts more than 200 parks, most linked by bike paths within the city limits—the largest city parks system in the country. In particular, the incredible Open Space Parks of Jefferson County, Colorado's most populated county, have been rated the best in the nation by the American Hiking Society. Nearly three fourths of Jefferson County lies in the Front Range. While the hills surrounding Denver offer riders more than

850 miles of paved and off-road trails, the city itself includes more than 450 miles of bike paths and lanes, all of which are frequently used by the Denver-based bicycle touring company Bikalope Tours; call (303) 483-5300 or visit www.bikalope.com.

The backbone of Denver's urban bicycling network includes the Platte River and Cherry Creek Trails. From these trails riders can link to all of Denver's bike paths and lanes, enabling riders to get anywhere in the city without having to compete with vehicular traffic. Receiving over 300 days of sunshine a year and warm Chinook winds periodically throughout the winter, Denver offers mountain bikers year-round riding. Not surprising then that *Bicycling* magazine consistently ranks Denver in the top twenty of its America's Top 50 Bike-Friendly Cities. And if that wasn't enough, Denver is one of the largest cities ever to have been honored by the League of American Bicyclists as a Silver Bicycling Friendly Community.

But cyclists beware. Denver also boasts one of the highest per-capita motor vehicle ownership rates in the country, which amounts to one licensed vehicle for every person in the city. Luckily, Denver provides bike transport on all of its buses.

Currently, the Denver metro area counts its population at over 2.5 million, three fourths of whom live in the suburban counties of Adams, Arapaho, Boulder, Denver, Douglas, and Jefferson. As the largest city between the Great Plains and the Pacific Coast, Denver offers all the amenities of a large city, while providing all the recreational activities normally found only in smaller mountain towns.

Local Bike Shops

Golden Bike Shop, Golden; (303) 278-6545, http://goldenbikeshop.com/

Peak Cycles, Golden; (303) 216-1616; www.bikeparts.com/peakCycles/peakCycles.asp

Big Ring Cycles, Golden; (877) RIDE-BIG; www.bigringcycles.com/

Any & All Bikes, Denver; (303) 995-3731; www.anyandallbikes.com/

Velosoul Cyclery, Denver; (720) 570-5039; http://velosoul.com/

Adventure Cycling, Denver; (303) 699-2514; http://adventurecycle.net/

Wheat Ridge Cyclery, Wheat Ridge; (303) 424-3221; http://ridewrc.com/

31 Mountain Lion Trail

Golden Gate Canyon State Park offers riders a network of prime singletrack. The Mountain Lion Trail stands the test of time and continues to invite more advanced riders to challenge themselves on its rocky and narrow singletrack. Weaving across meadows, through forests, up hillside climbs, and down creek sides, the Mountain Lion Trail offers a lot of incredible terrain that will challenge even the most seasoned rider.

(**Note:** As of this writing, the Deer Creek section of the Mountain Lion Trail is closed due to the flooding of 2013. For updates contact Golden Gate Canyon State Park Visitor Center at (303) 582-3707.)

Start: The Burro trailhead at Bridge Creek
Distance: 8.2-mile loop
Elevation gain: 1,300 feet
Riding time: Advanced riders, 1.5 hours; intermediate riders, 1.5-2 hours
Fitness effort: Physically challenging due to the sustained climbing along wide doubletrack and singletrack
Difficulty: Technically challenging due to rockier sections along the creeks and steeper terrain
Terrain: Singletrack and doubletrack that pass through open meadows, along rocky creeks, and through mixed conifer forests
Fees and permits: $7 daily pass park fee

Seasons: June-Oct
Maps: *DeLorme: Colorado Atlas & Gazetteer*, page 39; Colorado State Parks maps: Golden Gate Canyon; *USGS:* Ralston Buttes, CO; USGS: Black Hawk, CO illustrates the Gilpin County side of Golden Gate Canyon State Park; *Trails Illustrated:* #100, Boulder, Golden, CO
Nearest town: Nederland
Other trail users: Hikers, horseback riders, picnickers, anglers, campers, and hunters
Dog friendly: Yes
Trail contact: Golden Gate Canyon State Park; (303) 582-3707

Getting there: From Golden drive north on CO 93 for roughly 3 miles before turning left onto Golden Gate Canyon Road. Drive on Golden Gate Canyon Road for roughly 13 miles before pulling off to the right to pay the daily use fee. After paying, bear right on 57 Road (Ralston Creek Road or Drew Hill Road) by the visitor center and drive for roughly 3 miles to the Burro trailhead at Bridge Creek. Trailhead GPS: N39 50.883' / W105 21.714'

The Ride

Golden Gate Canyon State Park includes 14,000 acres of sweeping meadows, mixed conifer and aspen forests, and high-mountain peaks. Elevations within the park range from 7,600 feet to 10,400 feet.

The trail begins by climbing steadily on the Burro Trail, heading in a northnorthwest direction across south-facing meadows. Within the first mile of riding, a right-handed switchback delivers steep, sandy, and rocky terrain before leveling off atop a ridge.

Arriving at the site of the old Tallman Ranch.

Soon after connecting with the Mountain Lion Trail, the route travels through a tall stand of ponderosa pine. Here the trail is much smoother than the rockier and sandier sections of the Burro Trail. After passing the turnoff for the City Lights Ridge, riders descend on wide singletrack through stands of aspen and over occasionally rocky terrain before beginning their climb again at roughly 1.6 miles. Soon thereafter riders reach the site of the old Tallman Ranch.

The area surrounding the ranch has been occupied by four generations of Swedish descent. Anders Tallman and his family homesteaded the land in 1876. Here the Tallman family raised milk cows, beef cattle, and chickens. To supplement their income, the Tallmans also cut timber and kept a garden whose produce they would sell to residents of the nearby town of Black Hawk.

Originally, Anders homesteaded this site because it reminded him of his homeland in Sweden. When they came of age, Anders's son Nells and daughter Anna homesteaded neighboring land to a combined Tallman ranch holding of 400 acres. It would appear as though riders were climbing through all 400 of these acres as they make their way up the meadow toward a cool stand of aspen trees.

At about 2.7 miles the trail narrows to singletrack and climbs more steeply as it switches back toward Windy Peak over physically and technically challenging terrain. Riders are rewarded with views of the Continental Divide along the way, however, before entering into a thick ponderosa pine forest at nearly 3 miles into

Mountain Lion Trail

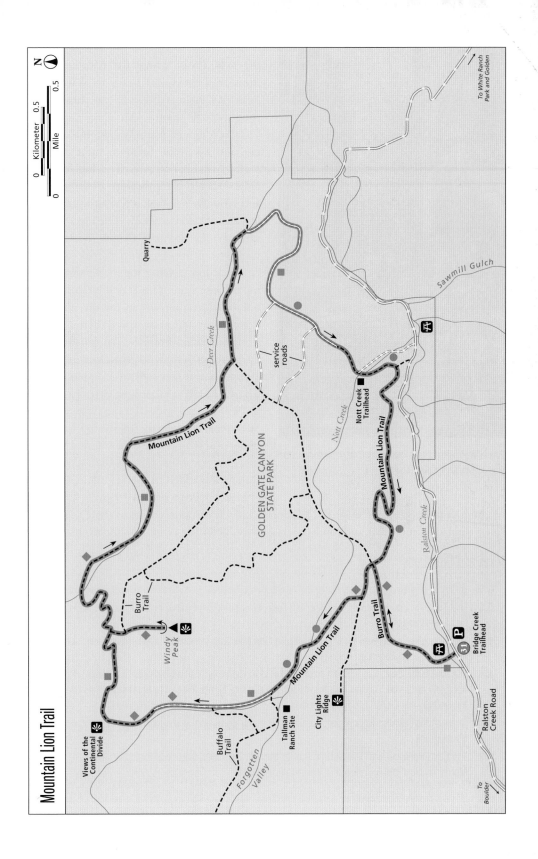

Darting through the rooted and rocky woods on the Mountain Lion Trail.

the ride. From where the Mountain Lion Trail forks and heads to Windy Peak, it's a short burst to the top at roughly 9,000 feet.

The descent from Windy Peak is fast and takes the form of tight and rocky switchbacks, as well as big root ledges. Riders blaze through a meadow and cross Deer Creek a few times, following it downstream. During the summer the Tallman family diverted water from nearby Nott Creek and channeled its cooling waters across the milk house floor. This was the family's only refrigeration system for the milk, eggs, butter, and meat stored there.

Descendants from the Tallman family continued to work this land until 1955, when it was sold to a developer. The first section of park was purchased in 1960, and a decade later the Colorado State Parks bought the remaining land, preserving it for future generations. Due to its historical significance, the Tallman Ranch was added to the State Registry of Historic Properties in 1995.

After crossing Deer Creek at the Mountain Lion Trail's intersection to the Quarry, riders climb on doubletrack and pass two service roads before descending to their vehicles.

Miles and Directions

0.0 Begin by climbing along the Burro Trail singletrack, heading in a north-northwest direction.

0.1 The Burro Trail comes to a fork. Bear left here, continuing your climb and heading in an easterly direction.

1.2 The Burro Trail intersects with the Mountain Lion Trail. Turn left onto the Mountain Lion Trail, heading toward Forgotten Valley.

1.4 The trail forks. Continue straight here on the Mountain Lion Trail as it heads in a more northerly direction. The left fork heads toward the City Lights Ridge. No horses or bikes are allowed on the City Lights Ridge section.

1.9 Arrive at the Tallman Ranch site. Continue climbing north on the Mountain Lion Trail's doubletrack.

2.2 The trail intersects with the Buffalo Trail to the left. Bear right here, continuing on the Mountain Lion Trail and heading toward Windy Peak.

3.3 The trail forks at a rock wall. Bear right (straight) here and continue along the out-and-back trail to Windy Peak.

3.6 Arrive at Windy Peak. Turn around and backtrack to where the Mountain Lion Trail forked.

4.0 Arrive at the Mountain Lion fork for Windy Peak and the trail's continuation to Nott Creek. Bear right here, heading in a northerly direction. Careful inspection of the area will reveal a yellow trail sign that reads MOUNTAIN LION TRAIL TO KNOTT CREEK and points in the correct direction.

5.6 The trail intersects with the Burro Trail. Continue descending on the Mountain Lion Trail.

6.3 The Mountain Lion Trail forks. Bear right, crossing Deer Creek, and begin climbing in a southerly direction. The left fork is an out-and-back to the Quarry.

7.1 Pass a service road.

7.3 The trail intersects with a service road. Bear left here, continuing on the Mountain Lion Trail, descending in a southerly direction and following the Nott Creek parking sign.

7.7 Arrive at the Nott Creek trailhead. Ride through the parking area and continue on the singletrack on the other side, located near the restroom.

8.2 Arrive at your vehicle.

Ride Information

Trail Information

Golden Gate Canyon State Park, Golden; (303) 582-3707
   Colorado State Parks; (303) 866-3437

Local Events and Attractions

Panorama Point Scenic Overlook group events; (303) 582-3707

Mining towns of Black Hawk and Central City, 6 miles south of the park on CO 119

Restaurants

Black Forest Restaurant, Nederland; (303) 258-8089
   Cool Beans at Happy Trails, Nederland; (303) 258-3435

32 White Ranch

White Ranch offers grueling climbs; steep, narrow descents; and tight switchbacks. The route described here includes all of these aspects but is still only a small sampling of what White Ranch has to offer. With steep grades, loose rock, and plastic erosion bars strewn across the trail, the initial climb from the parking lot is one of the toughest on the Front Range. From there riders are offered fast descents along precipitously sloping terrain and through mixed conifer and piñon forests.

   (**Note:** As of this writing, the Mustang Trail is closed. Contact Jefferson County Open Space at (303) 271–5925 for more information.)

Start: Parking lot off Pine Ridge Road
Distance: 8.4-mile lariat, with many options to add and/or subtract from this distance
Elevation gain: 1,600 feet
Riding time: Advanced riders, 1.5 hours; intermediate riders, 2-2.5 hours
Fitness effort: Physically challenging due to the climbing involved in exposed and hot terrain
Difficulty: Technically moderate to challenging due to its steep and rocky climbs and descents with many tight switchbacks
Terrain: Singletrack and doubletrack that run over very rocky terrain as well as very smooth, forested terrain

Seasons: Apr-Nov
Maps: *DeLorme: Colorado Atlas & Gazetteer*, page 40; *USGS*: Golden, CO, and Ralston Buttes, CO; *Trails Illustrated*: #100, Boulder, Golden, CO; Jefferson County Open Space White Ranch Park map
Nearest town: Golden
Other trail users: Hikers, horseback riders, campers, and picnickers
Dog friendly: Yes, but bring plenty of water for the pooch. Dogs must be on a leash at all times.
Trail contact: Jefferson County Open Space; (303) 271-5925

Getting there: From Golden drive north on CO 93 for 3-5 miles until you see the White Ranch Open Space sign to your left. Turn right before the sign onto 56th Avenue. Drive for approximately 1 mile on 56th Avenue before turning right again onto Pine Ridge Road, which will lead you to the lower White Ranch parking lot. Trailhead GPS: N39 47.946' / W105 14.915'

The Ride

Once a cattle operation, today White Ranch is a 3,040-acre Open Space Park. Taking its name from a local homesteader, Paul R. White, the park includes roughly 18 miles of multiuse trails. Only a half mile northwest of Golden, White Ranch offers mountain bikers living in the Denver metro area a great escape from the city grind.

   The majority of the park is exposed, particularly the east side, which traverses a steep slope, so White Ranch receives ample sunlight, making it one of the first mountain bike areas of Colorado's higher foothills region to open each year. Because of the jump on the season, White Ranch tends to get sandy toward the end of summer.

The steep and rocky initial climb of Belcher Hill Trail.

The wide-open trails can be brutally hot in the summer, so bring plenty of water and sunscreen.

From the bottom of the trail, White Ranch offers intermediate to advanced riding. But beginners can drive around to the top to avoid the long climbs and enjoy the nicest parts. Rugged and rocky steep climbs challenge even the best of riders, while smooth and gentle meadow shots tempt weary neophytes to release the death grip on the brakes. From the many vantage points in the park, mountain bikers are offered sweeping views of the Great Plains and the Denver skyline.

The first part of the route ascends a steep, sandy, and rocky doubletrack. Even the best riders will feel the burn after 2.4 miles of this kind of climbing. Luckily, the singletrack descent of Mustang Trail to Longhorn Trail offers a brief respite. After passing the continuation of the Longhorn Trail and continuing to climb up the Shorthorn Trail, the route winds its way through a dense pine forest. The terrain of the singletrack here is narrow and smooth. The trail eventually exits the forest and winds its way north along an east-facing slope.

Along the slope you'll find patches of a Class C invasive weed that is sometimes called Indian T.P. (toilet paper), though the proper name is mullein. The plant's soft, wide leaves account for the nickname. Tea made from brewing mullein leaves is said to relieve respiratory problems.

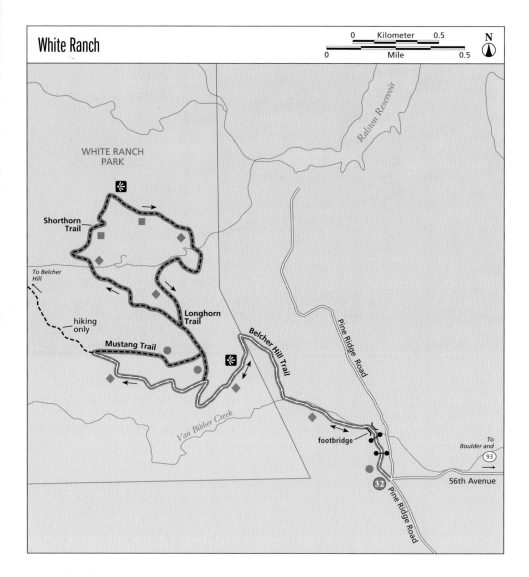

At mile 4.3 the northern junction of Shorthorn and Longhorn Trails marks the beginning of your return. The most challenging part of this entire route begins once you turn onto the Longhorn Trail. At mile 5.0 the route hits a steep and rocky descent, followed by tight switchbacks and big drop-offs, eventually delivering you to the bottom of a steep-walled drainage. What follows is a steep and rocky ascent up the other side, with tight switchbacks. From here it's a fast race back to the Belcher Hill Trail and an even faster race back to the parking lot.

With elevations raging from 6,150 feet to 8,000 feet, White Ranch offers some tough climbing but rewards you with bombing singletrack. One note of caution: Because of the many narrow trails leading around blind curves, it's likely that you may run into someone. Control your speed while descending. Mountain bikers are responsible for yielding to all other trail users, and downhill riders yield to uphill riders.

Miles and Directions

0.0 Start from the parking lot at the trailhead of Belcher Hill Trail. You'll pass through two gates and cross Van Bibber Creek via a footbridge within the first half mile. Please close both gates behind you, and begin climbing up Belcher Hill Trail after crossing the creek.

1.8 Arrive at the junction of Longhorn (to your right) and Belcher Hill Trails. You will eventually return via Longhorn Trail, but for now forgo turning right onto Longhorn Trail and continue pedaling west up Belcher Hill Trail. This is one of the few loops in this book that only works well in one direction. To the east, views of the Denver skyline and its surrounding towns sprawl out before you.

2.4 Belcher Hill Trail intersects with Mustang Trail. Here is a good place to rest, as your initial climb has ended—not to mention there's a bench seat to sit on. Hang a right, now descending on the singletrack of the Mustang Trail.

3.0 Arrive at the junction of Mustang and Longhorn Trails. Veer left onto the Longhorn Trail, which within 0.25 mile will quickly Y: Longhorn to your right, Shorthorn to your left. Continue left and begin climbing, now on the Shorthorn Trail.

4.3 Arrive at the northern junction of Shorthorn and Longhorn Trails. Bear right onto the Longhorn Trail.

6.0 Arrive at the southern junction of Shorthorn and Longhorn Trails. Bear left, continuing your ride on Longhorn. Within 0.3 mile you will once again arrive at the junction of Mustang and Longhorn. Continue on Longhorn for another 0.1 mile.

6.4 Arrive at the junction of Longhorn and Belcher Hill Trails. Veer left onto Belcher Hill Trail and descend what you had climbed previously, back to the parking lot.

8.4 Arrive at the parking lot.

Ride Information

Great extensions to this standard ride include adding on the Mustang Trail and the Rawhide Trail. The Princess Anne viewpoint is well worth the visit.

Trail Information

Jefferson County Open Space Trails Hotline, Evergreen; (303) 271-5975

Jefferson County Open Space; (303) 271-5925

Local Events and Attractions

Coors Brewing Company Tours, Golden; (303) 277-2337 or (800) 642-6116; open Mon to Fri 10 a.m. to 4 p.m.

Restaurants

D'Deli, 1207 Washington Ave., Golden; (303) 279-8020; www.ddeligolden.com/

Woody's Wood-Fired Pizza, 1305 Washington Ave., Golden; (303) 277-0443; www.woodysgolden.com/

Table Mountain Inn and Grill, 1310 Washington Ave., Golden; (303) 277-9898; www.tablemountaininn.com/

33 Centennial Cone Park

Delivering smooth singletrack; tight, technical switchbacks; interesting rock features; subalpine meadows; vertigo-inducing exposure; mixed conifer forests; and views of 8,679-foot Centennial Cone above and Clear Creek below, Centennial Cone Park has it all. At 17.2 miles, this route is more akin to the Rocky Mountain interior's high-elevation rides. Although there are a few technical aspects in the form of tight and off-camber switchbacks, as well as trickier rock descents, the route is generally smooth with a high flow factor. That said, some of the singletrack provides a fair amount of exposure as it hugs the walls of Clear Creek Canyon. This isn't your typical go-up-and-come-down ride, as it provides a good mix throughout. As one of the Front Range's newer park systems that focus on recreational and wildlife sustainability, Centennial Cone Park follows an alternating use schedule on weekends: hikers only on odd days, mountain bikes only on even days. During the week it's open to all. However, the Elk Range Trail is closed until mid-June to provide winter range and calving habitat for elk.

Start: The Mayhem Gulch trailhead
Distance: 17.2-mile lariat
Elevation gain: 1,000 feet
Riding time: Advanced riders, 1.5 hours; intermediate riders, 2 hours
Fitness effort: Physically moderate to challenging due to the length of the ride
Difficulty: Technically moderate to challenging with a few off-camber switchbacks, exposure, and steeper, rockier terrain
Terrain: Singletrack that delivers exposed, steep, and rocky terrain, as well as smooth-running singletrack and doubletrack through meadows and forests
Seasons: May–Oct

Schedule: Open daily from dawn to dusk with an alternating use schedule: even-numbered weekend dates allow mountain biking, while odd-numbered weekend dates provide for hiking. Days during the week are multiuse. The park is closed Dec and Jan.
Maps: Jefferson County Open Space Centennial Cone Park map; *USGS:* Ralston Buttes, CO, and Evergreen, CO; *DeLorme: Colorado Atlas & Gazetteer,* page 39, B- and C-7
Nearest town: Golden
Other trail users: Hikers and equestrians
Dog friendly: Yes
Trail contact: Jefferson County Open Space Trails Hotline, Evergreen; (303) 271-5975

Getting there: From Golden (and the intersection of CO 58, 93, and US 6), drive west on US 6 through Clear Creek Canyon for roughly 9 miles and turn right into the Mayhem Gulch trailhead parking lot. The trail begins at the west end of the parking lot. Trailhead GPS: N39 44.234' / W105 22.304'

The Ride

The initial climb out of Clear Creek Canyon on the Mayhem Gulch Trail travels moderately over smooth singletrack and delivers a handful of easily negotiable

Jeff Williams negotiating his way down the more technical aspects of the Travois Trail.

switchbacks, which isn't always the case for this route. As you climb, you'll be rewarded with stunning views of Clear Creek and the canyon below.

Your first real descent, a welcome relief from the climbing, arrives at roughly 1.8 miles. After connecting with the doubletrack of the Elk Range Trail, cyclists ride through subalpine meadows with views of Centennial Cone off to their right. Centennial Cone has been a natural landmark to the area's human inhabitants for over 12,000 years. Paleo-Indians, the first peoples to inhabit the American continents, hunted wildlife and gathered food in this area. Centennial Cone proved attractive to these people for its 360-degree views; sheltering rock overhangs; and proximity to water, plant, and animal resources.

The area continued to be a travel route, hunting ground, and religious epicenter for Arapaho, Cheyenne, and Ute Indians. Religious rites were performed atop Centennial Cone, while below lie sacred underground crystal caverns. Carla Swan Coleman, pioneer and founder of the Clear Creek Land Conservancy, recalled stories told by her mother about Arapaho and Cheyenne sunrise ceremonies on the summit of Centennial Cone. Similarly, torchlight evening farewell ceremonies were also spotted from the Cone's crown.

Not only was the area of Centennial Cone Park a magnet for early hunter-gatherers, but according to local legend, Centennial Cone became a sanctuary and homestead to a family of former slaves who moved from the south following the Civil War and the passing of the Homestead Act of 1862. These "exodusters," as they were called, saw Centennial Cone as a new opportunity. Ruins of the family's "Plantation" include a root cellar, log structures, and stone walls found in the northeast section of the park.

After passing through the gates on the Elk Range Trail, riders are rewarded with a fun and fast descent through the meadowlands of Centennial Cone Park to intersect with the Travois Trail. To honor the semi-nomadic lifestyle of the area's earliest inhabitants, the Travois Trail is named after the conveyance for goods and belongings of early hunter-gatherers. Travois were constructed of a frame slung between trailing poles that were lashed together. Plains Indians would have their travois pulled by horses or dogs while they hunted and gathered food or traveled to camp. Imprints of these travois can still be seen today in the park, serving to connect the past with the present, as you lay down tracks of your own along this speedy descent.

After crossing Elk Creek, riders intersect with the Evening Sun Loop and bear right onto its southern hemisphere. This loop can be ridden in part, as this route describes, or in its entirety for an additional 1.3 miles. The singletrack here is gorgeous and narrow with some interesting rock features. Your climbing begins in earnest again as you rejoin with the Travois Trail. While not particularly technical, this singletrack climb is rocky, sandy, and moderately physical. At roughly 7.8 miles you reach a considerably rockier and more technical descent. The tight drop-offs and switchbacks are an interesting addition to an otherwise very flowy ride. From this rockier section the Travois Trail delivers a variety of tighter, off-camber switchbacks that also demand advanced bike-handling skills. Then it's a fast romp down smooth and tight singletrack. Nevertheless, there are some points where you need to be on your game, as this trail offers a fair amount of exposure and some blind and tight corners.

After crossing Elk Creek for a second time, you begin another moderate climb of roughly 3 miles through a mixed conifer forest and over smooth singletrack. Climb for roughly a mile, and another short and rocky technical section awaits, delivering embedded rock stairs. Finally, make your way down the singletrack that is pressed up against precipitously sloping terrain. The exposed route of this section allows for some vertigo-inducing riding. But once you reconnect with the Mayhem Gulch trail, it's a fast and furious drop to your vehicle.

Miles and Directions

0.0 From the Mayhem Gulch trailhead, begin climbing moderately in a northwesterly direction on the Mayhem Gulch Trail.

1.5 The Mayhem Gulch Trail intersects with the Juniper Gulch Trail. Go straight (left) onto the Juniper Gulch Trail.

Centennial Cone Park

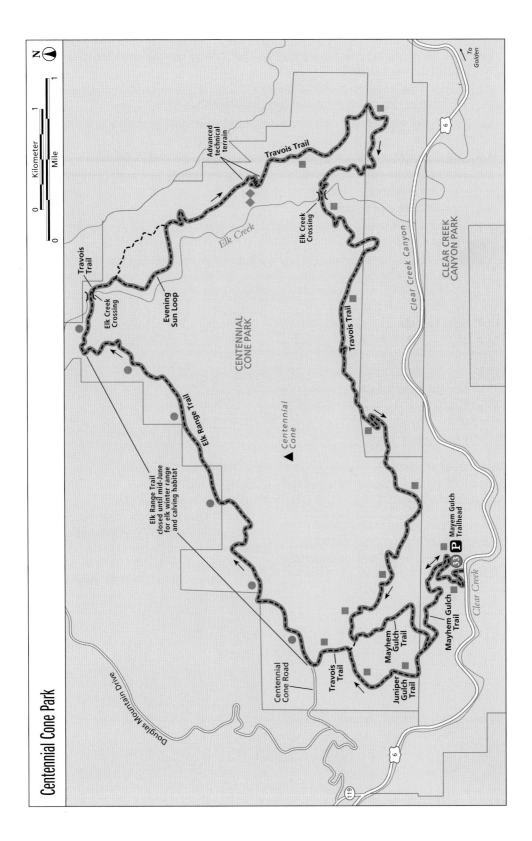

N

Kilometer
0   1

Mile
0   1

Travois Trail

Advanced
technical
terrain

Travois Trail

Elk Creek

Elk Creek
Crossing

Travois
Trail

Elk Creek
Crossing

Evening
Sun Loop

CENTENNIAL
CONE PARK

Travois Trail

Centennial
Cone

CLEAR CREEK
CANYON PARK

Clear Creek Canyon

Elk Range Trail
closed until mid-June
for elk winter range
and calving habitat

Elk Range Trail

Douglas Mountain Drive

Centennial
Cone Road

Travois Trail

Mayhem Gulch
Trail

Juniper
Gulch
Trail

Mayhem Gulch
Trailhead

Mayhem Gulch
Trail

Clear Creek

To
Golden

6

6

19

33

P

2.4 The Juniper Gulch Trail intersects with the Travois Trail. Bear left onto the Travois Trail, continuing your moderate climb.

2.7 The Travois Trail intersects with the Elk Range Trail. Bear right onto the Elk Range Trail, and ride in a northeasterly direction through subalpine meadows.

4.2 Pass through a gate. Bear in mind that the trail passes close to private property, so stay on the trail.

4.5 Pass through another gate, where there is a private residence and barn to your left.

5.8 Elk Range Trail intersects with the Travois Trail at the park's northernmost access point, with equestrian trailer parking. Bear right onto the Travois Trail.

6.2 Cross Elk Creek via a bridge.

6.4 The Travois Trail intersects with the Evening Sun Loop. Bear right, continuing your ride along the Evening Sun Loop.

7.1 The Evening Sun Loop intersects and rejoins with the Travois Trail. Bear right onto the Travois Trail, and head in a southeasterly direction. (**Option:** To add 1.3 miles, simply bear left onto the northern hemisphere of the Evening Sun Loop, effectively completing the loop and riding its lower half twice.)

10.4 Cross Elk Creek again via a bridge.

14.7 The Travois Trail intersects with the Mayhem Gulch Trail. Bear left onto the Mayhem Gulch Trail.

15.6 Reach the intersection of the Mayhem Gulch Trail and the Juniper Trail. Bear left, continuing on the Mayhem Gulch Trail, and return the way you came.

17.2 Arrive back at your vehicle.

Ride Information

Trail Information

Jefferson County Open Space Trails Hotline, Evergreen; (303) 271-5975

Local Events and Attractions

White Ranch Park, Golden; (303) 271-5925

Golden Gate Canyon State Park, Golden; (303) 582-3707

Restaurants

D'Deli, 1207 Washington Ave., Golden; (303) 279-8020; www.ddeligolden.com/

Woody's Wood-Fired Pizza, 1305 Washington Ave., Golden; (303) 277-0443; www.woodys golden.com/

Table Mountain Inn and Grill, 1310 Washington Ave., Golden; (303) 277-9898; www.table mountaininn.com/

34 Chimney Gulch Trail

The area surrounding Lookout Mountain, aside from being great for mountain biking, is also a well-known hang gliders' launching ground. But for those of us who prefer the terra firma to the terrifying, the Chimney Gulch Trail is perfect. The first part of this route takes riders over red dirt singletrack and through patches of scrub oak. The exposed terrain and many switchbacks make this initial approach a tough one. The next part of the trail climbs steadily as it snakes its way up to Windy Saddle. The last section of this route follows through dense stands of pine and aspen on its way to the top of Lookout Mountain. In short, Chimney Gulch offers a lot of bang for your buck. The initial descent from Lookout Mountain runs over a smooth bed of pine-needle singletrack before continuing over rocky and exposed terrain. A great option is to combine this ride with Apex Park (ride 35).

Start: The Chimney Gulch trailhead at the base of Lookout Mountain

Distance: 9.4-mile out-and-back

Elevation gain: 1,700 feet

Riding time: Advanced riders, 1-1.5 hours; intermediate riders, 1.5-2 hours

Fitness effort: Physically moderate to challenging due to the climbing through exposed terrain, with a good deal of tight and steep switchbacks

Difficulty: Technically moderate due to some steeper, short sections. There are also a number of water bars with which to contend.

Terrain: Singletrack that runs over exposed hillsides, around tight switchbacks, and through deep forests. Riders will also have to ride on a dirt drive and paved road for a short while.

Seasons: Mar-Nov; open daily from 8 a.m. to dusk. The nature center hours are Tues to Sun from 10 a.m. to 4 p.m.

Maps: *DeLorme: Colorado Atlas & Gazetteer,* page 40; *USGS:* Morrison, CO; Lookout Mountain Nature Center and Preserve map

Nearest town: Golden

Other trail users: Hikers and horseback riders

Dog friendly: Yes, although no dogs, bikes, or horses are allowed on the Forest Loop and Meadow Loop

Trail contact: Jefferson County Open Space, Golden; (303) 271-5925; http://jeffco.us/parks/parks-and-trails/; or City of Golden; (303) 384-8000

Getting there: From Denver drive west on I-70 for 8 miles before taking exit 265 to CO 58, following signs for Golden and Central City. Drive west on CO 58 for 5 miles to its intersection with US 6 at a stoplight in Golden. Bear left at the stoplight and drive south on US 6 for roughly a quarter mile before turning right into the dirt pullout of the Chimney Gulch trailhead. Park in the pullout by the trailhead. Trailhead GPS: N39 45.04' / W105 13.74'; trailhead terminus/turn-around GPS: N39 43.110' / W105 15.064'

The Ride

To the observant and ambitious rider, the Chimney Gulch Trail affords lessons in recycling and sustainable resources. At the end of the trail, riders are introduced to

Heading southwest from Windy Saddle toward the Lookout Mountain Nature Center.

the sustainable design of the Lookout Mountain Nature Center. From the Lookout Mountain Nature Center on Colorow Road riders can also easily access a second area ride in Apex Park before "re-cycling" back to the start. But these lessons begin even before you reach the top.

As you make your way up the initial switchbacks of the trail, you may notice a slight hint of roasting barley and malt wafting through the air. That's the Coors Brewing Company (now owned by Miller) just over your left shoulder, which has operated in Golden since 1873. So where's the lesson in recycling and economy, you might ask?

After World War II ended in 1945, Coors began looking into alternatives for packaging its product. Having relied exclusively on kegs and bottles up to this time, Coors introduced the country's first all-aluminum beverage can in 1959. Moreover, the company offered a penny for every can returned to the brewery. And thus, a recycling revolution was born. Today, Coors owns and is an operating partner in the world's largest aluminum-can manufacturing plant. Known as the Rocky Mountain Metal Container and founded in 2003, it is a joint venture between Ball Metal and Coors.

After a mile of steady climbing, the trail begins to level out a bit, offering a few rockier and more technical sections. After crossing the footbridge at 1.7 miles, you begin riding up Chimney Gulch. Sections of this ride offer shaded relief from the otherwise exposed terrain of the lower reaches of the trail.

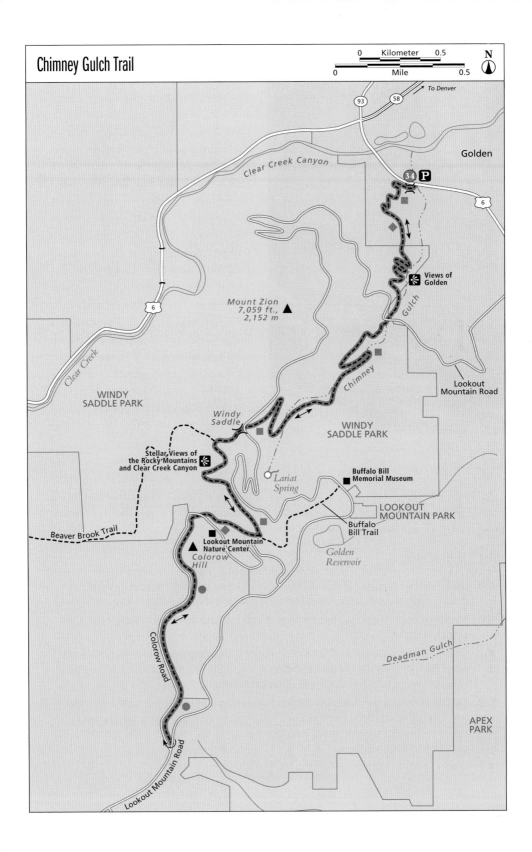

Chimney Gulch Trail

0   Kilometer   0.5
0   Mile   0.5

N

To Denver

93   58

Golden

34 P

Clear Creek Canyon

6

Views of Golden

Mount Zion
7,059 ft.,
2,152 m

Chimney Gulch

Lookout
Mountain Road

Clear Creek

WINDY
SADDLE PARK

Windy
Saddle

WINDY
SADDLE PARK

6

Stellar Views of
the Rocky Mountains
and Clear Creek Canyon

Lariat
Spring

Buffalo Bill
Memorial Museum

LOOKOUT
MOUNTAIN PARK

Beaver Brook Trail

Lookout Mountain
Nature Center

Buffalo
Bill Trail

Colorow
Hill

Golden
Reservoir

Colorow Road

Deadman Gulch

APEX
PARK

Lookout Mountain Road

Arriving at the Windy Saddle, you're offered stellar views of the Rocky Mountains and Clear Creek Canyon. This section of trail that leads from Windy Saddle is one of the most beautiful of the entire route. As it climbs steadily through thick stands of mixed conifers, the trail's singletrack is laden with pine needles and an occasional rocky section. After nearly 3 miles of riding, you pass a scree field where you're offered beautiful views of Golden to the east. As you near the top of Lookout Mountain, you're thrown a technical rock- and root-filled section as a last little test of your strength. Once atop Lookout Mountain, take time to explore the nature center.

Riders can continue from the nature center via the Lookout Mountain Trail to Apex Park. Should your stamina be sustainable, you might consider combining this ride with one through Apex Park. This combination is truly a Front Range epic. If

Amanda Hlawaty riding tall among the pines on the Lookout Mountain Trail.

you choose to save this epic for another day, you'll undoubtedly enjoy the fast descent from the top of Lookout Mountain to your vehicle.

Miles and Directions

0.0 Begin riding west, staying to the left of US 6, following a trail along the steel guardrail. Cross a small bridge that will deliver you to the start of the Chimney Gulch Trail.

0.2 After crossing the bridge, the trail climbs as it switches back a number of times in a southwesterly direction.

0.7 The singletrack of the Chimney Gulch Trail intersects with a dirt drive that leads to a private home. Bear left onto this dirt road and ride for roughly 50 feet before bearing right, following a trail marker sign, and continuing on the singletrack.

0.9 The Chimney Gulch Trail intersects with the paved Lookout Mountain Road. Cross the road and continue riding on the Chimney Gulch Trail, heading west. Use caution when crossing the road, as Lookout Mountain Road sees a good deal of vehicular traffic. It is also a popular road biking route.

1.7 Cross a creek via a footbridge.

2.0   Cross over another bridge as the trail continues through mixed conifer and aspen forests.

2.3   Arrive at the Windy Saddle. Here the Chimney Gulch Trail again intersects with the paved Lookout Mountain Road. Bear left onto the paved road and ride for roughly 50 yards before bearing right, following a sign for the hikers-only Beaver Brook Trail. At this point the Chimney Gulch Trail and the Beaver Brook Trail follow the same route.

2.6   Arrive at the point where the Chimney Gulch Trail breaks from the Beaver Brook Trail. The hikers-only Beaver Brook Trail bears right and continues heading in southwest. Bear left here, following a sign for the Jefferson County Conference and Nature Center. This section of trail is known as the Lookout Mountain Trail.

3.3   The Lookout Mountain Trail (aka Chimney Gulch Trail) intersects with the Buffalo Bill Trail to the left. Bear right and continue riding on the Lookout Mountain Trail, heading for the Lookout Mountain Nature Center.

3.6   Reach the top of Lookout Mountain and the Lookout Mountain Nature Center and Boettcher Mansion. Cross the paved Lookout Mountain Road, and continue riding on the Lookout Mountain Trail toward Apex Park.

4.2   Pass Ellsworth Park to your right.

4.7   Lookout Mountain Trail intersects with the Lookout Mountain Road trailhead to Apex Park. At this point turn back and retrace your path. (**Option:** You may wish to descend into Apex Park via the Apex Trail and Enchanted Forest Trail. See ride 35: Apex Park.)

9.4   Arrive back at your vehicle.

Ride Information

Trail Information

Jefferson County Open Space Trails Hotline, Evergreen; (303) 271-5975

Local Events and Attractions

Buffalo Bill Memorial Museum and Grave, Lookout Mountain; (303) 526-0744

Historic Boettcher Mansion, Lookout Mountain; (720) 497-7630

Lookout Mountain Nature Center Group Programs, Golden; (720) 497-7600

Restaurants

D'Deli, 1207 Washington Ave., Golden; (303) 279-8020; www.ddeligolden.com/

Woody's Wood-Fired Pizza, 1305 Washington Ave., Golden; (303) 277-0443; www.woodysgolden.com/

Table Mountain Inn and Grill, 1310 Washington Ave., Golden; (303) 277-9898; www.tablemountaininn.com/

35 Apex Park

Apex Park offers a network of trails within a short drive of Boulder, Denver, and Golden. Hence, it can get crowded on weekends. But don't let its proximity fool you into believing that this doesn't have some of the toughest trails surrounding the metropolitan area. Featuring rocky singletrack, steep climbs, and exposed hillsides, Apex Park delivers quintessential Front Range riding. On even-numbered days of the week, all the trails are multidirectional; however, on odd-numbered days of the week, cyclists must travel one way on certain segments of trail in the park.

(*Note:* As of this writing, all trails, except the lower section of Apex Trail, are now open in Apex Park.)

Start: The Apex Park trailhead by the Heritage Square Shopping Center

Distance: 5.5-mile lariat, with options to extend

Elevation gain: 1,600 feet

Riding time: Advanced riders, 30-45 minutes; intermediate riders, 1-2 hours

Fitness effort: Physically moderate to challenging due to some extended climbs over varied terrain in exposed areas

Difficulty: Technically moderate to challenging due to the rocky terrain, tight singletrack, and big drop-offs

Terrain: Singletrack with a good deal of large, loose rocks and sand

Seasons: Apr-Nov

Maps: *DeLorme: Colorado Atlas & Gazetteer,* page 40; *USGS:* Morrison, CO; Jefferson County Open Space Apex Park map

Nearest town: Golden

Other trail users: Hikers and horseback riders

Dog friendly: Yes

Trail contact: Jefferson County Open Space, Golden; (303) 271-5925; http://jeffco.us/parks/parks-and-trails/; or City of Golden; (303) 384-8000

Getting there: From Denver drive west on I-70 and exit at 265 onto CO 58. Drive west on CO 58 for 5 miles to its intersection with US 6 at a stoplight in Golden. Bear left at the stoplight and drive south on US 6 for roughly 2.3 miles before turning right onto Heritage Road (the Jefferson County Complex will be on your left). Drive on Heritage Road for 1 mile, and turn right into Apex Park, marked by a brown park sign. Park in the northeast corner of the Heritage Square Parking Lot. Trailhead GPS: N39 42.899 / W105 12.848'

The Ride

Apex Park offers outstanding views of the unique geological formations of Green Mountain (see ride 37: Hayden/Green Mountain Park), the Hogback (see ride 38: Dakota Ridge and Red Rocks Trail), and the Table Mountains. With nearly 7 miles of prime singletrack over 530 acres, Apex Park is sure to offer mountain bikers the good life.

Before setting out on the Apex Trail, take notice of the looming old cottonwood tree overhead. Word has it that a misguided rustler was hanged on one of its branches

Climbing the Pick N' Sledge Trail, with views of the eastern plains and the Denver skyline.

after he was caught stealing horses. In fact, the *Rocky Mountain News* of July 24, 1861, reported, "he was arrested yesterday and preparations were made to bring him to Denver to trial; but last night he was taken in charge by a body of men who preferred that his trial should cost nothing."

The site of the park used to be occupied by the town of Apex. During Colorado's mining craze of the late 1800s, a toll road ran through the town that connected to the gold mining districts of Central City, or as people of the day liked to call it, "Gregory Diggins." The Apex and Gregory Wagon Road through Apex Gulch was one of the area's first thoroughfares to the gold fields of Central City. The tolls were collected from miners on their way to strike it rich near where the Heritage Square Shopping Center stands today. The toll road remained in operation from the 1860s through the mid-1880s. While riding the trails, visitors to Apex Park may still catch glimpses of the old roadbed.

The Pick N' Sledge Trail is marked by steeper and more exposed sections than those the first mile of the ride has to offer. While the climb up the Pick N' Sledge Trail is serious, you are rewarded with sweeping views of the Great Plains and the Denver skyline to the east.

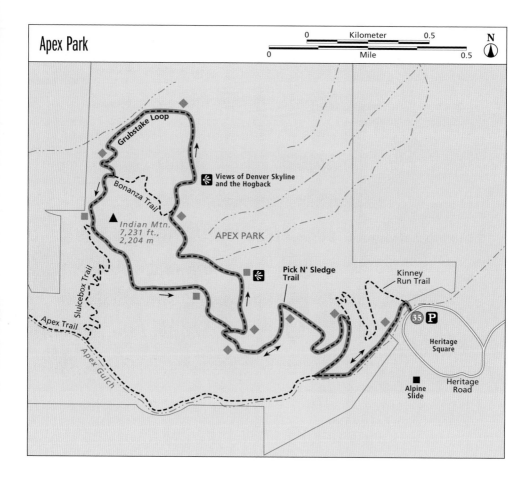

Once on the Grubstake Loop Trail, you're again offered views of the Front Range, the Great Plains, and the Denver skyline. More important, however, you're provided with shaded relief from the more exposed sections of the Pick N' Sledge Trail. The Grubstake Loop Trail courses swiftly over smooth singletrack as it runs through mixed conifer forests and skirts the perimeter of Indian Mountain. Sitting in Apex Gulch, near the confluence with Lena Gulch, the area surrounding Apex Park was a great value to early Native Americans. From the higher reaches of the park, as well as the nearby Hogback, Indians could stand watch over any invaders while they reaped the benefits of the numerous bison, deer, and elk that also inhabited nearby areas.

From the top of Indian Mountain, it's a speedy descent across a meadow, passing the intersection with the Grubstake Loop, to the Apex Trail. Your ride closes with a short and rocky descent along the Apex Trail to your vehicle.

Miles and Directions

0.0 Start from the Apex Park parking lot and trailhead and begin climbing in a westerly direction, crossing a small seasonal creek via footbridge. After crossing the creek, bear left by an Apex Trail sign.

0.6 The Apex Trail intersects with the Pick N' Sledge Trail. Bear right onto the Pick N' Sledge Trail, which takes a number of switchbacks as it continues to climb in a northwesterly direction.

1.6 The Pick N' Sledge Trail intersects with the Grubstake Loop. Continue on the Grubstake Loop as it descends in a northwesterly direction.

2.1 The Grubstake Trail intersects with the southern tip of the Bonanza Trail to your left. Continue straight on the Grubstake Trail as it descends in a northerly direction over smooth singletrack and through densely wooded forests.

2.6 You begin climbing again via a number of switchbacks, although this time you're in the shade.

3.0 The Grubstake Loop intersects with the northern tip of the Bonanza Trail to the left. Continue on the Grubstake Loop as it continues to the top of Indian Mountain.

3.1 The Grubstake Trail intersects with the Pick N' Sledge Trail and the Sluicebox Trail. Veer left onto the Pick N' Sledge Trail.

3.4 Reach the top of Indian Mountain. From here the trail descends in an easterly direction on smooth singletrack.

3.8 The Pick N' Sledge Trail intersects with the Grubstake Loop. Continue on the Pick N' Sledge Trail, keeping right, on your way to the Apex Trail.

4.8 The Pick N' Sledge Trail intersects with the Apex Trail. Bear left onto the Apex Trail and return to Apex Park trailhead.

5.5 Arrive at your vehicle.

Ride Information

Trail Information

Jefferson County Open Space Trails Hotline, Evergreen; (303) 271-5975

Local Events and Attractions

Astor House Museum, Golden; (303) 278-3557

Hakushika Sake Tours, Golden; (303) 278-0161; Mon to Fri 10 a.m. to 3 p.m.

Heritage Square Family Entertainment Village, Golden; (303) 279-1661; www.heritage square.info/

Restaurants

D'Deli, 1207 Washington Ave., Golden; (303) 279-8020; www.ddeligolden.com/

Woody's Wood-Fired Pizza, 1305 Washington Ave., Golden; (303) 277-0443; www.woodys golden.com/

Table Mountain Inn and Grill, 1310 Washington Ave., Golden; (303) 277-9898; www.table mountaininn.com/

36 Barbour Fork

The Barbour Fork Trail is one of the lesser-traveled trails in the Denver region. This may be due to the variety of trails that cross its main route. For this reason, riders should always be familiar with the trail's route and bring a map of the area. The trail supplies hillside meadows full of wildflowers, tall stands of aspen and mixed conifers, as well as—dare I say it—little in the way of other trail users. Combining doubletrack with prime singletrack, the trail travels up the Soda Creek drainage of Idaho Springs to connect with a looped singletrack trail. While not particularly long, this trail can be enjoyed by novice and advanced riders alike. The singletrack stands out among the best in the area. Perhaps more important, after the ride is over, riders can soak their sores away in the thermal pools of the Indian Springs Resort.

Start: The Barbour Fork trailhead
Distance: 5.0-mile lariat
Elevation gain: 1,100 feet
Riding time: Advanced riders, 45 minutes; intermediate riders, 1-1.5 hours
Fitness effort: Physically moderate to challenging due to the trail's steeper climbs along the four-by-four road
Difficulty: Technically moderate due to the significant amount of rocky sections both when climbing on the four-by-four Barbour Fork Road and when descending on the Barbour Fork singletrack

Terrain: Four-by-four road and singletrack that pass through dense woodland and open meadows
Seasons: June-Oct
Maps: *DeLorme: Colorado Atlas & Gazetteer,* page 39; *USGS:* Idaho Springs, CO; *Trails Illustrated:* #104, Idaho Springs, Georgetown, Loveland Pass, CO
Nearest town: Idaho Springs
Other trail users: Hikers, horseback riders, four-by-four vehicles, and ATVs
Dog friendly: Yes
Trail contact: Arapaho and Roosevelt National Forests and Pawnee National Grassland, Clear Creek Ranger District; (303) 567-3000

Getting there: From Denver drive west on I-70 for 30.6 miles to Idaho Springs, exiting at 241A, the first Idaho Springs exit. Drive through Idaho Springs on Colorado Boulevard for 1 mile, passing the Argo Gold Mine and Mill on your right and the Safeway on your left, before bearing left onto Miner Street. Here Miner Street and Colorado Avenue form the V of a Y intersection. Colorado Avenue splits to the right, and Miner Street continues to the left. After bearing left here onto Miner Street, a brown sign reading Steve Canyon will be on the right as you pass the Idaho Springs Visitors' Center. Drive past the visitor center for roughly 0.3 mile on Miner Street before turning left onto Soda Creek Road, heading underneath the interstate. You'll drive on Soda Creek Road for 1.6 miles, passing the Indian Springs Resort on your left, before the road turns to gravel at the county dump site. From the dump site drive for another 1.7 miles on the gravel Soda Creek Road before bearing left into the pullout parking space and the Barbour Fork trailhead. Park in the dirt pullout by the trailhead. Trailhead GPS: N 39 42.883' / W105 33.250'

The Barbour Fork singletrack.

The Ride

Although relatively short in length, the Barbour Fork Trail does dole out its share of technical and physical abuse. Riders can rest assured knowing that the healing waters of the Great Spirit pour forth just down the road at the Indian Springs Resort.

The first recorded mention of the hot springs was made by George A. Jackson, the man who first discovered placer gold in the Rockies. In his journal of 1859, Jackson wrote that he "camped at warm springs near mouth of small creek, coming in on south side." That small creek was none other than Soda Creek. But before Jackson was bathing in these hot mineral springs, the Arapaho and Ute Indian tribes used these healing waters as spiritual centers. In fact, Soda Creek divided the Ute and Arapaho Nations. Each nation, then, came to view the hot springs as neutral ground. Needless to say, once gold was discovered here, the Ute and Arapaho were soon permanently removed from the area.

Upon beginning the trail, riders are immediately tossed a grunt of a hill climb, as the trickling waters of the Barbour Fork of Soda Creek lend a teasing voice to the sound of your heavy breathing.

Far from any healing hot waters at this point, you pass through a dense evergreen forest. After about a mile of climbing, riders are greeted with a moderately physical and technical climb, complete with sand and loose rock. Soon thereafter, however, the trail levels out as it passes under the dark canopies of mixed conifers. After crossing the fork of Soda Creek at 1.2 miles, you ride into a beautiful meadow. Shortly after bearing left in the meadow, you'll bear right at an intersection and climb up a very steep and rocky technical section. As you near the top, Barbour Fork Road will come into view below before the trail lets out onto a wide-open plateau.

Once passing through a small aspen stand, you'll want to look for the singletrack that darts off to the right. Once you're on the Barbour Fork singletrack, you'll curve around to the right, nearly 180 degrees, back toward the direction from where you came.

The singletrack initially follows the edge of the clearing next to where you had just ridden on the road, delivering rocks and roots that eventually give way to smooth and

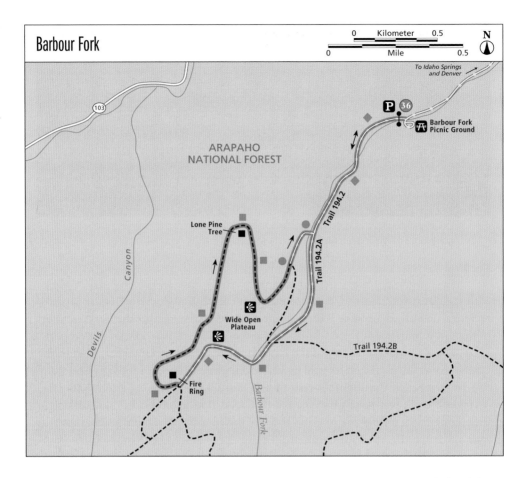

ARAPAHO
NATIONAL FOREST

Lone Pine
Tree

Wide Open
Plateau

Fire
Ring

Trail 194.2

Trail 194.2A

Trail 194.2B

Barbour Fork
Picnic Ground

To Idaho Springs
and Denver

Canyon

Devils

Barbour Fork

hard-packed trail. The trail descends in a northerly direction to deliver you behind the big boulder north of the grassy plateau. The descent becomes considerably faster from here as the trail's smooth surface invites riders to let go of their death grip on the brakes.

Upon entering into the meadow after 3 miles of riding, you'll again have to carefully look for the singletrack that veers off to the right. After connecting with this singletrack, the trail doubles back and drops into a pine forest below the trail on which you were just riding. This trail runs over smooth singletrack through dense evergreen forest to a logging skid road. Bearing left on the skid road and again onto trail 194.2, you return to your vehicle.

Miles and Directions

0.0 Ride out of the parking lot and bear left onto Soda Creek Road. Passing through a gate, begin climbing southwest up the four-by-four Barbour Fork Road.

0.7 The Barbour Fork Road comes to a trail intersection. Bear left here onto trail 194.2A (still the Barbour Fork Road), and pedal in a southwesterly direction through a hillside meadow awash with wildflowers. The trail to the right is listed as 194.2 and continues in a more immediate westerly direction as it crosses the fork of Soda Creek. You will eventually connect to 194.2, but not now.

1.2 Trail 194.2A (Barbour Fork Road) intersects with 194.2B to your left and climbs in an easterly direction. Bear right here, heading west and crossing the fork of Soda Creek. Once arriving in the meadow, intersect the 194.2 trail and bear left onto it, climbing in a southerly direction.

1.3 Trail 194.2 (Barbour Fork Trail) intersects with a road that cuts left through a pine forest and heads south. At this point bear right, continuing on the main Barbour Fork Trail as it climbs in a northwesterly direction along a technically challenging, steep climb.

1.5 Reach the top of an open and grassy plateau. Just beyond the big boulder to the north of the plateau lies the singletrack with which you'll eventually connect. For now, however, look to the southwest (left), where you'll continue riding along the main Barbour Fork Trail. There, in the woods, you may spy the remains of an old hunter's shelter. Bear left here, continuing on the main trail and heading southwest through the pine forest.

1.9 Pass through a small aspen stand. Here the Barbour Fork Road that you are on continues to the left, heading in a southeasterly direction as it passes through another tall stand of pines and begins to climb significantly over loose rock. At this point look to connect with the Barbour Fork singletrack on your right. The singletrack is identifiable by a large fire ring and an old rusted pipe. Bear right onto the singletrack and head in a southwesterly direction.

2.5 Arrive behind the big boulder located in the northernmost section of the grassy plateau. Bear left here, continuing on the singletrack, continuing your descent in a northerly direction.

3.3 Arrive at a ridge-top meadow. Ride slowly through the meadow for roughly 40 yards (at 3.4 miles) before veering right onto the inconspicuous singletrack that wraps around a lone pine tree to double back into the woods directly below the trail on which you were just riding. Should you miss this turnoff and continue straight on the more obvious trail, you'll still return to your vehicle, but at the expense of a couple of miles.

4.0 Arrive at an old logging skid road. Bear left, and continue on the skid road, heading in an easterly direction.

4.1 The skid road intersects with the 194.2 trail. Bear left onto 194.2.

4.3 Trail 194.2 crosses the fork of the Soda Creek and intersects with 194.2A (Barbour Fork Road). Bear left onto Barbour Fork Road and return to the start the way you came.

5.0 Arrive at your vehicle.

Ride Information

Trail Information
Arapaho and Roosevelt National Forests and Pawnee National Grassland, Clear Creek Ranger District; (303) 567-3000

Local Events and Attractions
Argo Gold Mine and Mill, Idaho Springs; (303) 567-2421

Mount Evans Scenic and Historic Byway; (303) 567-4660 or (800) 88-BLAST

Lodging
Indian Hot Springs Healing Waters Spa, Idaho Springs; (303) 989-6666

Restaurants
Jiggies Cafe, Idaho Springs; (303) 567-9942

Two Brothers Deli, Idaho Springs; (303) 567-2439

37 Hayden/Green Mountain Park

By offering smooth singletrack, beautiful views of Red Rocks Park and the Denver skyline, and a fast and sometimes rocky descent from the 6,800-foot summit, Hayden/Green Mountain Park is sure to please. With more than 2,400 acres of open space, Hayden/Green Mountain Park is Lakewood's second-largest park. It makes for a great introduction to mountain biking. Due to its proximity to Denver, the park can be crowded on weekends. During the spring and early summer riding season, Green Mountain is blanketed with wildflowers.

Start: The Florida trailhead on the north side of Alameda Parkway, just past Florida Avenue

Distance: 6.4-mile loop

Elevation gain: 900 feet

Riding time: Advanced riders, 30-45 minutes; intermediate riders, 1-2 hours

Fitness effort: Physically easy to moderate due to the modestly rolling nature of the terrain. There is one extended hill climb on the park's western slope that many will find challenging as they head to the summit.

Difficulty: Technically easy to moderate due to the smooth singletrack. There are some rockier and narrower sections of singletrack that might require an intermediate level of technical expertise.

Terrain: Mostly smooth singletrack with some varying rocky sections. Dirt roads lead to the top and extend across the summit of Green Mountain.

Seasons: Apr-Nov

Maps: *DeLorme: Colorado Atlas & Gazetteer*, page 40; *USGS*: Morrison, CO

Nearest town: Lakewood

Other trail users: Hikers and horseback riders

Dog friendly: Yes

Trail contact: Jefferson County Open Space, Golden; (303) 271-5925; http://jeffco.us/parks/parks-and-trails/; or City of Lakewood; www.lakewood.org/HaydenPark/

Getting there: From Denver drive west on US 6 (exit 209B from I-25) toward Lakewood for roughly 7 miles. Exit at Simms Street/Union Boulevard and bear left onto South Union. Drive south on Union for 1.7 miles before bearing right onto Alameda Parkway. Drive west on Alameda for 1.5 miles before bearing right into the Green Mountain trailhead. Park in the lot by the Florida trailhead. Trailhead GPS: N39 41.438' / W105 09.145'

The Ride

Offering more than 2,400 acres of lush hillsides awash with wildflowers and wildlife, Hayden/Green Mountain Park is an oasis set on the outskirts of an otherwise bustling metropolis. Aside from this, what makes Green Mountain Park special is that it is one of a few large parcels of Foothills ecosystem left in the Denver metro area.

Green Mountain sits at the terminus of two distinct regions: the easternmost edge of the Rocky Mountains and the westernmost edge of the short grass prairie. In a beautifully blended tribute to both regions, the 6,800-foot mountain is covered in a wavy plume of open grassland, highlighted at times with yucca and cacti.

Descending on the singletrack, with views of Red Rocks Park to the west.

Starting on Lonesome Trail, the first 3 miles offers relatively smooth terrain as it skirts the base of Green Mountain. Should you be riding during the spring and early summer season, you'll appreciate the green lushness of the hillsides. In full bloom Green Mountain reminds one of Marin County, California, one of mountain biking's birthplace.

Spring attracts a lot of attention to Green Mountain from nature lovers. In March you can find the red and purple blooming colors of cranesbill and alyssum. In keeping with the season's colors, red-tailed hawks return to nest at Green Mountain, as do robins. The territorial singing of the red-winged blackbird is often heard, while foxes and coyotes settle in dens with their pups. Later in the spring the lilac-colored locoweed begins to bloom. Love for locoweed is not shared by all, however, as the weed is a problem for ranchers because it is poisonous to many kinds of livestock. In fact, deriving from the Spanish word that means "crazy," the "loco" in locoweed recalls a long-standing belief that animals, particularly horses, that eat the weed become crazy and eventually die.

Spring wears on to uncover a rookery of nesting Swainson's hawks, night herons, pelicans, meadowlarks, and bluebirds. Butterflies become active flitting through forests of white and yellow sand lilies; purple, bell-shaped harebells; and the reds and oranges of Indian paintbrush and mallow.

Passing through this kaleidoscope for the senses, you're treated to stunning views of the Hogback and Dakota Ridge. These pleasantries soon fade, however, as you reach the Green Mountain Trail and start climbing to the top of Green Mountain.

Once reaching the summit of Green Mountain, you're offered 360-degree views of the Red Rocks Park, Dakota Ridge, and the higher Rocky Mountains to the west; Boulder and the Flatirons to the north; the Great Plains and Denver skyline to the east; and 14,110-foot Pikes Peak to the south. As you look around, realize that this area was once prime bison habitat. Today, the black-tailed prairie dog communities

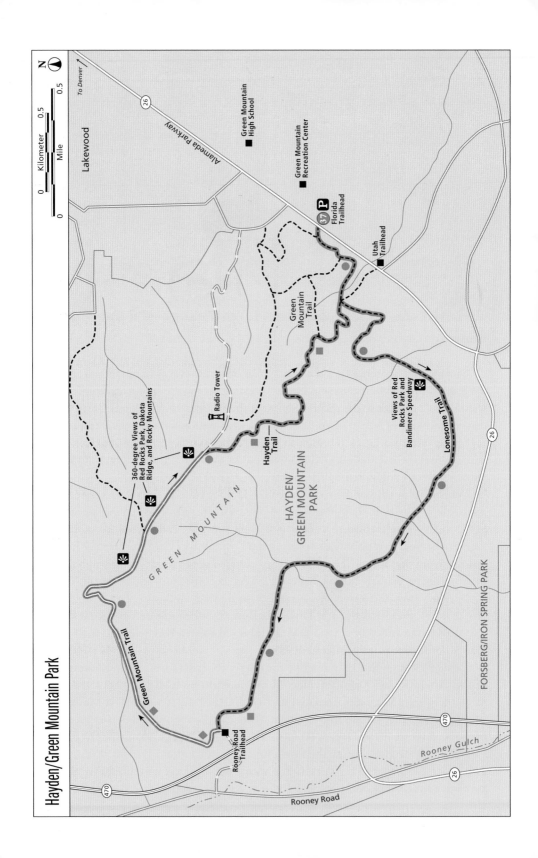

Hayden/Green Mountain Park

N

Kilometer
0   0.5

Mile
0   0.5

To Denver

Lakewood

Alameda Parkway

26

Green Mountain
High School

Green Mountain
Recreation Center

37 P

Florida
Trailhead

Utah
Trailhead

Green
Mountain
Trail

Radio Tower

360-degree Views of
Red Rocks Park, Dakota
Ridge, and Rocky Mountains

GREEN MOUNTAIN

Hayden
Trail

HAYDEN/
GREEN MOUNTAIN
PARK

Views of Red
Rocks Park and
Bandimere Speedway

Lonesome Trail

26

Green Mountain Trail

Rooney Road
Trailhead

470

FORSBERG/IRON SPRING PARK

Rooney Gulch

470

26

Rooney Road

surrounding the base of the mountain take up a good deal of that habitat. From your roost atop Green Mountain, however, you may see coyotes, hawks, and rattlesnakes, possibly even a mountain lion.

Upon connecting with the Hayden Trail from atop Green Mountain, you begin a savage descent over smooth and sometimes rocky terrain. While descending the eastern ridge of the park, the Hayden Trail continues to provide incredible views of Red Rocks Park. This speedy descent returns you to the Lonesome Trail. After basking in the beauty that Hayden/Green Mountain Park has to offer, bear left on the Lonesome Trail and return from a day well spent.

Miles and Directions

0.0 Begin climbing moderately in a southwesterly direction on the Lonesome Trail.

0.4 The Lonesome Trail intersects with the Utah Trail. Continue heading west on the Lonesome Trail.

0.6 You're offered an overlook of Red Rocks Park and Bandimere Speedway to the west and the Denver skyline to the east.

3.3 Lonesome Trail meets the Rooney Road trailhead and the beginning of the Green Mountain Trail. Bear right onto the dirt road of the Green Mountain Trail, and begin climbing in a northerly direction.

4.4 Reach the summit of Green Mountain, and continue a fast cruise on the Green Mountain Trail heading east.

4.9 The Green Mountain Trail intersects with the Hayden Trail on the right, roughly 100 yards before the tall radio tower. Only cairns mark the singletrack of the Hayden Trail. Bear right onto the Hayden Trail singletrack. If you pass the radio tower, there are other singletrack trails that lead to your vehicle.

5.6 The Hayden Trail intersects with the Green Mountain Trail at a T intersection. Bear right at the T, continuing your descent on the Hayden Trail as it crosses over water bars and occasional switchbacks.

5.9 The Hayden Trail intersects with the Utah trailhead and the Lonesome Trail. Bear left onto the Lonesome Trail and return toward your vehicle.

6.4 Reach your vehicle.

Ride Information

Trail Information

Bear Creek Lake Park Visitor Center, 14620 W. Morrison Rd., Lakewood; (303) 697-6159

Local Events and Attractions

Bandimere Speedway, Morrison; (303) 697-6001

Dinosaur Ridge, Morrison; (303) 697-3466; www.dinoridge.org/

Red Rocks Park and Amphitheatre, 18300 W. Alameda Pkwy., Morrison; (720) 865-2494; www.redrocksonline.com/

Restaurants

The Fort (specializes in big game entrees), Morrison; (303) 697-4771; www.thefort.com/

Taste of Denmark, 1901 S. Kipling St., Lakewood; (303) 987-8283; www.tasteofdenmark.net/

The Oven, 7167 W. Alaska Dr. at Belmar, Lakewood; (303) 934-7600; www.theovenpizzaevino.com/

38 Dakota Ridge and Red Rocks Trail

The Hogback is a popular mountain bike ride within easy reach of Denver or Golden. From its highest points you can see stunning views of Red Rocks Amphitheatre. The ride demands sound legs and technical skills. With some of the most technically challenging terrain in the Front Range, the Hogback is not for the faint of heart. Its rocky drop-offs and narrow singletrack, tightening atop a steep ridge of tilted strata, have left many cyclists crying "mommy." Once you descend from the Hogback, the ride continues within Red Rocks Park and among its beautiful, sanguine rocks.

Start: Village Walk parking lot of the Matthews/Winters Park
Distance: 6.5-mile loop
Elevation gain: 1,200 feet
Riding time: Advanced riders, 1 hour; intermediate riders, 2 hours
Fitness effort: Physically moderate to challenging due to some short but steep climbs
Difficulty: Technically moderate to challenging due to steep, sandy drop-offs and climbs
Terrain: Singletrack, dirt road, and paved highway. The terrain is very rocky and sandy in spots. This is a good early-season ride, as it tends to get too sandy after long dry spells. Not recommended as an autumn ride.

Seasons: Apr-Nov
Maps: *DeLorme: Colorado Atlas & Gazetteer,* page 40; *USGS:* Morrison, CO; Jefferson County Open Space Matthews/Winters Park map
Nearest town: Golden
Other trail users: Hikers, concert-goers, and picnickers
Dog friendly: Yes, (but watch out for the rattlesnakes). Dogs must be on a leash at all times.
Trail contact: Jefferson County Open Space, Golden; (303) 271-5925; http://jeffco.us/parks/parks-and-trails/; or City of Golden; (303) 384-8000

Getting there: From Denver head west on I-70 to exit 259, following signs to Morrison. Exit at 259 and turn left, driving under I-70. Now on CO 26, turn right into Matthews/Winters Park, marked by a brown sign on the right side of the road. Park at the Village Walk parking lot in Matthews/Winters Park. Trailhead GPS: N39 41.670' / W105 12.262'

The Ride

Dakota Ridge is part of the Dakota Group, a 14-mile-long ridge of steeply sloping or tilted strata—otherwise known as a "hogback." The ridge extends from Golden to Roxborough Park and is composed of Lower Cretaceous rock units. Formed roughly 66 million years ago, the hogback is the result of the upward thrust of the Rocky Mountains' Front Range. Due to the abundance of Jurassic dinosaur fossils this area has yielded, the section of the Dakota Hogback stretching from I-70 to the town of Morrison is now named Dinosaur Ridge, a famous national landmark.

Dinosaur discoveries near Morrison date back as early as 1877, when Arthur Lakes, a part-time professor at what became the Colorado School of Mines, found a stegosaurus vertebra with a 33-inch circumference. Aside from being the first

View of Red Rocks Amphitheatre, with Creation Rock (left), Shiprock (right), and Rock of Mnemosyne (center).

dinosaur fossils found in the western United States, many of the discoveries near Morrison were the first of their kind.

Riders begin their journey with an instant lung-buster to the top of the Hogback and onto the Dakota Ridge Trail. From this knife-like ridge, sweeping views of the High Plains lie to the east, marked distinctly by Green Mountain and Denver. The Rocky Mountains lie to the west, with Mount Morrison and Red Rocks Park in plain view. Plentiful patches of sand and rock, remnants of a 135-million-year-old sea, mark the crest.

The trail snakes atop the Hogback for roughly 2 miles. Rattlesnakes are occasionally spotted here, though they typically stick to the rock piles and tall grasses and are generally easily avoided. The southern end of the Dakota Ridge Trail delivers some of the trickiest rocky sections found along the entire route. At mile 2.1 there's a short rock face. The line to the left requires deft technical skills, particularly as it cuts sharply to the right along the edge of a big drop-off. The center line is attractive but delivers a strong blow to your front tire, not to mention your ego.

Ride for another mile before entering Red Rocks Park, en route to the Red Rocks Trail. The town of Morrison opened the park as "the Garden of the Titans" in

RATTLESNAKES

Colorado's Front Range generally offers a benign outdoor environment; however, mountain bikers should be vigilant at lower altitudes for pit vipers. The prairie rattlesnake or Western rattlesnake (*Crotalus viridis viridis*) and the Western diamondback (*Crotalus atrox*) make their home in the grasslands and rocky hillsides along Colorado's Front Range, mostly below about 6,000 feet. While the Western diamondback is the larger of the two, the prairie rattlesnake enjoys a larger range of habitat. Rattlesnakes are generally most active during the months of April through October, when they leave their winter dens to feed and mate.

These rattlesnakes grow as long as 5 feet, although adults will generally be between 3 to 4 feet in length. Their bodies can vary in color from light brown to green, with a yellowish underbelly. Dark, egg-shaped blotches run down the line of the back. The snake's head is triangular in shape, with black elliptical slits forming eyes that can detect movement from 40 feet away. Between the eyes and the nostrils of the rattlesnake are smaller "pits." These pit organs can locate potential prey in the dark by detecting the heat the prey gives off against its cooler surroundings. So keen are these thermoreceptor organs that they can detect temperature variances of several thousandths of a degree and can, in total darkness, sense warm-blooded prey up to 2 feet away.

No doubt a rattlesnake's most distinctive feature is the conical-shaped rattle at the end of its tail. The rattle looks like individual cups of fibrous material turned upside down and placed on top of one another. When threatened, the rattlesnake uses its tail muscles to shake the rattle. The sound one hears is made from these cup-like segments hitting each other, which in turn causes a few heartbeats to skip in most humans. Don't believe the myth that rattlesnakes will rattle their tails before striking.

Rattlesnakes don't deliberately harm people; they strike in self-defense and when threatened—as in the cases of the one third of bite victims who are dumb enough to handle or kill the snake. A rattlesnake can strike in any direction and from virtually any position. Its striking distance can cover up to 2 feet; however, that distance can increase if the snake is striking downhill.

A rattlesnake has two hollow fangs in which the venom is stored. As a hemotoxin, venom is primarily used for securing prey, as it affects the blood and lymphatic systems in the body. The degree of pain a victim experiences is a good indicator of the level of toxicity from the bite. The bites of younger rattlesnakes may possess up to twelve times the toxic levels as those of adult rattlesnakes.

Bite victims feel an immediate sharp pain, along with rapid swelling of the area. Effects include slower blood clotting, numbness and a metallic taste in the mouth, swelling of the hands and feet, and even nausea and vomiting.

If you are bitten, stay calm. Physical exertion helps spread the hemotoxic venom through your body. Cleanse the wound with water. Treat for shock and apply a loose-fitting tourniquet above the bite to prevent the venom from entering into your lymph system. If the bite is near a joint, splint the area to decrease

This prairie rattlesnake is defensively coiled and ready to strike just off to the side of the trail.
STEPHEN HLAWATY

movement. Seek medical care immediately. Antivenom therapy must be administered within 6 hours of bite. Never try sucking out the venom.

1906. Students studying mythology at nearby Episcopal College imagined the park to be the Titans' playground and ascribed fitting names to each rock formation.

To the north of the stage of the Red Rocks Amphitheatre stands the 400-foot monolith Creation Rock. Facing Creation Rock is Shiprock, so named because it looks like a sinking ship. The formation behind the stage is the Rock of Mnemosyne, named for the Greek goddess of song and memory. Iron oxide deposits are responsible for the many shades of red.

Today, Red Rocks Park is best known for its naturally formed amphitheater. Nestled between two 400-foot-high red sandstone formations, the amphitheater provides near-perfect acoustics. The 9,200-seat theater offers concert-goers an intimate listening experience—complete with a 30-mile panoramic view of hued plains and the stunning Denver city lights.

Once on the Red Rocks Trail, bear right (north) at all trail crossings. The Red Rocks Trail offers rolling hills and mild climbs mixed with some smooth descents. At mile 4.2 the Red Rocks Trail intersects with the Morrison Slide Trail at Cherry Gulch. Taking the Morrison Slide Trail on your left for 1.2 miles adds about a half mile and some more climbing to your route. Continue on the Red Rocks Trail until you reach the intersection with the Village Walk. This is a 1-mile loop that will lead you back to your vehicle, whichever way you decide to turn.

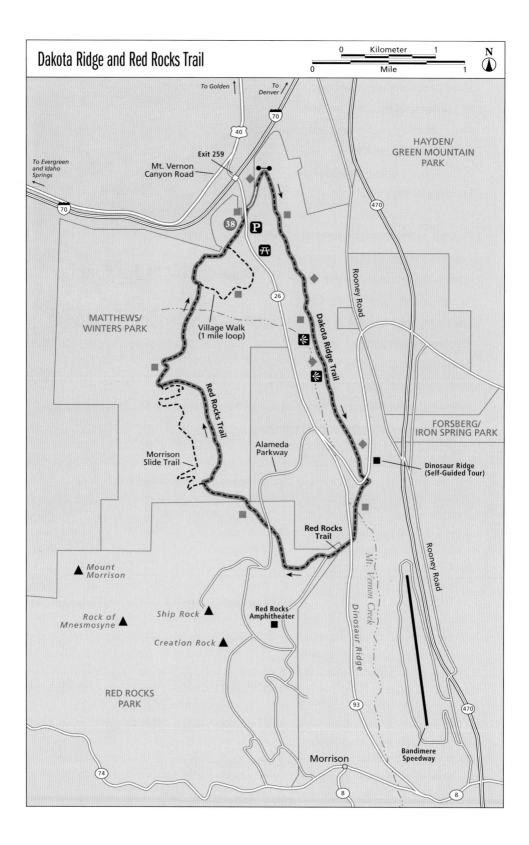

Dakota Ridge and Red Rocks Trail

0   Kilometer   1

0   Mile   1

N

To Golden

To Denver

70

40

Exit 259

Mt. Vernon
Canyon Road

To Evergreen
and Idaho
Springs

70

470

HAYDEN/
GREEN MOUNTAIN
PARK

38

P

Rooney Road

26

MATTHEWS/
WINTERS PARK

Village Walk
(1 mile loop)

Dakota Ridge Trail

Red Rocks Trail

Morrison
Slide Trail

Alameda
Parkway

FORSBERG/
IRON SPRING PARK

Dinosaur Ridge
(Self-Guided Tour)

Red Rocks
Trail

Mount
Morrison

Rock of
Mnesmosyne

Ship Rock

Creation Rock

Red Rocks
Amphitheater

Mt. Vernon Creek

Dinosaur Ridge

Rooney Road

RED ROCKS
PARK

Bandimere
Speedway

Morrison

93

470

74

8

8

Miles and Directions

0.0 Start at the Village Walk parking lot in the Matthews/Winters Park. Ride back out of the parking lot and cross CO 26. Begin ascending the rock- and sand-laden dirt road to the top of Dakota Ridge.

0.3 Bear right at the gate onto the Dakota Ridge Trail. Do not ride beyond this gate.

0.7 Reach the top of the Hogback. To your right will be I-70, leading west into the mountains. There are some big drop-offs from here until you reach a killer but short climb.

1.0 Reach the killer but short climb. What makes this climb difficult is its steep pitch coupled with large water bars across the trail.

2.2 The trail comes to a Y intersection. Hang a left. By continuing straight, you'll end up having to duck under a gate to get back onto the main trail. Ride down the trail with caution. Arrive at a staircase and bear right onto the paved road (Dinosaur Ridge). Ride to where the road curves to the right, cross over the cement barricade, and rejoin the trail on your left. Climb briefly and then descend sharply.

3.0 After riding down a fast singletrack, the trail once again lets out onto a paved road (Jefferson CR 93). Be cautious here and stay in control, as the trail leads you right onto the road. Bear right here again, following signs for the Red Rocks Trail. Cross the paved road and hang an immediate left onto an access road into the Red Rocks Park. Pedal for 0.2 mile and bear right onto the singletrack Red Rocks Trail.

4.2 At the junction of Morrison Slide Trail and Red Rocks Trail, bear right and continue on the Red Rocks Trail. (**Option:** Taking the Morrison Slide Trail on your left for 1.2 miles adds about a half mile and some more climbing to your route.)

5.8 At the second intersection with Morrison Slide Trail, stay to the right.

6.5 Arrive back at the Village Walk parking lot in the Matthews/Winters Park.

Ride Information

Trail Information

Jefferson County Open Space; (303) 271-5925; http://jeffco.us/parks/parks-and-trails/

Local Events and Attractions

Bandimere Speedway, Morrison; (303) 697-6001

Dinosaur Ridge, Morrison; (303) 697-3466; www.dinoridge.org/

Red Rocks Park and Amphitheatre, 18300 W. Alameda Pkwy., Morrison; (720) 865-2494; www.redrocksonline.com/

Restaurants

The Fort (specializes in big game entrees), Morrison; (303) 697-4771; www.thefort.com/

Willy's Wings, 109 Bear Creek Ave., Morrison; (303) 697-1232; www.willyswings.com/

Caretta Vieja, 9064 US 285, Morrison; (303) 697-8881

Red Rocks Grill, 415 Bear Creek Ave., Morrison; (303) 697-9290; www.redrocksgrill.com/

39 Argentine Pass

This trail leads to the top of the Continental Divide and the 13,132-foot Argentine Pass, the highest crossing of the Continental Divide in North America. From the top of the Divide, riders are rewarded with sweeping views of the Rocky Mountains, including 14,270-foot Grays and 14,267-foot Torreys Peaks to the northwest and 14,264-foot Mount Evans to the southeast. Because this trail travels above timberline, be ever mindful of rapidly changing weather conditions. By following the singletrack of the old railroad bed of the Argentine Central Grade, riders connect with FR 248, which leads to the Waldorf town site at 11,594 feet, before taking the very rocky and hazardous Argentine Pass Trail to the top. The entire route is fantastic, offering incredible singletrack, long climbs, stellar views, and a bit of Colorado mining history. This ride is best suited for well-conditioned riders.

Start: The Georgetown Loop Historic Mining and Railroad Park

Distance: 23.2-mile out-and-back

Elevation gain: 2,500 feet

Riding time: Advanced riders, 2-2.5 hours; intermediate riders, 3-3.5 hours

Fitness effort: Physically challenging due to a number of switchbacks as well as a long, extended climb at high elevations

Difficulty: Technically moderate to challenging due to some rockier sections through gullies and on sections nearest the trail's higher elevations

Terrain: Four-by-four road and singletrack. The singletrack passes over an old railroad grade through dense forest, while the four-by-four road climbs to elevations of more than 13,000 feet through rocky, above-timberline terrain.

Seasons: July-Sept

Maps: *DeLorme: Colorado Atlas & Gazetteer*, page 39; *USGS:* Georgetown, CO, Grays Peak, CO, and Montezuma, CO; Trails Illustrated: #104, Idaho Springs, Georgetown, Loveland Pass, CO

Nearest town: Georgetown

Other trail users: Hikers and horseback riders on the Argentine Central Grade; four-wheel-drive vehicles on FR 248

Dog friendly: No

Trail contact: Arapaho and Roosevelt National Forests and Pawnee National Grassland, Boulder Ranger District, Boulder; (303) 541-2500

Getting there: From Denver drive west on I-70 for 45 miles to the town of Silver Plume. Take exit 226 from I-70 and bear left at the end of the ramp. After driving under I-70, bear right and follow the historic site parking sign. Park in the Georgetown Loop Historic Mining and Railroad Park parking lot. Trailhead GPS: N39 41.678' / W105 44.016'; trailhead terminus/turnaround GPS: N39 37.515' / W105 46.945'

The Ride

Riders begin this trail by leaving the old Silver Plume depot that once served the tiny mining town. The depot began operating on September 11, 1884, and stayed in operation until 1939. Today, the depot still stands at the south edge of Silver Plume.

Waldorf town site.

As you leave the station, Republican Mountain lies to the right (north) across Clear Creek Canyon. A flock of bighorn sheep can often be seen on the mountain's south slope. The population of these sheep dwindled from the thousands during the early 1900s to just forty in 1950. Their decrease in numbers was due in part to development of local mountain towns, as well as to an invasion of the parasitic lung worm that caused many sheep to die of pneumonia. Luckily, the Colorado Division of Wildlife came to the flock's aid, restoring Colorado's state animal to its normal population.

Upon connecting with the singletrack of the Argentine Pass Trail, riders turn south underneath a canopy of aspen as they climb across Leavenworth Mountain. Along this route riders pass a number of relics from Colorado's bygone mining days: water tanks, abandoned mines, trestles, and mining roads. One such road appears as you near 1 mile. Here the trail becomes narrower as you pass the old mining road on your right. Continue straight, heading in an easterly direction and staying on the main trail. Generally speaking, railroad grades follow the path of least resistance and therefore travel along moderate inclines. Be sure to avoid any conspicuous roads that leave from the main trail.

Nearing 2 miles into the ride, the trail bears right and continues in a southwesterly direction, offering views of the famous Georgetown Loop.

Opened in 1884, the Georgetown narrow gauge railroad served the mining camps between Denver and Silver Plume. Aside from hauling freight, the rail line

NARROW GAUGE RAILROAD

As mountain bikers, we owe a debt of gratitude to the narrow gauge railroad lines whose beds have since become some of our finest mountain bike rides. The Argentine Pass Trail, the Switzerland Trail, and the Narrow Gauge Trail in Pine Valley Ranch Park all owe their existence to the narrow gauge railroad.

To circumvent the difficulties of construction along steep canyon walls and high-mountain passes, the narrow gauge railroads were built on a 3-foot-wide track bed, rather than the industry standard of a 4-foot, 8.5-inch track bed. Overall, this allowed the narrow gauge railroads greater flexibility in negotiating sharp curves and up and down steep grades.

In 1870 the Denver & Rio Grande Railroad (D&RGR) laid Colorado's first narrow gauge line, which extended north from Denver through Wyoming. Following the D&RGR's lead, and spurred by the growing mining industry, the Colorado Central Railroad was first in building a narrow gauge line that extended into the Rocky Mountain interior in 1872 to provide service for the booming mining industries up Clear Creek. At one third the expense of standard rail construction, the narrow gauge railroad soon became the standard for rail building in Colorado's Rocky Mountains.

The narrow gauge lines contributed to the expansion of mines throughout the western portion of Colorado during the 1870s and 1880s. A waning gold and silver mining economy, coupled with the higher costs of converting standard rails to narrow gauge rails, caused the eventual decline of the narrow gauge railroad by the mid-1890s. However, they remained a tourist attraction for passengers wishing to view the splendid mountain scenery. Indeed, the D&RGR included an Around the Circle tour that began in Denver and traveled south to New Mexico before heading northwest to Durango. From Durango passengers could board the Rio Grande Southern Railroad and experience a similar adventure throughout Colorado's southwest before returning to Denver.

also delivered passengers amazed at where these trains could run. Although Georgetown and Silver Plume lie only 2 miles from each other, it took 4.5 miles of track to cover the twisty 600 feet in elevation that separate the two towns. To achieve this, the 300-foot-long Devil's Gate High Bridge spans a gorge nearly 100 feet high as it crosses Clear Creek, and the track actually crosses over itself. Today, it has been reopened as a tourist attraction that includes a walking tour of the Lebanon Silver Mine, so you can sometimes hear the train whistle as you chug upwards.

About 3 miles into your ride, the contrasting views of the Continental Divide rising above and the tiny town of Silver Plume below are astounding when you consider what men and women had to endure during Colorado's early mining history.

Enjoying the sweet descent of the Argentine Central Grade.

These hardy men and women needed relief from the hardships of the day, which came in the form of a dance hall atop Pavilion Point. Today, all that remains is a free-standing stone fireplace and chimney.

Once it connects with FR 248, the route passes a variety of cascading hillside waterfalls, particularly if you're riding during June and early July. As you continue on FR 248, an old telegraph line will be to your left. Upon reaching the town site of Waldorf, it's a grueling 2.3 miles to the top of Argentine Pass.

Constructed in 1869 under the management of Stephen Decatur, Argentine Pass attempted to connect the ore smelters in Denver to the gold and silver mines near Breckenridge. When finished, the direct wagon route would cross the Continental Divide at 13,132 feet, making it the highest crossing of the divide in North America.

Once atop the pass, you're rewarded with incredible views. Looking to the northwest, the most prominent peak is 14,270-foot Grays Peak; 14,267-foot Torreys Peak lies just behind and to the right. Mount Evans, ever popular for the road to its 14,264-foot summit, lies to the southeast.

The descent from Argentine Pass is fast and rocky. Be careful of vehicular traffic along FR 248. The trail offers speed freaks a big-ring good time the whole way down.

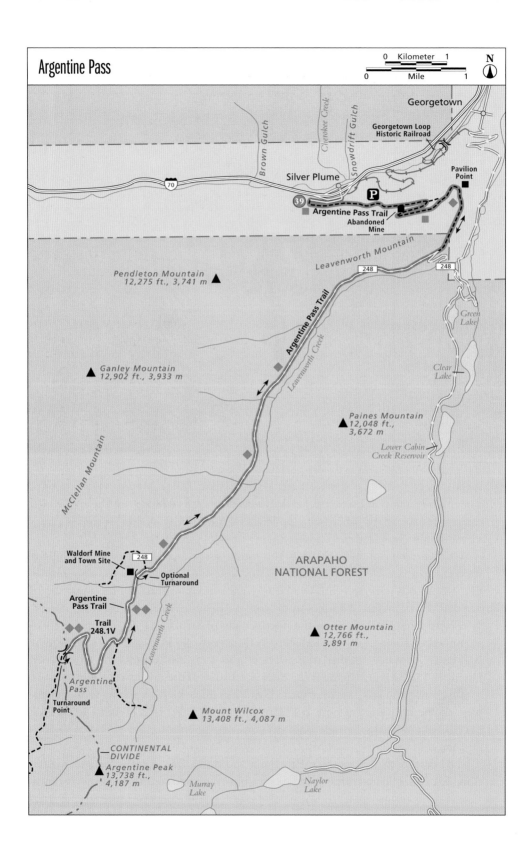

Argentine Pass

0 Kilometer 1
0 Mile 1

N

Georgetown

Georgetown Loop
Historic Railroad

Pavilion
Point

Silver Plume

P

39

Argentine Pass Trail

Abandoned
Mine

Cherokee Creek

Brown Gulch

Snowdrift Gulch

Leavenworth Mountain

248

248

Green
Lake

Clear
Lake

Pendleton Mountain
12,275 ft., 3,741 m ▲

Argentine Pass Trail

Leavenworth Creek

Ganley Mountain ▲
12,902 ft., 3,933 m

Paines Mountain
▲ 12,048 ft.,
3,672 m

Lower Cabin
Creek Reservoir

McClellan Mountain

**ARAPAHO
NATIONAL FOREST**

Waldorf Mine
and Town Site

248

Optional
Turnaround

**Argentine
Pass Trail**

**Trail
248.1V**

Otter Mountain
▲ 12,766 ft.,
3,891 m

Leavenworth Creek

*Argentine
Pass*

Turnaround
Point

Mount Wilcox
▲ 13,408 ft., 4,087 m

*CONTINENTAL
DIVIDE*

Argentine Peak
▲ 13,738 ft.,
4,187 m

*Murray
Lake*

*Naylor
Lake*

Miles and Directions

0.0 Starting from the Georgetown Loop Historic Mining and Railroad Park, begin riding westward along the frontage road.

0.4 Bear left, heading in a southeasterly direction, following the Argentine Pass Trail.

1.6 Pass an abandoned mine. Keep your eyes open here, as you'll eventually bear right before passing any other abandoned mines.

1.9 The route cuts to the right. While a path continues straight ahead and eventually passes a second abandoned mine on the right, you should bear right at this time, continuing your ride and heading in a southwesterly direction. The trail is considerably narrower singletrack than in the first 2 miles. If you pass this second mine, you've gone too far. Turn around and reconnect to the main route.

2.3 Arrive at a trail intersection. One trail cuts sharply to the left and heads east. Another trail crosses the Argentine Pass Trail and descends in a westerly direction. Be sure to continue climbing here on the main trail of the Argentine Central Grade.

3.3 Arrive at Pavilion Point.

4.2 The Argentine Pass Trail intersects with FR 248. Do not be put off by the sign at this intersection that identifies this road as 248.1. Regional maps identify this road as FR 248. Continue riding on FR 248 toward the Waldorf town site about 5 miles down the trail. Be advised that this road is open to vehicular traffic.

6.6-7.3 FR 248 forks two times. At each fork continue straight on FR 248.

9.3 Reach the town site of Waldorf. At this point FR 248 cuts right (north) on its way to McClellan Mountain. Continue heading straight, in a southerly direction, following the very steep and rocky Argentine Pass Trail to the top of Argentine Pass. (**Option:** The Waldorf town site makes for a good turnaround point for riders less than gonzo-abusive to their bikes and bodies.)

10.2 The trail forks. The left fork has a posted sign that reads 248.1U. The right fork has a posted sign that reads 248.1V. Bear right here onto Trail 248.1V, taking the higher of the two trails and switchbacking toward Argentine Pass.

11.6 Reach the top of Argentine Pass and the Continental Divide. Turn around here and return the way you came.

23.2 Arrive at your vehicle.

Ride Information

Trail Information

Georgetown Gateway Visitor Center; (303) 569-2405

Local Events and Attractions

Georgetown Loop Railroad; (888) 456-6777; www.georgetownlooprr.com

Hamill House Museum, Georgetown; (303) 569-2840

Hotel de Paris Museum, Georgetown; (303) 569-2311

Restaurants

The Alpine Restaurant and Bar, Georgetown; (303) 569-0200

A Whistle Stop Café, Georgetown; (303) 569-5053

Troia's Café, Georgetown; (303) 569-5014

40 Elk Meadow and Bergen Peak

The trails that weave through Elk Meadow Park are some of the finest in Jefferson County. While the climb to the top of Bergen Peak is a bit of a grunt, the views of Pikes Peak, Mount Evans, Mount Bierstadt, and the Continental Divide make it worth the effort. Not only that, the descent packs enough punch to make the climbing seem like a distant memory. The singletrack throws out smoother, softer sections, but you leave remembering the screaming descent of threading tight rock outcroppings and barreling over big drop-offs. Oh yeah, there are more switchbacks here than pine cones.

Start: The Sleepy S Trail at the Lewis Ridge Road parking lot and trailhead

Distance: 11.3-mile loop

Elevation gain: 1,900 feet

Riding time: Advanced riders, 1.5 hours; intermediate riders, 2-3 hours

Fitness effort: Physically challenging due to the climb to Bergen Peak

Difficulty: Technically moderate to challenging due to some tighter singletrack that weaves through rock outcroppings and over big drop-offs

Terrain: Wide and narrow singletrack and doubletrack that roll over smooth terrain through meadows; also steeper ascending and descending sections that roll over rocky terrain and through mixed conifer forests

Seasons: Late May-Oct

Maps: *DeLorme: Colorado Atlas & Gazetteer,* page 39; *USGS:* Squaw Pass, CO, and Evergreen, CO; Jefferson County Open Space Elk Meadow Park map

Nearest town: Bergen Park

Other trail users: Hikers, horseback riders, and picnickers

Dog friendly: Yes, with a dog training area located on the south side of Stagecoach Boulevard

Trail contact: Jefferson County Open Space; (303) 271-5925; http://jeffco.us/parks/parks-and-trails/; or Jefferson County Open Space Trails Hotline, Evergreen; (303) 271-5975

Getting there: From Denver drive west on I-70 for roughly 20 miles to exit 252 and the Evergreen Parkway. Drive east (heading south to the town of Evergreen) on the Evergreen Parkway (CO 74) for 4.5 miles through the town of Bergen Park. Bear right onto Lewis Ridge Road and then right again into the Elk Meadow Park parking lot. Park in the Lewis Ridge Road lot. Trailhead GPS: N39 39.802' / W105 21.535'

The Ride

The barn that stands in Elk Meadow Park speaks to a rich ranching history. As part of the Homestead Act of 1862, the US government awarded homesteaders Robert Strain, Charles Abbott, Thomas Audrey, and Charlotte Dow 160-acre tracts. Between 1905 and 1943 Theodore Johnson acquired these and other properties to build an 1,140-acre ranch. Darst Buchanan purchased the property in 1945 for his purebred Hereford cattle. In 1949 Cole Means bought the land from Buchanan as summer pasture for his Texas herds. Finally, in 1977 Jefferson County bought the land for its park system.

The diverse ecosystems of Elk Meadow also make for great mountain biking. The first mile of trail rolls over smooth, wide singletrack, climbing moderately in a northern direction. The Meadow View Trail passes through meadow and grassland ecosystems over wide singletrack, turning into doubletrack at roughly 1.5 miles. The less steep and lower elevations found within the meadow and grassland ecosystems provide riders with an abundance of grasses, shrubs, wildflowers, and wavy terrain. The Richardson ground squirrel, a relative of the prairie dog, thrives here. In fact, there are a number of squirrel colonies in the park.

As the Meadow View Trail continues to rise to meet the Too Long Trail, riders are introduced to a number of tough switchbacks. After these switchbacks riders begin to enter the transitional zone from meadow to forest. This ponderosa parkland ecosystem offers shelter and food to the many deer and elk that frequent this area during the winter months.

Navigating the rocky descent of the Bergen Peak Trail.

By 2.5 miles the trail gets a bit tougher as it continues to climb, delivering a number of rocky sections with which to contend. This section of trail leads through an aspen grove that introduces riders to the foothills zone, which features steeper slopes and densely populated Douglas fir, with islands of aspen groves thrown in the mix.

Eventually riders enter an incredible lodgepole pine forest. The singletrack here is soft with pine needles as the trail whips through these dense stands of evergreens in the montane zone.

After connecting with the Bergen Peak Trail, riders have to contend with a grueling climb to the top of Bergen Peak, where they are rewarded with westerly views of the Continental Divide and easterly views of the Great Plains. Bergen Peak introduces riders to the subalpine environment: little plant life, save for the green lichen that grows on exposed rock outcroppings.

Elk Meadow and Bergen Peak

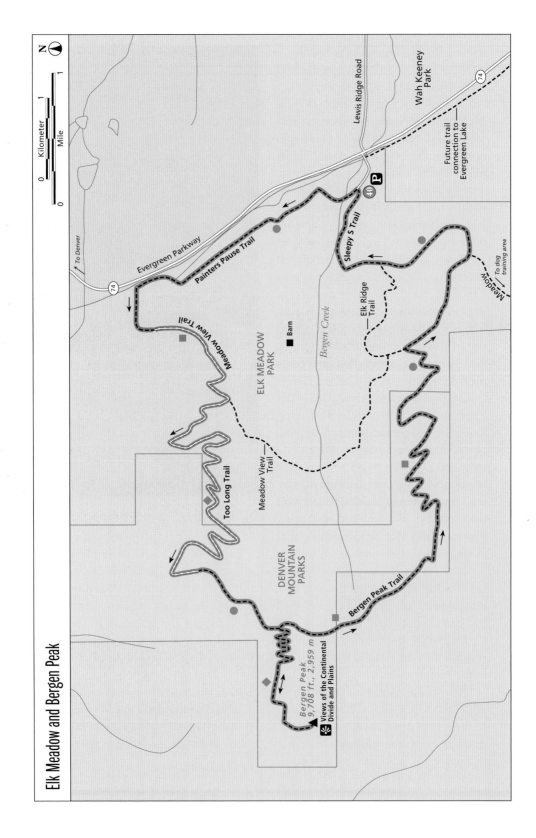

N

Kilometer
0   1
Mile
0   1

To Denver

Evergreen Parkway

74

Painters Pause Trail

Lewis Ridge Road

Wah Keeney Park

Future trail connection to Evergreen Lake

74

P
40

Sleepy S Trail

Meadow

To dog training area

Elk Ridge Trail

Meadow View Trail

ELK MEADOW PARK

Barn

Bergen Creek

Meadow View Trail

Too Long Trail

DENVER MOUNTAIN PARKS

Bergen Peak Trail

Bergen Peak 9,708 ft., 2,959 m

Views of the Continental Divide and Plains

The descent from Bergen Peak is a screamer. After a technical rocky section, riders reach the intersection of the Bergen Peak Trail and the Too Long Trail. Continuing south along the Bergen Peak Trail, riders have to negotiate some huge drop-offs, as well as tighter, rockier sections. After a fun switchback section, riders connect with the Meadow View Trail and return to their vehicles. Since the descent can be very fast, be aware of other trail users.

Miles and Directions

0.0 From the parking lot bear right and begin riding on the Sleepy S Trail, heading in an easterly direction toward the Evergreen Parkway.

0.1 The Sleepy S Trail intersects with the Painters Pause Trail. Bear left onto the Painters Pause Trail, and begin riding in a northerly direction.

1.1 The Painters Pause Trail intersects with the Meadow View Trail. Bear left onto the Meadow View Trail, and begin riding southwest.

2.1 The Meadow View Trail intersects with the Too Long Trail. Bear right onto the Too Long Trail, and begin climbing up the tight switchbacks.

3.2 Enter into Denver Mountain Parks.

4.5 The Too Long Trail intersects with the Bergen Peak Trail. Continue climbing on the Bergen Peak Trail in a westerly direction as it makes its way to the top of Bergen Peak.

5.6 Reach the top of Bergen Peak. From here backtrack to the intersection of the Bergen Peak Trail and the Too Long Trail.

6.7 Reach the intersection of the Bergen Peak Trail and the Too Long Trail. Bear right, continuing on the Bergen Peak Trail and heading in a southerly direction.

9.4 Bergen Peak Trail intersects with the Meadow View Trail. Bear right onto the Meadow View Trail.

10.1 Meadow View Trail intersects with the Sleepy S Trail. Bear left onto the Sleepy S Trail, and ride in a northerly direction.

10.8 The Sleepy S Trail intersects with the Elk Ridge Trail to the left. Stay on the Sleepy S Trail, continuing in a northerly direction.

11.3 Arrive at your vehicle.

Ride Information

Trail Information

Jefferson County Open Space, (303) 271-5925; http://jeffco.us/parks/parks-and-trails/

Local Events and Attractions

Evergreen Music Festival & Art Show at Evergreen Lake, July; (720) 515-8594

Hiwan Homestead Museum, Evergreen; (720) 497-7650

Restaurants

The Whippletree Restaurant, Evergreen; (303) 670-7348

Da Kind Soups, Evergreen; (303) 674-7687

Willow Creek Restaurant, Evergreen; (303) 674-9463

Tequila's Mexican Restaurant, Evergreen; (303) 679-1913

41 Mount Falcon Park

With 2,330 acres and 12.6 miles of trails to its credit, Mount Falcon Park delivers some of Denver's finest singletrack. The park's multiuse trail system leads visitors to a variety of historical sites and overlooks: the Summer White House ruins; the remains of John Brisben Walker's castle in the mountains; Eagle Eye Shelter; and the panoramic views of Mount Evans and the Continental Divide, the Great Plains, and Red Rocks Park. Riders cross meadows and gullies and pass red sandstone boulders on their climb up Mount Falcon. Picnic tables and restrooms are provided at trailheads.

Start: The eastern Mount Falcon trailhead

Distance: 9.6-mile lariat

Elevation gain: 1,700 feet

Riding time: Advanced riders, 1-1.5 hours; intermediate riders, 1.5-2 hours

Fitness effort: Physically moderate to challenging due to a few steep climbs

Difficulty: Technically easy to moderate due to wide singletrack and a moderate degree of rocks and roots on the trail

Terrain: Singletrack and doubletrack, mostly on smooth, hard-packed dirt; some rocks and roots with which to contend through semiarid conditions

Seasons: Apr-Nov

Maps: *DeLorme: Colorado Atlas & Gazetteer*, page 40; *USGS:* Morrison, CO

Nearest town: Morrison

Other trail users: Hikers and horseback riders; Turkey Trot Trail is a hikers-only trail

Dog friendly: Yes

Trail contact: Jefferson County Open Space; (303) 271-5925; http://jeffco.us/parks/parks-and-trails/; or Jefferson County Open Space Trails Hotline, Evergreen; (303) 271-5975

Getting there: From Denver drive west on I-70 for roughly 13 miles to the Golden/Morrison exit. Bear left (east) onto CO 26 and drive for roughly 4 miles to the town of Morrison. In Morrison bear right onto the one-way Stone Street and then right (west) again onto Main Street and drive through the town to CO 8. Bear left (south) onto CO 8 and drive for a little over a mile to Forest Avenue. Bear right (west) onto Forest Avenue and drive for 0.2 mile before taking your first right (north) onto Vine Avenue, following the signs to the trailhead and the eastern access of Mount Falcon. Park in Mount Falcon Park's east parking area off CO 8. Trailhead GPS: N39 38.810' / W105 11.804'

The Ride

Your ride begins immediately with a tough climb up Castle Trail. Although the singletrack is wide and smooth, the climb is particularly challenging because of the various water bars that cross the trail. As if that wasn't enough, the first few miles also deliver some intermittent rockier sections with which to contend before you retreat into the cooler confines of a mixed conifer forest.

As the Castle Trail switches back a number of times, you're offered beautiful views of the Denver skyline and Red Rocks Park. While riding up to Mount

Walker home ruins.

Falcon, you'll sometimes hear the high-winding engines of the race cars at nearby Bandimere Speedway.

Once you intersect with Walker's Dream Trail, you can hike or ride the short 0.3 mile to the Summer White House ruins. Named after John Brisben Walker, the trail leads to the site of his once-cherished dream: a summer home for the presidents of the United States.

With funds collected from 10-cent contributions by the children of Colorado, among other donations, Walker began the campaign for the presidents' home in 1911 by displaying the marble cornerstone—mined locally from Marble, Colorado—in Denver to generate local interest. After commissioning Denver architect J.B. Benedict to design the Summer White House, Walker funded the foundation himself. In the fall of 1914, the cornerstone for the Summer White House was positioned. However, President Woodrow Wilson declined to attend the ceremony, which should have been an omen.

Though thousands of dollars had been collected for the Summer White House project, construction never resumed due to the onset of World War I and Walker's dwindling financial resources. Today, all that is left of this dream is the foundation and the marble cornerstone, which reads "Summer home for the presidents of the United States, the gift of the people of Colorado, 1911."

From the site of the Summer White House, our ride continues southwest along the Castle Trail. From here to its intersection with the Meadow Trail, the Castle Trail

The yin-yang of mountain biking: Gotta go up to go down, with the Denver skyline as a backdrop.

becomes a smooth doubletrack as it runs through mixed conifer forests. The cruise is mellow and sweet along the ridgeline, offering views of the Continental Divide to the west and eastern plains to the east. At the intersection of the Castle and Meadow Trails, you can take a short hike to the ruins of Walker's castle home.

Begun in 1909, Walker's elaborate stone mansion included a northwest tower that encompassed a library, living room, master bedroom, and observation deck, while the north wing of the mansion included a reception room, dining room, and kitchen. The south wing provided a den, a large music room, and several bedrooms. Unfortunately, lightning struck the mansion in 1918, and the resulting fire burned it to the ground. Today, only the mansion's stone walls and numerous fireplaces remain.

At the intersection of the Castle and Parmalee Trails, you'll find a rest area with restrooms. Riding the tight singletrack of the Parmalee Trail, you descend through a beautiful mixed conifer forest over moderately technical terrain of rock and sand. After speeding through a clearing below the Eagle Eye Shelter, you cross a stream and are immediately thrown into a steep climb, complete with erosion-resistant water bars.

After climbing to the Parmalee Trail's intersection with the Meadow Trail, it's a short run back to the Castle Trail. The descent to your vehicle via the Castle Trail is an impressive one. While there are a number of opportunities to catch air, be aware of other trail users and check your speed.

Mount Falcon Park

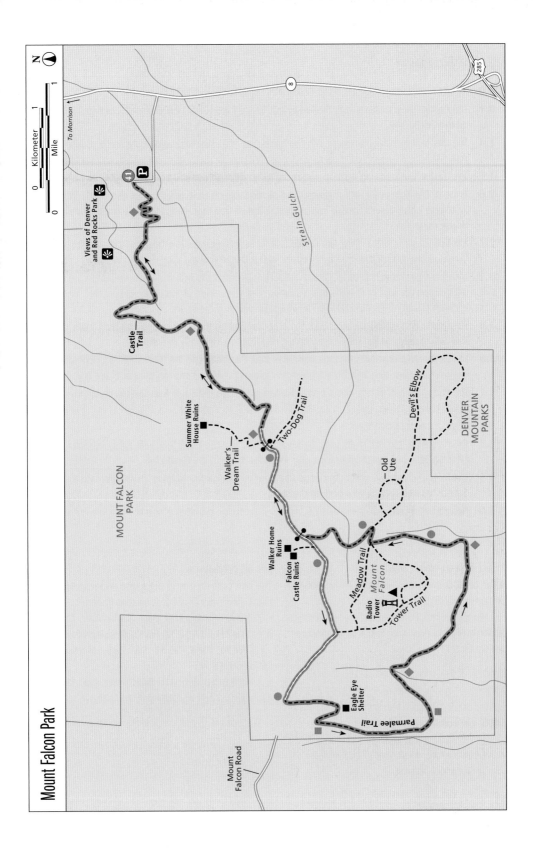

Miles and Directions

0.0 Heading west, begin riding on the Castle Trail singletrack.

0.1 The Castle Trail intersects with the Turkey Trot Trail, a hikers-only trail. Bear left, continuing on the Castle Trail.

1.4 The Castle Trail again intersects with the Turkey Trot Trail. Bear left, continuing on the Castle Trail.

1.7 The Castle Trail leads up a steep and rocky climb through a mixed conifer forest.

2.6 Arrive at the high point with a gazebo and picnic table off to your right. Here the Castle Trail intersects with Walker's Dream Trail, a short 0.3-mile trail that leads to the Summer White House ruins.

2.7 After passing through a gate, the Castle Trail intersects with the Two-Dog Trail to your left. Continue straight on the wide doubletrack of the Castle Trail.

3.1 After passing through another gate, the Castle Trail intersects with the Meadow Trail to the left and the Walker home ruins trail. (Caution: The foundation of the castle is unstable, so keep off.) Continue on the Castle Trail in a southwesterly direction.

3.5 The Castle Trail again intersects with the Meadow Trail on the left. Continue on the Castle Trail, which leads to the Eagle Eye Shelter, heading in a northerly direction.

3.8 The Castle Trail intersects with the Parmalee Trail. Bear left onto the Parmalee Trail, continuing in a southerly direction. The doubletrack rejoins the singletrack on the Parmalee Trail.

4.7 The Parmalee Trail enters into a clearing where you'll see the Eagle Eye Shelter, an old fire-watch tower.

5.8 Begin a switchback ascent.

6.1 The Parmalee Trail intersects with the Meadow Trail and the Tower Trail. Veer right onto the Meadow Trail, heading east toward your reconnection with the Castle Trail.

6.5 The Meadow Trail intersects the Castle Trail near the Walker home ruins. Bear right onto the Castle Trail and retrace your path to the start.

9.6 Arrive at your vehicle.

Ride Information

Trail Information

Jefferson County Open Space Trails Hotline, Evergreen; (303) 271-5975

Mount Falcon Park's trails are sometimes closed due to heavy rains. To check on closures, call (303) 271-5975.

Local Events and Attractions

Bandimere Speedway, Morrison; (303) 697-6001

Dinosaur Ridge, Morrison; (303) 697-3466; www.dinoridge.org/

Red Rocks Park and Amphitheatre, 18300 W. Alameda Pkwy., Morrison; (720) 865-2494; www.redrocksonline.com/

Restaurants

The Fort (specializes in big game entrees), Morrison; (303) 697-4771; www.thefort.com/

Willy's Wings, 109 Bear Creek Ave., Morrison; (303) 697-1232; www.willyswings.com/

Caretta Vieja, 9064 US 285, Morrison; (303) 697-8881

Red Rocks Grill, 415 Bear Creek Ave., Morrison; (303) 697-9290; www.redrocksgrill.com/

42 Alderfer/Three Sisters Park

Alderfer/Three Sisters Park offers riders a network of great trails. From smooth to rocky singletrack along speedy descents and tough climbs, the trails offer something for everyone. The rock formations of Three Sisters and the Brother have served as area landmarks for years and are an incredible sight. The summit of Evergreen Mountain rewards the rider with great views of the town of Evergreen. Offering a variety of picnic areas, restrooms, and terrain, this park can be great for families as well as loner mountain-bike types. As such, it can get pretty crowded on the weekends.

(**Note:** As of this writing, the western edge of the Wild Iris Loop is closed from Buffalo Park Road to its intersection with West Evergreen Mountain Trail due to flood damage.)

Start: The Alderfer/Three Sisters Park trailhead. Cross Buffalo Park Road and begin riding on the East Evergreen Mountain Trail on the south side of the road.
Distance: 7.7-mile loop
Elevation gain: 1,000 feet
Riding time: Advanced riders, 45 minutes; intermediate riders, 1-1.5 hours
Fitness effort: Physically moderate due to some extended climbs
Difficulty: Technically moderate due to the wide singletrack; more technical with rocks on the tight Three Sisters Trail
Terrain: Singletrack over sometimes smooth and wide or rocky and tight trail; rocky sections, meadows, and forests

Seasons: May-Oct
Maps: *DeLorme: Colorado Atlas & Gazetteer,* page 39; *USGS:* Evergreen, CO, and Conifer, CO; Jefferson County Open Space Alderfer/Three Sisters Park map
Nearest town: Evergreen
Other trail users: Hikers and horseback riders
Dog friendly: Yes
Trail contact: Jefferson County Open Space; (303) 271-5925; http://jeffco.us/parks/parks-and-trails/; or Jefferson County Open Space Trails Hotline, Evergreen; (303) 271-5975

Getting there: From Denver drive west on I-70 for around 20 miles to exit 252 and the Evergreen Parkway. Drive east (heading south to the town of Evergreen) on the Evergreen Parkway (CO 74) for 8.4 miles before turning right after Evergreen Lake onto Seventy-third Road. Drive on Seventy-third Road for 0.6 mile before turning right onto Buffalo Park Road, following the brown sign for Alderfer/Three Sisters Park. Drive on Buffalo Park Road for 1.5 miles to the east parking lot and trailhead on the right (a second parking lot is located another 0.5 mile up the road). Cross the road and begin riding. Trailhead GPS: N39 37.377' / W105 20.786'

The Ride

Alderfer/Three Sisters Park partly takes its name from E.J. Alderfer and his wife, Arleta, who moved into the Dollison ranch house in 1945. The Alderfers first raised silver fox and Aberdeen Angus cattle. In 1970 the Alderfers switched from raising

Author Stephen Hlawaty working through the rough stuff. AMANDA HLAWATY

silver fox to pasturing horses. Between 1977 to 1986 the Alderfer family donated a sizeable portion of their property to Jefferson County Open Space.

We begin riding in a clockwise direction along the East Evergreen Mountain Trail on the south side of Buffalo Park Road. The trail climbs moderately over wide, smooth singletrack as it switches back up Evergreen Mountain. All of these switchbacks are difficult but manageable to varying degrees. The water bars strewn across the trail add to the degree of difficulty. After crossing Wilmot Creek, riders are offered a fine overlook of the surrounding hillsides to the south. Once atop Evergreen Mountain, beautiful views of the Continental Divide are the climber's spoils.

The descent along the Summit Trail and the West Evergreen Mountain Trail is incredibly fast over smooth and wide singletrack and through mixed conifer forests. Parts of these forests have been thinned in an attempt to revitalize the forest. Before thinning, there were roughly 5,000 lodgepole pine per acre, which left little room for new trees to grow.

The Wild Iris Loop, Bluebird, and Homestead Trails offer easy rides through wide-open meadows. It's not until you get to the Sisters Trail that the route becomes considerably tougher. After 6 miles the terrain becomes very rocky as the trail climbs more steeply through large boulders on its way north to the Three Sisters rock formation.

Made of metamorphic rock of the Precambrian era, these outcrops consist largely of silver plume quartz. These dominant rock formations are a familiar landmark for Evergreen residents and lie in the park's northernmost corner. Spencer Wyant

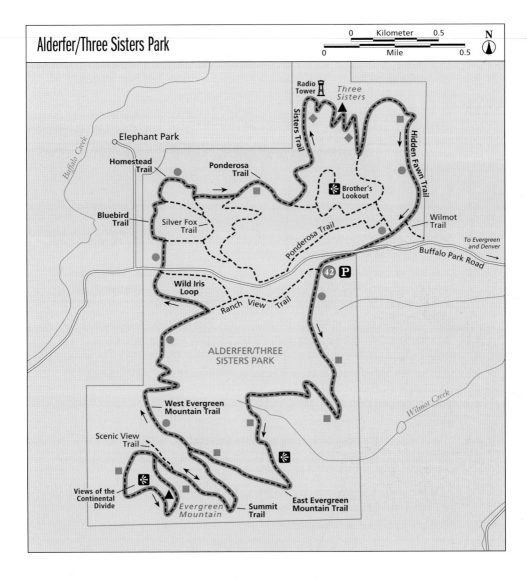

0   Kilometer   0.5

0   Mile   0.5

N

Radio Tower

Three Sisters

Sisters Trail

Hidden Fawn Trail

Elephant Park

Homestead Trail

Ponderosa Trail

Brother's Lookout

Bluebird Trail

Silver Fox Trail

Wilmot Trail

To Evergreen and Denver

Ponderosa Trail

Buffalo Park Road

Buffalo Creek

42 P

Wild Iris Loop

Ranch View Trail

ALDERFER/THREE SISTERS PARK

Wilmot Creek

West Evergreen Mountain Trail

Scenic View Trail

Views of the Continental Divide

Evergreen Mountain

Summit Trail

East Evergreen Mountain Trail

originally owned this area of the park, which includes the Three Sisters Peak. Luckily, he also donated much of his land to Jefferson County Open Space.

After arriving at the saddle between two of the Three Sisters summits, your troubles of climbing seem to vanish as you digest the meaning of the words inscribed in a nearby rock, "Meetings, whether between moments or lifetimes, are certain when you are friends." Wishing newfound friends well, riders descend south from the Three Sisters Peak along the Sisters Trail. The first part of this descent delivers tight, rocky sections; big drop-offs; and a number of steeps. After connecting with the Hidden Fawn Trail, the route offers a welcome contrast to the Sisters Trail in the form of a smooth and mellow cruise on wide singletrack back to your vehicle.

Miles and Directions

0.0 Start riding on the East Evergreen Mountain Trail, heading in a southwesterly direction.

0.2 The East Evergreen Mountain trail intersects with the Ranch View Trail. Bear left here, continuing on the Evergreen Mountain Trail heading south.

2.2 The East Evergreen Mountain Trail becomes the West Evergreen Mountain Trail and intersects with the Summit Trail on the left. Bear left onto the Summit Trail, passing the Scenic View Trail on your right. Just after passing the Scenic View Trail, bear right where the Summit Trail loops back to itself, heading up Evergreen Mountain in a counterclockwise direction. (**Option:** Riders can opt to take the short 0.2-mile Scenic View Trail to an overlook of an old ranch house.)

3.6 Return to the junction of the East/West Evergreen Mountain Trail and the Summit Trail. Bear left, continuing on the West Evergreen Mountain Trail.

4.7 The West Evergreen Mountain Trail intersects with the Wild Iris Loop Trail. Bear left onto the Wild Iris Loop Trail as it heads west through a meadow.

5.0 Cross Buffalo Park Road and enter into the west parking area of Alderfer/Three Sisters Park. Bear left onto the Bluebird Trail, heading in a northerly direction. (**Option:** At this point riders can also bear right onto the Buffalo Park Road and return to their vehicles.)

5.3 The Bluebird Trail intersects with the Homestead Trail. Bear left onto the Homestead Trail.

5.7 The Homestead Trail intersects with the Silver Fox Trail. Bear left onto the Silver Fox Trail, heading east.

5.8 The Silver Fox Trail intersects with the Ponderosa Trail. Bear left onto the Ponderosa Trail, continuing in an easterly direction.

5.9 The Ponderosa Trail intersects with the Sisters Trail. Bear left onto the Sisters Trail, heading north.

6.5 Reach the top of the Three Sisters rock formation. Descend via the Sisters Trail.

6.9 The Sisters Trail intersects with the Hidden Fawn Trail. Bear left onto the Hidden Fawn Trail as it continues north.

7.5 The Hidden Fawn Trail intersects with the Wilmot Trail on your left. Continue riding south on the Hidden Fawn Trail toward the trailhead.

7.7 Arrive at the trailhead and your vehicle.

Ride Information

Trail Information

Evergreen Park and Recreation District, Evergreen; (303) 674-6441

Jefferson County Open Space Trails Hotline, Evergreen; (303) 271-5975

Jefferson County Open Space, (303) 271-5925; http://jeffco.us/parks/parks-and-trails/

Local Events and Attractions

Evergreen Music Festival & Art Show at Evergreen Lake, July; (720) 515-8594

Hiwan Homestead Museum, Evergreen; (720) 497-7650

Restaurants

The Evergreen Inn, Evergreen; (303) 674-5495

The Whippletree Restaurant, Evergreen; (303) 670-7348

Da Kind Soups, Evergreen; (303) 674-7687

Willow Creek Restaurant, Evergreen; (303) 674-9463

Tequila's Mexican Restaurant, Evergreen; (303) 679-1913

43 Meyer Ranch Park

Meyer Ranch Park offers riders one of the milder singletrack rides in all of Jefferson County. As such, it makes for a great beginner's ride. However, the area network of trails accommodates riders of all abilities. The easier Owl's Perch and Lodgepole Loop Trails are ideal for beginners, while the Sunny Aspen and Old Ski Run Trails steadily climb to an overlook. There are no sections of the route that are particularly strenuous or technical, although riding in excess of 8,000 feet elevation does require one to be in good physical condition. The short 4.4 miles of this route take riders through wide-open meadows and dense woodland.

Start: The Meyer Ranch Park trailhead
Distance: 4.4-mile double lariat
Elevation gain: 830 feet
Riding time: Advanced riders, 30 minutes; intermediate riders, 30-60 minutes
Fitness effort: Physically easy to moderate due to the short length of the trail. The going gets tougher as you climb along the Sunny Aspen and Old Ski Run Trails, near the trail's high point.
Difficulty: Technically easy to moderate due to smoother, hard-packed singletrack that occasionally rolls over more technical rockier sections
Terrain: Singletrack and doubletrack through meadows and mixed conifer forests over hard and smooth terrain

Seasons: May-Oct
Maps: *DeLorme: Colorado Atlas & Gazetteer,* page 40; *USGS:* Conifer, CO; Jefferson County Open Space Meyer Ranch Park map
Nearest town: Aspen Park
Other trail users: Hikers, bird-watchers, and horseback riders
Dog friendly: Yes
Trail contact: Jefferson County Open Space; (303) 271-5925; http://jeffco.us/parks/ parks-and-trails/; or Jefferson County Open Space Trails Hotline, Evergreen; (303) 271-5975

Getting there: From Denver drive west on I-70 for roughly 15 miles to CO 470. Drive south on CO 470 for roughly 5.8 miles before bearing right and heading west onto US 285 (Hampden Avenue). Drive on US 285 for roughly 11.6 miles before turning right onto South Turkey Creek Road. Pull into the Meyer Ranch Park parking lot.
From South Denver drive west on US 285 (Hampden Avenue) for roughly 25 miles. Turn right onto South Turkey Creek Road and pull into the Meyer Ranch Park parking lot. Trailhead GPS: N39 32.766' / W105 16.353'

The Ride

Meyer Ranch Park takes its name from Norman and Ethel Meyer, who acquired the land in 1950 and operated a successful grazing and haying business until 1986, when Jefferson County Open Space acquired the land. Long before the Meyers moved in, the land was owned by Louis Ramboz, who purchased it from its original homesteader, Duncan McIntyre, in 1883. While Ramboz worked his ranch primarily

Cruising through the Old Ski Run Trail.

for hay, timber, and cattle until 1912, legend suggests that he leased parts of his ranch to the P.T. Barnum Circus as the winter quarters for circus animals. While remodeling the house in 1955, Norman Meyer stumbled across a wooden board inscribed with the words CIRCUS TOWN, 1889.

Riders begin by climbing through lush meadows that display a variety of wildflowers including columbine, shooting star, and wood lily. After connecting with the Lodgepole Loop Trail, riders continue climbing through evergreen and aspen forests along soft and smooth singletrack. The Sunny Aspen Trail challenges even the most accomplished of riders with moderately technical sections that include steep terrain and water bars.

Riders continue on the Old Ski Run Trail, which passes through a portion of the park that was once used as a ski hill in the 1940s. The climbing continues over wide, smooth singletrack and through mixed conifer and aspen forests.

The switchbacks that lie on the loop of the Old Ski Run Trail are moderately tight and offer a challenge before the trail begins its descent on smooth and fast singletrack. Shortly after passing the point where the Old Ski Run Trail forked to create its loop, a switchback lies in ambush of riders who are speeding too fast. The remaining descent offers little in the way of moguls. Riders can make short work of their speedy descents back to their vehicles.

Miles and Directions

0.0 Begin climbing in a westerly direction on the wide doubletrack of the Owl's Perch Trail.

0.1 After passing the restroom, the Owl's Perch Trail forks. Bear left onto the singletrack of the Owl's Perch Trail, and climb into a mixed conifer and aspen forest.

0.3 The Owl's Perch Trail intersects with the Lodgepole Loop Trail. Bear right onto the Lodgepole Loop Trail, heading west.

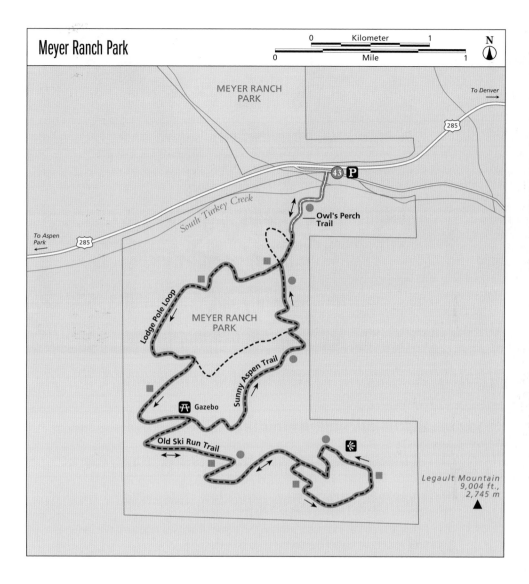

Kilometer

Mile

N

MEYER RANCH
PARK

To Denver

285

South Turkey Creek

Owl's Perch
Trail

To Aspen
Park

285

Lodge Pole Loop

MEYER RANCH
PARK

Sunny Aspen Trail

Gazebo

Old Ski Run Trail

Legault Mountain
9,004 ft.,
2,745 m

0.9 The Lodgepole Loop Trail intersects with the Sunny Aspen Trail. Bear right onto the Sunny Aspen Trail, and continue climbing in a southerly direction.

1.2 The Sunny Aspen Trail intersects with the Old Ski Run Trail by a gazebo. Bear right onto the Old Ski Run Trail, continuing your climb in a southerly direction.

2.0 The Old Ski Run Trail forks, creating a loop of itself. Bear right at the fork, climbing in a counterclockwise direction.

2.4 Arrive at a point where the Old Ski Run Trail meets a worn footpath. Here you can bear right and ride up the technically and physically challenging path or leave your bikes aside and walk up the short spur to rock outcroppings providing a bit of a view. After taking in the view, continue descending along the Old Ski Run Trail.

One of the few clearings in an otherwise densely forested trail with westerly views of Aspen Park and US 285.

2.6 Arrive at the fork where the Old Ski Run Trail creates a loop of itself. Continue your descent along the Old Ski Run Trail, heading in a westerly direction.

3.4 Reach the intersection where the Old Ski Run Trail intersected with the Sunny Aspen Trail by the gazebo. Bear right here, continuing your descent on the Sunny Aspen Trail.

3.9 The Sunny Aspen Trail intersects with the Lodgepole Loop Trail. Bear right, continuing on the Lodgepole Loop Trail, descending in a northerly direction.

4.1 The Lodgepole Loop Trail intersects with the Owl's Perch Trail. Bear right onto the Owl's Perch Trail, and return toward the start.

4.4 Arrive at your vehicle.

Ride Information

Trail Information

Jefferson County Open Space, (303) 271-5925; http://jeffco.us/parks/parks-and-trails/

Local Events and Attractions

Colorado Trail, 470-mile trail from Denver to Durango

Restaurants

Coney Dog Stand, Conifer; (303) 838-4210

Golden Stix, Conifer; (303) 838-5208

Brooks Place Tavern, Conifer; (303) 816-1499

DW's 285 Diner, Conifer; (303) 816-2515

44 Coyote Song Trail

The Coyote Song Trail offers an easy, short ride through wide-open meadows. The route travels along wide singletrack as it passes intriguing red rock formations. After connecting with a paved bike path, riders descend on a dirt road. From the dirt road riders connect to the Lyons Back singletrack, which crosses a low-lying ridge of Lyons Hogback. From the ridge top it's a moderately rocky descent to the wide singletrack that returns you to your vehicle. When combined with the riding in Deer Creek Canyon (ride 45), located just up the road, riders can extend their route to more than 14 miles.

Start: The Coyote Song trailhead on the north side of Deer Creek Canyon Road

Distance: 4.6-mile lariat

Elevation gain: 350 feet

Riding time: Advanced riders, 15-20 minutes; intermediate riders, 30-45 minutes

Fitness effort: Physically easy due to the trail's relatively short length and insignificant elevation gain

Difficulty: Technically easy with some rougher, rockier riding along the singletrack of the hogback

Terrain: Singletrack, dirt road, and paved bike path for mostly smooth riding through meadows

and over a hogback, passing red rock formations along the Rocky Mountain foothills

Seasons: Mar-Nov

Maps: *DeLorme: Colorado Atlas & Gazetteer,* page 40; *USGS:* Indian Hills, CO

Nearest town: Littleton

Other trail users: Hikers

Dog friendly: Yes, although trail passes through coyote country and provides no water

Trail contact: Jefferson County Open Space; (303) 271-5925; http://jeffco.us/parks/parks-and-trails/; or Jefferson County Open Space Trails Hotline, Evergreen; (303) 271-5975

Getting there: From Denver drive west on I-70 for roughly 15 miles to CO 470. Drive east on CO 470 to the Kipling Street exit. Exit southbound and drive on South Kipling Street until it bears right (west) and becomes West Ute Avenue at a stop sign. Drive for 0.2 mile on West Ute Avenue before bearing right onto Deer Creek Canyon Road. Drive on Deer Creek Canyon Road for roughly 2.1 miles before bearing left into a pullout just before South Valley Road. The Coyote Song trailhead will be directly across from where you parked on Deer Creek Canyon Road. Trailhead GPS: N39 33.077' / W105 08.349'

The Ride

The Coyote Song Trail is part of the 909-acre South Valley Park and is ideal for beginner mountain bikers. According to archaeologists, early hunter-gatherers began living in the area over 7,500 years ago.

From the trailhead riders begin by climbing moderately, passing through a small ridge of red rock formations. The trail continues over wide but sandy singletrack as it passes through meadows of piñon pine and scrub oak reminiscent of riding in Moab,

Walking it down the set of stone stairs of the Lyons Hogback.

Utah. Lending an air of authenticity to this Moab-like trail, these vertical red rock formations look like petrified whales breaching the surface of the earth.

Seventy million years ago these great sandstone ledges formed the beaches and sands of a vast inland sea. Over time the sand and sediment compressed under extraordinary pressure and heat into solid masses of sandstone rock. Folding and faulting of the earth's crust gradually raised these monolithic formations that slope as much as 90 degrees.

Among the notorious outlaws that lived in the Deer Creek Canyon area was Horsethief Thompson, a onetime member of the Hole in the Wall Gang. In fact, tales continue to circulate about a cache of loot that lies hidden in the area surrounding the site of Lockheed Martin.

Another resident of ill repute was alleged cannibal Alferd Packer. Having served a 17-year sentence at the state penitentiary for making a meal of his prospecting companions near Breckenridge, Packer in 1901 settled in to the sleepy little town of Critchell, along the south fork of Deer Creek. He worked as a hired hand on local ranches, always maintaining his innocence, and many of his neighbors took a liking to him. After his death in 1907, Packer was buried in a Littleton cemetery. Bishop Frank Hamilton Rice led a party of followers to Packer's grave in 1940. Rice's ceremony included an exorcism of Packard's sins, which were cast onto a goat tied to a nearby tree.

Nearing a mile into your ride, you may notice a coyote den off to your left. The den lies in a batch of scrub oak. Oftentimes, particularly between April and June, you can glimpse coyotes and their pups sitting outside of their den, identifiable by their rust-colored bodies with markings of white and gray on the throat and belly. Their vocalizations range from short yips to barks to extended clear howling. These songs call members of the pack together as well communicate their locations.

Generally, coyotes keep to themselves and are shy around humans. However, on rare occasions coyotes have been known to approach people and attack unattended pets. Should you see a coyote, it's best to just relax and enjoy the wildlife from a distance; however, if it comes near, speak in a loud and authoritative voice. Because coyotes are opportunistic hunters, never allow your pets to go unattended and never move toward a coyote. Should the coyote continue its approach, try throwing sticks and rocks to scare the animal away.

After connecting with the Cathy Johnson Trail, riders enter the Ken-Caryl Ranch Foundation Open Space. The trail runs through the valley of the Dakota and Lyons Hogbacks. Riders then connect with the Columbine Trail and climb to the top of the Lyons Hogback through oak thickets. As this area hosts a critical wildlife habitat, rare plants, archaeological sites, and nesting falcons, only the trail is open to public access, so take care when crossing over it.

The Lyons Back Trail descends from the ridge of the hogback over embedded granite and a set of stone stairs. After a short and fast descent over rocks and through sandy patches, connect with the Coyote Song Trail and return to your vehicle.

Miles and Directions

0.0 Begin riding in a northeasterly direction on the smooth, wide singletrack of the Coyote Song Trail. The trail immediately crosses over the ridge of some red rock formations. Caution: These rocks are closed to all public use.

0.4 The trail forks; bear right here, following a brown trail marker sign.

0.9 The Coyote Song Trail intersects with the Lyons Back Trail on the right. Continue heading north on the Coyote Song Trail. You'll eventually loop around and over the Lyons Hogback to this junction to return to your vehicle. Note: After passing the Lyons Back Trail intersection, you'll notice Lockheed Martin (advanced technology systems/aerospace) to your left.

1.1 The Coyote Song intersects with the Swallow Trail to the left. Continue riding on the Coyote Song Trail.

1.3 The Coyote Song Trail reaches the northern terminus of the park at South Valley Road. Bear right onto the paved bike path, and descend along South Valley Road.

1.9 The South Valley Road bike path intersects with the Cathy Johnson Trail on the right. Bear right onto the gravel road of the Cathy Johnson Trail.

2.4 The Cathy Johnson Trail intersects with the Columbine Trail to the right. Bear right onto the Columbine Trail, climbing up the Lyons Hogback. (**Option:** At this point you may choose to descend on the Cathy Johnson Trail, which will deliver you roughly 1 mile south of your vehicle on Deer Creek Canyon Road.)

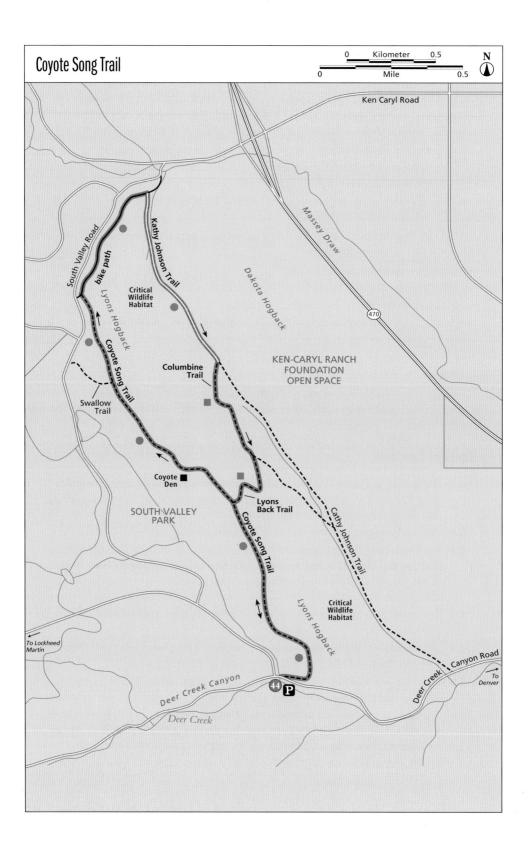

Coyote Song Trail

Ken Caryl Road

Massey Draw

South Valley Road

bike path

Kathy Johnson Trail

Dakota Hogback

470

Critical
Wildlife
Habitat

Lyons Hogback

Coyote Song Trail

Columbine
Trail

KEN-CARYL RANCH
FOUNDATION
OPEN SPACE

Swallow
Trail

Coyote
Den

Lyons
Back Trail

SOUTH VALLEY
PARK

Coyote Song Trail

Cathy Johnson Trail

Lyons Hogback

Critical
Wildlife
Habitat

To Lockheed
Martin

44 P

Deer Creek Canyon

Deer Creek

Deer Creek Canyon Road

To
Denver

Sharing the trail amid impressive red rock formations.

2.9 The Columbine Trail intersects with the Pass Trail and becomes the Lyons Back Trail. Bear right here and continue on the Pass/Lyons Back Trail, heading underneath a set of power lines.

3.2 Arrive at the summit of the Lyons Hogback and the boundaries of the Ken-Caryl Ranch Foundation Open Space and the Jefferson County Open Space. From here continue descending along the Lyons Back Trail.

3.5 The Lyons Back Trail intersects with the Coyote Song Trail. Bear left onto the Coyote Song Trail, and retrace your path to the trailhead.

4.6 Arrive at your vehicle.

Ride Information

Trail Information

Jefferson County Open Space, (303) 271-5925; http://jeffco.us/parks/parks-and-trails/

Denver Parks and Recreation, Parks Division; (720) 913-1311

Jefferson County Open Space, ranger staff; (303) 904-0249

Ken-Caryl Ranch Foundation Open Space, (303) 979-1876 ext. 129

Local Events and Attractions

Chatfield State Park, Littleton; (303) 791-7275

Deer Creek Canyon Park (ride 45)

Restaurants

Los Dos Portrillos, Highlands Ranch; (720) 529-0299

Café Terracotta, Littleton; (303) 794-6054

MC's Brooklyn Pizzeria, Littleton; (303) 763-8299

45 Deer Creek Canyon Park

Mountain bikers can access great singletrack trails in Deer Creek Canyon Park. The park encompasses 1,722 acres and 12.8 miles of trails. While the Meadowlark, Golden Eagle, and Homesteader Trails are reserved for hikers only, that still leaves roughly 7.5 miles of trails for bikers. When combined with the Coyote Song Trail (ride 44), located just down the road, riders can extend their route to more than 14 miles. The park offers some challenging terrain: loose, football-size rocks; steep climbs; and exposed areas. But it also offers fast descents on hard-packed terrain through ponderosa forests. In short, it's a great ride for intermediate to more advanced riders, offering views of the foothills' hogbacks and the Denver skyline.

Start: The Plymouth Creek Trail trailhead off Grizzly Drive

Distance: 9.6-mile double lariat

Elevation gain: 1,800 feet

Riding time: Advanced riders, 1.5 hours; intermediate riders, 2-2.5 hours

Fitness effort: Physically moderate due to the challenging climb to Red Mesa. Some sections are physically challenging, particularly the climbing that is required at the trail's outset.

Difficulty: Technically moderate to challenging due to the steeper and rockier sections when both climbing and descending

Terrain: Singletrack and doubletrack over loose sand and rock. While much of this trail is exposed, riders do enter into thick stands of ponderosa pine as they gain elevation.

Seasons: May-Oct

Maps: *DeLorme: Colorado Atlas & Gazetteer*, page 40; *USGS:* Indian Hills, CO; Jefferson County Open Space Deer Creek Canyon Park map

Nearest town: Littleton

Other trail users: Hikers and horseback riders

Dog friendly: Yes

Trail contact: Jefferson County Open Space; (303) 271-5925; http://jeffco.us/parks/parks-and-trails/; or Jefferson County Open Space Trails Hotline, Evergreen; (303) 271-5975

Getting there: From Denver drive west on I-70 for roughly 15 miles to CO 470. Drive east on CO 470 to the Kipling Street exit. Exit southbound and drive on South Kipling Street until it bears right (west) and becomes West Ute Avenue at a stop sign. Drive for 0.2 mile on West Ute Avenue before bearing right onto Deer Creek Canyon Road. Drive on Deer Creek Canyon Road for roughly 3 miles before bearing left onto Grizzly Drive. Drive on Grizzly Drive for 0.4 mile before bearing right into the parking lot. Park in spaces provided at the Deer Creek Canyon Park trailhead. Trailhead GPS: N39 32.592' / W105 09.125'

The Ride

The area surrounding Deer Creek Canyon Park once served as holdup and hideout for a variety of characters as colorful as the nearby sandstone is red. This area was once a campground for the Arapaho and Ute Indians. These nomadic tribes would spend their winters here, scouting out over the eastern plains looking for elk and buffalo as well as for raiding marauders.

Looking east onto the eastern plains from Plymouth Mountain Trail.

From the trailhead riders descend a short, sinuous track before starting their climb. The climb comes soon enough, offering switchbacks over wide singletrack strewn with water bars. After passing the intersection for the hikers-only Meadowlark Trail, riders have to negotiate a physically challenging and technically moderate hill climb before the trail becomes a smoother doubletrack. At this point riders pass through a cool riparian area of mixed vegetation and conifers. Adding to the lushness of this section are the wild raspberries that grow trailside.

Connecting to the Plymouth Mountain Trail, the route travels along narrow but smooth singletrack beneath the shade of an aspen and ponderosa pine forest. As the Plymouth Mountain Trail veers south, riders are greeted with views of the eastern plains, the Denver skyline, and tilting sandstone red rocks. Plymouth Mountain takes its name from John Williamson, who left Plymouth, England, to homestead the area in 1872.

Just to the southwest lies Sampson Mountain, named after the African-American minister who discovered gold there in 1874. Legend has it that Jesse James favored Sampson Mountain as one of his hideouts. While cooling off after a train robbery, James stumbled upon the Mielke family who lived on Sampson Mountain. James reportedly gave them a gold nugget for their hospitality.

After the sweeping views of Plymouth Mountain, riders continue climbing over a number of switchbacks that lead in a southerly direction. After passing the intersection with the Homesteader Trail, riders are rewarded with a fast descent.

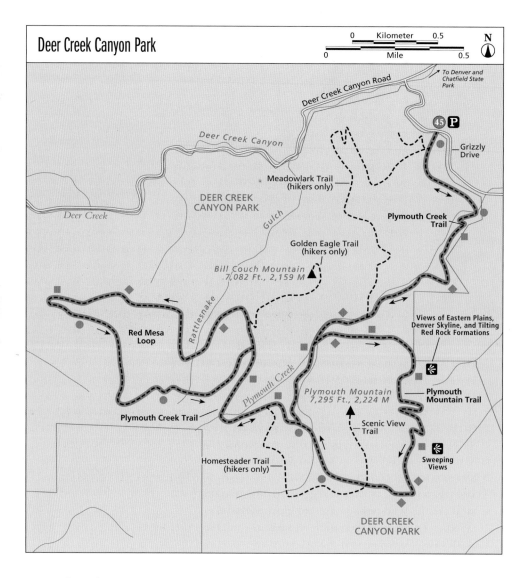

Deer Creek Canyon Park

0   Kilometer   0.5

0   Mile   0.5

N

To Denver and
Chatfield State
Park

45 P

Grizzly
Drive

Deer Creek Canyon Road

Deer Creek Canyon

Meadowlark Trail
(hikers only)

DEER CREEK
CANYON PARK

Deer Creek

Plymouth Creek
Trail

Gulch

Golden Eagle Trail
(hikers only)

Bill Couch Mountain
7,082 Ft., 2,159 M

Views of Eastern Plains,
Denver Skyline, and Tilting
Red Rock Formations

Red Mesa
Loop

Rattlesnake

Plymouth
Mountain Trail

Plymouth Creek

Plymouth Mountain
7,295 Ft., 2,224 M

Plymouth Creek Trail

Scenic View
Trail

Sweeping
Views

Homesteader Trail
(hikers only)

DEER CREEK
CANYON PARK

It is short-lived, however, as riders will climb once again, this time on the Plymouth Creek Trail.

From the Plymouth Creek Trail, riders link to the Red Mesa Loop, which extends to the park's western boundary. The initial climb up Red Mesa traverses thick forests and open meadows that reach farther west into Rattlesnake Gulch and the old Couch Ranch.

From the top of the mesa, riders descend rapidly over prime singletrack and through mixed conifer forests. The descent along the Plymouth Creek Trail is quite rocky and sandy, so check your speed, as other trail users may be coming up. There are also a few sandy switchbacks that don't present themselves until you're right above them, so ride within your limits when returning to your vehicle.

Miles and Directions

0.0 Begin riding south on the Plymouth Creek Trail.

1.1 The Plymouth Creek Trail intersects with the Meadowlark Trail to your right. Continue climbing on the Plymouth Creek Trail. The Meadowlark Trail is a hikers-only trail.

1.7 The Plymouth Creek Trail intersects with the Plymouth Mountain Trail to the left. Bear left onto the Plymouth Mountain Trail, continuing in an easterly direction as you continue climbing.

3.3 The Plymouth Mountain Trail levels off onto doubletrack as it starts heading northwest.

3.5 The Plymouth Mountain Trail intersects with the multiuse Scenic View Trail on the right, and shortly thereafter the hikers-only Homesteader Trail on the left. Continue riding in a northwesterly direction along the Plymouth Mountain Trail. (**Option:** Riders can choose to ride the 0.4 mile to the top of the Scenic View Trail, where they are offered 360-degree views. There is one steep section to this trail.)

3.9 The Plymouth Mountain Trail intersects with the Plymouth Creek Trail. Bear left here, continuing on the Plymouth Creek Trail and climbing in a northwesterly direction.

4.1 The Plymouth Creek Trail intersects with the Homesteader Trail. Continue on the Plymouth Creek Trail.

4.6 The Plymouth Creek Trail intersects with the Red Mesa Loop. Continue straight along the Red Mesa Loop, riding the loop in a counterclockwise direction.

4.8 The Red Mesa Loop intersects with the hikers-only Golden Eagle Trail to the right. Continue climbing along the Red Mesa Loop.

6.2 Reach the top of the mesa and begin descending.

7.2 The Red Mesa Loop finishes its loop and again intersects with the Plymouth Creek Trail. Bear right at this point onto the Plymouth Creek Trail, and return the way you came.

7.8 The Plymouth Creek Trail intersects with the Plymouth Mountain Trail. Bear left here, continuing on the Plymouth Creek Trail in a northerly direction.

8.2 The Plymouth Creek Trail again intersects with the Plymouth Mountain Trail on the right. Bear left here, continuing on the Plymouth Creek Trail toward the start.

9.6 Arrive at your vehicle.

Ride Information

Trail Information

Jefferson County Open Space, (303) 271-5925; http://jeffco.us/parks/parks-and-trails/
    Denver Parks and Recreation, Parks Division; (720) 913-1311
    Ken-Caryl Ranch Foundation Open Space, (303) 979-1876 ext. 129

Local Events and Attractions

Chatfield State Park, Littleton; (303) 791-7275
    Coyote Song Trail (ride 44)

Restaurants

Los Dos Portrillos, Highlands Ranch; (720) 529-0299
    Café Terracotta, Littleton; (303) 794-6054
    MC's Brooklyn Pizzeria, Littleton; (303) 763-8299

46 Waterton Canyon

Waterton Canyon is a favorite trail among Denver-area residents. As such, it may be crowded during the weekends. The trail begins on a wide, dirt service road as it travels through the canyon. Following the South Platte River, this section of the trail offers a mellow cruise, so it's a great family ride. The trail, however, becomes increasingly difficult, with steeper climbs and moderate switchbacks, as riders near the beginning of the 470-mile Colorado Trail.

Start: Trailhead of the Colorado Trail in Waterton Canyon

Distance: 17.5-mile lariat, with innumerable options off the 470-mile Colorado Trail. Note: If you do decide to continue on the Colorado Trail, special arrangements for your return must be considered, as these routes will not lead you back to your vehicle at the mouth of Waterton Canyon.

Elevation gain: 1,200 feet

Riding time: Advanced riders, 1.5 hours; intermediate riders, 2-2.5 hours

Fitness effort: Physically moderate. Although there isn't any significant elevation gain, there are a number of tougher and steeper climbs.

Difficulty: Technically moderate. The first 6 miles offers an easy, scenic ride along the South Platte River on an improved dirt road. The singletrack of the Roxborough Connection offers some tight ascending switchbacks, with sudden tight twists along the trail on the descent.

Terrain: Singletrack, doubletrack, and improved dirt road; the single- and double-track offer a variety of terrain: sand, rocks, and softened forest growth

Seasons: Open daily from 4 a.m. to 9 p.m. year-round (Roxborough Connection may only be available May-Oct)

Maps: *DeLorme: Colorado Atlas & Gazetteer,* page 50; *USGS:* Kassler, CO, and Platte Canyon, CO; *Trails Illustrated:* #135, Deckers, Rampart Range, CO; Waterton Canyon Map, Denver Water

Nearest town: Littleton

Other trail users: Horseback riders, anglers, campers, hikers, and picnickers

Dog friendly: No. Dogs are not allowed in the canyon for two reasons: they may contaminate drinking water, and they may disturb the resident herd of bighorn sheep in the canyon.

Trail contact: Pike National Forest, South Platte Ranger District, Morrison; (303) 275-5610

Getting there: From Denver take I-25 south to exit 207B, and then drive south on US 85, which will Y shortly after the exit; stay to your left. Take US 85 south for 10 miles until reaching CO 470. Veer right onto CO 470, heading west. Drive west on CO 470 for a few miles before exiting at Wadsworth Boulevard. Following signs for Waterton Canyon, bear left, driving under CO 470, and pick up CO 121 south. Drive south on CO 121 for roughly 4.5 miles before turning left into Waterton Canyon State Park. The parking lot will be on your left. Trailhead GPS: N39 29.455' / W105 05.642'

The Ride

The eastern end of the 470-mile Colorado Trail sits on an improved dirt road in Waterton Canyon. Following the former railroad bed of the Denver, South Park, &

Riders converge at the junction of the Colorado Trail and Roxborough State Park connection atop Russell Ridge.

Pacific Railroad through Waterton Canyon, the first 6 miles of this route is a mellow cruise along the South Platte River—admittedly, not the most technical. What this lacks in technical challenge, it delivers in natural beauty and historical significance.

On July 6, 1820, Stephen H. Long (remembered in the naming of Longs Peak) led an expedition to the mouth of what is now Waterton Canyon. As a member of the US Army Corps of Engineers, Long was instructed to find the headwaters of the Platte, Arkansas, and Red Rivers. His expedition camped at the site where the South Platte River emerges from the mountains. His camp would become the town of Waterton and even later the location of the Denver Union Water Company, forebear of the Denver Water Department—the largest water district in the Front Range. In 1912 the Kassler Treatment Plant, located at the mouth of Waterton Canyon, became the first slow-sand water filtration plant west of the Mississippi River and just one of three in the country with the technology.

About 3 miles from the trailhead and the mouth of the canyon, the Platte Canyon Intake Dam and the Marston Diversion Dam direct South Platte and Blue River water to Marston Reservoir. At mile 6.1 the Strontia Springs Dam rises 243 feet above the South Platte streambed and diverts water into a 3.4-mile-long tunnel under the mountains to the Foothills Water Treatment Plant.

As you head east from the Strontia Springs Dam, the road begins to climb. Within a mile the Colorado Trail's singletrack begins to your left. From here the trail rises out of the canyon to Russell Ridge (6,560 feet), offering a moderately challenging climb. Among this section's highlights are smooth-running singletrack, thick ponderosa pine forests, and switchbacks (which deserve special attention). Intermediate riders can manage the switchbacks with careful balance and control, while advanced riders can spin their way to the top with minimal effort. The last switchback, which breaks right

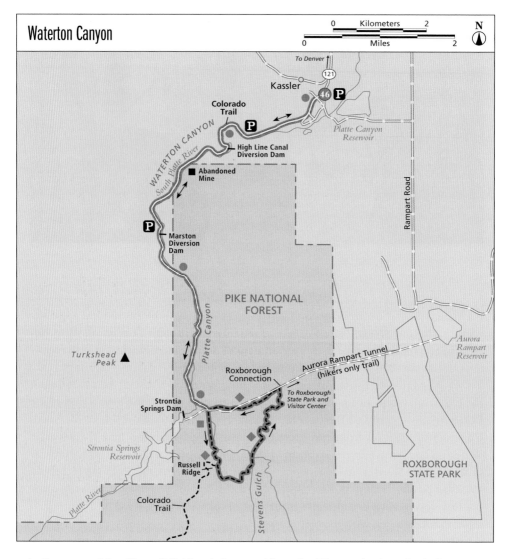

Waterton Canyon

0   Kilometers   2
0   Miles   2

N

To Denver

121

Kassler

46 P

Colorado
Trail

P

Platte Canyon
Reservoir

WATERTON CANYON

South Platte River

High Line Canal
Diversion Dam

■ Abandoned
Mine

Rampart Road

P

Marston
Diversion
Dam

PIKE NATIONAL
FOREST

Platte Canyon

Aurora
Rampart
Reservoir

Turkshead ▲
Peak

Roxborough
Connection

Aurora Rampart Tunnel
(hikers only trail)

To Roxborough
State Park and
Visitor Center

Strontia
Springs Dam

Russell
Ridge

ROXBOROUGH
STATE PARK

Strontia Springs
Reservoir

Platte River

Colorado
Trail

Stevens Gulch

before summiting Russell Ridge, is beset with rocks. Keep spinning, don't forget to smile, and you'll make it with relative ease.

Atop the ridge the Colorado Trail will continue southwest to Durango. To begin your return of the Waterton Canyon route, you'll have to turn off the Colorado Trail at this point and follow the sign marking Roxborough State Park.

The singletrack of this section of trail is sweet. Thick overgrowth at the section's beginning makes for very narrow and tight paths. The trail weaves its way through cool forests and offers riders a number of screams. One such scream comes at mile 8.2. The singletrack descent is steep and narrow as it hugs the slope of the ridge. For an added element of fear, a tree at the bottom welcomes any would-be tree-hugger. The trail winds through forests, over creeks, and through one meadow before delivering another tight spot at mile 10.8. A big, rocky drop-off invites you to take it down the center.

From here, ride for another mile through heavy forest. Finishing the Roxborough Loop leaves the rider with a feeling of pleasant amazement: How can such sweet singletrack be so close to a city? Arrive at the road where you started your ride. Bear right and top-ring it back to your vehicle.

Miles and Directions

0.0 Start at the parking lot of Waterton Canyon State Park. Ride back out of the parking lot and cross the road. The Colorado Trail sign marks the beginning of the ride into Waterton Canyon. Follow the trail around as it weaves itself onto the improved dirt road and into the canyon.

2.2 Pass an abandoned mine to your left.

3.3 Reach Marston Diversion Dam.

4.3 Cross Mill Gulch Bridge.

6.1 Reach Strontia Springs Dam and Reservoir. Beware the bighorn sheep that descend from the tall canyon walls, making their way to the Colorado Trail. A herd of twenty to thirty-five bighorn sheep lives in the canyon, remaining at low elevation all year, rather than typically traveling to higher elevation in the summer.

6.3 Reach the junction of the Roxborough Connection and the Colorado Trail. Here is where the route will return after the loop. For now, keep heading east, ascending straight on.

6.6 Reach the start of the Colorado Trail singletrack on the left side of the road. From this point the maintained dirt road is closed to public use.

8.0 Reach the top of Russell Ridge, the route's high point. At this point the Colorado Trail continues heading southwest all the way to Durango. Instead, bear left (east) onto the singletrack marked by the Roxborough State Park sign.

10.3 Here the singletrack T's. Bearing right will lead you to the Roxborough State Park and Visitor Center—however, this section of trail is off-limits to bikes. Instead, bear left and head toward Waterton Canyon. This way will lead you back to the improved dirt road on which you began your ride, just above the Strontia Springs Dam in Waterton Canyon.

11.2 As you reach the improved dirt road of the Colorado Trail in Waterton Canyon, bear right and return to your vehicle the way you came.

17.5 Arrive at your vehicle.

Ride Information

Trail Information
Colorado Division of Wildlife, Denver; (303) 291-7227

Local Events and Attractions
Chatfield State Park, Littleton; (303) 791-7275
    Roxborough State Park, Littleton; (303) 973-3959

Restaurants
Los Dos Portrillos, Highlands Ranch; (720) 529-0299
    Café Terracotta, Littleton; (303) 794-6054
    MC's Brooklyn Pizzeria, Littleton; (303) 763-8299

47 Kenosha to Georgia Pass

The Kenosha Pass to Georgia Pass ride includes awe-inspiring descents through hillside meadows and dense aspen forests, as well as technical rocky and rooty climbs. Views from the top of Georgia Pass and the Continental Divide are breathtaking, including the entire South Park basin below. The "town" of South Park, incidentally, was the inspiration for the quirky fictional town in Comedy Central's popular cartoon series *South Park*. It's actually a tourist attraction in the town of Fairplay that offers a glimpse into the life of a nineteenth-century Colorado mining town. The buildings are authentic but came from different nearby places—there wasn't actually a "town of South Park" until it opened in 1959.

Start: The trailhead for the Colorado Trail atop Kenosha Pass on the west side of US 285
Distance: 23.8-mile out-and-back
Elevation gain: 2,520 feet
Riding time: Advanced riders, 3 hours; intermediate riders, 4 hours
Fitness effort: Physically moderate to challenging due to the higher elevations at which you're riding
Difficulty: Technically moderate to challenging due to the abundance of exposed roots and rocks
Terrain: Singletrack and doubletrack. Most of this route rolls over smooth, soft forest earth. There are, however, a few rougher sections of roots and rocks. Aspen and evergreen forests,

high alpine valleys, and mountain passes form the backdrop to this incredible ride.
Seasons: July-Sept
Maps: *DeLorme: Colorado Atlas & Gazetteer,* pages 48-49; *USGS:* Jefferson, CO, and Boreas Pass, CO; *Trails Illustrated:* #105, Tarryall Mountains, Kenosha Pass, CO, and #109, Breckenridge, Tennessee Pass, CO; Pike National Forest map
Nearest town: Fairplay
Other trail users: Hikers, bikepackers, horseback riders, and backpackers
Dog friendly: Yes
Trail contact: Pike National Forest, South Park Ranger District, Fairplay; (719) 836-2031

Getting there: From Denver head west on US 285 for roughly 48 miles to Kenosha Pass. Turn right (west) into the Kenosha Pass Picnic Ground area. Park in the available spaces by the brown Colorado Trail sign. Drinking water and toilet facilities are available. Trailhead GPS: N39 24.773' / W105 45.534'; trailhead terminus/turnaround GPS: N39 27.547' / W105 55.470'

The Ride

Situated at the western edge of the Pike National Forest, the trail begins atop the 10,001-foot Kenosha Pass and continues to the 11,585-foot Georgia Pass on the Continental Divide. Aspens crowd the trail along its westerly route, making for a spectacular, although crowded, ride during the color change.

The first mile of the trail climbs moderately over smooth terrain through pine forest. The first technical section arrives soon enough. After descending rapidly through

South Park City.

a meadow and into an aspen grove, the trail switches back sharply to the left and over a group of large rocks, adding a nice wake-up call to the singletrack. After roughly 2.4 miles the singletrack exits the forest and opens up onto a hillside meadow sometimes awash with wildflowers. In view are the Continental Divide and Mount Gugot (13,370 feet), both straight ahead. Georgia Pass (11,585 feet) lies to the northwest, while all of South Park opens to the south.

South Park is an expansive 900-square-mile basin in a sea of rolling mountains. At the northwestern edge lies the small town of Fairplay, which is home to the South Park City Museum. After gold was discovered in 1859, eager prospectors flocked to the South Park Valley in droves. Within months mining camps such as Tarryall, Leavick, Eureka, and Buckskin Joe dotted the edge. With increased development and trade, these rough-and-tumble mining camps metamorphosed into flourishing communities until all the gold was gone. The restored mining camp of South Park City features thirty-four buildings and the businesses that made life in nineteenth-century Colorado livable. This museum invites you to take a step back in time and listen for the slightly out-of-tune piano heard from Rache's Place. Farther up the street you'll notice the Simpkins General Store, the Garo School, and Merriam's City Drug Store complete with all the early-day tinctures, remedies, and poultices.

After crossing Deadman Gulch, where seven prospectors were killed by Ute Indians in 1859, the trail becomes very narrow as it runs its course over large exposed roots. As you begin the last 6-mile push to Georgia Pass, the route climbs steadily.

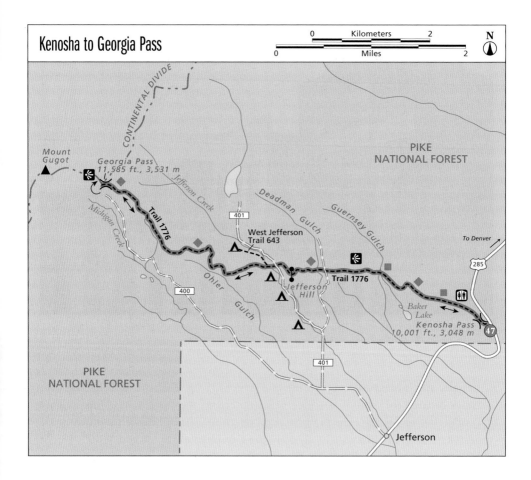

Upon reaching FR 400, bear left and pedal to Georgia Pass, where you turn around and enjoy the ride in reverse.

The descent from Georgia Pass to Jefferson Creek Road is fast and rocky. After crossing Deadman Gulch in the opposite direction, begin the tough climb through the meadow to the gate. From the gate it's a fast and smooth descent through clustered aspens to the floor of South Park Valley.

The final 1.5 miles to Kenosha Pass and your vehicle is perhaps the most exhilarating stretch. Smooth-running singletrack through quiet stands of aspen and pine offer the weary rider a certain peace-in-motion. The trail's narrow width, its smooth running course, and the close-standing trunks of pine and aspen enfold the rider into the forest's high society. Riders silently track their tires into the soft belly of the earth, revealing unto no one but themselves and the surrounding forest the simple pleasures shared by two.

Miles and Directions

0.0   Start at the Colorado Trail 1776 trailhead atop Kenosha Pass. Begin riding through serene groves of aspen and pine on smooth and hard-packed singletrack.

2.5   Cross Guernsey Creek and continue riding on the singletrack.

4.3   Cross Deadman Gulch and continue riding in a westerly direction, negotiating through a tough root singletrack section as it winds its way up a hillside marked by a miniature forest of pine saplings.

5.1   Pass through a gate, closing it behind you, and continue riding through a moderately technical rocky singletrack section.

5.8   Descend through lush forests of pine and aspen before arriving at FR 401 (Jefferson Creek Road). Cross FR 401 and Jefferson Creek, continuing on the Colorado Trail to Georgia Pass. Just after crossing Jefferson Creek, ride to where the singletrack intersects with a doubletrack. Bear right onto this doubletrack, following signs for the Colorado Trail and Georgia Pass.

6.0   Notice the continuation of the Colorado Trail singletrack bearing left into the pine forest. A sign on the right reads WEST JEFFERSON TRAIL 643, JEFFERSON CREEK CAMPGROUND AND GEORGIA PASS VIA TRAIL 643. Continue to follow signs for the Colorado Trail and Georgia Pass, veering left onto the singletrack. At this point you're about 6 miles from Georgia Pass.

7.7   The Colorado Trail intersects with the Michigan Creek Road Trail. Continue on the Colorado Trail in a northerly direction, passing the Michigan Creek Road Trail on your left (west).

10.5   Near the timberline, with views of Mount Gugot and Bald Mountain immediately to your left. Continue climbing over tundra-like terrain to Georgia Pass. Since the area is treeless, cairns mark the path of travel.

11.9   Arrive at FR 400. Bear left and ride to the top of Georgia Pass. Turn around here and retrace your tracks back to your vehicle.

23.8   Arrive back at your vehicle.

Ride Information

Trail Information

Pike National Forest, South Park Ranger District, Fairplay; (719) 836-2031

Local Events and Attractions

Fairplay Beach Recreation Area, Fairplay; (719) 836-4279

Forest Service Mountain Bike Trails, Fairplay; (719) 836-4279

South Park City Museum, Fairplay; (719) 836-2387

Restaurants

Brown Burro Café, Fairplay; (719) 836-2804

Silver Scoop Creamery, Fairplay; (719) 836-3403

Mason's High Country BBQ, Fairplay; (719) 836-3465

48 Kenosha Pass to Lost Creek Wilderness

The stretch of the Colorado Trail that extends from the top of Kenosha Pass to the Lost Creek Wilderness Area is one of the best fall foliage rides. Aside from riding through thick stands of aspen, the trail opens out onto views of the entire South Park Valley and Tarryall Mountains, where numerous stands of aspen dot the landscape. The trail rolls over hard-packed and sometimes sandy singletrack through forests and meadowlands before ending at the Lost Creek Wilderness Area, where no bikes are allowed. While not offering the elevation gain nor the 360-degree views of its west side cousin (ride 47: Kenosha to Georgia Pass), the Kenosha Pass to the Lost Creek Wilderness Area stretch offers a colorful ride guaranteed to satisfy.

Start: The trailhead for the Colorado Trail atop Kenosha Pass on the east side of US 285.

Distance: 13.2-mile out-and-back

Elevation gain: 1,200 feet

Riding time: Advanced riders, 2 hours; intermediate riders, 2.5-3 hours

Fitness effort: Physically moderate to challenging due to some extended hill climbs at elevations exceeding 10,000 feet

Difficulty: Technically moderate to challenging in spots due to some steeper, rockier sections

Terrain: Singletrack that rolls through mixed conifer forests, aspen glens, and meadows; rocks and a good deal of roots line the trail

Seasons: July-Oct

Maps: *DeLorme: Colorado Atlas & Gazetteer*, page 49; *USGS:* Jefferson, CO, Mount Logan, CO, and Observatory Rock, CO; *Trails Illustrated:* #105, Tarryall Mountains, Kenosha Pass, CO; Pike National Forest map

Nearest town: Fairplay

Other trail users: Hikers, horseback riders, and backpackers

Dog friendly: Yes, although the trail atop Kenosha Pass that leads to the wetland is off-limits to dogs and other pets

Trail contact: Pike National Forest, South Park Ranger District, Fairplay; (719) 836-2031

Getting there: From Denver head west on US 285 for roughly 48 miles to Kenosha Pass. Turn left (east) into the Kenosha Pass Picnic Ground area. Park in the available spaces by the brown Colorado Trail sign. Drinking water and toilet facilities are available. Trailhead GPS: N39 24.773' / W105 45.534'; trailhead terminus/turnaround GPS: N39 21.737' / W105 41.257'

The Ride

The nomadic tribes of the Ute Indians often crossed Kenosha Pass in their search for bison, elk, deer, and other large game that flourished in the South Park basin. With the discovery of gold in 1859, towns like Fairplay, Leadville, and Tarryall sprang up almost overnight. The Kenosha Pass Road used the already worn hunting path as a toll road and stage line that serviced the mining camps in the area. Needless to say, the race for transportation to and from the mining towns in the interior Rockies became a heated battle.

Soon after beginning the trail, riders enter a large grove of aspen trees. Soon the Tarryall Mountains and the entire South Park Valley explode into view before the trail starts climbing moderately.

Following a brief warm-up, riders awake to face the physical and technical challenge of climbing over very steep terrain of loose rock and sand. After roughly 2.5 miles of riding, however, the trail begins to descend over loose and rocky terrain before letting out onto an open meadow. As the trail wears on, the route becomes more challenging.

Here football-size rocks and tentacle-like roots threaten your progress, as the expansive views of the Tarryall Mountains tempt you to lift your eyes from the ground. From here it's a speedy descent through Johnson Gulch. This descent through aspen glens and hillside meadows is as good as any singletrack descent you're likely to come across and is, in a word, fantastic.

After crossing the creek, riders climb for roughly a half mile before reaching the

Doubletrack through aspens along the aspen-lined trail.

Lost Creek Wilderness Area boundary. The Lost Creek Wilderness Area covers roughly 120,152 acres and received protective wilderness status in 1980. From the boundary riders turn around and follow their path back to their vehicles. You'll discover that the ride takes on a different character on the return, so it is equally enjoyable.

Miles and Directions

0.0   Begin riding on the singletrack of the Colorado Trail, heading in a southeasterly direction.

0.3   Arrive at Jason Jameson Sealy's Statement on Life.

1.7   Arrive at a vista of the South Park Valley and the Collegiate Peaks.

3.0   Continue descending through Johnson Gulch, heading in a southeasterly direction.

6.0   Descend to cross the creek and arrive at a cattle-grazing area. Continue climbing on the other side of the creek.

6.6   Arrive at the Lost Creek Wilderness Area boundary. Turn around to return the way you came.

13.2   Arrive at your vehicle.

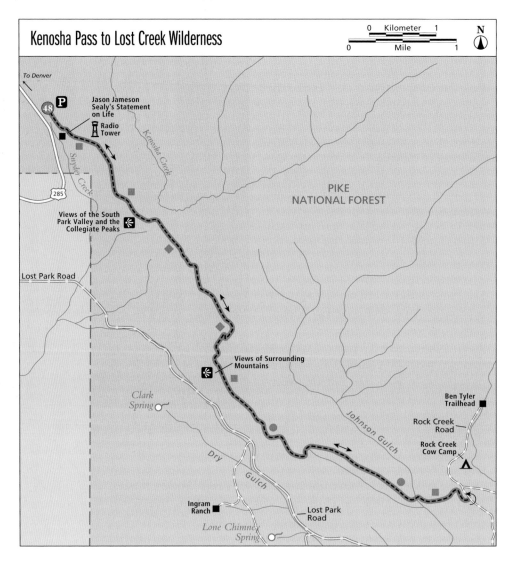

Ride Information

Trail Information

Pike National Forest, South Park Ranger District, Fairplay; (719) 836-2031

Local Events and Attractions

Fairplay Beach Recreation Area, Fairplay; (719) 836-4279

Forest Service Mountain Bike Trails, Fairplay; (719) 836-4279

South Park City Museum, Fairplay; (719) 836-2387

Restaurants

Brown Burro Café, Fairplay; (719) 836-2804

Silver Scoop Creamery, Fairplay; (719) 836-3403

Mason's High Country BBQ, Fairplay; (719) 836-3465

49 Pine Valley Ranch to Buffalo Creek

Pine Valley Ranch Park serves as an excellent access point into the northern sector of Buffalo Creek Recreation Area. Delivering the cool, rushing waters of the North Fork of the South Platte River, picnic tables, restrooms, potable water, and 6.1 miles of trails, the 820-acre Pine Valley Ranch Park offers riders a pleasant oasis in the otherwise more crowded Buffalo Creek Recreation Area. The park is truly one of Jefferson County's most beautiful, particularly Pine Lake. The route described here incorporates two trails found in Pine Valley Ranch Park and combines them with six trails in the Buffalo Creek Recreation Area, making for a 13.4-mile loop. In general, the singletrack here is well groomed and marked.

Start: The Pine Valley Ranch Park
Distance: 13.4-mile loop
Elevation gain: 1,000 feet
Riding time: Advanced riders, 1.5-2 hours; intermediate riders, 2-3 hours
Fitness effort: Physically moderate due to the lesser degrees of elevation gain. The trail also alternates its ascents and descents.
Difficulty: Technically easy, as the trail rolls over consistently smooth gravel singletrack. Sections do require some technical skills, however, as the trail also includes rocky and sloping terrain.
Terrain: Singletrack and doubletrack that roll over hard-packed trails and loose granite and through burned sections of the Pike National Forest caused by the Hi Meadow Fire of 2000

Seasons: May-Oct
Maps: *DeLorme: Colorado Atlas & Gazetteer*, page 49; *USGS:* Pine, CO; *Trails Illustrated:* #105, Tarryall Mountains, Kenosha Pass, CO; Buffalo Creek Recreation Area map; Pine Valley Ranch Park map
Nearest town: Pine Junction
Other trail users: Hikers, horseback riders, anglers, and picnickers
Dog friendly: Yes
Trail contact: Pike National Forest, South Platte Ranger District, Morrison; (303) 275-5610; or Jefferson County Open Space Trails Hotline, Evergreen; (303) 271-5975; or Jefferson County Open Space; (303) 271-5925; http://jeffco.us/parks/parks-and-trails/

Getting there: From Denver head west on US 285 for roughly 22 miles. Turn left onto Pine Valley Road (Road 126) at the light in Pine Junction. Drive on Pine Valley Road for 6 miles before turning right onto Crystal Lake Road, following the sign for Pine Valley Ranch Park. Drive on Crystal Lake Road for 0.6 mile before entering the park. Parking spaces are available. Trailhead GPS: N39 24.495' / W105 20.830'

The Ride

Part of what makes Pine Valley Ranch Park one of the more exquisite Jefferson County Open Space Parks is the historic Pine Valley Lodge. Nestled in the timbers above the parking lot, the historic lodge incorporates native rock and white spruce into its exterior and interior construction.

The pack heads home via the Miller Gulch Trail.

The lodge was the brainchild of William A. Baehr, who bought Pine Valley Ranch in 1925. Inspired by the natural surroundings, noted Denver architect J.B. Benedict designed the lodge to reflect the manor homes found in Germany's Black Forest. Known as the "Baehrden of the Rockies," the lodge includes intricate wrought iron detailing and wood highlighted with pyrographic etchings.

Riders begin their route heading west on the Narrow Gauge Trail, which parallels the North Fork of the South Platte River. Before Baehr's arrival, Charlie Eggert ran an ice company here. He bought the land in 1908 and started producing ice by diverting water from the river into man-made lakes. The ice was then cut into large blocks and transported to Denver via the Colorado & Southern Railroad, which the Narrow Gauge Trail now follows.

After intersecting with the Buck Gulch Trail, riders climb moderately over wide singletrack dusted with loose granite rock to the Strawberry Jack Trail. This section provides views of the fire-scarred Pike National Forest. Backed by winds in excess of 60 mph, the Hi Meadow Fire ripped through this area in 2000 and consumed 10,500 acres while destroying fifty-one homes and seven other structures. The blaze traveled quickly, scorching all in its path with high-intensity heat. Fortunately, many of the trees' root systems were saved. Thus, the nutrient-rich soils that naturally occur after a blaze enabled the trees and underbrush to recover.

Nevertheless, the fire made this area particularly prone to flooding. Parts of the Strawberry Jack Trail can get quite sandy and rutted after heavy rains. The loss of much of the forest canopy has made this trail particularly hot and dry.

Once they intersect with the Homestead Trail, riders travel over narrower single-track as it passes through a large boulder field. The trail descends quickly over granite-gravel singletrack. This gravel has a nasty ball-bearing effect, so check your speed. Nearing 5 miles into your ride and after negotiating moderately rocky and root-filled terrain, you will enter a pleasant riparian section of the Homestead Trail.

Riders soon connect with the unmarked Miller Gulch Trail and then climb gradually on wide doubletrack. Luckily, after 1 mile a Miller Gulch Trail sign does appear on the right, relieving any route uncertainty.

After its second intersection with Charlie's Cutoff Trail, the Homestead Trail descends swiftly over smooth doubletrack and through a variety of meadows before returning riders to the Strawberry Jack and Skipper Trails.

The Skipper Trail descends to Buck Creek via moderate switchbacks before rising up from it again. This is possibly the sweetest section of trail. From the creek, riders have to negotiate over physically challenging and technically moderate terrain, as the trail rising from the creek bed is rutted and sandy.

Although the descent on the Buck Gulch Trail is very fast, the water diversion ditches that stretch across the trail provide both good bunny-hop potential and bum-blasting potential. The trail switches back a few times along a north-facing, slippery slope before arriving at its intersection with the Strawberry Jack Trail. Riders continue their descent along the Buck Gulch Trail to its intersection with the cool-running waters of the South Platte River. From this intersection it's an easy flow back to your vehicle.

Miles and Directions

0.0 Descend from the parking lot, pass the restrooms, and begin riding west on the double-track, multiuse Narrow Gauge Trail.

0.3 The Narrow Gauge Trail intersects with the North Fork View Trail and the Buck Gulch Trail. Cross over the river via the bridge, and continue riding straight in a southerly direction on the singletrack of the Buck Gulch Trail.

0.8 The Buck Gulch Trail (Trail 772) enters the Pike National Forest and intersects with the Strawberry Jack Trail (Trail 710). Bear left onto the Strawberry Jack Trail, crossing a creek, and continue climbing more arduously in a southeasterly direction.

1.4 The Strawberry Jack Trail intersects with the hikers-only Park View Trail to the left. Continue riding south along the Strawberry Jack Trail. The Park View Trail descends to Pine Valley Ranch Park.

3.0 The Strawberry Jack Trail intersects with the Skipper and Homestead Trails. Bear left (east) onto the Homestead Trail and continue riding on plush singletrack.

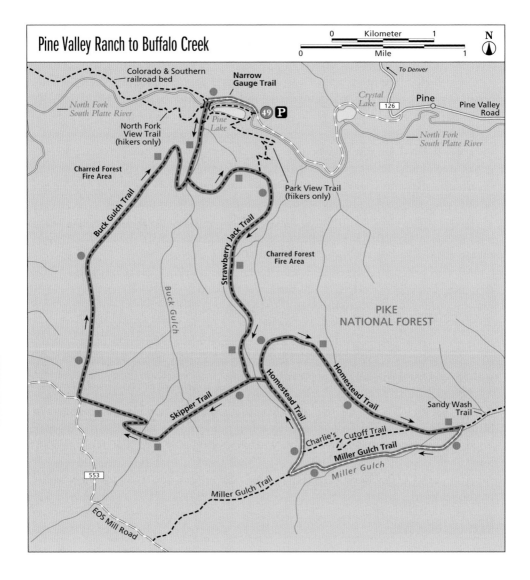

Pine Valley Ranch to Buffalo Creek

Colorado & Southern railroad bed

Narrow Gauge Trail

To Denver

Crystal Lake

Pine

126

Pine Valley Road

North Fork South Platte River

Pine Lake

49 P

North Fork View Trail (hikers only)

North Fork South Platte River

Charred Forest Fire Area

Buck Gulch Trail

Park View Trail (hikers only)

Strawberry Jack Trail

Charred Forest Fire Area

Buck Gulch

PIKE NATIONAL FOREST

Homestead Trail

Skipper Trail

Homestead Trail

Sandy Wash Trail

Charlie's Cutoff Trail

Miller Gulch Trail

Miller Gulch

553

Miller Gulch Trail

Miller Gulch

EOS Mill Road

N

4.6 The Homestead Trail intersects with the Charlie's Cutoff Trail on the right. Continue riding on the Homestead Trail as it makes its descent to the Sandy Wash Trail.

5.1 The Homestead Trail leads into the Sandy Wash Trail. Continue riding on the Sandy Wash Trail.

5.8 After a short and moderately technical climb, the Sandy Wash Trail reaches its high point and intersects with the Miller Gulch Trail on the right. At this point the Miller Gulch Trail is unmarked and goes off in a westerly direction, while the Sandy Wash Trail continues its descent in a southeasterly direction. Bear sharply to the right here, switchbacking above the route that you had been following along the Sandy Wash Trail, and continue on the unmarked, wide doubletrack of the Miller Gulch Trail, heading west.

6.7 The Miller Gulch Trail curves to the right as riders pass a brown MILLER GULCH TRAIL sign on the right: welcome evidence of being on the correct trail.

7.9 The Miller Gulch Trail intersects with the Homestead Trail (Trail 728) on the right. Bear right here onto the Homestead Trail, and continue riding in a northerly direction.

8.0 The Homestead Trail intersects with Charlie's Cutoff Trail on the right. Continue straight here on the Homestead Trail.

8.8 The Homestead Trail intersects with the Strawberry Jack and Skipper Trails. Bear left here, choosing the Skipper Trail.

10.2 The Skipper Trail intersects with Service Road 553 and the Buck Gulch Trail. There is no sign for the Buck Gulch Trail at this intersection, but there will be a sign reading PINE VALLEY that points in a northerly direction. Bear right onto the Buck Gulch Trail by the pine valley sign, and descend in a northerly direction.

12.6 The Buck Gulch Trail intersects with the Strawberry Jack Trail. At this point continue your northerly descent along the Buck Gulch Trail back to the trailhead.

13.4 Arrive at your vehicle.

Ride Information

Trail Information

Pike National Forest, South Platte Ranger District, Morrison; (303) 275-5610

Jefferson County Open Space; (303) 271-5925; http://jeffco.us/parks/parks-and-trails/

Front Range Mountain Bike Patrol; www .frmbp.org/

Local Events and Attractions

Colorado Trail, 470-mile trail from Denver to Durango

Denver Firefighters Museum, Denver; (303) 892-1436

Restaurants

Coney Dog Stand, Conifer; (303) 838-4210

Golden Stix, Conifer; (303) 838-5208

Brooks Place Tavern, Conifer; (303) 816-1499

DW's 285 Diner, Conifer; (303) 816-2515

50 Baldy Trail to Gashouse Gulch Trail

The Buffalo Creek Recreation Area includes a network of outstanding singletrack within an hour's drive of Denver. Most of the riding rolls through thick forests over smooth and tacky singletrack. Some sandy sections appear along the way, but they don't last long. Charred trees mark the path of a forest fire that devastated much of this area. Despite the burn scars, the Buffalo Creek Recreation Area remains a mountain biker's playground. A variety of campsites dot the region in case you want to turn your day ride into an overnighter.

Start: Junction of FR 550 and FR 543

Distance: 7.7-mile loop, with options to connect to a host of other singletrack trails

Elevation gain: 600 feet

Riding time: Advanced riders, 45–60 minutes; intermediate riders, 1.5 hours

Fitness effort: Physically easy to moderate due to the short mileage but moderate climbing

Difficulty: Technically easy to moderate due to occasional sandy and rocky sections

Terrain: Improved dirt roads, doubletrack, and singletrack. The terrain consists of mostly smooth-running singletrack, but there are a number of sandy patches to ride through, particularly at the route's onset. Two small rocky sections along the Gashouse Gulch Trail offer a challenging ride.

Seasons: May–Oct

Maps: *DeLorme: Colorado Atlas & Gazetteer*, pages 49–50; *USGS:* Green Mountain, CO; *Trails Illustrated:* #135, Deckers, Rampart Range, CO; Buffalo Creek Recreation Area map

Nearest town: Buffalo Creek

Other trail users: Anglers, hikers, campers, and picnickers

Dog friendly: Yes

Trail contact: Pike National Forest, South Platte Ranger District, Morrison; (303) 275-5610; or Jefferson County Open Space Trails Hotline, Evergreen; (303) 271-5975; or Jefferson County Open Space; (303) 271-5925; http://jeffco.us/parks/parks-and-trails/

Getting there: From Denver head west on US 285 for roughly 22 miles. Turn left onto Pine Valley Road (Road 126) at the light in Pine Junction. Drive on Pine Valley Road for 13.9 miles. Turn right onto FR 550 roughly 4 miles past the town of Buffalo Creek. Once on FR 550, drive for another 5 miles before parking your vehicle at the junction of FR 550 and FR 543. Park on the right side, along Buffalo Creek. There is additional parking at the nearby Meadows Group Campground. The ride begins on FR 543 after crossing Buffalo Creek. Trailhead GPS: N39 20.520' / W105 19.867'

The Ride

Just 30 miles southwest of Denver lies a mini metro–mountain biking mecca. Commonly referred to as the Buffalo Creek Recreation Area, this part of the Pike National Forest provides a vast network of fine singletrack. Acclaimed for its smooth and easily negotiable singletrack, the 7.7-mile Baldy to Gashouse Gulch route provides satisfying sweetness.

Racing out of the scorched forest.

Within the first 0.5 mile, the route delivers a fast and cool descent on FR 543, following Buffalo Creek downstream. After a mile you come upon the charred remains of the Buffalo Creek forest fire. On Saturday, May 18, 1996, a campfire left for dead atop Gashouse Gulch turned into a wind-whipped wildfire. Ten miles long and 2 miles wide, the fire raged for 5 days and destroyed 12,000 acres at a cost of $2.8 million. The effects of such an inferno are still visible. Beginning at mile 1.5, the Baldy Trail weaves its singletrack course in between the standing corpses of ponderosa pine. As the Baldy Trail scratches its sandy way to higher ground, islands of roundleaf bluebell and invasive mullein reaffirm nature's recuperative powers.

About 2 miles into the ride, the trail enters a wonderful ponderosa pine forest and climbs gradually. The singletrack narrows, and the forest opens up a bit. The trees here seem taller and less crowded—a welcome contrast to the charred skeletons that introduced your ride.

As you near the summit and the junction of Baldy and Gashouse Gulch Trails, the singletrack exits the forest and crosses a huge rock face. Pushing its way up into overlying metamorphic rocks, this granite batholith remains as a tremendous intrusion of molten magma. Continue your fire-ride by scaling this formerly molten magma, and

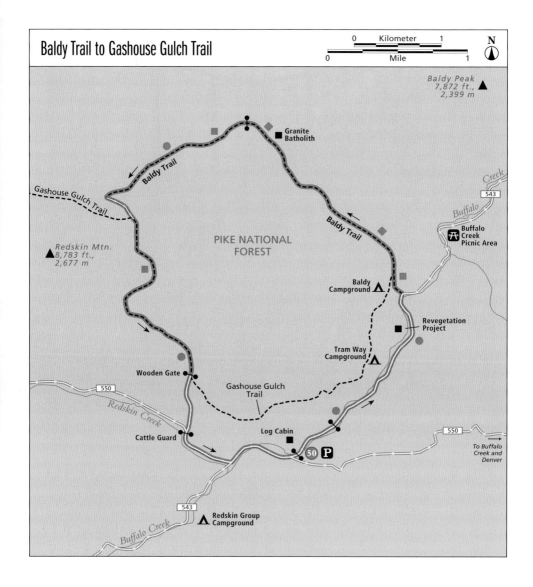

then veer to the left. By mile 3.7 the forest has been overtaken by boulders. A natural grotto to your left provides a dry respite from sudden thunderstorms.

From this point the trail takes you over grassy knolls and through meadows and flat-surfaced forests. While the Gashouse Gulch Trail began as a dirt road, it eventually disintegrates into a rough-looking doubletrack before connecting to a singletrack trail leading off to the left. The Gashouse Gulch singletrack offers fast descents, tight switchbacks, creek crossings, and one very technical rocky section at mile 5.8. Pass through the wooden gate and enjoy a fast ride on the road to FR 550, hitting as many jumps as possible. From there FR 550 takes you back to your vehicle.

Miles and Directions

0.0 Start at the gate at FR 543. Go under the gate and begin your ride, with Buffalo Creek to your right. A beautiful alpine log home will be to your left. Fashioned after the Euro-style log homes of old, this private residence backs up to a collection of enormous rocks.

0.4 Go around another gate and cross Buffalo Creek a second time.

1.3 Arrive at the sandy bottom. Following FR 543 downstream, you'll notice a large sandy area to your left. Strewn across this area are four large rocks embedded in the sand. Veer left off FR 543, riding between these rocks, and continue through the sand heading into the burned forest. The singletrack will begin to your left shortly thereafter, marked by the Gashouse Gulch trail sign.

1.5 At the junction of the Gashouse Gulch and Baldy Trails, veer right onto Baldy Trail.

3.7 Cross a wire gate. The area here is distinct for its large rock formations—a great place to mix bouldering in with your day of riding. If you scurry to the tops of these boulders to your right, you'll be treated to a killer view of Baldy Peak.

4.5 Reach the junction of Gashouse Gulch and Baldy Trails. Gashouse Gulch will lead both to the right and to the left. Take the left route. At this point the trail will become a rough-looking dirt road.

5.1 The rough doubletrack/dirt road intersects with a singletrack veering off to the left. Veer left onto this singletrack.

6.1 Cross another wire fence.

6.8 Arrive at FR 550. Veer left onto FR 550, crossing the cattle guard at 6.9 miles.

7.2 FR 550 intersects with FR 543 to your right. Bear left, continuing on FR 550.

7.7 Arrive back at your vehicle.

Ride Information

Trail Information

Pike National Forest, South Platte Ranger District, Morrison; (303) 275-5610

Jefferson County Open Space; (303) 271-5925; http://jeffco.us/parks/parks-and-trails/

Front Range Mountain Bike Patrol; www.frmbp.org/

Pike and San Isabel National Forests, Pueblo; (719) 523-6591

Local Events and Attractions

Colorado Trail, 470-mile trail from Denver to Durango

Denver Firefighters Museum, Denver; (303) 892-1436

Restaurants

Coney Dog Stand, Conifer; (303) 838-4210

Golden Stix, Conifer; (303) 838-5208

Brooks Place Tavern, Conifer; (303) 816-1499

DW's 285 Diner, Conifer; (303) 816-2515

51 Jackson Creek Loop

The Jackson Creek Loop is a mellow ride through some of metro Denver's most remote woodlands and mountains. Combining relatively easy road ascents, ridge rides of touring ease, fast and furious descents, and steady climbs through mountain-flanked canyons, this route offers the most bang for your buck for all mountain biking generalists. The descent toward Watson Park and Jackson Creek is a blast, delivering sandy sections, rooty sections, and a number of dips, while the climb from Jackson Creek to your cars will have you churning your pedals like an arthritic pioneer woman does butter. For those packing a lunch, the optional out-and-back spur will lead you to Watson Park, a great place for a picnic. Should your visit to Jackson Creek include camping out, this ride passes Jackson Creek Campsite at 11.2 miles into your ride.

Start: The junction of Rampart Range Road (FR 300) and Jackson Creek Road (FR 502). Notice the brown PIKE NATIONAL FOREST CAMPGROUND: JACKSON CREEK sign, and begin your ride ascending the Rampart Range Road from there.
Distance: 12.8-mile loop
Elevation gain: 1,300 feet
Riding time: Advanced riders, 1 hour; intermediate riders, 1.5-2 hours
Fitness effort: Physically easy to moderate. Although there is little elevation gain, the last 0.5-mile climb to your vehicle is tougher than any previous climbs along the trail.
Difficulty: Technically easy due to the well-maintained forest road. There are some sandy and rooty sections, but none that are overly technical.

Terrain: Forest Service roads and jeep roads, which are typically smooth; however, some sections include sand, roots, and larger rocks, along with a variety of dips and road washouts
Seasons: Apr-Nov
Maps: *USGS:* Devil's Head, CO, and Dakan Mountain, CO; *DeLorme: Colorado Atlas & Gazetteer,* page 50, B- and C-2; *Trails Illustrated:* #135, Deckers, Rampart Range, CO
Nearest town: Sedalia
Other trail users: Horseback riders, hikers, campers, pine cone collectors, and motorcyclists
Dog friendly: Yes
Trail Contact: Pike National Forest, South Platte Ranger District, Morrison; (303) 275-5610

Getting there: From Denver take I-25 south to exit 207B (US 85 south). Stay in the left three lanes of US 85 south, since it Y's soon after you exit onto it. Drive on US 85 south for 21 miles before turning right onto CO 67 west in Sedalia just before the Sedalia Grill. After about a mile turn left onto CO 105 south, which turns into Perry Park Road. Keep driving south on Perry Park Road for another 1.5 miles. Turn right onto Jackson Creek Road (CR 38). After 2 miles Jackson Creek Road turns to dirt. In another mile Jackson Creek Road forks, with Hidden Valley Road veering off to the left. Head right, continuing on Jackson Creek Road. Driving for another 4.5 miles from this fork, you will arrive at a stop sign where Jackson Creek Road merges with Rampart Range Road. Veer left, continuing on Rampart Range Road until you arrive at a three-sided wooden sign in the middle of the road. Bear right, following signs to Woodland Park. (Going straight ahead will bring you to Devil's Head Campground and trailhead, a great hike to the top of a fire tower overlooking the Front Range.) Finally, you'll arrive at the junction of Rampart Range Road (FR 300) and Jackson Creek Road (FR 502). Park behind the Pike National Forest Campground: Jackson Creek sign. Trailhead GPS: N39 13.989' / W105 05.760'

Under the Devil's Head.

The Ride

The Jackson Creek Loop offers the perfect mellow, out-of-town ride. Its out-of-the-way status lends itself to a quiet and peaceful ride that is neither technically frustrating nor physically demanding. A ride the whole family can enjoy, the Jackson Creek Trail travels over well-maintained forest and jeep roads.

From the trailhead parking begin the route by climbing the moderately pitched Rampart Range Road. This road was built by the now defunct Civilian Conservation Corps (CCC) in the 1930s, during America's Great Depression. Part of President Franklin Roosevelt's New Deal project to jump-start the American economy, the CCC provided employment for out-of-work, physically fit, unmarried men between the ages of 18 and 25. Although the bivouacking workers each received a weekly salary of $30, every man had to send $25 home to ensure that his family was provided for. Dotting much of the road are the CCC's original handmade rail fences. The route along Rampart Range Road continues for 2.7 miles before intersecting with FR 563.

Veer left onto FR 563 and begin a fast 0.5-mile descent that provides a number of embankments for you to ride high on—along with an engineering safety net so that mountain bikers can scream around curves while minimizing the threat of crashing.

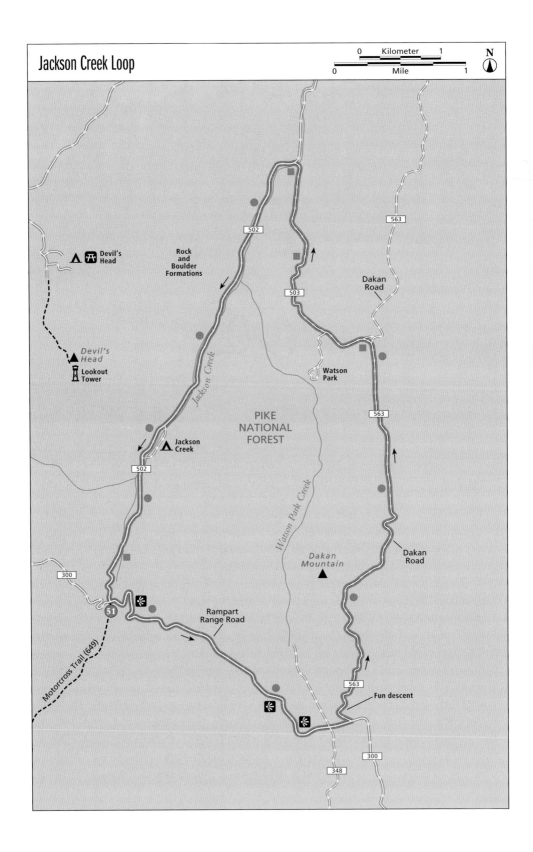

Jackson Creek Loop

0   Kilometer   1

0   Mile   1

N

563

502

Devil's
Head

Rock
and
Boulder
Formations

503

Dakan
Road

Devil's
Head

Lookout
Tower

Jackson Creek

Watson
Park

563

Jackson
Creek

PIKE
NATIONAL
FOREST

502

Watson Park Creek

300

Dakan
Mountain

Dakan
Road

51

Rampart
Range Road

563

Motorcross Trail (649)

Fun descent

300

348

The route eventually climbs through a dense lodgepole pine forest with occasional views of Castle Rock and the plains to the east. From this point (about 4.5 miles) the trail descends again. Here you're offered a chance to practice your bunny-hop, as a number of whoop-di-doos cross your path.

After 6.5 miles veer left onto FR 503. This section of the Jackson Creek Loop is the steepest part of the entire route. Luckily, it's all downhill. FR 503 does have, however, some thick, sandy sections, so take care at warp speeds. At mile 7 FR 503 Y's. Veering left here and riding for a half mile will deliver you to Watson Park, an idyllic picnic spot. Jackson Creek Loop, however, continues to the right as it drops to Jackson Creek. After crossing the creek, veer left onto Jackson Creek Road (FR 502) and ride upstream.

This section of the loop passes through a canyon with ghoulish rock formations to your right, the most prominent of which is named for the master of the netherworld. Devil's Head Mountain was once a fire lookout station. The mile-and-a-quarter hike is moderately challenging. Once at the summit, scale the steps to the top of the fire lookout tower and breathe in one of Colorado's best panoramic views.

Devil's Head Mountain will be to your right after passing the Jackson Creek Campground. From the campground FR 502 gradually ascends, with the last half mile being a bit of a grunt to your vehicle.

Miles and Directions

0.0   Start at the junction of Jackson Creek Road (FR 502) and Rampart Range Road (FR 300). The route begins as a gradual ascent along the Rampart Range Road.

2.5   FR 300 meets with FR 348. Ride straight ahead on FR 300, climbing the short hill in front of you.

2.7   Reach the junction with FR 563, and veer left onto it.

6.5   Reach the junction with FR 503, which you also take to the left.

8.6   Reach the junction with FR 502 (Jackson Creek Road), and take another left.

11.2   Jackson Creek Campsite will be to your left. Continue riding upstream.

12.8   Arrive back at your vehicle.

Ride Information

Trail Information

Pike National Forest, South Platte Ranger District, Morrison; (303) 275-5610

Local Events and Attractions

Devil's Head Tower and trail. Backtrack on Rampart Range Road for 4.8 miles from where you parked your car. Bear right at the three-sided wooden sign in the middle of the road, heading toward Devil's Head Campground and trailhead.

Restaurants

Bud's Café & Bar, Sedalia; (303) 688-9967
Gabriel's Restaurant & Tuscan Bar, Sedalia; (303) 688-2323
O'brien's Café, Sedalia; (303) 688-4672

Honorable Mentions

Denver Region

Six more rides in the Denver region deserve mention, even though they didn't make the "A" list. They may be a bit out of the way or more heavily traveled, but they still deserve your attention when considering a destination.

◯ Kingston Peak Loop

The Kingston Peak Loop is a popular four-wheel-drive vehicle route, but that doesn't deter cyclists from making it a popular high-mountain ride. Beginning in the old mining town of Alice, the route travels to 12,000 feet as it makes its loop around 12,147-foot Kingston Peak. Be advised, however, that a good deal of this route travels above timberline, so it's best to get an early start on the day.

Some riders may appreciate the loop's proximity to St. Mary's Glacier. At 11,000 feet high, St. Mary's Glacier provides a permanent 10-acre snowfield, offering year-round skiing and snowboarding. For the adventurous type, you can complement a day's riding in the saddle with a day's riding in the snow.

To reach the Kingston Peak Loop, drive west on I-70 and take exit 238 (Fall River Road). Bear right onto Fall River Road, and drive for roughly 9 miles. Pass Alice Road on your left, and drive for another 0.5 mile before parking in the dirt pullout area on the left side of the road near an old chairlift. Return to Alice Road and begin riding toward the town of Alice.

For more information on the Kingston Peak Loop, contact the Roosevelt National Forest at (303) 444-6600.

P South Platte River Greenway

As one of the first greenway systems in America, downtown Denver's South Platte River Greenway is truly a success story. This 30-mile paved bike path follows the South Platte River from Chatfield State Park through Denver to the river's confluence with Clear Creek. The river runs for 10.5 miles through the downtown, residential, and industrial neighborhoods of Denver.

Since its inception, the South Platte River Greenway Foundation has created 150 miles of trails, boat launches, chutes, and parks in four counties and nine municipalities, and it has served as an example for more than a dozen greenways across the nation.

For more information contact the Greenway Foundation, South Platte River Commission at www.thegreenwayfoundation.org/web/.

Q Cherry Creek Singletrack

The Cherry Creek Singletrack is a hidden jewel of a trail in an otherwise urbanized landscape. The trail parallels Cherry Creek, as well as the paved Cherry Creek Bike Path, from Colorado Boulevard to the Highline Canal. The paved bike path extends for 15 miles. The trail may be closed periodically due to flooding during the spring runoff season. The singletrack itself offers narrow and rocky sections that sometimes fall steeply to the creek. Should any sections be too challenging to risk riding, riders can bail to the paved bike path, which is always, for the most part, close at hand. This trail is ideal for the family whose preferences are split between riding on pavement and riding on dirt. This trail offers some tasty singletrack that pierces directly through the heart of Denver—and isn't that incentive enough?

From downtown Denver drive south on Speer Boulevard for roughly 4.3 miles, crossing University Avenue, to the Cherry Creek Mall. Park behind the south side of the mall, and pick up the Cherry Creek Bike Path.

For more information visit Denver Bike Trails at www.denver.org/what-to-do/sports-recreation/denver-bike-trails or contact Denver Region Council of Government Pedestrian Bicycle Committee at (303) 455-1000.

R Chatfield Reservoir State Park

Chatfield Reservoir State Park offers riders a mellow cruise on its multiuse trails, many of which are wheelchair-accessible. Over 30 miles of trails crisscross throughout the park. The reservoir is primarily a haven for Denver urbanites, accommodating more than 1.5 million visitors a year.

As one of the most complete parks in all of Colorado, Chatfield Reservoir State Park offers the metro area 5,600 acres of land and 1,450 acres of water. The park is popular for horseback riding, hiking, boating, swimming, fishing, camping, picnicking, and bird-watching.

For more information contact Chatfield State Park, (303) 791-7275.

To get to Chatfield Reservoir State Park, drive south on Wadsworth Boulevard (CO 121) past CO 470, and turn left into the park at the Deer Creek entrance. You can also reach the park by driving south on Santa Fe Boulevard and turning right (west) onto Titan Road. Drive about 3 miles on Titan Road before turning right again (north) onto Roxborough Park Road, entering the park via the Plum Creek entrance.

S Castlewood Canyon State Park

Castlewood Canyon State Park serves as a reminder that mountain biking need not take place in the mountains. While providing views of 14,110-foot Pikes Peak to the south and 14,255-foot Longs Peak to the north, the trails here course through prairie grasses and past juniper and piñon trees.

The Castlewood Canyon Loop follows a dirt road through the park for more than 25 miles. While the loop is long, it isn't tough, as there are no significant elevation gains. The route begins in Castle Rock and travels south on Gilbert Street before connecting with Castlewood Canyon Road (CR 51) through the park. Once through the park, riders connect with CO 86 and return to Castle Rock.

Located in the Black Forest of central Colorado, Castlewood Canyon State Park has as its centerpiece the old Castlewood Canyon Dam. In 1890 Cherry Creek was dammed for irrigation. When the dam broke on August 3, 1933, the subsequent flooding claimed two lives and caused $1 million in damages. What remained, however, was an exquisite canyon with unique ruins. Where the reservoir once lay behind the dam now is an open prairie dotted with Douglas fir and ponderosa pine trees. The many cliffs, bluffs, and overlooks make for incredible photo opportunities and invite the skilled rock climber.

There are also a number of scenic hiking trails that descend to the bottom of the canyon and those that traverse its rim. The park also offers a visitor center.

To reach Castlewood Canyon State Park, drive south from Denver on I-25 to exit 181 in Castle Rock. Bear right onto CO 83. Drive south on CO 83 for 7 miles to the main entrance, roughly 5 miles past the intersection with CO 86. The entrance is on the right (west).

For more information contact Castlewood Canyon State Park at (303) 688-5242 or Colorado Parks and Wildlife at (303) 866-3437.

Ridgeline Open Space

The 370-acre Ridgeline Open Space offers users roughly 13.5 miles of multiuse and singletrack trails that are ideal for families and beginner mountain bikers. Likewise, intermediate riders who enjoy interval workouts and want to run laps will enjoy a great aerobic if nontechnical workout. The trails weave through grasslands, valleys, and ridgelines and past stands of Gambel oak. Riders enjoy a relatively smooth trail system that delivers no significant extended climbs but does offer expansive views of the Front Range and the town of Castle Rock to the west. The trails at Ridgeline Open Space are marked A to O. Though easy, there are some tighter, looser switchback sections coupled with a few short climbs. For those living in Castle Rock, this makes for a great quick getaway. This "in-town" ride does have the potential to get crowded, so check your speed.

Located within the Meadows neighborhood in Castle Rock, there are several places to access the trail system. However, consider parking at the Coachline Road trailhead. In Castle Rock drive roughly 1.5 miles south from I-25 on Wolfensberger Road to Coachline Road. Bear right onto Coachline Road and drive for roughly 0.5 mile to the Ridgeline Open Space. The trailhead will be to the left. For more information contact Ridgeline Open Space at (303) 814-7444 or the trail maintenance group Ridgeline Wranglers at (303) 814-7456.

Colorado Springs Region

Colorado Springs is surrounded by such majestic mountain beauty that it inspired Katharine Lee Bates to compose "America the Beautiful" while standing atop Pikes Peak more than a century ago. But while Colorado Springs sits at the foot of Pikes Peak, there are a variety of other spectacular geological points of interest. The Garden of the Gods is a free, city-owned park comprising spectacular, 300-foot-tall red sandstone fins and spires. The Cave of the Winds is another natural wonder that was discovered in 1881 by two young brothers on a church outing. The commercial caves are encrusted with colorful stalactites, stalagmites, and flowstone curtains.

Also nearby are the Manitou Cliff Dwellings. Ancestral Puebloans lived in these dwellings between 1100 and 1300 AD and crafted some of this country's finest early pottery. Needless to say, these Ancestral Puebloans—followed by the Ute, Cheyenne, Kiowa, and Arapaho Indians—were the earliest residents of the area. While many of these tribes were hostile toward one another, they all laid down their weapons upon entering the sacred grounds of nearby Manitou Springs and Garden of the Gods.

General William Jackson Palmer, a Civil War veteran from Pennsylvania, founded the city of Colorado Springs in 1871 as a tourist destination. He also founded the Denver & Rio Grande Railroad in that same year. Palmer envisioned Colorado Springs becoming a world-class resort destination and went so far as to nickname the new town "Little London." But it was the 1890 discovery of gold near the mining town of Cripple Creek, southwest of Pikes Peak, that brought the hordes. By 1900 Colorado Springs was the leading mining exchange center of the world and received a new nickname—"City of Millionaires"—and for good reason. By 1904 Colorado Springs was home to thirty-five of the country's one hundred millionaires from gold mined in Cripple Creek. But Palmer would have his day yet. Following the end of the gold rush in 1903, Colorado Springs' sunny conditions and dry, mild climate attracted many visitors, and they continue to do so today.

Today, tourism is Colorado Springs' third-largest industry, employing more than 14,400 people and contributing more than $800 million to the local economy. More than 6 million people visit Colorado Springs each year. With a population of well over 400,000, Colorado Springs is the state's second-largest city.

The Springs, as it is commonly called, offers residents and tourists alike incredible outdoor recreational opportunities. Nearby Pikes Peak, North and South Cheyenne Canyon Park, Manitou Springs, and Woodland Park offer outdoor enthusiasts a varied assortment of bike-riding opportunities. Among its other accolades, Colorado Springs can boast ranking number one as Men's Fitness's "Fittest City in America" and being ranked in the top ten for best places to live, work, and play by *Frommer's Travel Guide, Kiplinger's Personal Finance*, and MSNBC, as well as earning the distinction as a Silver Bicycle Friendly Community by the League of American Bicyclists.

Local Bike Shops

Old Town Bike Shop, Colorado Springs; (719) 475-8589

Colorado Springs Bike Shop, Colorado Springs: (719) 634-4915

Ascent Cycling, Colorado Springs; (719) 597-8181

Bicycle Village, Colorado Springs; (719) 265-9346

Nick's Bikes, Pueblo; (719) 647-1150; www.nicksbikes.com

Vance's Bicycle World, Pueblo; (719) 566-6925; vancesbicycleworldllc.com

52 Raspberry Chautauqua Mountain Trail

Also called the Limbaugh Canyon Loop by locals, the Raspberry Chautauqua Mountain Trail is an underappreciated gem. The beginning of the ride includes a steady climb up Mount Herman Road. Aside from a moderate warm-up to the day ahead, the road offers views of Elephant Rock, Monument Rock, and the US Air Force Academy (see ride 53: Falcon Trail). Once the road intersects with the Raspberry Chautauqua Mountain Trail, a singletrack weaves a sinuous path through Limbaugh Canyon and skirts Chautauqua Mountain. The trail can be quite technical in spots, offering tight singletrack, steep grades, and large rock drop-offs. While the trail is mostly hidden in dense tree cover, there is one section (Inspiration Point) that offers riders views of the town of Monument and the Palmer Lake area. The route can be challenging to navigate, so be aware.

Start: Red Rocks Drive
Distance: 9.7-mile loop
Elevation gain: 1,200 feet
Riding time: Advanced riders, 1.5 hours; intermediate riders, 2 hours
Fitness effort: Physically moderate due to sustained climbs on Mount Herman Road
Difficulty: Technically moderate to challenging due to the tight and rocky singletrack
Terrain: Dirt road and singletrack, which is tight and technical and runs over large rocks and through dried creek beds and open meadows

Seasons: May-Oct
Maps: *DeLorme: Colorado Atlas & Gazetteer,* page 50; *USGS:* Palmer Lake, CO; *Trails Illustrated:* #137, Pikes Peak, Cañon City, CO; Monument/Palmer Lake Trails map
Nearest town: Monument
Other trail users: Hikers and campers
Dog friendly: No, due to the vehicular traffic along this route
Trail contact: Pike and San Isabel National Forests, Pikes Peak Ranger District, Colorado Springs; (719) 636-1602

Getting there: From Colorado Springs drive north on I-25 for 19.5 miles, and then take exit 161 for Monument and Palmer Lake. At the end of the ramp by the stoplight, bear left onto CO 105 and drive west, crossing over I-25. This road becomes Second Street. Pass straight through a stoplight and continue driving west on Second Street for roughly 1 mile to Mitchell Avenue at a T intersection. Bear left onto Mitchell, following signs for Monument Fire Center, Mount Herman Road, and FR 320, and drive roughly half a mile before bearing right onto Mount Herman Road. Drive 2.4 miles on Mount Herman; then bear right onto Red Rocks Drive. Immediately bear right again into the parking lot pullout. Trailhead GPS: N39 05.312' / W104 54.660'

The Ride

Shortly after leaving your vehicle on Red Rocks Road, you'll begin climbing up Mount Herman Road. This is a popular thoroughfare for weekend enthusiasts and offers residents of Monument an immediate access point to the mountains. Founded in 1879, the town of Monument began as a train stop and has since flourished.

Monument Rock.

Continue riding up Mount Herman Road through fields of scrub oak before reaching the higher elevations with Douglas fir and ponderosa pine. As you ride, you may notice the bald spot atop Mount Herman, which was caused by a wildfire that spread across its crown in the late 1980s. The road continues through much of the fire's path, distinguishable if not by the sometimes barren and burned scrub oak fields then most certainly by the Monument Fire Center that lies just off to your left.

As you start gaining elevation on the road, you may notice Elephant Rock to the northeast. Located in the town of Castle Rock, this formation is the namesake of the annual Elephant Rock Cycling Festival, which draws about 7,000 cycling enthusiasts the first Saturday in June and offers a variety of road and off-road cycling events and races for all ages and abilities.

Higher along the road you may catch a glimpse of the Air Force Academy to the south, noticeable by its distinctively pointed-roofed chapel. Designed by Walter Netsch in 1954 and constructed in 1963, the modern expressionist Air Force Academy Chapel's seventeen silvery aluminum spires stand more than 150 feet tall. The chapel was designed to resemble a phalanx of fighter jets shooting up into the sky.

Once you intersect with the Raspberry Chautauqua Mountain Trail, continue climbing over marble-size Pikes Peak granite through dense forests of ponderosa pine and Douglas fir. Upon reaching the fork and the dried creek bed, bear left to climb the final push before arriving at the three-way intersection.

From here the trail is fast and rutted as it descends through tall stands of aspens to Monument Creek and through Limbaugh Canyon. Raspberry Mountain lies to the east, while Chautauqua Mountain lies to the northwest. Once you cross the creek, however, your ride mellows a bit as it runs through open meadows and intermittent stands of aspen. About 5.5 miles into your ride, the trail travels along precipitously sloping terrain to your right. The trail here is quite narrow and rocky. Your technical descent is rewarded, however, upon reaching a beautiful overlook of Palmer Lake at roughly 7 miles into your ride.

Leading an army expedition through the Rocky Mountains in 1835, Colonel Henry Dodge originally named it Summit Lake. The lake was renamed Divide Lake before receiving its present name. It is located on the Palmer Divide, where a watershed drainage separates the waters of the Platte River to the north and the Arkansas River to the south. The lake served as a water supply for the steam engines of the Denver & Rio Grande Railroad, and ice houses at the south end supplied ice for the railroad's dining cars. In 1882 the lake was enlarged to its present-day size of 10 acres, and a boathouse, park, fountain, and covered pavilion were added to attract tourists to the area.

From the overlook you'll dive into your final descent on steep singletrack to Colonel's Road before riding through Red Rocks Ranch and returning to your vehicle.

Miles and Directions

0.0 Start by bearing left from Red Rocks Drive to Mount Herman Road.

0.1 Red Rocks Drive intersects with Mount Herman Road. Bear right onto the dirt Mount Herman Road, and begin climbing in a southerly direction.

1.5 Arrive at an overlook with views of Monument Rock to the north and the Air Force Academy to the south.

3.0 Mount Herman Road intersects with the Raspberry Chautauqua Mountain Trail (715, aka Limbaugh Canyon Loop Trail) on your right, marked by a NO SHOOTING sign. Bear right onto the Raspberry Chautauqua Mountain Trail, and begin climbing northward on hard-packed singletrack.

3.1 The trail forks at a sandy wash and dried creek bed. Bear left here and continue climbing toward the three-way intersection and the continuation of the Raspberry Chautauqua Mountain Trail. (Bearing right and choosing to ride up the dried creek bed delivers a grueling 0.4-mile climb through sandy and rutted terrain to a saddle where there are some interesting rock formations.)

3.6 Arrive at the three-way intersection and the continuation of the Raspberry Chautauqua Mountain Trail, marked by a bullet-riddled NO MOTORCYCLES sign on your right. Continue straight here onto the Raspberry Chautauqua Mountain Trail through Limbaugh Canyon.

4.5 Cross Monument Creek via a footbridge and portage your bike over some larger boulders.

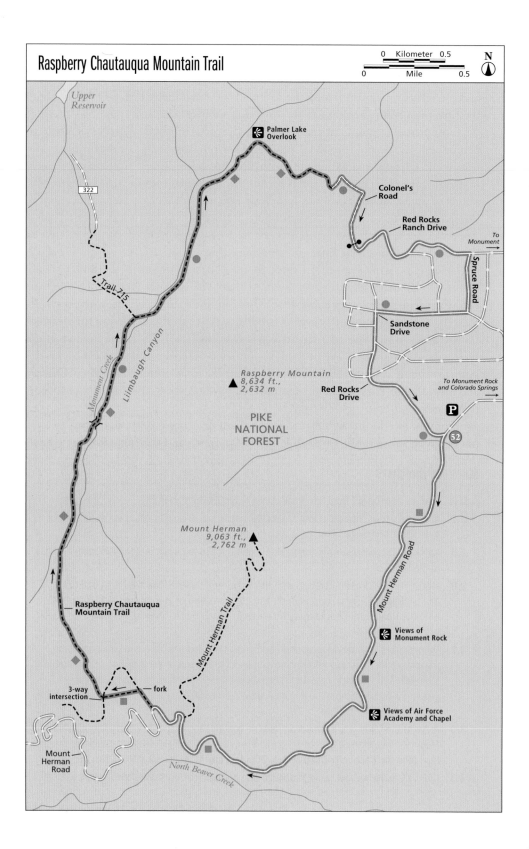

Raspberry Chautauqua Mountain Trail

Upper Reservoir

Palmer Lake Overlook

322

Colonel's Road

Red Rocks Ranch Drive

To Monument

Spruce Road

Trail 715

Sandstone Drive

Monument Creek

Liimbaugh Canyon

Raspberry Mountain
8,634 ft.,
2,632 m

Red Rocks Drive

To Monument Rock
and Colorado Springs

P

52

PIKE
NATIONAL
FOREST

Mount Herman
9,063 ft.,
2,762 m

Mount Herman Road

Raspberry Chautauqua
Mountain Trail

Mount Herman Trail

Views of
Monument Rock

3-way
intersection

fork

Views of Air Force
Academy and Chapel

Mount
Herman
Road

North Beaver Creek

N

Kilometer
0   0.5

Mile
0   0.5

6.9 Arrive at an overlook (Inspiration Point) with views of Palmer Lake. Continue descending on the Raspberry Chautauqua Mountain Trail.

7.3 The Raspberry Chautauqua Mountain Trail intersects with an old watershed access road. Bear left here onto the road and pass through the aluminum fence.

7.4 The old watershed access road intersects with Colonel's Road at a T intersection; bear right onto Colonel's Road and pass beyond a metal link gate. After the gate Colonel's Road turns into Red Rocks Ranch Drive. Bear left onto Red Rocks Ranch Drive, and descend through the Red Rocks Ranch area.

8.4 When Red Rocks Ranch Drive intersects with the paved Spruce Road, turn right onto Spruce and begin climbing.

8.6 Spruce Road intersects with Sandstone Drive. Bear right onto Sandstone Drive.

9.0 Sandstone Drive intersects with Red Rocks Drive at a four-way stop. Bear left onto Red Rocks Drive.

9.7 Arrive at your vehicle.

Ride Information

Trail Information

Pike and San Isabel National Forests, Pikes Peak Ranger District, Colorado Springs; (719) 636-1602

Local Events and Attractions

Subaru Elephant Rock Cycling Festival, June, Castle Rock; http://elephantrockride.com
 Palmer Lake; (719) 481-2953
 Santa Fe Regional Trail, a 14-mile trail that runs south from Monument to the US Air Force Academy
 US Air Force Academy, Colorado Springs; (719) 333-1110

Restaurants

Wisdom Tea House, Monument; (719) 481-8822
 Pike's Peak Brewing, Monument; (719) 208-4098
 Rosie's Diner, Monument; (719) 481-3287
 A Taste of Mexico, Castle Rock; (719) 660-2014

53 Falcon Trail

There's good reason why Colorado Springs' Falcon Trail is gaining classic status among local mountain bikers. Its close proximity to town, its cool factor for being located inside the US Air Force Academy, and its sinuous singletrack that is accessible to riders of any level all add up to an awesome mountain bike trail. In fact, Colorado Springs residents have voted it as one of the best mountain biking trails in the city. Although the Falcon Trail can be ridden in either direction, this route describes riding the loop in a counterclockwise direction. Know that identification is required to enter the US Air Force Academy.

Start: The Falcon trailhead off Academy Drive

Distance: 13.4-mile loop

Elevation gain: 733 feet

Riding time: Advanced riders, 1 hour; intermediate riders, 1.5 hours

Fitness effort: Physically easy to moderate with little significant elevation gain

Difficulty: Technically easy to moderate with a few rockier sections. There is one hike-a-bike section, but it can be avoided if an alternate route is taken at 8.4 miles.

Terrain: Singletrack that delivers exposed plateau riding as well as shaded forest riding. A brief section of dirt road is included in the route. The trail crosses paved roads several times.

Seasons: Apr-Oct

Schedule: Open to the general public from 8 a.m. to 6 p.m. daily. Active duty and retired military members and their families can use the trail from 5 a.m. to sundown.

Maps: US Air Force Academy visitor's map; *USGS:* Pikeview, CO; *Trails Illustrated:* #137, Pikes Peak, Cañon City, CO; *DeLorme: Colorado Atlas & Gazetteer,* page 63, B-4

Nearest town: Colorado Springs

Other trail users: Hikers and runners

Dog friendly: Yes

Trail contact: Barry Goldwater Air Force Academy Visitor Center, Colorado Springs; (719) 333-2025

Getting there: From Colorado Springs drive on I-25 and take exit 156B (Air Force Academy north gate). Drive west on Northgate Boulevard to the entrance gate of the Air Force Academy. Be sure all riders have identification ready to show the guards at the gate. After driving roughly 1 mile, bear left onto Stadium Boulevard. Drive south on Stadium Boulevard for roughly 1.3 miles, and turn right onto Academy Drive. Drive west on Academy Drive for roughly 0.5 mile, and bear right into the Falcon Trail parking lot and trailhead. The trailhead is located at the west end of the parking lot. Trailhead GPS: N39 00.013' / W104 51.036'

The Ride

The Falcon Trail has undergone much-needed restoration and grooming in recent years by the Air Force Center for Engineering and the Environment. This is part of a larger effort to restore and maintain the large network of publicly accessible trails that crisscross the academy for base residents and the public to enjoy.

The initial singletrack delivers a fast and smooth descent through forest to the grasslands. Here riders travel briefly on a dirt road before reconnecting with the

Author Stephen Hlawaty hammering some technical terrain on the Falcon Trail. JEFF WILLIAMS

singletrack. Roughly 2 miles into your ride, the terrain becomes a bit rockier, with switchbacks, as you begin a more moderate climb up an exposed plateau and along slopes full of Gambel oak.

Upon reaching the top of the plateau, riders will pass intermittent views of the Air Force Academy's chapel to the west. The descent from here provides riders with switchbacks, as well as some rocky, sandy, and moderately technical sections. From this point the trail travels westward, passing the Cadet Fieldhouse and Falcon and Holaday Athletic Centers to the right.

After you reach the intersection with the Chapel Overlook Trail, a short ride takes you to a view of the most-photographed building at the Academy, which is visited by more than half a million people every year. The seventeen aluminum, glass, and steel spires of the chapel soar upwards for over 150 feet. While the chapel was originally designed to provide Christian, Jewish, and Buddhist worship areas, in 2011 it opened its newest worship area: the Falcon Circle. This provides a place for worshipers of Earth-centered religions like Paganism, Druidism, and Wicca.

Continuing on your own Falcon circle of sorts, you begin to climb. Here the trail delivers some technical rockier sections before snaking its way through ponderosa pine woodlands. Soon you enjoy a fast run through a mixed bag of smooth-running

Author Stephen Hlawaty ripping through the riparian section along West Monument Creek and before a hole-riddled wall. JEFF WILLIAMS

and technical singletrack. The section of trail starting at roughly 8.5 miles is perhaps the route's most interesting, as it passes through a cool riparian landscape. The trail hugs a hole-riddled rock wall and delivers a short hike-a-bike section over large granite rocks as it winds along West Monument Creek. This area is prime habitat for the Preble's meadow jumping mouse and is protected under the Endangered Species Act. The mouse lives near the streams throughout the Academy, and its habitat is shrinking due to upstream, off-base development. From here riders make their way over trickier and rockier terrain before crossing another footbridge.

After crossing Community Center Drive, riders begin a steady climb to cross a dirt road. From this point the route delivers a sweet and fast descent on sinuous singletrack. Be mindful of trail users coming in the other direction.

The Pioneer Cabin, roughly 12 miles into your ride, was built in the 1870s by pioneer and homesteader Bill Burgess. The cabin's hand-hewn logs joined by wooden pegs instead of nails, as well as the fireplace's hand-set stones, reflect a kind of industry and craft that are rare in today's technological world. Burgess's original homestead included 160 acres, and he lived in this cabin with his wife, Adaline, and five children for 20 years. Listed on the National Register of Historic Places, the cabin was restored in 1992 and is the oldest building at the Academy and one of the oldest dwellings in the Pikes Peak region. Although the cabin's grounds include the tombstones of five members of the Capps family, and the cabin is frequently referred to as the Capps Cabin, the Cappses lived near the south end of what is now Falcon Stadium. The stadium's 50-yard-line was the original site of the Capps' interment before they were exhumed and relocated.

From the cabin continue a bit and cross Academy Drive to your vehicle.

Falcon Trail

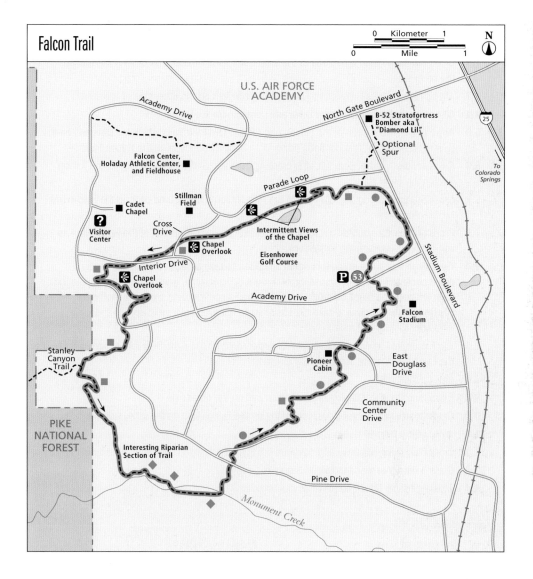

0   Kilometer   1

0   Mile   1

N

U.S. AIR FORCE ACADEMY

Academy Drive

North Gate Boulevard

B-52 Stratofortress Bomber aka "Diamond Lil"

25

To Colorado Springs

Optional Spur

Falcon Center, Holaday Athletic Center, and Fieldhouse

Parade Loop

Stillman Field

Cadet Chapel

Cross Drive

Visitor Center

Intermittent Views of the Chapel

Chapel Overlook

Eisenhower Golf Course

Interior Drive

Stadium Boulevard

Chapel Overlook

P 53

Academy Drive

Falcon Stadium

Stanley Canyon Trail

Pioneer Cabin

East Douglass Drive

Community Center Drive

PIKE NATIONAL FOREST

Interesting Riparian Section of Trail

Pine Drive

Monument Creek

Miles and Directions

0.0 Start riding from the west end of the parking lot on the Falcon Trail. While this loop begins on the north side of Academy Drive, it will end on Academy Drive's south side across the road from your vehicle.

0.3 The Falcon Trail intersects with a dirt road. Bear right onto the dirt road for 0.1 mile before bearing left onto the singletrack of the Falcon Trail.

1.4 The Falcon Trail intersects with a spur trail that leads to the B-52 Stratofortress bomber (aka "Diamond Lil") displayed at the southeast corner of North Gate Boulevard and Stadium Boulevard. Bear left here, continuing on the Falcon Trail loop. (**Option:** Riders can opt to park at the B-52 bomber, where there are restroom facilities, and ride this short spur to and from the main loop to lengthen their ride by roughly 1 mile.)

1.7 Cross the paved road that leads to the Eisenhower Golf Course, and pick up the trail on the other side.

3.7 After crossing Cross Drive, continue on the Falcon Trail on the other side of the drive.

4.1 Cross Faculty Drive and Interior Drive and continue on the Falcon Trail.

5.0 Arrive at the intersection of the Falcon and Chapel Overlook Trails. Academy Drive will be to your right. Bear right and continue riding in an easterly direction on the Falcon Trail.

5.9 Cross Academy Drive. Bear left after crossing the road, and continue riding on the Falcon Trail on the other side.

6.8 Cross Stanley Canyon Trail dirt road in the Pike National Forest, and pick up the Falcon Trail on the other side.

7.9 Cross Stanley Canyon Trail dirt road and continue on the singletrack of the Falcon Trail as you descend over smooth singletrack.

8.4 The Falcon Trail splits and offers riders an option to take an easier route, marked by a green circle before a creek crossing, or a more difficult route, marked by a black diamond. Bear left onto the black diamond section of the Falcon Trail, and cross the footbridge. (**Option:** Riders wanting to take the easier route will eventually meet up with the main loop after roughly 0.2 mile.)

8.6 The Falcon Trail again intersects with its easier route on the right. Bear left, continuing on the Falcon Trail, riding in an easterly direction.

8.9 Cross a footbridge.

9.8 Cross Pine Drive, continuing on the Falcon Trail on the other side.

10.0 Cross Community Center Drive, continuing on the Falcon Trail on the other side.

11.9 Arrive at the Pioneer Cabin.

12.1 Cross East Douglass Drive and continue riding on the Falcon Trail on the other side.

12.6 Cross a road that leads to Falcon Stadium.

13.4 Cross Academy Drive and arrive at your vehicle.

Ride Information

Trail Information
Barry Goldwater Air Force Academy Visitor Center, Colorado Springs; (719) 333-2025

Local Events and Attractions
US Air Force Academy, Colorado Springs; (719) 333-1110

Garden of the Gods, Colorado Springs; (719) 634-6666; free admission

Pikes Peak; www.experiencecolorado springs.com

Restaurants
Phantom Canyon Brewing, Colorado Springs; (719) 635-2800

PB & Jellies Restaurant, Colorado Springs; (719) 465-2686

Uchenna, Colorado Springs; (719) 634-5070

Il Vicino, Colorado Springs; (719) 475-9224

54 Lovell Gulch Trail

Resembling the shape of a lollipop, the Lovell Gulch Trail is a popular ride located in the heart of Woodland Park. This trail offers a scenic route through a large, open valley and some of the area's best views of Pikes Peak. Camping is permitted at undeveloped sites along the trail. Climbing out of Lovell Gulch offers a moderate workout, but one well worth the effort as you intersect with the Rampart Range Road and the beginning of a screaming descent beneath power lines. The trail is well marked by National Forest trail signs.

Start: The Lovell Gulch trailhead
Distance: 5.5-mile lariat
Elevation gain: 950 feet
Riding time: Advanced riders, 30 minutes; intermediate riders, 45-60 minutes
Fitness effort: Physically easy to moderate due to lack of any significant elevation gains. The climb through Lovell Gulch, however, is physically moderate.
Difficulty: Technically easy to moderate due to the trail's predominantly smooth terrain; some sections of rock, loose sand, and roots, particularly after passing the interesting rock formations on the left just under 2 miles into your ride
Terrain: Singletrack and doubletrack over mostly smooth terrain through mixed conifer

forests. There are some rockier and sandier sections, with one stream crossing. Parts of the trail, like many trails in the Colorado Springs area, are covered in Pikes Peak granite.
Seasons: Apr-Nov
Maps: *DeLorme: Colorado Atlas & Gazetteer*, page 50; *USGS:* Mount Deception, CO; Pike National Forest; *Trails Illustrated:* #137, Pikes Peak, Cañon City, CO
Nearest town: Woodland Park
Other trail users: Hikers and horseback riders
Dog friendly: Yes
Trail contact: Pike and San Isabel National Forests, Pikes Peak Ranger District, Colorado Springs; (719) 636-1602

Getting there: From Colorado Springs drive west on US 24 for 17.7 miles before bearing right onto Baldwin Road in Woodland Park. Baldwin Road runs behind McDonald's and eventually turns into Rampart Range Road after passing Woodland Park High School on the right. Drive on Baldwin Road for 2 miles, and then turn left into the Lovell Gulch trailhead, next to the City Road Maintenance Building. Park in the designated parking lot by the trailhead. Trailhead GPS: N39 01.093' / W105 02.460'

The Ride

The first mile climbs gradually over smooth singletrack and through aspen and lodgepole pine forests. As you ride north out of Woodland Park along the edge of the timber, you'll pass private residences on your right. There are a number of campsites along the way as well.

Just under a mile into your ride, you'll pedal through thicker stands of aspen and ponderosa pine over soft and smooth singletrack. Here the trail can be very quiet and

View of Pikes Peak.

calming. If you look carefully, you might spy a white cross standing roughly 60 feet from the trail on the left. Upon closer inspection, you'll notice that the cross is topped with a crown of barbed wire and has nails hammered into its arms. Underneath the nails lie scraps of paper containing handwritten notes, reportedly written by schoolchildren.

After passing the cross at 0.7 mile, the trail narrows considerably. While narrow, the trail isn't particularly straight, but it's fun nevertheless. Vegetation gets thicker the closer you get to the stream at the bottom of Lovell Gulch. Once you cross the stream, the trail forks where a sign describes the loop ahead as being 3.75 miles around. From here the trail climbs moderately as it travels upstream through the narrow valley. The trail isn't too technical and travels over smooth singletrack. As you pass the interesting rock formations to your left just under 2 miles into your ride, you face the trail's first moderately technical climb, with loose rocks and exposed roots.

Soon you'll reach another challenging section of exposed roots, deep ruts, and steep terrain. Your hard work pays off, however, as you intersect with Rampart Range Road at the top of the ridge. Riding along the ridgeline, you are offered spectacular views of Pikes Peak, along with a thrilling descent beneath towering power lines over smooth singletrack.

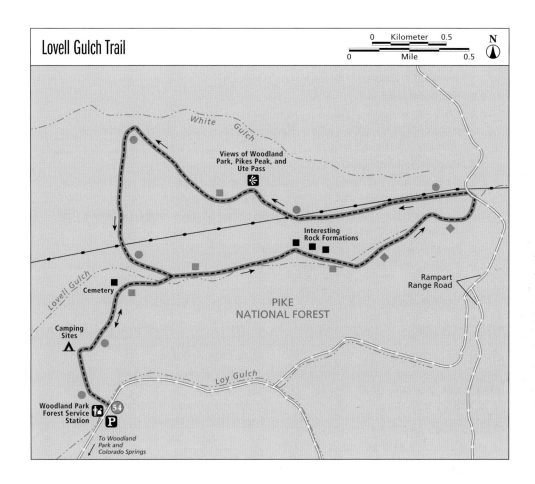

Lovell Gulch Trail

White Gulch

Views of Woodland
Park, Pikes Peak, and
Ute Pass

Interesting
Rock Formations

Lovell Gulch

Cemetery

Camping
Sites

PIKE
NATIONAL FOREST

Rampart
Range Road

Loy Gulch

Woodland Park
Forest Service
Station

54

To Woodland
Park and
Colorado Springs

Just under 3 miles into the ride, the trail once again leads into a mixed conifer and aspen forest along wider singletrack. By 3.4 miles you'll climb a short but moderate hill under a thick canopy to the top of a grassy knoll where you can enjoy views of Woodland Park, Pikes Peak, and Ute Pass.

A Ute legend offers an explanation for the origins of Pikes Peak. It is said that the Great Spirit poured snow and ice through a funnel in the sky to form the Great Peak. Using the mountaintop as a stepping-stone to retreat from the heavens to Earth, the Great Spirit poked holes with his fingers into the mountainside, in which the plants and trees could grow. The Great Spirit's daughter would later be taken by a giant grizzly bear; their offspring became the Ute Indian Nation. They believed the Great Spirit resides in Manitou Springs, as evidenced by his blowing bubbles in the mineral springs.

From the knoll it's a quick descent on smooth and steep singletrack. The trail runs speedily under tall stands of aspen to rejoin the stream. From the stream it's a mellow cruise back to your vehicle.

Miles and Directions

0.0 Start by passing through the gate and descending on the wide doubletrack, heading in a northwesterly direction to the singletrack on the right.

0.5 Pass under power lines.

0.8 Cross a small stream and reach the beginning of the loop by the Lovell Gulch Trail Loop sign. Bear right, riding the loop in a counterclockwise direction and following the trail upstream in an easterly direction.

1.7 Pass some interesting rock formations to your left.

2.4 The Lovell Gulch Trail intersects with Rampart Range Road beneath high power lines. Bear left under these power lines, and continue riding on the singletrack in a westerly direction.

3.6 Reach the top of a grassy knoll, where you are offered the route's best views of Pikes Peak and the town of Woodland Park.

4.4 The trail meets a private fence line and parallels the fence.

4.6 Return to the beginning of the loop. Bear right. Cross the stream and return the way you came.

5.5 Reach your vehicle.

Ride Information

Trail Information

Pike and San Isabel National Forests, Pikes Peak Ranger District, Colorado Springs; (719) 636-1602

Local Events and Attractions

Crystola Canyon, off US 24 behind the Crystola Inn

Florissant Fossil Beds National Monument, Florissant; (719) 748-3252; admission $3 (fees subject to change)

Garden of the Gods, Colorado Springs; (719) 634-6666; free admission

Ute Pass Cultural Center and Historical Society, Midland; (719) 686-7512

Restaurants

Bierwerks Brewery, Woodland Park; (719) 686-8100

Joanie's Bakery & Delicatessen, Woodland Park; (719) 686-9091

The Donut Mill, Woodland Park; (719) 687-9793

Grandmother's Kitchen, Woodland Park; (719) 687-3118

55 Rampart Reservoir Shoreline Loop

The Rampart Reservoir Shoreline Loop offers mountain bikers of any ability the chance to test their skills on a variety of terrain. From sand to gravel to soft forest earth, the loop delivers it all. Within a stone's throw of the reservoir, this trail follows the shoreline all the way around, providing opportunities for fishing and picnicking. A favorite among locals, the Shoreline Loop can get crowded on the weekends. It's best that mountain bikers ride the trail in a clockwise direction so as not to come upon riders unexpectedly around the many tight and rocky curves.

Start: The Rampart Reservoir Shoreline Loop trailhead

Distance: 15.3-mile lariat

Elevation gain: 160 feet

Riding time: Advanced riders, 1.5 hours; intermediate riders, 2-2.5 hours

Fitness effort: Physically moderate due to a modest elevation gain

Difficulty: Technically moderate to difficult due to a few tight rocky sections

Terrain: Improved dirt road and singletrack. The singletrack is covered in Pikes Peak granite, pebble-like rocks that absorb water, keeping trails in good shape during wet weather. These rocks are like ball bearings under your tires, making it tough to get out of steeper climbs.

Seasons: Apr-Nov

Maps: *DeLorme: Colorado Atlas & Gazetteer,* page 62; *USGS:* Woodland Park, CO, and Cascade, CO; *Trails Illustrated:* #137, Pikes Peak, Cañon City, CO; Team Telecycle map; *Selected Colorado Hiking Trails:* Pikes Peak Series

Nearest town: Woodland Park

Other trail users: Hikers, anglers, picnickers, boaters, horseback riders, campers, and seasonal ski tour groups

Dog friendly: Yes

Trail contact: Pike and San Isabel National Forests, Pikes Peak Ranger District, Colorado Springs; (719) 636-1602

Getting there: From Colorado Springs take I-25 north to exit 141. After exiting, continue heading west on US 24 for 17.8 miles to the WELCOME TO WOODLAND PARK sign on your right. Turn right onto Baldwin Road, taking you behind McDonald's. After passing Woodland Park High School on the right, Baldwin Road becomes Rampart Range Road. After 2.9 miles Rampart Range Road forks; take the right fork, and then turn right again onto the dirt road and the continuation of Rampart Range Road at 4.4 miles, following signs to the reservoir. Having driven 6.8 miles from when you turned onto Baldwin, you will see the trailhead on your left. Pull into the lot for the Rampart Reservoir Shoreline Loop and begin your ride beyond the wooden gate. Trailhead GPS: N38 58.688' / W105 00.558'

The Ride

Due in part to the eye-catching pink granite pebbles blanketing this trail's 12-mile stretch of singletrack, the Rampart Reservoir Trail is a popular mountain biking ride among Colorado Springs riders. This trail's singletrack is made of Pikes Peak granite, a

Rocky passes the big boulder on the loop's rockier side.

rock consisting of interlocking crystals of glasslike quartz, flat-surfaced white and pink feldspar, and a dash of black flaky mica.

Aside from its aesthetic appeal, the crushed granite doesn't hold water, so the trails stay dry and in good shape, even after the wettest of weather. This feature allows the loop to remain open when most other trails are closed. However, those pebbles also act as ball bearings. With the Rampart Reservoir's many roller-coaster dips, up and around protruding boulders and in and out of a variety of creek beds, the Pikes Peak granite singletrack does make for a physically challenging ride.

The ride begins at the Rampart Reservoir Shoreline Loop trailhead. As you pass the wooden gate, the trail begins with a fast, easterly 1.5-mile run through stands of quaking aspen to the pipeline spillway and the bridge. Bear left and continue on the north side of the spillway. On your right the spillway brings water from mountain runoff to Rampart Reservoir.

After 4 miles you cross Monument Creek and confront huge granite formations along the banks of the reservoir. Just beyond these rocks is a thick evergreen forest, complete with coiling roots and moist earth. This section quickly fades as the trail dries and leads into a tricky rocky section before offering a beautiful view of Pikes Peak. Part of the Rampart Reservoir Trail's appeal is its flirtatious skirting around huge boulders and through tight rocky sections. Pick your lines carefully.

By mile 8.4 the trail leads to what local riders call the Dip. Large boulders lie in front of you as the trail descends to meet the banks of the reservoir. When the water is high, you'll have to take the left spur of the singletrack, traversing up and over these rocks. If the water level is low, after carefully negotiating the tight rocky section just before these boulders, lift your bicycle and scramble over the rocks to rejoin the trail above. Just beyond this section is the Triple Squeeze. These tight rocky sections keep you honest on a trail as user-friendly as this. Once you reach the dam, be careful because vehicles also use this road.

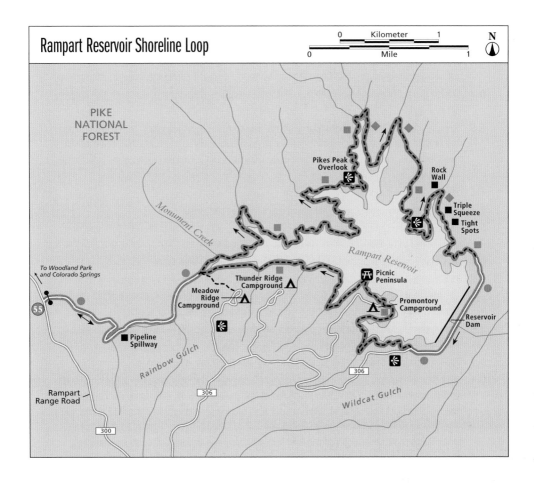

Rampart Reservoir Shoreline Loop

As a holding tank, Rampart Reservoir supplies Colorado Springs with water via a 12-foot-wide tunnel. A Swedish engineering firm bored Rampart Reservoir's shaft and its connecting tunnel. They bet city planners that the shaft and the tunnel would connect within 1 inch of specifications. The Swedes hit it right on the nose—an impressive display of engineering acuity if you consider the 20 miles the tunnel had to travel.

After rejoining the Rampart Reservoir singletrack just beyond the Wildcat Wayside Pike National Forest sign, continue through the ponderosa pine forest. Cross a stone culvert before arriving at Picnic Peninsula—a picnic area offering tables, water spigots, and shoreline views. Continue on the singletrack, veering right as it passes in front of the picnic table with the large boulder backdrop. This area contains many offshoots from the main trail. Know that the shoreline loop generally follows the land contour through here. Passing through Picnic Peninsula, you're rewarded with a fast and smooth singletrack descent to the bridge. Veer left by the bridge and return to your vehicle.

Miles and Directions

0.0 Start at the trailhead located to the left of the parking lot. Go through the wooden gate and begin riding on the fast-descending Rampart Reservoir Shoreline Road to the spillway.

0.7 Reach the spillway and bear left over it. Continue riding downstream, now with the spillway on your right.

1.5 Reach a footbridge. This footbridge also marks the point to which you'll be returning. Pass the bridge and keep heading straight—we're going clockwise. (You have the option of riding the trail in a clockwise or counterclockwise direction, but it's more rideable in a clockwise direction.)

1.7 The singletrack begins.

2.3 Reach a marshy area. Cross this marshy area via a footbridge.

5.4 Encounter a technical rocky section. The middle line offers the best results. This trail does have some tight rocky sections, so pick your lines carefully.

6.3 Arrive at a beautiful place to take your rest and a view of Pikes Peak.

6.8 The trail divides here, leading into another marshy, forested area. The tendency is to follow the trail to the left, which will soon thereafter lead into a meadow, ultimately dead-ending. Instead, bear right, scouting out the trail, and cross the creek.

8.4 Reach the Dip. Here a rock wall blocks immediate passage. You'll have to portage your bicycle up and around this wall.

9.7 Reach the dam. Cross it and pick up the singletrack on the other side.

10.4 Come to the wildcat wayside (pike national forest) sign. The singletrack trail continues 10 yards past the sign, on the right, just beyond the parked cars. At this point you can take the road back to your vehicle. Although far less technical, this option does add some mileage to your ride, as well as a significant amount of climbing. Bear right onto the singletrack. Note that this section of the trail has a higher level of foot traffic, so be cautious.

11.6 Reach a sweet picnic spot, offering picnic tables and water spigots. Here the trail Y's. A hiking trail veers to the left and splits the two picnic tables, and the Rampart Reservoir Loop Trail keeps to the right, passing the picnic table with the large boulder behind it.

13.8 Reach the bridge. Bear left and climb back up the road the way you came.

15.3 Arrive back at your vehicle.

Ride Information

Trail Information

Pike and San Isabel National Forests, Pikes Peak Ranger District, Colorado Springs; (719) 636-1602

Local Events and Attractions

Crystola Canyon, off US 24 behind the Crystola Inn

Florissant Fossil Beds National Monument, Florissant; (719) 748-3252; admission $3 (fees subject to change)

Garden of the Gods, Colorado Springs; (719) 634-6666; free admission

Ute Pass Cultural Center and Historical Society, Midland; (719) 686-7512

Restaurants

Bierwerks Brewery, Woodland Park; (719) 686-8100

Joanie's Bakery & Delicatessen, Woodland Park; (719) 686-9091

The Donut Mill, Woodland Park; (719) 687-9793

Grandmother's Kitchen, Woodland Park; (719) 687-3118

56 Waldo Canyon Trail

The Waldo Canyon Trail, although primarily a hiker's trail, does invite gonzo-minded mountain bikers to strut their stuff. What makes this trail particularly appealing to tough riders is its steep climbs out of creek beds and its fast and rocky descent. Views from its highest point include Pikes Peak, Colorado Springs, and NORAD (North American Aerospace Defense Command). Its location right beside US 24 makes for a speedy assault of the trail for those in transit.

(*Note:* As of this writing, Waldo Canyon is indefinitely closed due to the 2012 Waldo Canyon Fire and the potential for flash flooding.)

Start: The Waldo Canyon trailhead
Distance: 7.0-mile lariat
Elevation gain: 1,000 feet
Riding time: Advanced riders, 1 hour; intermediate riders, 1.5-2 hours
Fitness effort: Physically challenging due to the variety of climbing and portaging of your bicycle over rocky creeks
Difficulty: Technically moderate to challenging due to the many rocky sections and big drop-offs
Terrain: Singletrack that covers a variety of different terrain: various kinds of rock surfaces, hard-packed dirt, wet forest earth, large roots, Pikes Peak granite

Seasons: May-Oct
Maps: *DeLorme: Colorado Atlas & Gazetteer,* page 62; *USGS:* Woodland Park, CO, and Cascade, CO; *Trails Illustrated:* #137, Pikes Peak, Cañon City, CO
Nearest town: Colorado Springs
Other trail users: Campers, but this trail is primarily used by hikers—a good reason to stay clear of the mountain bike riding in this area on the weekends
Dog friendly: Yes
Trail contact: Pike and San Isabel National Forests, Pikes Peak Ranger District, Colorado Springs; (719) 636-1602

Getting there: From Colorado Springs take I-25 to exit 141 and US 24 west. Drive west on US 24 for 7.8 miles before reaching the turnoff for Waldo Canyon on your right. Park your vehicle here. You'll have to portage your bicycle up a set of stairs to the registration box and the trailhead before beginning your ride. A $1 donation is requested for trail maintenance.

From Woodland Park, starting from the intersection of US 24 and Baldwin Road, head east on US 24 toward Colorado Springs. At 9.9 miles you'll arrive at the turnoff for the Waldo Canyon trailhead on your left. The trailhead will be to the north side of US 24, so you'll have to cross US 24's westbound traffic. Trailhead GPS: N38 52.878' / W104 56.960'

The Ride

At its worst, Waldo Canyon is a crowded thoroughfare for weekend hikers. At its best, it's a grunt of a climb to some of the area's best unobstructed views of Pikes Peak. The tireless mountain biker is rewarded with a singletrack descent of titillating switchbacks, past a veritable smorgasbord of drop-offs. After carrying your bike up the

Bike snuggling up against the trail and its natural beauties prior to the Waldo Canyon Fire of 2012.

steep wooden steps, begin riding up the switchbacks. You will parallel US 24 for roughly a mile and then climb steadily, your tires relentlessly spinning through the ball-bearing-like Pikes Peak granite that blankets the trail. As the trail turns away from the highway, you're given your last look at civilization for a while.

Riding through tall stands of leafy greens, you descend into a cool meadow area, complete with campfire rings. Once you arrive at the Waldo Canyon Loop sign, bear left. In so doing, you'll be riding the loop in a clockwise direction, choosing to climb in the shade rather than in the more exposed areas of Waldo Canyon. From here the work begins.

A mile of steep climbing awaits you. The large rocks, knotty tree roots, and creek crossings make it a grunt by anyone's standards—a true trial rider's dream. By mile 2.5 the trail Y's before sending you up another set of wooden stairs. This time the stairs are a bit more manageable, as long as you hug the left side. Bear right at another Waldo Canyon sign and continue ascending through the ponderosa and fir forest. Areas of this trail are severely loaded with rocks, so be aware on the approach. By the third mile the trail levels out and offers incredible views of Pikes Peak.

By mile 3.4 you come upon an example of an "unconformity," which refers to a break in the geological record in which two kinds of rock are found in abnormal succession. In this case Precambrian metamorphic rock (granite) sits directly beneath Pennsylvanian red sandstone, with no sign between of the Ordovician, Silurian, Devonian, or Mississippian periods. With 500 million years of time apparently lost, a crucial piece in the earth's geological jigsaw puzzle remains missing. Possible explanations for this mysterious absence are severe erosion, folding, and faulting.

From the unconformity the trail traverses the sun-exposed hills above Williams Canyon before snaking its way back down into Waldo Canyon. Williams Canyon cuts

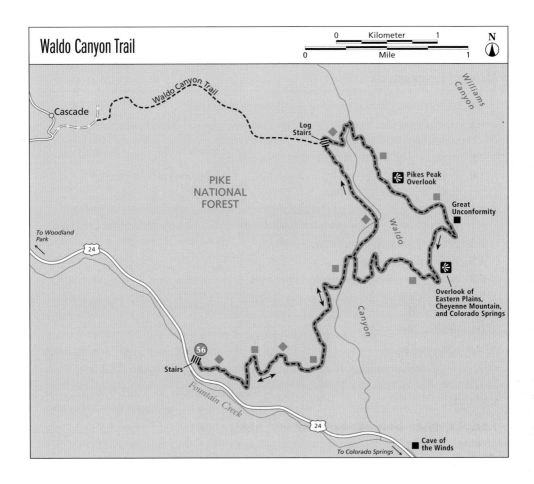

through the hillside in which the Cave of the Winds is located. The trail passes gorgeous views of the eastern plains, Colorado Springs, and the hollowed-out Cheyenne Mountain—home to NORAD, the underground facility that monitors foreign aircraft, missiles, and space systems that could threaten US security. Aside from the vast array of antennae on top, Cheyenne Mountain is virtually indistinguishable from any other mountain in Colorado. The trail from this point is packed with dirt and thick with overgrowth as it begins its descent back into Waldo Canyon.

This descent is fast and fun as it travels over a variety of terrain, keeping you on your toes. Manitou limestone–sprinkled switchbacks, precipitously sloping Sawatch sandstone, crowded Peerless dolomite sections, and carvable Pikes Peak granite turns—all conspire against the cyclist. Riders are afforded a crash course in geology as a host of interpretive signs explains the pedigree of each of these sections.

By mile 5.3 you arrive at a tributary of Fountain Creek and the Waldo Canyon Loop sign. Bear left and make a short climb out of this valley; the descent to your vehicle is sweet and fast, offering blind corners and a number of rocks. You'll arrive at the trail register at 7 miles. If you're feeling lucky, try doing the stairs down to the parking lot.

Miles and Directions

0.0 Start at the registration tower and box at the top of the stairs.

0.1 Waldo Canyon Trail bears left. To the right is an overlook of US 24 and a description of the composition of Pikes Peak granite.

0.8 Cross the ridge and begin descending into a clearing.

1.6 Arrive at a brown sign reading WALDO CANYON LOOP, 3 ½ MILES. Bear left here. You'll return to this spot after completing the loop.

2.5 Reach the second set of log stairs leading to an intersection with another trail. Veer right, as the left route will lead you out of Waldo Canyon and to the town of Cascade.

3.4 Here's a good example of an unconformity.

4.9 Begin your switchback descent.

5.3 Arrive at the creek and the Waldo Canyon sign.

7.0 Arrive back at the trail registration tower and box.

Ride Information

Trail Information

Pike and San Isabel National Forests, Pikes Peak Ranger District, Colorado Springs; (719) 636-1602

Local Events and Attractions

Crystola Canyon, off US 24 behind the Crystola Inn

Florissant Fossil Beds National Monument, Florissant; (719) 748-3252; admission $3 (fees subject to change)

Garden of the Gods, Colorado Springs; (719) 634-6666; free admission

Ute Pass Cultural Center and Historical Society, Midland; (719) 686-7512

Restaurants

Bierwerks Brewery, Woodland Park; (719) 686-8100

Joanie's Bakery & Delicatessen, Woodland Park; (719) 686-9091

The Donut Mill, Woodland Park; (719) 687-9793

Grandmother's Kitchen, Woodland Park; (719) 687-3118

57 Captain Jack's Trail

This trail is certainly one of Colorado Springs' best, offering a good climb and a fast, and somewhat technical, descent. Area riders divide Captain Jack's Trail into Upper and Lower sections and often combine it with the Chutes and Buckhorn Trail for an extended tour. While either of the Upper and Lower sections can be ridden alone, this description combines both sections. High Drive Road divides the two sections of Captain Jack's Trail.

Start: The Captain Jack's trailhead

Distance: 7.2-mile loop

Elevation gain: 1,200 feet

Riding time: Advanced riders, 1 hour; intermediate riders, 1.5-2 hours

Fitness effort: Physically moderate due to some longer climbs at higher elevations

Difficulty: Technically moderate to challenging due to some tighter, rockier sections over steep and precipitously sloping terrain

Terrain: Singletrack and dirt road that lead through a rocky canyon over sometimes tight and rocky terrain

Seasons: North Cheyenne Canyon Park is open May 1 to Oct 31 from 5 a.m. to 11 p.m. and Nov 1 to Apr 30 from 5 a.m. to 9 p.m.

Maps: *DeLorme: Colorado Atlas & Gazetteer,* page 62; *USGS:* Manitou Springs, CO; *Trails Illustrated:* #137, Pikes Peak, Cañon City, CO

Nearest town: Colorado Springs

Other trail users: Hikers and motorcyclists

Dog friendly: No, due to the preponderance of vehicular travel both on the singletrack and on Gold Camp Road

Trail contact: Pike and San Isabel National Forests, Pikes Peak Ranger District, Colorado Springs; (719) 636-1602; or North Cheyenne Canyon Park & Stratton Open Space; (719) 385-6086

Getting there: From Colorado Springs drive west on I-24 from its intersection with I-25 for 1.5 miles; then bear left onto Twenty-first Street, heading up the hill, and drive for 0.8 mile. Turn right at the stoplight onto Lower Gold Camp Road, and continue for 1.2 miles before arriving at a four-way stop intersection. Here Lower Gold Camp Road turns into Gold Camp Road. Drive through the intersection and continue driving on Gold Camp Road for 4.2 miles. The road turns to dirt as you enter North Cheyenne Canyon Park. Continue on the dirt Gold Camp Road for roughly 2 miles before turning right into the parking lot, just before the first tunnel. Trailhead GPS: N38 47.941' / W104 53.020'

The Ride

Begin by riding through North Cheyenne Canyon Park on the dirt Gold Camp Road. Views of the eastern plains and Colorado Springs lie to your left as you pass through the first of two tunnels. Gold Camp Road climbs gradually and offers a comfortable warm-up to the climbing that lies ahead. Be advised that there is vehicular traffic on Gold Camp Road, so be careful.

Checking out the view from the Cheyenne Mountain overlook.

In the early 1900s this served as a rail bed for the narrow gauge Colorado Springs & Cripple Creek District Railway Company (CS&CCD), whose trains carried gold ore mined in Cripple Creek to Colorado Springs. The CS&CCD, or "Short Line," ran 46 miles between Colorado Springs and the Cripple Creek–Victor Mining District. The rails are long since gone, but you can marvel at this century-old engineering achievement as you ride to the beginning of the singletrack.

Having passed through the parking lot, you connect with the trail's singletrack (some refer to this singletrack as the beginning of the Buckhorn Trail, while others refer to it as Upper Captain Jack's Trail). This marks the start of a moderately tough climb over a saddle where Upper Captain Jack's Trail intersects with the Jones Park Trail (alternately known as the Buckhorn Trail). Leading to this saddle, the trail switches back over smooth but narrow singletrack that falls precipitously to the right. After roughly 3.5 miles, ponderosa pine give way to taller stands of Douglas fir as you continue grunting your way to the saddle.

While the saddle offers good reason to rest and wait for straggling riders, it doesn't offer much in the way of views. For the overlook reward continue riding on Upper

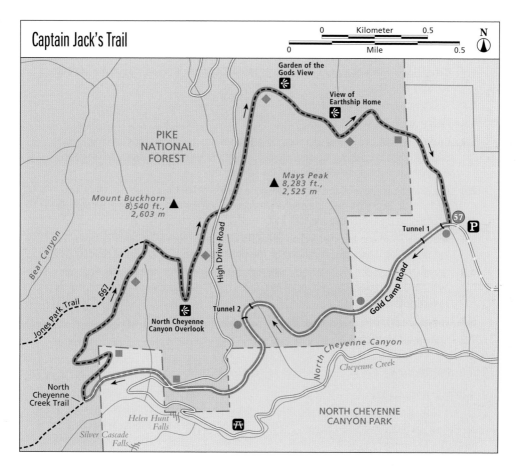

Captain Jack's Trail

Garden of the Gods View

View of Earthship Home

PIKE NATIONAL FOREST

Mays Peak
8,283 ft.,
2,525 m

Mount Buckhorn
8,540 ft.,
2,603 m

Bear Canyon

Jones Park Trail

667

High Drive Road

Tunnel 1

57 P

Gold Camp Road

Tunnel 2

North Cheyenne
Canyon Overlook

North Cheyenne Canyon

Cheyenne Creek

North
Cheyenne
Creek Trail

Helen Hunt
Falls

Silver Cascade
Falls

NORTH CHEYENNE
CANYON PARK

Captain Jack's to a beautiful North Cheyenne Canyon Park overlook to your right. Here you can enjoy the views of Mount Baldy and Cheyenne Mountain.

Descend from this overlook over fast and technical terrain. The trail combines granite-laden singletrack with a narrow and sloping surface. This section of trail includes some of the more technical sections of the entire route. Once you intersect and cross High Drive Road, continue your ride on Lower Captain Jack's Trail, which parallels the road before bearing in a more easterly direction. The singletrack on this section of trail can be quite fast and sinuous, offering beautiful views of the Garden of the Gods after 5.5 miles into your ride.

From this viewpoint, ride through a very narrow, steep, and high-walled section of trail. Like riding through a 15-foot-long miniature gorge, the terrain is technical and tight. Then you'll ride another short grunt to another easterly overlook before descending the rest of the way to your vehicle.

There are a variety of other trail options in this general vicinity. One such trail is called the Chutes. It begins across Gold Camp Road and the parking lot to Captain Jack's Trail and descends on technical and fast terrain back to town.

Miles and Directions

0.0 From the parking lot of the Captain Jack's trailhead, bear right onto the dirt Gold Camp Road and begin climbing through North Cheyenne Canyon, heading in a south-westerly direction.

0.1 Pass through the first tunnel.

1.0 Pass through the second tunnel.

1.7 Gold Camp Road intersects with High Drive Road by the second parking lot on your right. Bear right into the parking lot, and intersect with the Upper Captain Jack's Trail's wide doubletrack in the northwest corner of the parking lot.

2.4 The wide doubletrack intersects with the continuation of the Upper Captain Jack's Trail on the right. Bear right onto the narrow singletrack, and continue climbing in an easterly direction on the Upper Captain Jack Trail.

3.7 Reach a saddle and the intersection of the Upper Captain Jack's Trail and the Jones Park Trail on the left. Bear right, continuing on the Upper Captain Jack's Trail and heading east.

4.6 Upper Captain Jack's Trail intersects with High Drive Road, which divides Upper Captain Jack's Trail from Lower Captain Jack's Trail. Cross High Drive Road and continue riding on Lower Captain Jack's Trail.

5.7 Pass through the trail's miniature gorge.

7.2 Arrive at your vehicle.

Ride Information

Trail Information

Pike and San Isabel National Forests, Pikes Peak Ranger District, Colorado Springs; (719) 636-1602

Starsmore Discovery Center, North Cheyenne Canyon Park, Colorado Springs; (719) 385-6086; open Apr 1 through Nov from 9 a.m. to 5 p.m.

Local Events and Attractions

Florissant Fossil Beds National Monument, Florissant; (719) 748-3252; admission $3 (fees subject to change)

Garden of the Gods, Colorado Springs; (719) 634-6666; free admission

Helen Hunt Falls Visitor Center, North Cheyenne Canyon Park, Colorado Springs; (719) 633-5701; open Memorial Day through Labor Day from 9 a.m. to 5 p.m.

Restaurants

Phantom Canyon Brewing, Colorado Springs; (719) 635-2800

PB & Jellies Restaurant, Colorado Springs; (719) 465-2686

Uchenna, Colorado Springs; (719) 634-5070

Il Vicino, Colorado Springs; (719) 475-9224

58 Cheyenne Mountain State Park

Cheyenne Mountain State Park is a one-stop shop for outdoor enthusiasts who want to mountain bike, hike, camp, picnic, or establish a base camp for exploring what Colorado Springs has to offer. The route described here uses seven of the park's sixteen trails and covers 12.1 of its 20 miles. This route incorporates the southern and central portions of the park, leaving its trails in the more populated north for future exploration. This route generally combines easy and moderate terrain, although there are options for more technical terrain. Those wanting to test their trial–riding expertise can check out the Medicine Wheel Trail, the park's most technical terrain. Since these trails are all interconnected, riders can shorten, lengthen, or alter routes. This is a particular benefit for a family or a group of riders, as it offers flexibility in accommodating riders of different skill levels. Moreover, each of the park's trails is color-coded on its map, as well as on posts staked in the ground along the trails. And if that weren't enough to keep you from getting lost, GPS coordinates are posted along each of the trails, as well as on the park map at trail intersections.

Start: The Talon trailhead
Distance: 12.1-mile loop, with several side trails that make shorter lariats
Elevation gain: 753 feet
Riding time: Advanced riders, 1.5 hours; intermediate riders, 2 hours
Fitness effort: Physically easy to moderate due to the lack of any significant elevation gain
Difficulty: Technically easy, with a few more moderately technical sections along Blackmer Loop and Cougar's Shadow Trails.
Terrain: Singletrack and doubletrack that delivers generally smooth terrain with some sandier and rockier sections as it travels through low-lying exposed meadows and shaded forests

Seasons: Apr-Oct
Maps: Cheyenne Mountain State Park map; *USGS:* Cheyenne Mountain, CO; *Trails Illustrated:* #137, Pikes Peak, Cañon City, CO; *DeLorme: Colorado Atlas & Gazetteer,* pages 62-63, B- and C-3 and -4
Nearest town: Colorado Springs
Other trail users: Hikers, campers, and picnickers
Dog friendly: No
Trail contact: Cheyenne Mountain State Park, Colorado Springs; (719) 576-2016; or Medicine Wheel Trail Advocates, Colorado Springs; www.medwheel.org/

Getting there: From Colorado Springs drive on I-25 to exit 135. Drive west on Academy Boulevard for roughly 2 miles before turning left onto CO 115. Drive south on CO 115 for roughly 2 miles to the first stoplight, and turn right onto JL Ranch Heights Road: the entrance to Fort Carson Mountain Post will be on your left. Drive west on JL Ranch Heights Road to the park entrance. From the visitor center and fee station, drive another 0.2 mile and bear left, following the sign that reads LIMEKILN GROVE TRAILHEAD. Park in the Day Use trailhead parking lot. Trailhead GPS: N38 43.879' / W104 49.284'

Ralph Welz descending along the Talon Trail with Cheyenne Mountain as a backdrop.

The Ride

The 1,680-acre Cheyenne Mountain State Park is situated in a transitional zone between grasslands, shrublands, and montane forests. These varied ecosystems provide for a variety of terrain and wildlife. The most diverse wildlife exists within the montane ecosystem of the park.

As you begin your ride, bear left onto the short-lived Talon Trail before it connects with the Zook Loop. The initial ascent is over a wide trail covered with Pikes Peak gravel, easy terrain as it weaves playfully over low-lying grasslands and in and out of scrub oak stands.

The first half of this route includes a steady but easy climb as it snakes its way through mixed conifer forests and scenic overlooks. The singletrack of the South Talon Trail is laden with pine needles and delivers shorter, tight curves, which preclude one from riding too fast.

Once you bear onto the North Talon Trail, the climb continues. But at this point the climbing travels through shaded forest over smooth terrain, which is a welcome relief from the more exposed terrain of the lower elevations. A short, rocky section— with more on the way—wakes you from your shaded reverie at roughly 4 miles. After taking in the views of Cheyenne Mountain from the top of a rocky knoll, descend on the North Talon Trail, passing another scenic overlook to your left. This is a rip-roaring fast descent to the intersection of the North Talon and Talon Trails.

The Sundance Trail provides easygoing terrain over generally flat singletrack. By the time this intersects with the Little Bear Trail, you might begin to notice the lot where you parked. Riders wishing to end their ride early can do so once the Sundance Trail intersects with the Zook Loop, roughly 7 miles into the ride.

The intersection of the Zook Loop and the Blackmer Loop, identifiable by the rock garden, is a good place to refuel with some food. The Blackmer Loop climbs moderately, requiring you to negotiate through a couple of rockier sections than those you experienced earlier in the day. These rockier sections arrive around tight and sometimes blind curves, requiring a rider to practice deft bike-handling skills.

After bearing right onto the Cougar's Shadow Trail, riders are immediately delivered some rockier and more technical terrain. And while these sections are technically advanced, they are very short-lived. The Cougar's Shadow Trail is considerably narrower than were the trails previously ridden. Upon reconnecting with the Blackmer Loop, it's a fast descent to its completion along the Zook Loop.

Miles and Directions

0.1 Start riding from the Day Use trailhead on the Talon Trail. You'll ride for no more than 200 yards before intersecting with the Zook Loop.

0.1 Bear left onto the Zook Loop trail, crossing a footbridge. The Zook Loop intersects with the Talon Trail. Bear left after crossing the footbridge onto the Talon Trail as you begin your gradual climb in a southerly direction.

0.3 The Talon Trail intersects with the Little Bear Trail on your right. Continue riding on the Talon Trail.

0.5 The Talon Trail intersects with the southern terminus of the Turkey Trot Trail on the right. Continue riding on the Talon Trail.

1.2 The Talon Trail intersects with the Sundance Trail for the first time on your left. Veer right, continuing your climb on the Talon Trail. Shortly after this point the Talon Trail will intersect with the Sundance Trail for a second time on your right. You will access the Sundance Trail at this second intersection upon your return at 6.1 miles.

2.3 The Talon Trail intersects with the North Talon Trail on your right. Continue riding on the Talon Trail, noting the point at which you will be completing the North Talon Trail upon your return.

2.6 The Talon Trail intersects with the South Talon Trail. Bear left onto the South Talon Trail as you descend in a southerly direction.

3.6 South Talon intersects with the North Talon and Talon Trails. Bear left onto North Talon.

5.0 The North Talon Trail intersects with the Talon Trail. Bear left onto the Talon Trail, retracing your route to the Talon's intersection with the Sundance Trail.

6.1 The Talon Trail intersects with the Sundance Trail. Bear left onto the Sundance Trail, and ride in a northeasterly direction.

7.1 The Sundance Trail intersects with the northern terminus of the Turkey Trot Trail on your right. Bear left and continue riding on the Sundance Trail.

7.2 The Sundance Trail intersects with the Little Bear Trail on the right. Veer left, continuing on the Sundance Trail.

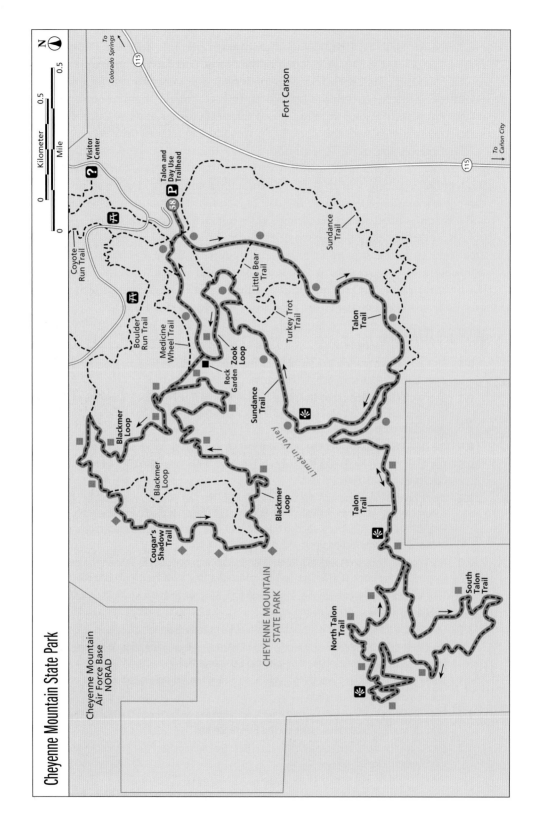

Cheyenne Mountain State Park

7.3 The Sundance Trail intersects with the Zook Loop trail. Bear left onto the Zook Loop.

7.7 Arrive at the intersection of the Zook Loop trail and the Blackmer spur trail. This intersection lies within a forested rock garden, complete with sitting bench and informational placard. Riders should bear left, riding between the bench and informational placard and over the rocks to pick up the Blackmer spur trail that leads to the loop of the same name.

7.8 The Blackmer spur trail intersects with the Medicine Wheel Trail on the right. Continue on the Blackmer spur trail to the beginning of its loop.

7.9 The Blackmer spur trail arrives at the beginning of the Blackmer Loop Trail. Bear right, riding the Blackmer Loop in a counterclockwise direction.

8.7 The Blackmer Loop intersects with the Boulder Run Trail on your right. Veer left, continuing your climb on the Blackmer Loop.

9.0 The Blackmer Loop intersects with the Cougar's Shadow Trail. Bear right onto the Cougar Shadow's Trail. Next to the Medicine Wheel Trail, the Cougar's Shadow Trail delivers riders the most technical terrain in the area. Riders not wishing to challenge themselves with this trail can opt to continue on the Blackmer Loop.

9.9 The Cougar's Shadow Trail intersects and rejoins with the Blackmer Loop. Bear right onto the Blackmer Loop, and descend to its intersection with the Blackmer spur trail.

11.4 Return to the beginning of the Blackmer Loop. Bear right onto the Blackmer Loop spur trail to the rock garden and its intersection with the Zook Loop trail.

11.5 The Blackmer Loop spur trail intersects with the Medicine Wheel Trail. Rock hounds wanting more abuse or to practice their trial riding can bear left onto the Medicine Wheel Trail and rejoin the group later on the Zook Loop at mile 11.9 of this route description. Otherwise, continue riding on the Blackmer Loop spur trail to its intersection with the Zook Loop trail.

11.6 The Blackmer Loop spur trail reconnects and intersects with the Zook Loop. Bear left onto the Zook Loop trail.

11.9 The Zook Loop intersects with the Medicine Wheel Trail on the left. Continue riding on the Zook Loop.

12.0 The Zook Loop intersects with the Coyote Run Trail on the left. Continue riding on the Zook Loop to your vehicle. Otherwise, riders can opt to ride the 1.3-mile Coyote Run Trail to lengthen their ride, which will take them to the park's northern part.

12.1 Arrive at your vehicle.

Ride Information

Trail Information

Cheyenne Mountain State Park, Colorado Springs; (719) 576-2016

Medicine Wheel Trail Advocates, Colorado Springs; www.medwheel.org/

Local Events and Attractions

Garden of the Gods, Colorado Springs; (719) 634-6666; free admission

Pikes Peak; www.experiencecolorado springs.com

Restaurants

Phantom Canyon Brewing, Colorado Springs; (719) 635-2800

PB & Jellies Restaurant, Colorado Springs; (719) 465-2686

Uchenna, Colorado Springs; (719) 634-5070

Il Vicino, Colorado Springs; (719) 475-9224

59 Shelf Road

The Shelf Road is a historic stagecoach toll road that connects Cañon City with the gold-mining camps of Cripple Creek and Victor. The Shelf travels precipitously along the limestone cliffs of Helena Canyon and then descends into the canyon to run through incredibly tall red-rock walls. Here is a mellow ride that offers a lot of spinning. The Shelf Road area is also world-renowned for its rock climbing. Bighorn sheep abound within Helena Canyon and most often can be spotted drinking from Fourmile Creek at dusk. The return from Cripple Creek or Victor is fast, offering a number of blind curves and washboard sections of road, with the last push to the parking area one burly climb.

Start: The Banks-Shelf Road parking area; take the right fork (Shelf Road)

Distance: 27.2-mile out-and-back

Elevation gain: 3,000 feet

Riding time: Advanced riders, 3.5 hours; intermediate riders, 4.5-5 hours

Fitness effort: Physically easy to moderate due to some degree of climbing

Difficulty: Technically easy with no major obstacles

Terrain: Shelf Road Trail follows an old wagon and stagecoach toll road; aside from the occasional washboard effect, the road is relatively smooth; at times it is very exposed

Seasons: Apr-Oct

Maps: *DeLorme: Colorado Atlas & Gazetteer*, page 62; *USGS:* Cooper Mountain, CO, and Cripple Creek South, CO; *Trails Illustrated:* #137, Pikes Peak, Cañon City, CO

Nearest town: Cripple Creek

Other trail users: Horseback riders, hikers, four-wheelers, bighorn sheep viewers, climbers, and gamblers

Dog friendly: No, due to vehicular traffic on Shelf Road

Trail contact: Bureau of Land Management, Royal Gorge Resource Area, Cañon City; (719) 269-8538

Getting there: From Colorado Springs drive south on I-25 for 45 miles to Pueblo. In Pueblo drive west on US 50 to Cañon City. Make a right onto Dozier Avenue near the Wal-Mart. (If you're coming from the west, make a left onto Dozier.) After 0.5 mile Dozier turns west and becomes Central. Continuing on Central (Dozier), drive west for 1.6 miles and then turn right onto Fields Avenue. It turns into a dirt road at 11.6 miles. Continue on Fields for another 2.3 miles before arriving at the Banks—a limestone cliff area located near the beginning of Shelf Road and known internationally for its incredible sport climbing. Park here and begin your ride, taking the right fork (Shelf Road). Trailhead GPS: N38 36.881' / W105 13.490'; trailhead terminus/turnaround GPS: N38 44.796' / W105 10.700'

The Ride

Originally built in 1892 as a wagon and stagecoach toll road, Shelf Road now offers the mountain biker a chance to experience history from his or her mountain bike. Colorado in the 1890s was home to America's last great gold rush. Towns such as Cripple Creek, Victor, Florence, McCourt, Adelaide, and Wilbur all popped up soon after Bob Womack discovered gold in October of 1890 in Poverty Gulch west of Pikes Peak.

Throughout its gold-mining days, Cripple Creek enjoyed a standard of living never before seen in Colorado. By 1899 the district had yielded $59 million, and by the end of the gold rush in 1903, area gold mines had produced $432 million—making it the fourth-largest gold-producing camp in the world. The town established itself as a social center as well. Grand opera houses hosted a variety of musicians. Jack Dempsey drew huge crowds to his boxing bouts in town. Even President Teddy Roosevelt visited and panned for gold. Today, Cripple Creek offers limited-stakes gambling complete with buzzing bells, neon lights, and gross excess.

Just a few miles away, Victor remains true to its roots. Its century-old streets offer quiet, non-gambling relief from Cripple Creek while retaining much of the area's 1890s authenticity. The original brick buildings, built by residents

Riding through Helena Canyon.

after a fire destroyed their town in 1898, still stand. Even the hillsides are dotted with original miners' homes, visual echoes recalling the town's illustrious past.

Connecting Colorado's past with its present is Shelf Road. Six hundred feet above Fourmile Creek, it cuts through Helena Canyon's limestone cliff walls. The initial 4 miles is perhaps the most dramatic section of the entire route. If you fear heights, this section could be difficult since it has little margin for error.

As you descend to the canyon floor and the banks of Fourmile Creek, a feeling of peace overcomes you as the exposed road gives way to juniper, scrub oak, and lush cottonwoods. From here one begins the extended 10-mile push to Cripple Creek. Shelf Road gradually climbs as it winds its way up Fourmile Creek.

By mile 6 the steeper part of the climbing begins and leads you through forests of lodgepole pine. After passing a number of abandoned mines between miles 10 and 11.4, Shelf Road forks at mile 11.8, where you will find the remains of the El Paso Mine. Victor is to the right and Cripple Creek to the left. This makes a good turn-around spot unless you cherish the touristy gambling town or are desperate for food; it's about 1.5 miles away.

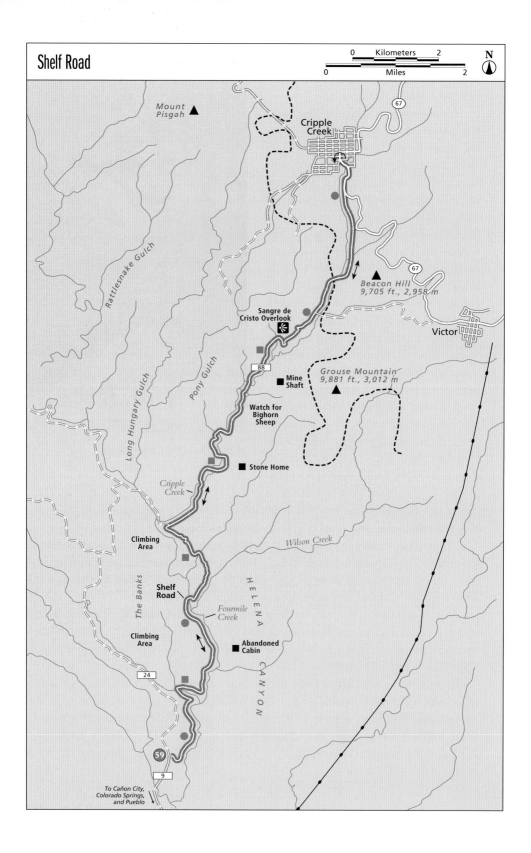

Shelf Road

Kilometers
0   2
Miles
0   2

N

Mount
Pisgah

Cripple
Creek

67

Beacon Hill
9,705 ft., 2,958 m

67

Victor

Rattlesnake Gulch

Sangre de
Cristo Overlook

88

Mine
Shaft

Grouse Mountain
9,881 ft., 3,012 m

Long Hungry Gulch

Pony Gulch

Watch for
Bighorn
Sheep

Stone Home

Cripple
Creek

Wilson Creek

Climbing
Area

The Banks

Shelf
Road

Fourmile
Creek

H
E
L
E
N
A

C
A
N
Y
O
N

Climbing
Area

Abandoned
Cabin

24

59

9

To Cañon City,
Colorado Springs,
and Pueblo

Your return trip is fast and bumpy. Be cautious of your speed, as the descent on Shelf Road offers many tight turns. The many washboards are sure to test your shocks. Enjoy the ride.

Miles and Directions

0.0 Start at the Banks-Shelf Road parking area. Take the right fork and begin climbing up Shelf Road.

2.0 Riding along the steep limestone walls of Helena Canyon, you'll notice an old abandoned cabin from the late 1800s on the canyon floor.

4.0 Shelf Road eventually widens and leads into the floor of Helena Canyon, affording additional parking to climbers and those who would like to forgo the initial, narrow descent to the canyon bottom. (The crags behind you offer great climbing opportunities and can be accessed via a variety of foot trails.)

5.0 The remains of an old stone home are on your right.

8.1 Come to an old abandoned mine shaft to your right.

10.0 Take in the beautiful vista of the Sangre de Cristo Mountains off to the west.

11.4 Cross Cripple Creek.

11.8 Shelf Road forks. Here signs to the town of Cripple Creek point to the left fork, while signs for Victor point to the right fork. Take the left fork and ride toward Cripple Creek. Pass the Scenic Byway sign, marked by a Colorado columbine.

13.3 Shelf Road connects to CO 67. At the stop sign, bear left onto CO 67 and ride into Cripple Creek.

13.6 Reach the corner of Second Street and Bennett Avenue, downtown Cripple Creek. Turn around here and return the way you came.

27.2 Arrive at your vehicle.

Ride Information

Trail Information

Bureau of Land Management, Royal Gorge Resource Area, Cañon City; (719) 269-8538

Local Events and Attractions

Donkey Derby Days, last full weekend in June with donkey races, greased pigs, and fun, Cripple Creek; (877) 858-4653

Fiddlers on the Arkansas, July, Cañon City; (719) 275-0593

Gold Belt Tour, year-round, Cañon City; (719) 275-2331

Victor Gold Rush Days, third weekend in July, Victor; (719) 689-3553 or (855) 643-8216; www.victorcolorado.com/goldrushdays.htm

Restaurants

The Creek, Cripple Creek; (719) 689-9595

Ralf's Break Room, Cripple Creek; (719) 689-9195

McGills Pint & Platter, Cripple Creek; (719) 689-0303

Midland Depot, Cripple Creek; (719) 689-2561

60 Lake Pueblo State Park

Lake Pueblo State Park is worth exploring over a few days. The park provides over 4,600 acres of water, 60 miles of shoreline, almost 10,000 acres of land, a swim beach, campsites, and nearly 40 miles of singletrack. This route captures a portion of everything that the park offers—rolling cross-country terrain, steep and rocky technical climbs and descents, and views of Lake Pueblo and the surrounding buttes—with suggestions to explore other trails. The ride delivers a continuous pedal with short, levels-training-type bursts of ascents and descents complemented by some technically advanced descending and climbing over rockier terrain. While the trails are generally well marked, there are some unidentified offshoot trails. As a general rule, follow the main trail when in doubt. The climate here is generally hot and dry, which allows for almost year-round access to mountain biking. But when wet, the park's thick clay takes on the consistency of chunky peanut butter. Riders should consult the park for current trail conditions.

Start: The South Shore trailhead at Arkansas Point

Distance: 21.7-mile loop, with several options to make shorter or longer routes

Elevation gain: 202 feet

Riding time: Advanced riders, 1.5 hours; intermediate riders, 2.5 hours

Fitness effort: Physically moderate to challenging due to the length of the ride

Difficulty: Technically easy to challenging owing to the variety of surface conditions at the park

Terrain: Singletrack and dirt road that deliver flat, wide, steep, narrow, sandy, rocky conditions over generally exposed terrain

Fees and permits: Entrance into Lake Pueblo State Park requires a $7 daily park pass

Seasons: Mar-Oct

Maps: Southern Colorado Cycling Club maps of Lake Pueblo State Park's South and North Shore Trails, http://lakepueblotrails.org; *USGS:* Swallows, CO, and Northwest Pueblo, CO; *DeLorme: Colorado Atlas & Gazetteer*, page 73, B-4 and -5

Nearest town: Pueblo

Other trail users: Hikers, runners, boaters, campers, anglers, swimmers, and hunters

Dog friendly: No

Trail contact: Lake Pueblo State Park, Pueblo; (719) 561-9320

Getting there: From Colorado Springs drive south on I-25 and take exit 101 to US 50. Drive west on US 50 for roughly 2.5 miles before turning left onto Pueblo Boulevard (CO 45). Drive south on Pueblo Boulevard for approximately 3.7 miles, and turn right onto Thatcher Avenue (CO 96). Drive west on Thatcher Avenue for roughly 3.7 miles, and bear right onto South Marina Road by the brown LAKE PUEBLO STATE PARK sign. Drive another 1 mile before arriving at the entrance and tollbooth of the park. From the tollbooth drive another 0.1 mile and turn left onto Arkansas Point Road to the South Shore trailhead. Trailhead GPS: N38 15.076' / W104 44.151'

The Ride

Lake Pueblo State Park is truly a land of contrasts. Receiving only 12 inches of annual precipitation, the park is a semiarid desert. But the rainfall on July 14 and 15,

The author dropping into Skull Canyon. Jeff Williams

2013, brought a 12-foot wall of water through Rock Creek Canyon that destroyed the 1-month-old wooden-planked bridge crossing the creek, cutting off access to Voodoo Loop. Likewise, the rains also washed away the footbridge that crossed Boggs Creek. These creeks are typically dry except for when the spring runoff is high, which is usually about every 3 years or when severe thundershowers occur.

Lake Pueblo State Park is geologically and biologically diverse. A keen eye can find 60-million-year-old marine fossils, such as ammonites—squid-like creatures that lived inside coil-shaped shells and had a ring of tentacles surrounding sharp, beak-like jaws. Moreover, the shale and limestone buttes and bluffs of the surrounding area are home to several plant species that can only be found near Lake Pueblo: golden blazing star, Arkansas Valley evening primrose, roundleaf four o'clock, and Pueblo goldenweed.

The South Shore Trail provides a fair amount of fun little rollers that offer riders terrain that is reminiscent of Fruita and Moab. The rock outcroppings of the South Shore Trail provide habitat for the rare triploid checkered whiptail, a foot-long lizard with a black checker pattern on a neutral yellowish or brownish background. This all-female species clones itself to reproduce and is the rarest reptile in Colorado.

After connecting with the Waterfall Trail, riders have to negotiate a rocky and narrow shale- and limestone-laden arroyo. The intersection with Log Drop Trail provides two log bridges that drop an expanse of over 3 feet. Such bridges can also be found in Keyhole Canyon and Free Ride. Just beyond this intersection lies steep and rocky terrain that is technically advanced but manageable by experienced riders.

The Pronghorn, Voodoo, and Route 96 Trails share similar terrain, traveling over tabletops that depart from the rockiness of Waterfall. Voodoo views of Rock Creek Canyon are impressive. It isn't until the Outer Limits Trail that the terrain becomes more consistently lined with shale and limestone as it snakes its way alongside the tops of limestone cliffs that rim Lake Pueblo. Tires rolling over shards of shale sound like riding over broken glass. As you skirt the tops of the canyon walls above the crystal blue waters of Lake Pueblo, views of Greenhorn Mountain, the tallest peak in the Wet Range, lie to the southwest and the imposing Pikes Peak to the north. The Inner Limits Trail takes you away from the lake and delivers more technical terrain. Riders can opt to ride the Buttes, which is a technically advanced, partial out-and-back trail that eventually reconnects with the Inner Limits.

While on Driftwood, riders wind along singletrack past large mounds of dead stumps. The logs on driftwood were cut from the Arkansas River shoreline, which feeds the 11-mile-long Lake Pueblo, before it was filled to clear the lake for boating. Another 15-mile loop is planned that will connect to Voodoo Loop and includes a pile of logs ten times bigger than those on Driftwood. Riders are rewarded with several playful log bridges to maneuver over along what is otherwise smooth singletrack.

After crossing Boggs Creek at the intersection of South Shore, Cuatro Sinko, and Creekside Trails, riders negotiate a short, technical climb. Aside from the initial short climb, Cuatro Sinko is a relatively smooth ride with a lot of flow factor. But don't get mesmerized, as this area is in no short supply of rattlesnakes, which have been known to appear in the middle of the trail around blind corners.

In contrast, the descent through Keyhole Canyon delivers log bridges down 4-foot drops, rocky shelves, and tight, off-camber terrain that requires steady cornering and balancing: a satisfying part of the route for any technically minded, advanced rider. The climb through Rock Canyon should likewise satisfy as it passes several other trails en route to Arkansas Point and Skull Canyon Trails.

The initial descent through Skull Canyon is an excellent example of trail building in high-consequence terrain. The shale rock gardens are quite negotiable by advanced riders' standards. The canyon will also pass several other trails—Quick Draw, Bones, Rattle Snake, and Free Ride—which are short but very fun, technical trails.

After reconnecting with South Shore Trail, riders climb a final hill before descending to their vehicles. You can add an additional 2.5 miles to this epic ride by riding up Watertower to Conduit to The Duke and down through Hooters Canyon, another trademark canyon ride.

Miles and Directions

0.0 Begin riding on the dirt road of the South Shore Trail. Riders will see three possible trails: a singletrack spur trail on the left that climbs to its connection with the Conduit Trail; the singletrack South Shore Trail in the middle, which will be the trail down which you will return; and the wide dirt road segment of the South Shore Trail on the right. Bear right onto the dirt road segment of the South Shore Trail, and ride in a southerly direction.

1.5 The South Shore Trail intersects with the Creekside Trail. Bear right onto Creekside.

1.7 The Creekside Trail intersects with the Waterfall Trail on the right. Cross the creek via a footbridge, and continue riding on the Waterfall Trail.

2.2 The Waterfall Trail comes to a four-way intersection with the Inner Limits Trail (south), Pedro's Point Trail, and Pronghorn Trail. Continue riding west on the Pronghorn Trail;

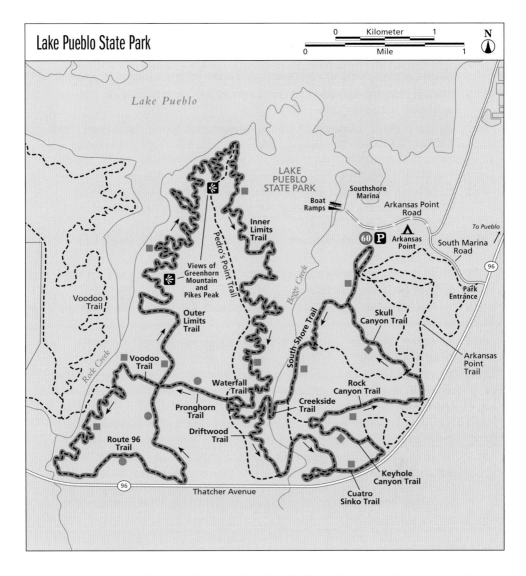

0 Kilometer 1

0 Mile 1

N

Lake Pueblo

LAKE
PUEBLO
STATE PARK

Southshore
Marina

Boat
Ramps

Arkansas Point
Road

Inner
Limits
Trail

Arkansas
Point

To Pueblo

South Marina
Road

96

Views of
Greenhorn
Mountain
and
Pikes Peak

Park
Entrance

Voodoo
Trail

Outer
Limits
Trail

Skull
Canyon Trail

Arkansas
Point
Trail

Voodoo
Trail

Waterfall
Trail

Rock
Canyon Trail

Pronghorn
Trail

Creekside
Trail

Route 96
Trail

Driftwood
Trail

96

Thatcher Avenue

Keyhole
Canyon Trail

Cuatro
Sinko Trail

Pedro's Point Trail

Baggs Creek

South Shore Trail

Rock Creek

however, know that you will also be riding Inner Limits (north and south) and portions of Pedro's Point upon your return (see mileage 16.1).

2.7 The Pronghorn Trail intersects with the Voodoo Trail. Continue riding on the Voodoo Trail, heading south.

3.2 The Voodoo Trail intersects with a detour trail that leads to the Voodoo Loop. Continue riding in a southerly direction on the Voodoo Trail. (**Option:** Riders wishing to extend their ride by 10 miles can bear right onto the detour trail and ride the 0.5-mile detour trail to the 9-mile Voodoo Loop, that is, if Rock Creek is crossable.)

4.6 The Voodoo Trail intersects with CO 96 on the left. Bear left onto the Route 96 Trail as it travels east and parallels CO 96.

5.5   The Route 96 Trail intersects with the Pronghorn Trail on your left. Bear left onto the Pronghorn Trail, and ride in a northerly direction.

6.6   The Pronghorn Trail returns to the intersection of the Voodoo and Outer Limits Trails. Continue straight, intersecting with the Outer Limits Trail and riding in a northerly direction.

11.5   The Outer Limits Trail intersects the Pedro's Point and Inner Limits (north) Trails. Continue riding south on the Inner Limits Trail.

16.1   The Inner Limits Trail intersects with the four-way intersection of the Waterfall, Pedro's Point, and Pronghorn Trails (see mileage 2.2). Bear left onto the wide doubletrack of Pedro's Point and continue riding south for roughly 75 yards before bearing left onto the singletrack of the Driftwood Trail.

17.2   The Driftwood Trail intersects with Pedro's Point Trail, with CO 96 off to your right. Bear left onto Pedro's Point Trail, descending away from the highway to the intersection of the Pedro's Point and South Shore Trails.

17.3   The Pedro's Point Trail intersects with the South Shore Trail on the left. Bear left onto South Shore.

17.5   The South Shore Trail intersects with the Cuatro Sinko Trail. Cross Boggs Creek and bear right onto the Cuatro Sinko Trail.

18.9   The Cuatro Sinko Trail intersects with the Keyhole Canyon Trail. Bear left onto the Keyhole Canyon Trail.

19.4   The Keyhole Canyon Trail intersects with the Rock Canyon Trail. Bear right and ascend through Rock Canyon.

20.3   The Rock Canyon Trail intersects with the Arkansas Point Trail off to your left and by a gate and CO 96, as well as the Cuatro Sinko Trail to your right. Bear left onto the flat and easy Arkansas Point Trail.

20.4   The Arkansas Point Trail intersects with the Skull Canyon Trail. Bear left onto the Skull Canyon Trail.

21.2   The Skull Canyon Trail intersects with the South Shore Trail. Bear right onto South Shore, climbing the singletrack in a northerly direction. (This will cut off the road section of the South Shore Trail with which you began your route. (**Option:** Add an additional 2.5 miles by riding up Watertower to Conduit to The Duke and down through Hooters Canyon.)

21. 7   Arrive at your vehicle.

Ride Information

Trail Information
Lake Pueblo State Park, Pueblo; (719) 561-9320

Local Events and Attractions
Historic Arkansas Riverwalk of Pueblo, Pueblo; http://puebloriverwalk.org

Pueblo Zoo, Pueblo; (719) 561-1452; www.pueblozoo.org

Pueblo Weisbrod Aircraft Museum, Pueblo; (719) 948-9219; www.pwam.org

Restaurants
Shamrock Brewing Company, Pueblo; (719) 542-9974

Bingo Burger, Pueblo; (719) 225-8363

Rocco's Riverside Deli, Pueblo; (719) 582-1616

Mr. Tandori Urban Bar & Grill, Pueblo; (719) 544-3000

Honorable Mentions

Colorado Springs Region

Other notable rides in the Colorado Springs area deserve consideration. These may be shorter rides or ones generally considered common knowledge but deserving of your consideration nevertheless.

U Ute Valley Park

Ute Valley Park offers a short network of singletrack trails within one of Colorado Springs' city parks. The area is a great trail for beginners taking to the trail for the first time. Ute Valley Park packs a lot into a little space, offering a great combination of fast and wide trails and sometimes more technical terrain. Popular among bikers and hikers alike, Ute Valley Park offers open meadows and interesting rock formations. Because most of the park's trails average less than 0.5 mile, you would best be served by riding laps around the park and connecting with several different trails, which would allow for an easy 4-mile loop. Otherwise, the entire park can be ridden well within 30 minutes.

The park is open May 1 to October 31 from 5 a.m. to 11 p.m. and November 1 to April 30 from 5 a.m. to 9:00 p.m.

To reach Ute Valley Park from Colorado Springs, drive west on Woodmen Road, which will become Rockrimmon Road. Follow Rockrimmon Road for roughly 1.5 miles before bearing right onto Vindicator. Drive on Vindicator for 0.75 mile to the parking lot and trailhead. For more information contact Ute Valley Park at (719) 385-5940 or Friends of Ute Valley Park at friendsofutevalleypark.com.

V Palmer Park

A great and huge city park in the middle of downtown Colorado Springs, Palmer Park offers a vast network of interconnected trails. While there are some maps available for the park, they are not very accurate or easy to read. It's best that you go to Palmer Park, at least for your first time, and explore. Otherwise, go with someone who knows the area.

The trail is mostly singletrack, with some dirt road and doubletrack, over hard-packed dirt and rocky terrain, as it courses through scrub oak, piñon pine, and ponderosa pine trees and yucca plants. Watch out for hikers and horseback riders, as this is a very popular trail. You're offered incredible views of Pikes Peak.

To reach Palmer Park from Denver, drive south on I-25 and take exit 150 at Academy Boulevard (CO 83). Drive south on Academy for roughly 7 miles before bearing right onto Maizeland Road. Drive 0.2 mile on Maizeland before taking your next right into the park and onto Paseo. Paseo Road splits the park in half and runs through to Mark Reyner Stables on the other side of the park.

To reach Palmer Park from downtown Colorado Springs, drive east on Platte Avenue for roughly 5.5 miles before bearing left onto Academy Boulevard. Drive north on Academy Boulevard for 1.9 miles before bearing left onto Maizeland Road. Drive on Maizeland for 0.2 mile before making your next right into the park.

Park your vehicle and begin riding.

The park is open May 1 to October 31 from 5 a.m. to 11 p.m. and November 1 to April 30 from 5 a.m. to 9 p.m. No alcoholic beverages are allowed. Dogs must be on leash. Park in designated areas only. No vehicles off roadways. No illegal dumping, golfing, or excessive noise. No firearms. No camping. No wood burning or gathering. For more information contact Palmer Park at (719) 385-5940.

W Garden of the Gods

The riding in the spectacular Garden of the Gods can be described as a bittersweet experience for mountain bikers. The Garden of the Gods is open to mountain biking in a very limited capacity but offers incredibly beautiful and stunning landscapes. The southeast corner of the park offers several trails that provide spectacular scenery, for example, Ute Trail. Riders have limited access to roughly 5 miles of trails in the southeast section of the park. Some of the trails can be narrow and sinuous in spots, making for a fun family ride.

To ride the Garden of the Gods is almost an afterthought, but one well worth considering. The 1,350-acre city-owned park delivers spectacular views of Pikes Peak framed by magnificent sandstone rock formations that are more than 300 million years old.

To reach the Garden of the Gods from Colorado Springs, drive west on the Garden of the Gods Road to 30th Street. Bear left onto 30th Street, and drive to the Garden of the Gods Visitors Center. For more information contact the Garden of the Gods at (719) 634-6666.

X Barr Trail

The Barr Trail is a Colorado Springs classic, but it's not for the weak of heart. The Barr Trail combines a grueling 11-mile climb, over sometimes technically and physically challenging terrain, to the top of Pikes Peak (14,110 feet). It offers an impressive 4,000-foot elevation gain in just 6.5 miles. Most of the Barr Trail is in good shape, with only a few unrideable sections, the most notable of which comes just before reaching the summit. Not everyone reaches the summit, however, nor do they ever intend to. Many riders choose to return after reaching Barr Camp, which is the midway point to the summit. People have made it somewhat a tradition to offer a donation to the caretaker of the camp. As traditions go, this is one that is worth the effort. Since the trail is very popular with hikers, riders should take care when descending.

To access the Barr Trail, drive west on US 24 to the Manitou Springs exit. Drive west on Manitou Avenue and turn left onto Ruxton.

Y Section 16

Section 16 is part of Bear Creek Regional Park and offers a network of scenic trails with beautiful easterly views of Colorado Springs. Two trails that are accessible from Section 16 include Palmer Red Rock Loop (6 miles) and Forest Overlook (2 miles). The Palmer Red Rock Loop offers some steeper, technical sections, while the Forest Overlook Trail is a bit more reserved. Also accessible from Section 16 is the Intemann Trail, which travels to Manitou Springs.

To reach Section 16 drive west on I-24 from its intersection with I-25 for 1.5 miles. Turn left onto 21st Street, heading up the hill for 0.8 mile. Bear right at the stoplight onto Lower Gold Camp Road. Drive on Lower Gold Camp Road for 1.2 miles to a four-way-stop intersection. Here Lower Gold Camp Road turns into Gold Camp Road. Drive through the intersection and continue driving on Gold Camp Road for 0.8 mile before bearing right into the Section 16 parking lot.

Section 16 gets its name from the official US term for land measurements. All of the land in this country is identified within a series of sections and townships. A section is 1 square mile in size and contains 640 acres of land. Townships consist of 36 sections. In 1876, the year Colorado became a state, the federal government deeded to Colorado all the section 16's and section 36's for the purpose of generating revenue for the state.

The El Paso County Park Department currently leases "Section 16." Income derived by the state from the lease or sale of Section 16 is deposited into a fund to support public schools. Presently, approximately 3 million acres of land throughout Colorado are under lease.

Z The Chutes

Running from the South Suburban Reservoir in Stratton Open Space to Gold Camp Road and North Cheyenne Mountain, the Chutes is a fast but short downhiller's dream, although portions of this ride deliver some strenuous climbing. If one were to start from Gold Camp Road, a rider could easily rip down the banked turns on his or her way to Stratton Open Space, making the ride feel more like a bobsled run than one through a mountain drainage channel. Do not ride up the drainage because of the cyclists bombing down. A better option is to ride the Chamberlin Trail, which runs parallel to the Chutes, for 4 miles from the South Suburban Reservoir. Taking a steep spur trail will connect riders to the last mile of the Chutes. Some riders combine this trail with the Captain Jack's Trail (ride 57) or the Columbine Trail to make it a loop. While this is a classic Colorado Springs ride and one of the more epic downhill runs of the region, it is not particularly family-friendly.

AA   Elk Park Trail 652

Elk Park Trail in the Pike and San Isabel National Forests is a short, 5.2-mile trail that follows an old road and heads southeast to North Pit, an abrupt glacier-carved cirque. Riders should also know that this trail connects to Barr Trail (Honorable Mention X) or that it can be ridden as an out-and-back, making for a 10.4-mile ride. Riders should expect moderate or greater difficulty, as this trail reaches above 11,000 feet. As such, it has oftentimes been the training ground for runners of the Pikes Peak Marathon. The riding is easier if ridden from Elk Park to Barr Camp and more difficult if ridden in reverse. Of special note, riders can access a short spur to an abandoned mining town. Nearing the top, riders are offered a ringside seat to the pink granite crown of Pikes Peak perched roughly 3,000 feet overhead.

To get to Elk Park Trail, drive west on CO 24 from Colorado Springs for roughly 10 miles to the Pikes Peak Highway tollbooth. Drive on the Pikes Peak Toll Highway for roughly 13 miles, and pull into the trailhead on the left, near mile marker 14. For more information contact the Pike and San Isabel National Forests at (719) 636-1602.

AB   Red Rock Canyon Open Space

The city of Colorado Springs purchased the Red Rock Canyon property in 2003 from the Bock family, who had owned it for more than 75 years. Today, it's a local favorite and is attracting much attention for its excellent riding opportunities. Situated on the west side of town, Red Rock Canyon Open Space delivers on its namesake with towering red sandstone spires. Its access to the Intemann Trail and Section 16, another Colorado Springs classic mountain biking destination, make for an all-around winning combination. The area provides riders with a variety of trails that vary in length and difficulty. Some of the trails deliver short, technical climbs on beautiful singletrack, while others allow for a more casual ride on old roadbeds. Throughout the Open Space, riders will be rewarded with views of the Garden of the Gods to the north, Pikes Peak to the west, and Cheyenne Mountain to the south.

To reach Red Rock Canyon Open Space, drive west on CO 24/Cimarron Street. Bear left onto Ridge Road. Red Rock Canyon is located on the south side of the street, with parking available at the end of Ridge Road. For more information visit www.springsgov.com and click on the Parks, Recreation & Cultural Services link, or call (719) 385-5940.

Appendix A: Bicycle Organizations

Alpine Bicycle Club & The Colorado Rough Riders; (303) 279-8558

American Alpine Club, 710 Tenth St., Golden, CO 80401; (303) 384-0110

American Trails; www.americantrails.org

Bicycle Colorado, 1525 Market St., Ste. 100, Denver, CO 80202; (303) 417-1544; http://bicyclecolorado.org

Bicycle Racing Association of Colorado; (303) 458-5538; www.coloradocycling.org; provides a list of resources and contact information for bicycle clubs throughout the Front Range

Bike Fort Collins; http://bikefortcollins.org

Bikepacking.net; contact Scott Morris at www.topofusion.com

Bikes del Pueblo, Pueblo, CO; http://bikesdelpueblosd.blogspot.com

Boulder Area Trails Coalition (BATCO); (303) 485-2162; www.bouldertrails.org

Boulder Bicycle Commuters, 4820 Thunderbird Circle #108, Boulder, CO 80303; (303) 499-7466; dallured@indra.com

Boulder Mountainbike Alliance, PO Box 4954, Boulder, CO 80306; http://boulder mountainbike.org

Clear Creek Land Conservancy, Golden, CO; (303) 279-4462

Colorado Bicycle Advisory Board, 4201 E. Arkansas Ave., Denver, CO 80222; (303) 757-9982

Colorado Bicycle Program, 4201 E. Arkansas Ave., Rm. 212, Denver, CO 80222; (303) 757-9982

Colorado Bicycle Racing Association for Seniors (COBRAS), 7963 S. Vance St., Littleton, CO 80128; (303) 866-3894; http://cobrascycling.org

Colorado Department of Transportation Bicycle and Pedestrian Program, (303) 757-9982; www.coloradodot.info/programs/bikeped

Colorado HeartCycle Association, PO Box 100743, Denver, CO 80210; (303) 267-1112; www.heartcycle.org

Colorado Mountain Club, 710 Tenth St., #200, Golden, CO 80401; (303) 279-3080 or (800) 633-4417

Colorado Springs Cycling Club, PO Box 49602, Colorado Springs, CO 80949-9602; (719) 266-0776 or (719) 351-3205; www.bikesprings.org

Colorado Springs Mountain Biking Club, Colorado Springs, CO; www.meetup.com/Colorado-Springs-Mountain-Biking-Club/

Colorado Trail Foundation, 710 Tenth St., Rm. 210, Golden, CO 80226; (303) 384-3729

Continental Divide Trail Coalition, PO Box 552, Pine, CO 80470; (720) 340-2382; www.continentaldividetrail.org

Denver Bicycle Touring Club, PO Box 101301, Denver, CO 80250-1301; (303) 756-7240; www.dbtc.org

Friends of Cheyenne Cañon; (719) 385-6086; http://cheyennecanon.org

Friends of Cheyenne Mountain State Park; www.cmspfriends.org

Front Range Mountain Bike Patrol; www.frmbp.org

Highlands Ranch Cycling Club; www.ridehrcc.com

International Mountain Bicycling Association (IMBA), 4888 Pearl East Circle, Ste. 200E, Boulder, CO 80301; (303) 545-9011; www.imba.com

League of American Bicyclists; (202) 822-1333; www.bikeleague.org

Medicine Wheel Trail Advocates, Colorado Springs, CO; www.medwheel.org

National Center for Bicycling & Walking; (973) 378-3137; www.bikewalk.org

National Off-Road Bicycling Association (NORBA), 210 USA Cycling Point, Ste. 100, Colorado Springs, CO 80909; (719) 434-4200; www.usacycling.org

Overland Mountain Bike Club, PO Box 1543, Fort Collins, CO 80522; (970) 430-5336; www.overlandmtb.org

PEDAL (Peoples' Efforts to De-emphasize Autos in Loveland); http://pedalclub.org

Pedestrian and Bicycling Info Center; www.pedbikeinfo.org

People for Bikes, 207 Canyon Blvd., Suite 202, Boulder, CO 80303, (303) 449-4893, www.peopleforbikes.org/

Rocky Mountain Cycling Club; (303) 738-1958; www.rmccrides.com

Seniors on Bikes; (303) 443-7623; www.seniorsonbikes.com

Southern Colorado Cycling Club (SCCC), formerly the Southern Colorado Trail Builders (SCTB), Pueblo, CO; http://lakepueblotrails.org

Team BOB (Babes on Bikes); www.coteambob.com

Team Evergreen Bicycle Club Inc.; http://teamevergreen.org

Trails and Open Space Coalition, 1040 S. 8th St., Ste. 101, Colorado Springs, CO 80905; (719) 633-6884; www.trailsandopenspaces.org

United States Cycling Federation, 210 USA Cycling Point, Ste. 100, Colorado Springs, CO 80909; (719) 434-4200; www.usacycling.org

USA Cycling Inc., 210 USA Cycling Point, Ste. 100, Colorado Springs, CO 80909; (719) 434-4200; www.usacycling.org

Velo-One Cycling of Colorado

Volunteers for Outdoor Colorado, 600 S. Marion Pkwy., Denver, CO 80209-2597; (303) 715-1010; www.voc.org

Appendix B: Bicycle Camps and Clinics

Alison Dunlap Adventure Camps; alison@alisondunlap.com; www.alisondunlap.com; skills clinics in the Colorado Springs region

Better Ride; (970) 335-8226; http://betterride.net/

Bikalope Tours; (303) 483-5300; www.bikalope.com/

Challenge Unlimited, Colorado Springs; (719) 633-6399 or (800) 798-5954; www.bikithikit.com

FasCat Coaching, 4550 N. Broadway St., Unit C-3B, Boulder, CO 80304; (720) 406-7444; www.fascatcoaching.com

New World Sports, 119 E. Mountain St., Fort Collins, CO 80524; (970) 224-5857; www.newworldsportsllc.com

Pikes Peak Mountain Bike Tours, 306 S. 25th St., Colorado Springs, CO 80904; (719) 337-5311; www.bikepikespeak.com

Appendix C: Ride Finder

Best Rides for Great Views
Ride 1: Killpecker Trail
Ride 12: Crosier Mountain Trail
Ride 30: Rollins Pass
Ride 33: Centennial Cone Park
Ride 39: Argentine Pass
Ride 40: Elk Meadow and Bergen Peak
Ride 47: Kenosha to Georgia Pass
Ride 48: Kenosha Pass to Lost Creek Wilderness
Ride 60: Lake Pueblo State Park

Best Rides for Wildlife Viewing
Ride 2: North Lone Pine Trail
Ride 3: Elkhorn Creek Trail System
Ride 21: Sourdough Trail
Ride 39: Argentine Pass
Ride 40: Elk Meadow and Bergen Peak
Ride 52: Raspberry Chautauqua Mountain Trail
Ride 54: Lovell Gulch Trail

Best Rides for Families with Children
Ride 4: Mount Margaret Trail
Ride 19: Boulder Valley Ranch
Ride 20: East Boulder Trail/White Rocks
Ride 26: Marshall Mesa/Community Ditch Trail
Ride 37: Hayden/Green Mountain Park
Ride 43: Meyer Ranch Park
Ride 44: Coyote Song Trail
Ride 55: Rampart Reservoir Shoreline Loop
Ride 58: Cheyenne Mountain State Park

Best Rides for Cyclists with Dogs
Ride 2: North Lone Pine Trail
Ride 13: Coulson Gulch Trail
Ride 19: Boulder Valley Ranch
Ride 20: East Boulder Trail/White Rocks
Ride 26: Marshall Mesa/Community Ditch Trail
Ride 43: Meyer Ranch Park
Ride 54: Lovell Gulch Trail
Ride 55: Rampart Reservoir Shoreline Loop

Best Rides for Flowy Singletrack

Ride 2: North Lone Pine Trail
Ride 10: Blue Sky Trail
Ride 16: Picture Rock
Ride 17: Heil Valley Ranch
Ride 23: Betasso Preserve
Ride 33: Centennial Cone Park
Ride 40: Elk Meadow and Bergen Peak
Ride 43: Meyer Ranch Park
Ride 49: Pine Valley Ranch to Buffalo Creek
Ride 50: Baldy Trail to Gashouse Gulch Trail
Ride 55: Rampart Reservoir Shoreline Loop
Ride 58: Cheyenne Mountain State Park

Best Rides for Technical Trails

Ride 1: Killpecker Trail
Ride 8: Mill Creek Trail
Ride 9: Bobcat Ridge
Ride 12: Crosier Mountain Trail
Ride 15: Hall Ranch
Ride 31: Mountain Lion Trail
Ride 32: White Ranch
Ride 35: Apex Park
Ride 38: Dakota Ridge and Red Rocks Trail
Ride 57: Captain Jack's Trail
Ride 60: Lake Pueblo State Park

Appendix D: Rides at A Glance

1–5 Miles

Ride 2: North Lone Pine Trail

Ride 14: Rabbit Mountain

Ride 24: Meyers Homestead Trail

Ride 28: Eldorado Canyon State Park

Ride 35: Apex Park

Ride 36: Barbour Fork

Ride 43: Meyer Ranch Park

Ride 44: Coyote Song Trail

5–10 Miles

Ride 4: Mount Margaret Trail

Ride 7: Hewlett Gulch

Ride 9: Bobcat Ridge

Ride 11: Devil's Backbone

Ride 13: Coulson Gulch Trail

Ride 17: Heil Valley Ranch

Ride 18: Ceran Saint Vrain Trail

Ride 19: Boulder Valley Ranch

Ride 20: East Boulder Trail/White Rocks

Ride 23: Betasso Preserve

Ride 25: Walker Ranch Loop

Ride 26: Marshall Mesa/Community Ditch Trail

Ride 31: Mountain Lion Trail

Ride 32: White Ranch

Ride 34: Chimney Gulch Trail

Ride 37: Hayden/Green Mountain Park

Ride 38: Dakota Ridge and Red Rocks Trail

Ride 41: Mount Falcon Park

Ride 42: Alderfer/Three Sisters Park

Ride 45: Deer Creek Canyon Park

Ride 50: Baldy Trail to Gashouse Gulch Trail

Ride 52: Raspberry Chautauqua Mountain Trail

Ride 54: Lovell Gulch Trail

Ride 56: Waldo Canyon Trail

Ride 57: Captain Jack's Trail

10-15 Miles
Ride 1: Killpecker Trail
Ride 3: Elkhorn Creek Trail System
Ride 5: Lower Dadd Gulch Trail
Ride 6: Young Gulch
Ride 8: Mill Creek Trail
Ride 10: Blue Sky Trail
Ride 12: Crosier Mountain Trail
Ride 15: Hall Ranch
Ride 16: Picture Rock
Ride 21: Sourdough Trail
Ride 27: Doudy Draw Area
Ride 29: Fourth of July Road
Ride 40: Elk Meadow and Bergen Peak
Ride 48: Kenosha Pass to Lost Creek Wilderness
Ride 49: Pine Valley Ranch to Buffalo Creek
Ride 51: Jackson Creek Trail
Ride 53: Falcon Trail
Ride 58: Cheyenne Mountain State Park

15 Miles and Up
Ride 22: Switzerland Trail
Ride 30: Rollins Pass
Ride 33: Centennial Cone Park
Ride 39: Argentine Pass
Ride 46: Waterton Canyon
Ride 47: Kenosha to Georgia Pass
Ride 55: Rampart Reservoir Shoreline Loop
Ride 59: Shelf Road
Ride 60: Lake Pueblo State Park

Ride Index

About the Author

Local cyclist and outdoor adventurer Stephen Hlawaty has spent over 35 years honing his craft of experiential living and sharing those experiences with others. A poet and writer, he has written outdoor adventure stories and technical articles for *Near Excessive, Rocky Mountain Sports Magazine, Outdoor, Skier, Steamboat Springs Magazine, KoffeeTalk, Scene, Boulder Weekly, Real Life, INsite Magazine, North Forty News, All-America City Yearbook,* and *Instructional Design for Web-based Training.* Stephen is the author of Falcon Guides' *Mountain Biking Colorado* and *Mountain Biking Colorado's Front Range.*

Stephen has taken his love for writing and enthusiasm for the outdoors to the classroom, where he teaches high school Language Arts. His outdoor resume includes heli-skiing the Chugach Mountains of Alaska; backcountry skiing the Wasatch Mountains of Utah, the Teton Range of Wyoming, and the Rocky Mountains of Colorado; as well as mountain biking throughout the American west. Also an avid boater, backpacker, and hiker, Stephen has logged countless days in the water, woods, and wilderness alone and with his wife, Amanda, and their two boys, Ethan and Benjamin, in the hills of the great state of Colorado. When not in hot pursuit of his next adventure, Stephen enjoys picking and sliding on his guitars or throwing and rolling at Aikido of Colorado in Fort Collins, where he trains under Victor Hung Sensei in the traditional Japanese martial art.